W9-CIB-732

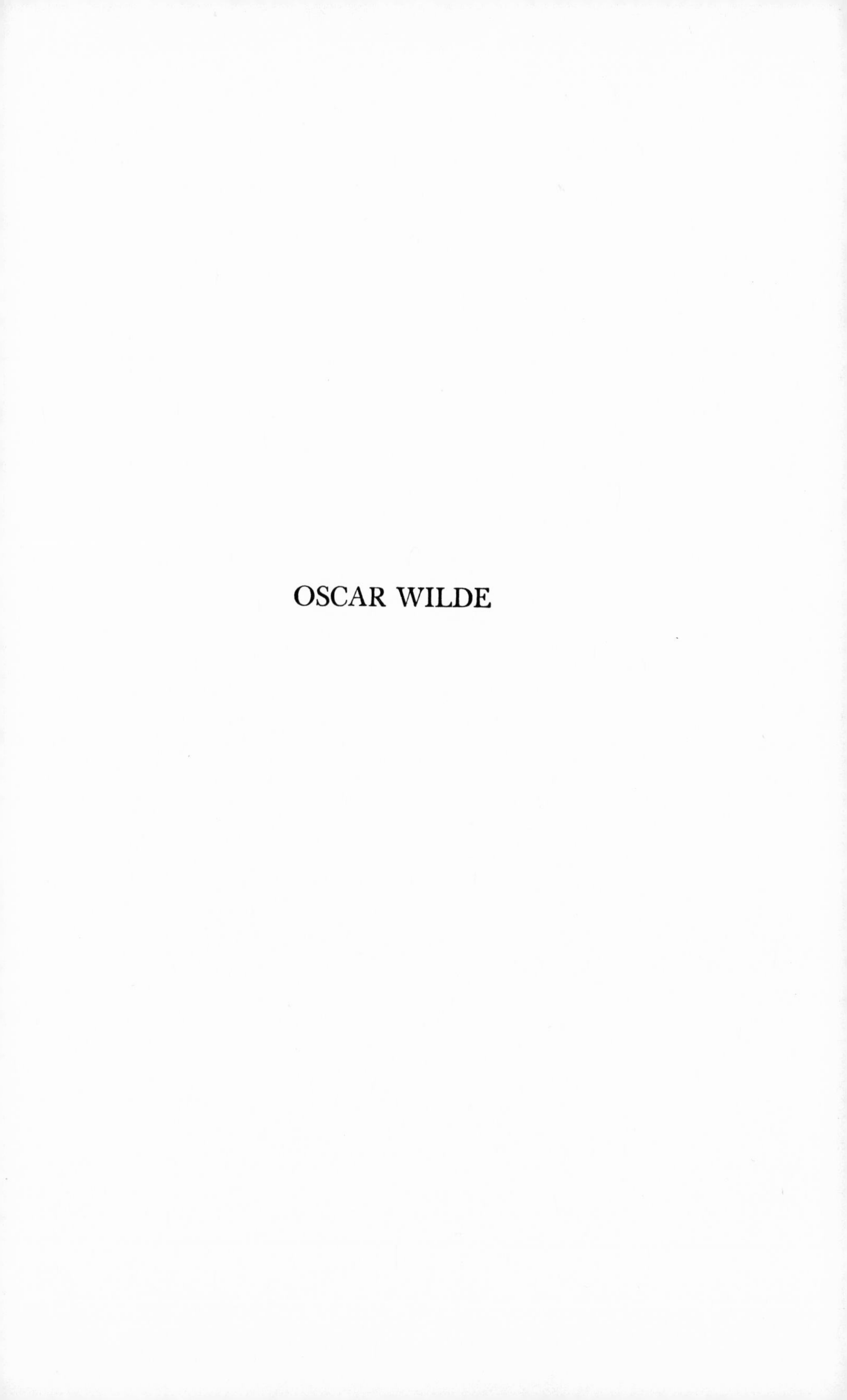

OSCAR WILDE

OSCAR WILDE

THE MAN – THE ARTIST

THE MARTYR

BORIS BRASOL

OCTAGON BOOKS

A DIVISION OF FARRAR, STRAUS AND GIROUX

New York 1975

Reprinted 1975
by special arrangement with Charles Scribner's Sons

OCTAGON BOOKS
A DIVISION OF FARRAR, STRAUS & GIROUX, INC.
19 Union Square West
New York, N.Y. 10003

Library of Congress Cataloging in Publication Data

Brasol, Boris Leo, 1885-
Oscar Wilde: the man, the artist, the martyr.

Reprint of the ed. published by Scribner, New York.
"Works by Oscar Wilde": p.
Bibliography: p.
Includes index.
1. Wilde, Oscar, 1854-1900.

[PR5823.B68 1975] 828'.8'09 75-23335
ISBN 0-374-90940-7

Manufactured by Braun-Brumfield, Inc.
Ann Arbor, Michigan
Printed in the United States of America

ACKNOWLEDGMENTS

In the course of the preparation of this book I have had the benefit of consulting several persons whose advice I greatly treasure. In this connection I wish to express my sincere thanks to Eleanore Brasol, my wife, and particularly to Mr. Robert Harborough Sherard, the valiant friend of Oscar Wilde. By placing at my disposal many first-hand data on the life of the English poet, Mr. Sherard has greatly facilitated my task, which I never regarded as an easy one. I also owe a debt of profound gratitude to Mr. Vyvyan Beresford Holland, the administrator of the estate of the late Oscar Wilde, for his generous permission to use in this book extracts from certain unpublished letters by Wilde from my own and other private collections. Further, Mr. Holland has allowed me to use extracts from the published works of Wilde, without which the publication of such a study as this would have been made difficult, if not impossible.

Messrs. Maggs Brothers, Messrs. Dulau & Co., Ltd., and Mr. Gabriel Wells proved extremely helpful in their willingness to let me read and refer, in the text of this volume, to some of Wilde's letters in their possession.

Finally, I feel it my pleasant duty to record here my appreciation of Miss Parker McCormick's studious library research on many a problem relating to the biography of the ill-starred "apostle of beauty."

Boris Brasol.

CONTENTS

ILLUSTRATIONS

INTRODUCTORY

FOR ages, the subject of homosexuality has been strenuously banished from the forum of public discussion, and society in civilised countries has always hypocritically pretended that it had no knowledge of any such vice. The only official recognition of its existence was found in the various penal Codes. Such, in most countries, is also the present-day condition. The male homosexual is regarded as a common law criminal, and, in fact, he is treated more severely and with greater contempt than the ordinary offender. To cite but one example: in the State of New York the punishment for assault in the first degree and for burglary in the second degree is imprisonment for a term not exceeding ten years (Sections 241 and 407 of the Penal Code), whereas sodomy may be punished with imprisonment for a term as long as *twenty years* (Sections 690, 691). On the other hand, though lesbianism has rarely been legally prosecuted, it is considered a thing so hideous and so shameful that its very mention makes *comme il faut* people blush. The result of this conventional silence has proved altogether disastrous, having given birth to countless false attitudes toward, and grave misinterpretations of, a universal phenomenon which does not belong to the field of either ethics or jurisprudence.

The confusion prevailing on the subject is at once unbelievable and appalling: homosexuality is mistaken now for exhibitionism, now for incest, now for necrophilia, now for sexual murder. Laurence Housman tells the story of a famous British bacteriologist who only recently—some twenty years ago—solemnly proclaimed that sexual inversion comes "from meat-eating" and that the problem might be adequately met by putting all homosexuals to death. The blockheaded obstinacy with which people insist that these victims of biological maladjustment be treated as felons of the lowest order is all the more incomprehensible as even before Freud had solved many a riddle of man's unconscious mind, psychiatry had discovered in sexual inverts a series of symptoms which, in their conjunction, unmistakably yield a psychopathological picture. "From the first dawn of sexual feeling in youth"—we read in Forel's classic, *The Sexual Question*—"male inverts have the same feelings as girls toward other boys. They reveal the need for passive submission; they become easily enraptured over novels and dress; they like to occupy themselves with feminine pursuits, to dress like girls and to frequent women's societies . . . they are fond of religious forms and ceremonies; they admire fine clothes and luxurious apartments; they dress their hair and 'fake' themselves with a coquetry which often exceeds that of women." This description, though merely approximate and quite incomplete, as will later be seen, admirably sums up the early bizarre traits of Wilde's behaviour. In addition, from the time of boyhood, he developed that feeling of narcissism which is usually indicative of an exaggerated auto-erotic interest; unsublimated, it becomes not only the basis of egotism, but often leads to strange twists in the sexual instinct.

In the light of modern knowledge, there is, of course, not the slightest doubt that homosexuality both among men and women is one of the many forms of *psychopathia sexualis,* and while its origin is not always traceable to any particular physiological malformation, whether in the thyroid gland or in the genital zone, it invariably constitutes a psychosis, and to this extent should be conceived as a mode of insanity in general. Mental imbalance of this kind is sometimes difficult of detection, particularly among tribades or female inverts. But even uranism does not necessarily manifest itself in marked effemination: men of unquestioned virility and moral fortitude have been victims of morbid perversion. Alexander the Great, Hamilcar, Hannibal, Condé and Charles XII of Sweden, those bold conquerors and intrepid soldiers, were homosexuals, while

Julius Cæsar, the man of iron will, "unshak'd of motion" and "constant as the Northern Star," was described by a contemporary Roman writer as "every man's wife and every woman's husband."

Wilde, whose mentality and physique were strongly characteristic of his own sex, sought sexual gratification with lads of girlish appearance. At the same time, the fact should also be borne in mind that he did not experience that repugnance for women which has frequently been observed among male perverts. On the contrary, he was fond of associating with women; among his dearest friends there were several ladies of genuine mental refinement; he married Miss Constance Lloyd, a young woman of loveliness and feminine charm, for whom he had a sincere affection and by whom he had two sons. His, then, was a typical case of bi-sexualism or incomplete inversion, very similar to that of Lord Francis Bacon.

It goes without saying that sodomy and sapphism being what they are—distinctly pathological phenomena—should never be dealt with by criminal courts. In mediæval times it may have been thought proper to send lunatics, "sorcerers," "witches" and other "heretics" into the flames of a glorious *auto-da-fé,* but, in our would-be enlightened age, to have inverts subjected to hard labour and kept behind iron bars seems unbelievable and shocking.

Nevertheless, in both England and America, where homosexualism seems to be more widespread than in any other country on the globe, the censors of public morals steadily sought to attribute these deviations from the standard pattern of sexual behaviour to inherent wickedness or acquired immorality. Accordingly, when, as in the case of Oscar Wilde, a man is charged with the offence of pederasty, the press, the public and the courts give full vent to their indignation and then their virtue, to quote Macaulay's words, "becomes outrageous." On the part of the rank and file this, no doubt, is due to superstitious ignorance; but the really remarkable aspect of such paroxysms of mass folly is the despicable cowardice which men of learning, psychiatrists, pedagogues, sociologists, churchmen, criminologists and the like, have always displayed on such occasions.

Floods of hysterical denunciation of Wilde accompanied and followed his three trials, but not a single sane voice was raised in defence of science and common sense. No one from among England's distinguished medical experts has dared to inform the public that androcentrism, far from being a sign of moral depravity, is a complex resultant of psycho-physiological and environmental factors which deflect one from heterosexuality, or the biologically normal attraction for persons of the opposite sex. Nor has any writer of distinction attempted to show that in all fairness to Art the work of an artist should never be judged by the things which he may or may not have done in his private life. In our day, certainly, it would be considered sheer imbecility to challenge the beauty of the Sapphic metre because Sappho, its inventress, was addicted to lesbian love; or to question the genius of Tchaikovsky on the ground that he was a homosexual. For we have at last reached that stage of cultural development and intellectual freedom where we no longer need to invoke the authority of the vicar in order to render our verdict on a question of æsthetics or the merits of a philosophical system.

Much as homosexuality may be, and indeed is, repugnant to a wholesome person, the fact cannot be denied that this aberration is extraordinarily common. Professor N. H. B. Stoddart and Havelock Ellis state that it is being *admitted* (what about those who will not admit it?) "by about 5 per cent. of males and 10 per cent. of females." Taking this estimate for granted, one should have to conclude that in a country such as the United States, with its population of about 130,000,000, there must be some 3,500,000 lesbians, and well over 1,000,000 pederasts, or close to 5,000,000 men and women suffering from this sad anomaly! These theoretical figures seem to find support in the findings of a case survey of the sex life of 1200 unmarried American college women which, in 1934, was conducted under the supervision of Doctor Ira S. Wile.[1]

It has been furthermore observed that a large number of sexual inverts are endowed with unusual brain power and exquisite artistic talents which, however, remain more or less latent until the unnatural craving eventually finds a definite outlet in some form of homosexual practice. In other words, there appears to be a peculiar correlation between the abnormal sexual appetite and its intellectual, especially æsthetic, irradiations, a relationship, which though obscure, is nevertheless persistent and real. To many of these lords of language and sovereigns of thought, mankind owes a debt of eternal gratitude for their sublime visions and noble achievements in virtually every field of human endeavour.

What would philosophy have been without Parmenides, Zeno, Socrates and Plato? And where would our poor logic be without Aristotle, its immortal Euclid? What would have been the political destiny of ancient Greece without Solon, probably the sagest of all law-givers, Aristides, Epaminondas and Alcibiades? How much would poesy have lost if Theocritus, Pindar, Thucydides, Bion, Anacreon, Vergil, Ovid, Horace, Hafiz and Verlaine had been banished by Themis from Parnassus? Who will undertake to measure Leonardo's, Michelangelo's and Cellini's contributions to the treasury of universal Art? Who could have replaced Aristophanes, Æschylus, Euripides and Sophocles in world dramaturgy? Should we also forget how greatly the progress of German music has been enhanced by Louis II of Bavaria, that generous philharmonic? —And yet, all these men of genius admittedly were homosexuals, and each one of them is known to have indulged in the same habits for which, on the eve of the twentieth century, Oscar Wilde was sent to Reading Gaol.

Now, we can easily imagine what would have happened to a Walt Whitman or Andersen, that gentle teller of children's fairy tales, if either of them had been dragged into an English court of justice on a charge of homosexuality to be tried before so merciful a judge as Sir Alfred Wills who, having sentenced Wilde to two years of hard labour, the severest sentence that the law allowed, said, with a sigh of regret, that in his judgment the punishment was "totally inadequate." *Fiat justitia—pereat mundus.* If it had only been in his power, he would no doubt have sent to Devil's Island not only a profound moralist like La Rochefoucauld, or a distinguished naturalist such as Alexander Humboldt, or Rosa Bonheur, the famous French painter, or Renée Vivien, the honey-tongued weaver of *Cendres et Poussières,* or that marvellous dancer Nijinsky, but St. Augustine himself, and he would have told them exactly what he did tell Wilde, that "people who can do these things must be dead to all sense of shame."

It is time for the wise legislators in England and America to make a mental effort—the Lord knows how difficult this is —to grasp the plain fact that homosexuality, like any other illness of the mind, cannot be adequately dealt with by the criminal courts and that, accordingly, the place for homosexuals is not in prisons, but in hospitals, if their behaviour offends public morals; or . . . on Olympus, if by reason of their genius, they have won immortality.

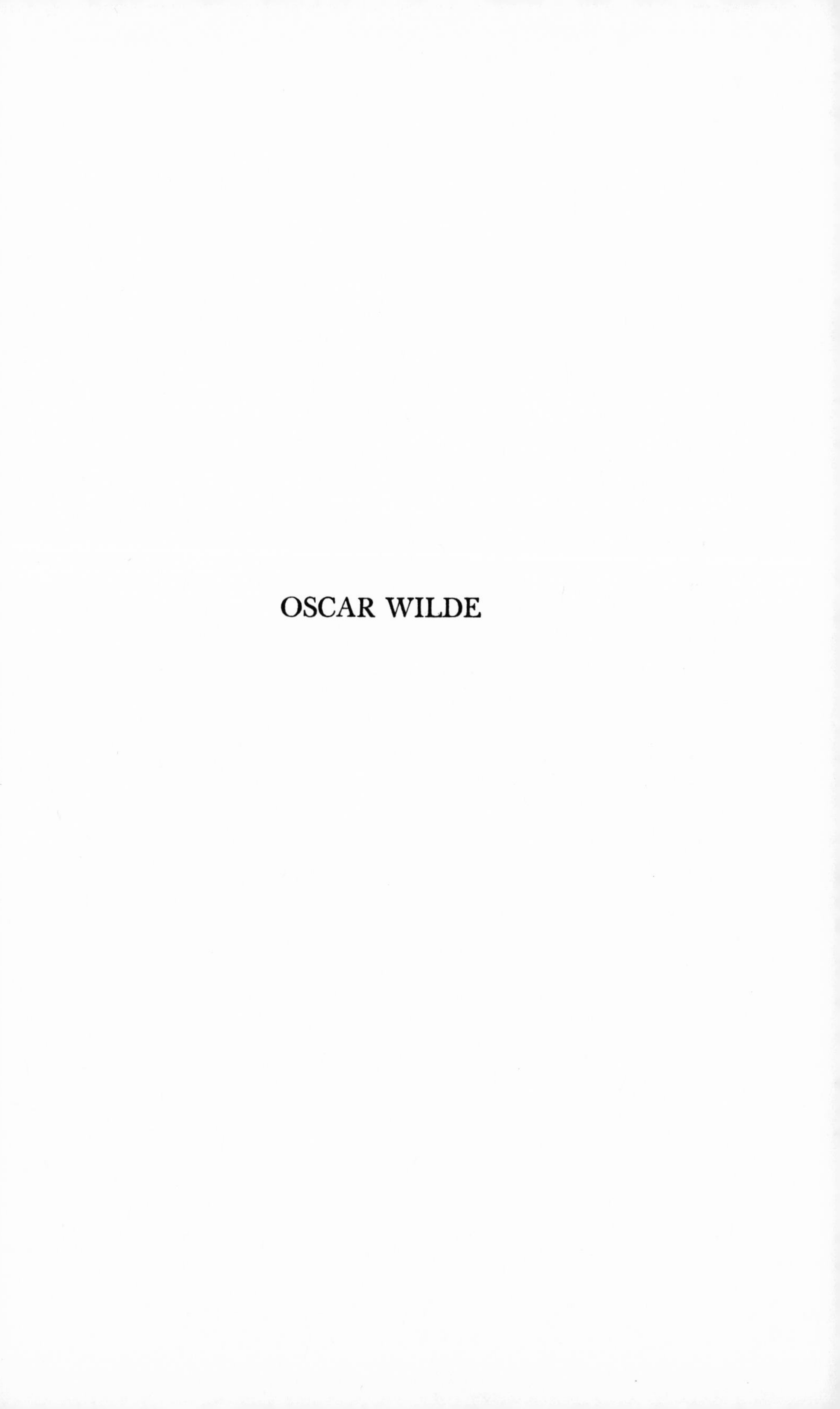

OSCAR WILDE

CHAPTER I

UNREST IN THE GOLDEN CAGE

THE august Victorian era, with its radiance and glamour, is justly considered England's Golden Age. The British then seem to have achieved everything which a nation, honourable and enterprising, may reasonably hope to attain: at no time was their international prestige so unquestioned, and their statesmanship so envied, as in those days of Gladstone, Palmerston and Disraeli. For were not both the Paris Treaty of 1856, and the Berlin Congress of 1878, England's greatest diplomatic triumphs? At no time, outwardly at least, was prosperity so solid and contentment as widespread on those Isles across the Channel, as during the three or more decades which marked the middle of Queen Victoria's long reign. At no time—not even during the Elizabethan epoch—had the British genius yielded as many illustrious characters and profound thinkers as in the years when Dickens reigned supreme in literature, Darwin in science, Irving on the stage, Spencer, Ruskin and Mill in the vast domain of abstract thought, and when Gordon, Wolseley and Roberts were scoring signal victories on the battlefields of three Continents.

What a galaxy of splendid names, brilliant careers and great deeds! The majestic empire had then reached a level of almost unexcelled fame, proudly towering amongst the nations of the world like its own mighty Rock of Gibraltar.

As we look back at the England of the Sixties and Seventies, we see her felicitous and calm, governed, guided and inspired by "saints and seers and poets and painters," all striving to lead their countrymen toward things noble and of good repute. This was a state of equilibrium, social and moral, where society, wrapped in the mantle of enlightened conservatism, was sure of its impregnable fortitude, and had no inclination to let anything, be it from within or from without, disturb its habitual modes of living.

The storms that threatened Britain's existence early in the nineteenth century had blown over, leaving in their wake the honour of Trafalgar and the glory of Waterloo, bequeathing to the nation the imperishable laurels of Wellington and Nelson.

The Continental thunders of 1848, of which the Chartist Rebellion was but an echo, died away without loosening the rivets of England's historical structure: on the surface, life there as ever remained still, Sabbatarian and pacific. The noisy agitation of the Forties, stirred by the inflammatory orations of O'Brien, was soon forgotten and safely buried under what Sir William Watson called "the dust of vanished collisions."

With internal peace restored, English society settled down to bring order into its own house. Above all, the people wanted to devise a moral code which they, as a body, could safely practice and to which they could faithfully adhere. The Queen herself had set a very precise *modus vivendi* which, to the average Englishman, carried an immediate appeal. Benson justly remarked that Victoria,

> both as a Queen and as a housewife, conducted her life on broad, simple principles, hating anything flamboyant or "extraordinary," quite uninterested in problems of human nature and the dim mysterious yearnings which inspire art and music; simple and sincere in her religion, troubled neither by ecstasy nor by theological complexities, bringing up her children with affection and firmness in the fear of God and of herself.

The Prince Consort was not merely the Queen's "intimate and sole secretary," as Guizot styled him, "but her loyal and worthy counterpart." Lieutenant-General C. Grey made this observation about Albert's exemplary conduct:

> He . . . from the first laid down strict, not to say severe, rules for his own guidance. He imposed a degree of restraint and self-denial upon his own movements, which could not but have been irksome had he not been sustained by a sense of the advantage which the throne would de-

rive from it. . . . Scandal itself could take no liberty with his name. . . . The country in general knew how to estimate and admire the beauty of domestic life beyond reproach, or the possibility of reproach.

The reign of Victoria was one of virtuous domesticity, unshaken common sense and respectability incarnate. She was anything but a dreamer: both her policies and personal habits were calculated, though unconsciously perhaps, to please the middle class which she recognised as the real power of her realm. Of course, the Queen had no quarrel with the aristocracy. She knew that royal insignia and armorial bearings, even as the precious crown, which on state occasions she wore with so much dignity, were the necessary and revered trappings of any Monarchy. But with her clear vision she discerned unmistakable signs of the impending decomposition of England's hereditary peerage long before this fact became apparent to both the rulers and the ruled. And so she made up her mind to draw her chief support from the bourgeoisie which, throughout Europe, had been acquiring an ever-increasing political weight. She had the happy knack of divining the fads and leanings of that Puritan *tiers-état* which in Arnold's estimate was "still the best stuff in the nation." In return, the commoners regarded their Queen with unwavering respect and enthusiastic devotion. They sought to emulate her example by creating in their own homes an atmosphere of accentuated decency and good manners such as pervaded the whole mid-Victorian era, and which only a few decades later, in the Queen's own words, "alas, was no longer the fashion."

With all the advantages which such a *status quo* unmistakably possessed, it was necessarily fraught with shortcomings, all the more embarrassing since the petty niceties of the daily etiquette and the humbug of domestic conventions *à la longue* had grown tedious. And in a community where decency and virtue are being ardently practiced and assiduously advertised, there is always the danger of hypocrisy, pedantry and Philistinism eventually coming to blossom. Besides, no nation has ever lastingly endured the curse of glutted fecundity with the boredom of a social Paradise. Whenever these, after much labour, struggle and pain, had been ultimately attained, people began to experience a peculiar feeling of restless nervosity, and they would start looking for some sort of change, knowing not whither they should turn. This is true of all eras of economic affluence and political complacence: such was the end of "the glory that was Greece" and the sad finale of Marcus Aurelius' righteous reign; the same fate befell Bismarck's illustrious epoch, and such was also the dénouement of the stately Victorian drama.

A strange force, sometimes described as social dynamics, appears to be always challenging the stability of national existence at the very moment when its aims seem to have about reached their complete realisation. The disruptive currents find their source in the individual who, though part of the social texture, seeks, in an effort of self-assertion, to drift away from that body to which he naturally belongs. Secure immobility causes in him a condition of dissatisfied fatigue; and gradually, inner unrest diffuses itself among ever more numerous groups, whose incongruous oscillations, at first, lead to nothing but an aimless imbalance amidst a world of inert dogmas and outworn traditions.

It often happens that the spirit of rebellion against a highly respectable civic order—before it affects those who, by quaint avocation, are addicted to politics, or are professionally engaged in the queer occupation of overthrowing monarchies, makes its first outburst amongst those so called "shy wooers of the fair Muses," who, ostensibly, stand farthest from the monotonous vicissitudes of parliamentary conflicts and the lively experiences of soapbox combats.

In England, too, the earliest signs of protest against the stiff comfort provided by the golden cage of the Victorian epoch revealed themselves in the bohemian sets of the artistic *milieu.*

As far back as in 1847, the banner of dissension from conventional æsthetics was hoisted by three then obscure young men—William Holman Hunt, John Everett Millais and Dante Gabriel Rossetti.[1] Hypnotised by the bewitching eloquence of

[1] For notes, see Appendix.

Ruskin, they proclaimed a new symbol of faith in which all painting subsequent to Raphael was declared defective and was unhesitatingly swept into the discard.

These enthusiasts were earnestly convinced that the pictorial craft had deteriorated and turned banal because it had abandoned its primitive simplicity. According to them, the eclectic school of Carracci; or that of Veronese with the crowded luxury of his palette; or the sensually prolific Rubens, and even the divine Raphael himself, had lost the secret of the true sense of line and colour of the earlier masters—Orcagna, Gozzoli and others—who faithfully copied only that which they actually perceived in Nature. And was it not Ruskin, the zealous prophet of the new cult, who had boldly declared that Nature is the most beautiful and the most majestic manifestation of Divine Providence? And did he not preach that it was the duty of the artist to absorb with painful diligence the minutest details of the material which he endeavours to reproduce on his silent canvases?

Nor were Ruskin's sermons addressed to painters only. For it was he who, referring to the architect and speaking of the things he should be taught, came forth with this advice:

> Send him to our hills and let him study there what nature understands by a buttress and what by a dome.

And it was also he who urged the student to envisage Nature with his heart open and his mind concentrated on the one task of penetrating into her profound mysteries, piously accepting her lessons, "rejecting nothing, neglecting nothing and scorning nothing."

This was the creed which Wordsworth so beautifully expressed in his well-known lines:

> One impulse from the vernal wood
> Can teach us more of man,
> Of moral evil and of good,
> Than all the sages can.

Nebulous though this novel doctrine was, it conveyed a strong impetus to the determination of Hunt and his young friends to test the technique proposed by Ruskin, and they went about their task like conspirators clandestinely gathering under the dark mantle of the night.

About these actors in the English drama La Sizeranne said:

> They were quite gifted by nature, passionately longing for success. The trio constituted an accomplished whole: Hunt possessed faith, Rossetti—eloquence, Millais—talent. The Italian more than anything was a poet; Millais—more than anything a painter; Hunt—more than anything a Christian.

The three formed the nucleus of the Pre-Raphaelite Brotherhood, a secret order, which hid its identity under the innocent initials "P. R. B."

Hunt selected as a subject for his début the historical scene of Rienzi taking the oath to avenge his murdered brother; Rossetti, the theme of "Childhood of the Holy Virgin," and Millais, Keats' lovely and mournful poem *Isabella.*

Millais and Hunt exhibited their pictures at the Royal Academy, and Rossetti sent his to the Chinese Gallery at Hyde Park Corner, where Madox Brown was just then causing a sensation among the stolid Londoners by "The Fate of Cordelia," a chef d'œuvre inspired by the Shakespearean tragedy.

At first, the critics, the public and even the wise Royal Academicians took the rebels with a good deal of tolerance. No one, apparently, was dumbfounded by their realistic manner, while the mysterious letters, "P. R. B.," on the joist of Isabella's chair, remained altogether unnoticed. The young painters met with such success that some of their pictures were even purchased by private English collectors.

However, the secret aims of the Brotherhood soon began to leak out, and then a flood of indignation burst over English society.

For a group of juvenile artists to have had the courage to challenge the authority of Raphael, and still more, the sanctity of England's æsthetic constitution, was an unheard of blasphemy which provoked sharp resentment amongst the guardians of British manners. The press promptly instituted a campaign against the Pre-Raphaelites, to which even Dickens added his voice of protest. He attacked Millais for his "Christ in the Home of His Parents." The painter's naturalistic treatment of the adolescent Jesus and all the other personages, including the Holy Virgin and St. Anne, utterly shocked the Dean of the English writers, and he came out with this tirade:

> You come in this Royal Academy Exhibition, . . . to the contemplation of a Holy Family. You will have the goodness to discharge from your minds all Post-Raphael ideas, all religious aspirations, all elevating thoughts, all tender, awful, sorrowful, ennobling, sacred, graceful or beautiful associations; and to prepare yourselves, as befits such a subject—Pre-Raphaelly considered—for the lowest depths of what is mean, odious, repulsive and revolting.

Altogether, public opinion unequivocally condemned the Pre-Raphaelite conspiracy: the brethren were suspected of being dangerous dreamers threatening the safety of the Realm. No one really knew what their theory of painting was and why it had to be opposed or mocked, but to the rank and file Victorian the idea itself of innovation was intolerable as it carried the preposterous suggestion that anything either should or could be improved in an order of things which was based upon a set of certainties and on immutable finality.

Inasmuch as the Pre-Raphaelites were an overwhelming minority, theirs was a truly precarious situation, and for a while it seemed that the barrage opened against their front would crush their resistance. Still, the very tumult of the battle contributed clamorous novelty to their aims and issues, making people talk, and some of them even think, about a subject which hitherto had hardly ever been either noticed or discussed.

In his tranquil retreat at Denmark Hill, Ruskin kept silent, maintaining an attitude of watchful neutrality toward the contending parties. But, from the moment when war had been declared, he realised that at the bottom of the whole controversy lay the deeply rooted animosity of mummified conservatism—of which the Academy was then the doughty stronghold—toward the freedom of the artist's self-expression. And to him coercion of this kind was repugnant.

So, it was at the darkest hour of the Pre-Raphaelite retreat that Ruskin took up his pen in their defence. His two letters to the editor of the omnipotent *Times* in vindication of the insurgent school created a real sensation.

Rather cleverly, and with utmost candour, in discussing, for instance, Hunt's "Valentine and Sylvia," Ruskin uncovered its various defects, but, at the same time, he stressed the "marvellous truth of detail," "the intense harmony of colour," and "the most perfect ease of touch and mastery of effect" that characterised the new pictorial genre. The Pre-Raphaelite canvases, in his opinion, were blessed with that "freedom of execution" which he deemed a sign of "modern excellence." And he claimed this quality to be lacking even in so great a master as Van Eyck.

Ruskin concluded his plea with the prophecy that, notwithstanding all their errors and imperfections, the Pre-Raphaelites eventually would "lay in our England the foundations of a School of Art nobler than the world has ever seen for three hundred years."

Coming as it did from a recognised student and honoured teacher, Ruskin's rebuttal supplied the Pre-Raphaelite movement with increased vigour. Many a critic was compelled to revise his sympathies and test his idiosyncrasies. Step by step, the Brotherhood managed to recapture the position it had lost. And, finally, nothing else was left for artistic officialdom than to acknowledge the *fait accompli* of its own defeat. The Liverpool Academy went so far as to confer honours on Hunt for that very picture which Ruskin had so ingeniously advertised. And then, only one year later, Millais scored a momentous triumph when he unveiled to the public his "Ophelia," as she emerged to him from the "weeping brook" in which "from her melodious lay" she was dragged "to muddy death."

Not only was Pre-Raphaelitism saved, but soon its ranks were strengthened by the intervention of such sparkling talents Burne-Jones, George Watts, and Alma-Tadema, whose works today adorn the walls of both the Tate and the National Galleries.

Now, the battles which raged in the field of painting were but a repercussion of that inner commotion which threatened the ideological stability of the Anglo-Saxon world. Blomfield is right when he states that the Pre-Raphaelite venture was not exclusively an artistic affair and that at a rather early date it had been taken over by the literati. As time went on, the seemingly innocent palette and brush incident grew into a mighty challenge to the whole array of political, social, ethical and philosophical principles which constituted the foundation, the Alpha and Omega, of the Victorian era.

Paraphrasing Poushkin's well-known lines it might be said that the first P. R. brethren

> . . . . disregarding worlds' relations,
> Like lawless comets, in their course,
> Swept right along with reckless force,
> Amidst well-settled constellations.

The psychological effect of their mutiny was so great that it actually led to a *Götterdämmerung,* if not to a complete dethroning, of the recognised Olympian gods.

Revolt was everywhere: not merely in the Brotherhood's vague longing for a spiritual revival of art, or in Ruskin's *mot d'ordre* for the return to Nature, in his fiery protest against the shabby ugliness of unrestricted industrialism; but also in Arnold's craving for culture and in Pater's subtly conceived and delicately etched meditations about the sinfully fascinating epoch of the Renaissance; in Mill's worship of Liberty; in Carlyle's deification of strength and in the creations of Morris, "the idle singer of an empty day," the aimless wanderer to some "nameless city in a distant sea," with his Gothic taste and strange fondness for medievalism; in the obscure phantasms of Browning, who, like Beethoven, suffered from an over-abundance of ideational content, and in Swinburne's rhythmical affectations and effete mannerism, in his reverent hymns to Hugo's "magnificent forest of verse" and his bold rejection of everything that tends to restrain the self-divulgence of the human spirit. And even Dickens, despite his apparent *Gemütlichkeit,* domesticity and good-natured humour, was amongst those "movers" and "shakers" who, unconsciously perhaps, were labouring for the undermining of the solid Victorian structure. For Dickens—whose rise Chesterton so aptly compares with the rising o fa vast mob—Dickens, too, could see no compromise with a society where the poor were adjured from the pulpit the practice of "an impossible thrift." And his very realism, the faithful mirroring of the common fellow in English everyday life, produced, on the whole, a shocking picture of a highly explosive character.

The newly aroused critical instinct which, for so many decades, had been kept suppressed by the heavy load of Victorian virtue, suddenly converted every truism of public ethics and every axiom of national philosophy into a complex theorem or an insoluble riddle.

Everywhere there appeared menacing signs of discontent with the gilded glory of material wealth, the chills of self-infatuated Puritanism, and that state of things which Macaulay described as "the Paradise of cold hearts and narrow minds."

Of these troubled moods Carlyle's passionate and impatient protest:

> I do not want cheaper cotton, swifter railroads—I want, what Novalis called—"God, Freedom, Immortality,"

was indeed representative. Quite in line with Ruskin's condemnation of England's urban civilisation and its "rattling, growling, smoking, stinking, ghastly heap of fermenting brickwork," the British began to lose faith in the infallibility of those modes of existence which they had set up for themselves.

> Forward, backward, backward, forward
> in the immeasurable sea,
> Sway'd by vaster ebbs and flows than
> can be known to you or me,

may have been a true description of man's impotence before the eternal Sphinx of Life. But only a few continued to find relief in such fatalistic formulæ: the spirit of adventurous pioneering forcibly diverted the younger Victorians from that well-settled and self-sufficient Toryism which by the middle of the nineteenth century had become less a philosophy than a mere habit of the public mind.

The antiquated catechism of British morality and æsthetic taste, like Carthage, had to be destroyed by the blows and stings of a new generation devoid of the gift of compromise, and craving like that Rebel-Sail of Lermontov for storms *quand-même*—"as though in tempests there is peace."

It was only reasonable to expect that, sooner or later, there should have appeared in the limelight of England's national stage someone who, even at the price of public ridicule, would carry the protest against Victorian conventionalism to its bitter end.

The person who assumed this embarrassing rôle was Oscar Fingal O'Flahertie Wills Wilde, whose career, brilliantly though it had begun, could not have culminated, at least on British soil, in anything but complete disaster.

Tempi passati!

The crusades of olden days no longer stir our imagination or excite our feelings. The battle-cries which then sounded daring and defiant, today are either forgotten or bear the stamp of academic approbation—and this last, as a rule, is but a polite token of general oblivion. We meditate over the things our fathers looked upon as delightfully intriguing with a sigh of regret, a sigh for that "lovely toy, so fiercely sought," which

. . . lost its charm by being caught.

CHAPTER II

THE ILLUSTRIOUS PARENTS

ALL-PACIFYING time has enabled the present-day biographer of Oscar Wilde to inquire into his enigmatic personality and to treat of his literary legacy *sine ira et studio,* with an objectiveness that could hardly have been expected from earlier commentators who stood too close to the memorable events which marked the tragic end of a career once crowned with unparalleled success and with fame that was greater perhaps than the man himself.

Belonging, as we do, to a generation at once remote from the Victorian era and altogether free from its prejudices and conventions, we are in a better position to judge Wilde than those who were either sympathetic or scornful spectators of his drama which, with a cruelty so patent and futile, was wrought upon him and cynically exhibited to the world by an inherently hypocritical society.

When, in our day, one's behaviour is diagnosed, it is customary to take into account not merely the man's bare acts, but also his psycho-genetic background and that complex gamut of external circumstances which exercises a potent influence upon character formation. After all, it is only by this somewhat elaborate method that light may be shed upon the obscure process of *Personalausbildung,* or personality development, a theme which, incidentally, has become so popular amongst our contemporaneous crime explorers.

In a volume such as this, where an attempt is made to combine the unusually intriguing life story of an artist with a critical evaluation of his sophisticated literary record, the ætiological approach becomes not only legitimate but imperative; all the more so as Wilde has revealed in his writings, with remarkable candour, the emotional tone of his many-faceted ego—the cryptic workings of his soul, the clandestine longings of his heart, the intimate leanings of his mind. And Wilde's genius was pre-eminently the outgrowth of his personality—brilliant though superficial, artistic but artificial, unilateral in its manifestations and yet mosaically eclectic,—a strange conglomeration of most contradictory attitudes, a queer psychological pattern like that of Poushkin's Onegin, about whom it was said that,

> Absorbed by vanity, he also possessed a kind of arrogance which made him view with equal indifference the bad things as well as the good—a posture which was due to a feeling of superiority, imaginary perhaps.

Despite his noble impulses and innate kindness, Wilde took delight in advertising his egotism, the absence in him of any ethical sympathy and kindred "virtues." "A heart," he proclaimed, "does not suit me. Somehow, it doesn't go with modern dress."

Of course, this utterance was but one of the innumerable manifestations of his pose, about which so many droll anecdotes have been recounted and scrupulously recorded. And yet his bravura was sincere and he permitted it to taint even his style, the one thing which he did take seriously in life. Carefully preconceived dandyism was the key to his philosophy and it left a peculiar stigma upon many of his creations, possibly without his being aware of this, or cognizant of the truth that no art is ever perfect if it is at all pretentious.

Even though textbooks on genetics may disagree on the extent to which mental traits and temperamental leanings are inheritable, it appears certain that Oscar, physiologically and psychologically, was a faithful product of both his parents, each of whom contributed a generous share to the moulding of their son's manners, habits and predilections.

Both Sir William and Lady Wilde were unusually intellectual and endowed with urbane refinement. Both were known for their remarkable erudition in widely divergent fields of learning, and both had striking accomplishments to their credit.

Doctor Wilde was honoured by royalty both at home and

abroad. In 1857, the Order of the Polar Star was conferred upon him by Oscar I, the King of Sweden. Not only was Sir William a brilliant physician of European repute who had been called "the father of modern otology," but he had also laboured fruitfully and intensely as an archæologist and litterateur, an ingenious collector of Irish folklore, and a most gifted statistician, to whom, in 1864, Lord Carlisle, then Viceroy of Ireland, addressed these significant words:

> Mr. Wilde, I propose to confer on you the honour of knighthood, not so much in recognition of your high professional reputation . . . but to mark my sense of the services you have rendered to Statistical Science, especially in connection with the Irish census.

Sir William was also awarded the Cunningham Medal of the Royal Irish Academy, a well-earned reward for his distinguished work in the field of the history of Celtic culture. With remarkable perseverance he studied the legends of Ireland and the superstitions of her people. He had a pronounced taste for antiquarian research, and he used to spend much of his time roaming about the ancient Irish castles, forts and caves around Castlerea and in the valley of Ruthcragan. Oscar sometimes accompanied his father on these journeys, and the site of the many mysterious places which they visited must have made a profound impression on the romantic nature of young Wilde.

A writer of great talent, Doctor Wilde left behind him a scientific heritage that is still, after many decades, treasured and explored by students of Ireland's past. Sir William died on April 19, 1876; he was then working on a life of Béranger which was subsequently completed by Lady Wilde. She was not biased when she gave this estimate of her late husband's distinguished achievements:

> There was probably no man of his generation more versed in our national literature, in all that concerned the land and the people, the arts, architecture, topography, statistics and even the legends of the country; but above all, in his favoured department, the descriptive illustration of Ireland, past and present, in historic and prehistoric times, he has justly

SIR WILLIAM ROBERT WILLS WILDE

(1815-1876)

gained a wide reputation as one of the most learned and accurate, and at the same time one of the most popular, writers of the age on such subjects. In misty cloudland of Irish antiquities, he may especially be looked upon as a safe and steadfast guide.

But perhaps the noblest piece of this illustrious man's life work was the foundation of the Royal Victoria Eye and Ear Hospital in Dublin, his native city, where he had started and vigorously pursued his career. To the improvement and growth of that institution he had disinterestedly contributed many years of assiduous labour and considerable sums of money. All this made him a popular figure in Ireland, particularly beloved by the poor who, in thousands, have benefited by his wise medical advice.

Still, it is a matter of common knowledge that Sir William Wilde was a man of amoral, not to use the word "immoral," proclivities, and some writers, notably Frank Harris, in their accounts of him, have relished every minute detail of his alleged trespasses against the moral, if not, indeed, the criminal, code. To what extent, for instance, the notorious "Miss Travers" incident was, or was not true, is a matter of little importance, since it appears undeniable that Sir William could not have been classed amongst the really staunch supporters of the monogamic principle, and that, being over-sensual, he actually did indulge in a fervent and somewhat unrestrained affection for the ladies. In his usual reserved manner, Sherard tells us that Sir William "left besides his legitimate children, a number of natural offspring." And Oscar Wilde himself, with an air of unperturbed innocence, gave out to the world the story of a mysterious "veiled and silent woman" in deep mourning, who, notwithstanding the presence of Lady Wilde, used to appear every morning with a nurse's punctiliousness, at Sir William's dying bed.

Searching biographers have also noted that, even in a stronger measure than most nineteenth-century Irishmen, Sir William was addicted to alcohol so that "though never intoxicated, he was rarely sober."

As for Lady Wilde, née Jane Francesca Elgee, her reputation as an ardent, if not violent, Irish nationalist, though overrated, was partly justified by her fiery appeal to arms which, in July 1848, appeared under her *nom de plume* "Speranza," in *The Nation,* a weekly published at the time in Dublin. In that article she did urge her countrymen to burn the Castle, which —if one were to take her statements seriously—was "the keystone of English power" and a symbol of oppression, something like that old Bastille.

However, aside from this *faute de jeunesse,* Speranza did hardly anything at all to vindicate her claim to political martyrdom, and she is not known either to have murdered a British Viceroy, or bitten an English "bobby," or even set fire to Buckingham Palace.

Be that as it may, the Irish like to think of Speranza as a really uncompromising iconoclast. In support of this contention time and again they have cited with pride her *Resurgam,* a poem in which she expressed sublime confidence in the triumph of justice:

> For our right is might
> In the deadly fight
> We wage with the powers of evil,
> And our thunder-words
> Are like lifted swords
> To war against man or devil.

But notwithstanding her rebellious ire, her avowed intention to shake the British throne and to tread the path of "our martyred dead," Speranza did not divorce her husband after he had been knighted, and she accepted Ladyship with a graceful smile, though perhaps not without a subdued sigh.

The truth of the matter is that Lady Wilde was a woman of culture and unquestioned mental ability, who wrote a number of books on this and that—on driftwood from Scandinavia and ancient charms of Ireland, on social topics and "the first temptation," the glacier land and the French Revolution, not to speak of a volume of poems in which she exhibited genuine poetic talent.

But in the case of Lady Wilde, too, the fine qualities of her mind strangely blended with the most queer and grotesque characteristics. From the various accounts of her career it is safe to deduce that she had an irresistible craving for mannerism which converted her mode of living into a perpetual pose. As she grew older—and no woman forever stays young, though most of them will not admit it—this attitude of artificiality assumed almost maniacal proportions. Even such a sincere admirer of the "noble Speranza" as Anna, Comtesse de Brémont, in her most sympathetic sketch of Lady Wilde, was forced to admit that her manners and quaint attire, the "towering headdress of velvet, the long gold earrings," her huge bracelets of turquoise and gold—her whole appearance, produced a painful impression of conspicuous purposiveness. More impartial observers, like Miss Hamilton or Miss Corkran, have furnished us with ample data on this bizarre twist of Lady Wilde's otherwise brilliant mind.

When we now think of that kindhearted and, in many ways, brave woman, we cannot dissociate her picture from "the voluminous crinolined skirt of crimson red," the blue black glossy hair covered with a crown of laurels; a face overladen and overloaded with paint "too thick for any ordinary light"; the yellow lace fichu crossed on her breast with a string of miniature brooches which made her look like "a vast terrifying person with a strangely toned voice," as Mr. W. B. Maxwell describes her, a "walking family mausoleum," or "a tragedy Queen of a suburban theatre."

No doubt, all this subterfuge, those petty tricks to which Lady Wilde resorted in her daily "make-up," must have contagiously affected Oscar.

Besides, it is said that the good lady desperately tried to conceal the fact that she had first reached, and then passed, the Balzac mark of *une femme de trente ans*. Thus, having before him the example of an aging yet pathologically juvenescent mother, Oscar after all was right when he coined his immortal epigram:

> London society is full of women of the very highest birth who have, of their own choice, remained thirty-five for years.

Another thing that added to Lady Wilde's incongruity was her distasteful admiration of titles and pageantry. Most assuredly, this was inconsistent with her record as an Irish ex-revolutionist. As she gradually skied down the social ladder from her Merrion Square mansion to that "dingy house" in Oakley Street, her weakness for the *beau monde* became more pathetic.

A spirited and self-denying hostess, Speranza combined the gift of a subtle *diseuse* with the defect of an incurable talker. It was one of her life ambitions to acquire the reputation of a London Madame Récamier, and for a while at least her "crushes" were quite in vogue. The English snobs, in those days, considered it "smart" to be sandwiched in Lady Wilde's Chelsea drawing room between some shabby art critic and a stage star of second magnitude. Yet it is doubtful if she really had what Sherard calls *l'art de faire le salon:* her Saturday receptions, crowded though they were, far from gaining the distinction of genuinely aristocratic affairs, became a meeting place of obscure celebrities who were seeking to advertise their mediocre talents to London Society.

Unwittingly perhaps, Wilde painted in *Lord Arthur Savile's Crime* an amusingly true picture of a London medley which must have strikingly resembled Lady Wilde's gatherings in Oakley Street:

> Gorgeous peeresses [says he] chatted affably to violent Radicals, popular preachers brushed coat-tails with eminent sceptics, a perfect bevy of bishops kept following a stout primadonna from room to room; on the staircase stood several Royal Academicians, disguised as artists, and it was said that at one time the supper room was absolutely crammed with geniuses.

Speranza's propensity for social climbing exercised an ineradicable influence upon Oscar's conduct, and it added to his own posing an element of the *ridicule,* which, in turn, exposed him to just public censure, making him more vulnerable to satiric arrows and unpleasant notoriety at a time when it would have been best for him to have dwelt in the shadow of public oblivion.

CHAPTER III

OSCAR'S CHILDHOOD

OSCAR FINGAL O'FLAHERTIE WILLS WILDE descended from straight Irish parentage: there might have been a slight admixture of Italian blood on his mother's side, but it is certain that in his father's lineage there was a somewhat remote Saxon strain, since Ralph Wilde, Sir William's grandfather, was the son of a Durham resident, who left England about the middle of the eighteenth century, proceeded to Connaught, and settled in Castlerea. Although both Oscar's parents were Protestants, and not Roman Catholics, their Celtic origin predetermined their filial affection for Ireland and her unhappy people.

This racial factor also proved a dominant trait in Oscar's psychic constitution, colouring his whole mental fabric with an unmistakable Irish impress:—flashing wit without the tempering counsel of true wisdom; sparkling humour lacking the mitigating influence of sound judgment; intense longing for effect devoid of the sobering restraint of genuine passion; and last, but not least—alert shrewdness, deliberately evading the effort of earnest planning. Altogether, his was an orientation of the mind which the Irish themselves must have suspected in the fox, "whose skin," they claim, "despite his cunning, is often sold."

It is a well-known fact that Lady Wilde, when she was pregnant with her second child, had set her heart upon a daughter, and she was profoundly grieved over the birth of a boy. It is said that she continued to dress up Oscar in petticoats and treat him as a girl long after the period customary in her day. She even used to hang jewels on her little son which, according to Georges Claretie,[1] made him look like a miniature Hindoo idol.

Anna de Brémont laid much stress upon Lady Wilde's strange aversion to male progeny. She sought to explain this phenomenon by the nebulous contention that Speranza had a "masculine soul." To this one can only say, "Who knows?"— Nor is there much to sustain the theory that Oscar "possessed the feminine soul."

> This [said the Countess] was the ghost that haunted his house of life, that sat beside him at the feast and sustained him in the day of famine: the secret influence that weighted down his manhood and enervated his hope: the knowledge that he possessed the feminine soul; that he was a slave to the capricious, critical feminine temperament, the feminine vanity and feminine weakness to temptation, the feminine instinct of adaptability, the feminine impulse of the wanton's soul, gave him the lust for strange, forbidden pleasures and imparted to his final repentance the sublime abnegation of the Magdalene.

And then, continuing her analysis, she drew this arbitrary conclusion:

> He was doomed before his birth, hence, the strange maternal spirit of divination that urged his mother to wish that the child she was about to bring to the world would be a girl. The mother instinct sensed the feminine soul that had taken form within her.

It is possible that, influenced by Plato's provocative legend of the "androgene" or by Weininger's more recent and less imaginative conjectures about the interrelation of sex and character, Countess de Brémont conceived the bold idea that the mystery of Wilde's inverted personality may be adequately explained by the preponderance in him of the feminine over the masculine element, which may or may not have been so. Still, abstractions such as these can neither be proved to be fallacious nor demonstrated to be true, and in the case of our poet, they are more apt to becloud the issues than to clarify them. Nor is there much need for invoking either Freud or Plato or Jung in order to appreciate the fact that Oscar's entourage, the whole trend at his parents' home, the sum total of the environmental influences to which he was subjected,

"SPERANZA," LADY WILDE, OSCAR WILDE'S MOTHER

(1826-1896)

would eventually generate in him queer attitudes and erratic impulses of the most hazardous kind.

From the very day when, on October 16, 1854,[2] Oscar was born into this world at 21 Westland Row, Dublin,[3] he had been imbibing an orthodox Irish atmosphere permeated with lavish and loose hospitality—delightful in a way, but careless, fascinating, and yet lacking that order or system which, in family life, goes to make for stability and good demeanour.

Brilliant though Sir William Wilde was, his influence upon Oscar's character could not have been entirely beneficial; not only, as we know, was his moral credo of a dubious fortitude, but his habits as a convivial drinker made it impossible for him to give the proper attention to his children's education. This was all the more regrettable since his wife was busily engaged in catering to her improvised salon, and wasting her extraordinary eloquence and iridescent intellect on a crowd of men and women who were recruited from rather mixed strata of Dublin society—medical men and artists, publishers and writers, politicians and mere drinkers—some of whom not only laid no claim to fame but even exhibited no indications of an earmarked profession. Literary talks were often followed by late suppers at which much wit was displayed by both hosts and guests, but where considerable quantities of liquor were also merrily consumed.

As Oscar and his brother Willy, who was two years his senior, grew older, they were warmly admitted to these unceremonious parties, where they eagerly absorbed many a risqué idea which was freely expressed and heatedly debated by the members of those half-sober conclaves.

The following passage is taken from a biographical note of Oscar Wilde which thus refers to his adolescent period.

> . . . The boy before his eighth year had learnt the ways to "the shores of old romance," had seen the apples plucked from the tree of knowledge, and had gazed with wondering eyes into the "younger day." This upbringing suited his idiosyncrasy; indeed with his temperament it is impossible to conceive what else could have been done with him.

To be sure, there is no printed record of the things that transpired in the Wilde mansion, at 1 Merrion Square, yet, one is inclined to share Sherard's view that ethics occupied but a secondary place in the daily routine of that distinguished household, so that Oscar was perhaps not far from the truth when he once said to a fellow undergraduate of his at Trinity College: "Come home with me, I want to introduce you to my Mother. We have founded a Society for the Suppression of Virtue."

Neither Sir William nor his wife was capable of building up in the children those mechanisms of self-defence which ordinarily perform the function of powerful deterrents to the temptations of the world. It is upon these deeply rooted moral principles and carefully conceived rational convictions that man's character is altogether dependent. To Oscar, however, all considerations of ethical order were indifferent, if not actually boring.

What his parents transmitted to him was a pronounced intellectualism, a sincere admiration for classicism with a keen appreciation of literary taste and style. Oscar's early wanderings with Sir William over Ireland, where he first learned the romance of archæology and the charm of a folk tale; his journeys across the Channel, now to Germany—that land of ancient sagas and medieval castles, now to France, with her lovely scenery and cultural refinement, the graceful lightness of her literature and the elusive fascination of her art—all these, indeed, were at once rare and most instructive experiences in a boy's life. For a mind as quick and susceptible as that with which Oscar was endowed, the multi-coloured impressions which were thus accumulated during his early youth must have proved suggestive of many a fertile idea, which, later, he exploited so admirably in his creations.

And yet, no one taught him that man's earthly existence, far from consisting merely of pleasurable privileges and reverently acknowledged rights, is a long chain of rigid duties toward kin and neighbour, society and State, God and himself. From the dawn of his days, Oscar had been observing in his parents' house avowed contempt for restraint, complete lack of inner discipline, and that "indifference towards the good things as well as the bad" which is typical of superficial, though at times sparkling liberal mentality. No one spoke to him about the sighs of silent grief and the tears of despairing woe that make heads turn grey and hearts grow cold. So the child could hardly have been blamed for not understanding the horror of misery and misunderstanding the meaning of compassion for other people's pain. And when, many years later, Lady Wilde, who was then facing troubles of her own, would start reminding her son of Goethe's lines:

> Who never ate his bread in sorrow,
> Who never spent the midnight hours
> Weeping and waiting for the morrow,
> He knows you not, ye heavenly powers,

he would listen to her with impatience, and at one time he confessed: "I do not want to eat my bread in sorrow, or to pass any night weeping and watching for the dawn." Not before the Reading tragedy did he discover the true value and purifying dignity of human suffering. Only in *De Profundis* did he finally succeed in lifting his spirit above the shallow commonplace of self-satisfied and satiating egotism, and then, swayed by his own humiliation, he exclaimed:

> Where there is sorrow, there is holy ground. Some day people will realise what that means. They will know nothing of life till they do.

When at last he had reached in his philosophy this lofty point, alas, it was too late for him to have remodelled his past or rationally fashioned his future. Before he had been taught that pathetic lesson, he continued to maintain a selfish attitude toward the world around him, and gradually, he even developed a real distaste for everything that reminded him of duty. Certainly, he was very much in earnest when he cynically declared: "The only way to get rid of temptation is to yield to it." To him, then, the line of least resistance became the only intelligible method of dealing with the conventional intricacies of a social existence.

This, indeed, was a dangerous path to choose, particularly for a man of Wilde's mental pattern who firmly believed that his intellectual equipment was far above that of any ordinary mortal. He made his conviction so conspicuous that it was at once seized by his Catos and turned against him. *Punch,* for instance, satirising the interview of the reporter for *The World* with Wilde on the occasion of his arrival in New York, struck the right keynote in attributing to him these words:

> Precisely. I took the Newdigate. Oh, no doubt, every year some man gets the Newdigate; but not every year does the Newdigate get an Oscar.

But one doesn't have to quote *Punch* in order to grasp the full extent of Wilde's vanity. For he himself evinced it in his *The Disciple,* that charming poem in prose about the death of Narcissus and the Pool whose "cup of sweet waters" changed "into a cup of salt tears."

> But I loved Narcissus, whispered the Pool, because as he lay on my banks and looked down at me, in the mirror of his eyes I saw ever my own beauty mirrored.

This super-narcissism developed in Wilde step by step, slowly but with tragic fatality, as a result of that moral vacuum in which he dwelt throughout his tender years, and where he caught his first glimpses of Sir William's incurable nonchalance and his mother's vexing eccentricities.

CHAPTER IV

OSCAR AT PORTORA

WILDE was about ten when, in 1864, his parents sent him as a boarder to the Portora Royal School at Enniskillen, where his brother Willy, commonly called "Blue-Blood," was spending his second year.

Little is known about Oscar's record there, except that he remained at the school seven years, graduating with honours that opened to him the doors of Trinity College in Dublin. From a letter of Sir Edward Sullivan to Frank Harris, we learn that, on the whole, Oscar was a good-tempered, kindly and generous lad. He promptly gained among his schoolmates the reputation of an unusually entertaining *raconteur* and a wit, quick at inventing mordant nicknames. He was a capable student of Latin and Greek, but had no gift for mathematics or any leaning toward sports.

Unfortunately, his witticisms were sometimes ill-chosen if not really tactless. Even in those days he seems to have possessed an almost maniacal craving for idle banter, with no regard for the consequences to which a *bon mot* might lead. Some of his epigrammatic remarks were repeated outside the school walls, and were justly resented by the victims of his stinging wit.

On one occasion, he said about an Irish writer:

> He has no enemies, but he is bitterly disliked by his friends.

Speaking of a Jew who, inflated with social ambitions, after expatriating himself from Russia, had settled in England, Oscar commented "He came to London in the hopes of founding a salon; he has succeeded only in opening a saloon." Such pleasantries of an unbridled tongue certainly could have contributed little to young Wilde's popularity.

Too tall for his age, heavily built and "flopping about ponderously," Oscar was never a favourite among the other boys, principally because he would not participate in their games, and he explained once that he resented "kicking and being kicked at." But to his youthful companions an attitude such as this was a grave sin against a long-standing tradition. Nor did the pupils like his long hair, his *tiré à quatre épingles* attire and above all, that black top hat of the latest style which he wore with stubborn persistence.

To this meagre account it might be added that even at Portora, Oscar took a strange interest in rare editions and artistically bound books of which he had a small collection of his own; among other things, a beautiful large-paper copy of Æschylus. Insignificant though this bent of the mind may seem, it was an indication of Oscar's æstheticism at that happy age when, as Poushkin put it, children

> Will read with fervour Apulleius,
> Neglecting Cicero with zeal,

and when their hearts and thoughts are staunchly set on nothing but some rough game in the back yard of their Alma Mater.

Aside from these innocent peculiarities, the boy evinced hardly any traits that would have placed him in a class of his own. He was a kindhearted and tender little fellow, deeply attached to his sister Isola who died in 1867, at the age of eight, when he was only twelve. Alluding to this event, the doctor who attended the child in her illness noted:

> Ossie was an affectionate, gentle, retiring, dreamy boy whose lonely and inconsolable grief found its outward expression in long and frequent visits to his sister's grave in the village cemetery.

During his last year at Portora, when Oscar had just reached the age of sixteen, his thirst for knowledge and his keen receptivity became a matter of general comment. On this point Mr. Sherard gives some interesting details:

> Often when Mr. Purser was instructing the class in history or in geography, Oscar Wilde would contrive by means of some cleverly put question to lead the master into a disquisition on some topic on which he desired to gain information. The subject in hand would be forgotten; the master, ever prompted by his pupil, would unbosom himself of his store of learning. Sometimes the whole of the hour would be thus absorbed. At other times the master would bring the discussion back to the subject of the lesson, and then it was a sight to see the lad, all alert, thinking and planning how, next day, he could turn the master once more on to the question in which he needed instruction—questions often as abstruse as the relative definitions of nominalism and realism.

In Oscar's time Portora was considered a model institution. It was a sectarian school which functioned under the supervision of a Protestant Board of Education. Apparently the tutoring system was calculated to instill in the pupils a feeling of contempt for everything that was even remotely associated with Irish national aspirations. It is a matter of conjecture to what extent the Lord Bishop of Clogher, then Chairman of the Board, was actually wielding his influence to destroy in the children entrusted to his care such love for Ireland as they may have acquired in their parents' homes. Still, no fervent imagination is required to divine that both the pious Bishop and his worthy associates must have had small respect for ideas like those which Speranza—to take but one example—poured forth in the columns of *The Nation,* where she prudently counselled her compatriots to "burn the Castle" and "starve the English garrison."

Thus, there was a striking contrast between the atmosphere at 1 Merrion Square, where everything bearing the Celtic stamp was ardently revered, and that at Portora, permeated with snobbish and sneering disdain for the orthodox Irish. No doubt, this rabid "Rule Britannia" attitude was painfully felt by Oscar's unripe and still fermenting mind; all the more so, as the boy always had a tender feeling for his mother of whose nationalistic record he was proud and whose intellectual achievements he greatly treasured.

At Portora, it was not merely a matter of the deep-rooted controversy—Ireland *vs.* England: the thing that must have struck young Wilde as the sharpest dissonance was the whole school routine, tainted with ultra-Protestant bigotry and stuffed with chilly Sunday sermons; these could have lent but little encouragement to that loose philosophy, professed and practiced at home, upon which his mother's "Society for the Suppression of Virtue" was evidently founded.

Oscar's tutors at school preached to him the honour of virtue and the disgrace of vice which, of course, was the proper thing to do; yet, the fact itself that virtue was extolled and wickedness denounced by those for whose opinions he had practically no respect aroused in the boy's mind a whole range of provocative thoughts, fostering in him a morbid curiosity about the fascinating garment of sin. And, in his later life, he found strange pleasure in imbibing the poisonous breath of the *"fleurs du mal"* whose aroma intoxicated his soul and induced him to compose such hymns to evil as that essay on Wainewright, or *The Picture of Dorian Gray,* or *La Sainte Courtisane,* and many others, all of which dealt in some way or other with the forbidden fruit of knowledge and cultivated a perverted taste for irresponsible amorality.

Still, from a narrow biographical viewpoint, the years Oscar Wilde spent at Enniskillen were altogether uneventful. His school record, while good, strangely enough revealed nothing conspicuously brilliant about his English compositions, and only in the field of classical languages did he evince an extraordinary ability, which won him the enviable Gold Medal.

Nor did Wilde show any signs of moral aberration. The only hint of his possible homosexual leanings at this early period of his life is found in an anecdote, obviously fabricated by Frank Harris, about a Portora undergraduate who fell in love with Oscar shortly before he had entered Trinity College. The youngster, according to Harris, went to see Wilde off at the station, and, just as the train was starting for Dublin, he caught

Oscar's face "in his hot hands," and kissed him on the lips. Harris concludes his narrative by quoting Wilde as having said to him:

> I was trembling all over. For a long while I sat, unable to think, all shaken with wonder and remorse.

Even in this account, if it were to be taken literally, there is nothing to sustain the suspicion that, in Wilde's own attitude toward his junior schoolmate, he had transgressed in any respect the rigid precepts of either ethics or convention.

For all we know, Oscar left Portora in 1871, not only with his Gold Medal, but also with a reputation that was irreproachable.

Many years later, when Wilde was in public disgrace, the enlightened Fermanagh Protestant Board of Education was prompt in its decision to efface his record from the tablet on which, in gold letters, the honours he had won at school were inscribed. However, "outraged Nature herself had forestalled" the execution of this verdict, at once silly and distasteful, by mysteriously causing the slab to crack across the ill-reputed name. This incident may have helped to obliterate Wilde's scholarly achievements from the parochial minds of his Enniskillen censors, but it emphatically failed to dim his world fame as a great artist and an unrivalled master of that tongue in which Shakespeare, Milton and Byron bequeathed to posterity their immortal creations.

CHAPTER V

TRINITY COLLEGE

HAVING received an exhibition from Portora Royal School, Oscar, on October 10, 1871, matriculated as a "junior freshman" at Trinity College, Dublin. Some two weeks later he passed with distinction an entrance scholarship examination and in November he was elected a "Queen's Scholar." It may be noted here that among his college mates there was one Edward Henry Carson, who, many years later, representing the Marquis of Queensberry during the Old Bailey trial, dealt the deathblow to Wilde's social reputation.

At Trinity, Oscar's latent talents began to reveal themselves gradually, but with unmistakable vigour. As usual, he showed no interest in the dry and hopelessly precise world of integers, and a German schoolmaster would have said of him: *Kopfrechnung schwach.* But he did possess that natural gift for the ancient languages which had already been evident at Portora. This aptitude now placed him in the limelight of official recognition, and it was not long before he became known as a "thoroughly good classical scholar of a brilliant type." In fact, shortly after entering College, he obtained a composition prize of £2 for Greek verse, and he was also awarded a "premium for composition at the term lectures." On January 31, 1872, in the "Examination for Honours" he was third out of eight in the First Class, and on April 29 of the same year he won the Michaelmas prize in classics, while his marks in *Viva Voce* Tacitus, Thucydides, the Latin comedians and Greek tragedians were next to the best. An exercise book used by him in 1873 clearly shows his keen interest in the classics. Among other things it contains a number of Greek proverbs extracted from the fragments of the ancient dramatists, some construing from Latin and also a few original Greek verses. On June 9 of that year, in recognition of his successful studies, he was elected to a University Scholarship on the Foundation which entitled him to an annual sum of £20.

In 1874, Wilde took the Berkeley Gold Medal, of which he was quite proud, for an examination in "The Fragments of the Greek Comic Poets as edited by Meineke." Incidentally, we are told that Doctor George Berkeley, Bishop of Cloyne, and the founder of the prize, denied—*horribile dictu*—the existence of matter, an assertion for which, no doubt, he would have been instantly executed by the Marxian rulers of present-day Russia, and which prompted Byron to utter the caustic remark that "when Bishop Berkeley says that there is no matter, it really is no matter what he says."

Wilde's life at Trinity was fraught with no momentous events, and biographical details regarding this period of his growth are indeed very scanty. All the more reason for quoting here Sir Edward Sullivan's account of the boy's college record:

> He had rooms in College at the north side of one of the older squares, known as Botany Bay. These rooms were exceedingly grimy and ill-kept. He never entertained there. On the rare occasions when visitors were admitted, an unfinished landscape in oils was always on the easel in a prominent place in his sitting room. He would invariably refer to it, telling one in his humorously unconvincing way that "he had just put in the butterfly." Those of us who had seen his work in the drawing class presided over by "Bully" Wakeman at Portora were not likely to be deceived in the matter. . . .

At Trinity, Oscar met a man who was destined to exercise a signal influence upon his mental orientation. This was Reverend John Pentland Mahaffy, Precentor and Junior Dean of the College, who became the young lad's tutor and teacher in Greek. A sincere admirer of Hellenic art, it was he who initiated his talented pupil into the cult of that noble beauty which Keats, through the prism of his poetic dreams, perceived in the silent form of the Grecian urn with its "cold pastoral" and the undying "Attic shape." In 1874, Professor

Mahaffy published his *Social Life in Greece from Homer to Menander,* and in the preface he acknowledged his indebtedness to Wilde who had "made improvements and corrections all through the book." Mahaffy was a minister of the Evangelical denomination, and possibly because of this, a staunch anti-Catholic. He had all the earmarks of a rabid *libre penseur,* and the extravagances of his atheistic catechism used to shock even his agnostic co-religionists, so that only once was he permitted to deliver a sermon at the College Chapel.

Wilde became sincerely attached to Mahaffy, and it was to him perhaps more than to the two Oxford celebrities, Pater and Ruskin, that he really owed his greatest debt of gratitude. It is significant that after he had left Dublin, his friendly relations with Mahaffy did not cease, and it was under his dangerously enlightened chaperonage that Wilde, in 1877, made his journey to Greece. But this adventure will be discussed elsewhere in this volume.

While in College, Oscar contracted a fondness for English literature, both classical and modern. He read extensively, and it seems that these studies greatly helped to improve his mastery of the language, particularly in relation to the technique of composition.

Even in those early days he exhibited a distinct predilection for eclecticism: his enthusiasm for Shakespeare did not in the least prevent him from becoming a zealous admirer of Swinburne's Muse, in whose ornamental style, "not golden but gilded," he must have scented the spicy essence of effete æstheticism. With time, this indiscretionary tolerance assumed a focal significance in Wilde's ideological leanings and artistic speculations.

As a member of "The Philosophical," a junior debating circle at Trinity, he distinguished himself little, if at all, and throughout this whole period he preserved a chaste innocence of either politics or anything remotely bearing upon the disturbing quests and queries of his time. No doubt, thanks to this happy mental disposition and his scintillating wit, amiable, though somewhat heavy, appearance, good manners, and moderate habits, he was at once recognised as a *bien venu* by Dublin society, with which he readily mixed.

Wilde was never known to have been a "telltale" or a "squealer." But, much in the same way as at Portora, he cared little for strictly college, if not really academic, functions, like football or cricket. For this he was either despised or looked upon with suspicion by his fellow students. On the other hand, Oscar was in no sense impressed with the average mentality of those boys, and without resorting to any profound Simon or Binet tests, he solemnly gave them this *testimonium paupertatis:*

> They thought of nothing but . . . running and jumping; and they varied these intellectual exercises with bouts of fighting and drinking. If they had any souls, they diverted them with coarse amours among barmaids and the women of the streets; they were simply awful.

There probably was a great deal of truth in this not too generous statement, and yet, the verdict reveals on the part of Wilde a lack of that spirit of sympathetic camaraderie which is the cement of good fellowship and lasting friendships among school boys. After all, a dose of deviltry or a bit of frolicsome mischief is a good thing for healthy lads to have, and it is *à l'âge de chérubin* that adolescents should be permitted to blow off steam as a precautionary measure against "repressed complexes" of all kinds.

Oscar's was an instinctive and deeply imbedded reaction against the crude deification of sport—so typical in the annals of English life—which has made the name of a Tom Cribb more popular with John Bull than that of Byron or Keats.

It should not be forgotten that only a few decades before the advent of the Victorian era, one John Mytton, a Shropshire squire, undoubtedly a gentleman of great "abdominal dignity," who typified, though a bit hyperbolically, the English gentry, much to the delight of his neighbours, engaged in the most extraordinary pursuits and extravagant adventures, which made him as a man "without fear and one utterly regardless of the ordinary limitations of nature," imperishable in the memory of his countrymen. We are told, for instance, that "he would deliberately smash the gig he was driving against a bank or gallop a tandem at a turnpike gate; he would go duck shooting in the snow with nothing on but his night-shirt" or "ride into his drawing room mounted on a bear"; or, finally, "cure himself of the hiccups by setting his shirt on fire, a feat that all but cost him his life and did cost him his reason."

Now, all these things were fresh in England's social records, and amongst the younger generation, particularly its intellectual strata, there was a growing feeling that this *manière de vivre* was really disgraceful even if the gravestones of the Myttons were adorned with the traditional inscription:

Lived respected—died lamented.

Not that Oscar, at this youthful age of eighteen, could have clearly comprehended the vulgarity of such practices, but he did have an innate revulsion—an idiosyncrasy if you please—from the over-emphasis of the "physical culture" tendency in English everyday life.

However, a few words refuting Oscar's alleged dislike of all sports might be added. Some of his unpublished letters, dating back to his Trinity days, furnish ample evidence that our poet was then extremely fond of tennis and fishing. Thus, in a letter written to Richard Harding from Bringham Rectory, Notts., we read:

> These horrid red marks are strawberries—which I am eating in basketfuls, during intervals of lawn tennis, at which I am awfully good.

Again, giving an account of his proposed trip to Galway, Oscar remarked:

> I am rather tired of sea bathing and lawn tennis and shall be glad to be down for the 12th—after this rain too there will be a lot of fish up.

So much for tennis!

Now, as for the rod. Wilde owned a fishing lodge called Illaunroe near Lough Fee in Connemara, where he used to spend many a happy day. He stayed there some time in the summer of 1877, with two of his friends, Jack Barrow and Dick Trent. Here is his account of the trio's strenuous activities:

> I have been here fishing for the last three weeks. . . . The fishing has not been so good as usual—I only got one salmon, about 7½ lbs.—the sea trout however are very plentiful, we get a steady average of over four a day and lots of brown trout, so it is not difficult to amuse oneself and as no fish are going in any of the neighbouring lakes I am fairly pleased. . . .
>
> One week more of this delightful, heathery, mountainous, lake-filled region! Teeming with hares and trout! Then to Longford for the partridge, then Home.

Is not this a typical sportsman's letter?—And does it not prove that Oscar, like a young sylvan faun, enjoyed to the fullest measure the great happiness of outdoor life, with its wilds and rivers and lakes, singing in unison with Nature, and "teeming with hares?"

Yet, Oscar's instinct for the beautiful and the fascination which the unique held for him did raise a barrier between him and many of those roughneck "jumpers" and "runners," who reigned supreme over Trinity, making of it a playing ground rather than a temple of learning.

There, within the college walls, Wilde felt himself in a state of psychological isolation which rendered it impossible for him to develop in a standard fashion, along the lines sanctified by Holy Convention and approbated by ossified routine. His, unquestionably, was a case of maladjustment to the *milieu,* neither too cultured nor over-intellectual, on whose stage, by a caprice of fate, he was later destined to play a leading part in the drama of life. At Trinity he was a stranger amidst the playful company of under-developed colts, chiefly because there was in him that trait of mental senility which usually is a prelude to pathological aversion to normal experiences and natural passions. And—this in passing—it is a striking fact that in Wilde's entire literary heritage, the theme of love is altogether absent, while the eternal tale, the sweet murmur of two fusing hearts, never found its way into our poet's own soul, empty of happy song.

Long before Oscar had adopted the pose of a professional æsthete and habitual wit, he had been "spotted" by his Victorian contemporaries, to whom everything that deviated, even slightly, from the deep-grooved rut—was anathema and taboo. It was all right, in their opinion, to mix, after college hours, with half-sober barmaids and loose street mermaids, but it was all wrong for a young man to take any interest in the "stilled sounds of the heavenly Grecian tongue" or the lasting grace of a Doric column. This, decidedly, was "too awful."

Wilde was justified in his contention that such a *status quo* was the by-product of an outworn tradition. But he erred very definitely when he decided that he could do without the community of which he was an integral part; subsequent events conclusively proved how well that community could and did do without him.

And, though inherently Oscar had in him no streak of the iconoclast nor any characteristics of the social rebel, he started slowly drifting away from that vast and almighty "conglomerated mediocrity" which, at all times and in every land, has constituted the backbone of so-called respectable society.

CHAPTER VI

OXFORD

WILDE was only twenty when, after leaving Trinity, he went to Oxford, won a demyship to which an annual income of ninety-five pounds was attached, and matriculated at Magdalen College on October 17, 1874.

In the whole group of the lovely Oxford structures, Magdalen Tower is perhaps the most famous and certainly one of the noblest monuments of Gothic architecture. Anthony à Wood, a devout lover of Oxford, speaking of the water walks around and about Magdalen, remarked that they are "delectable as the banks of Eurotas where Apollo himself was wont to walk," and J. Wells added that "in Magdalen, if anywhere, might the Platonic dream be realised as to the influence of Beauty in education, for here is Beauty on every side."

The soft green which holds that College as in some velvety frame; the venerable trees along the silent Cherwell and throughout the pensive Deer Park; the quaint Kitchen Staircase and the modest Open Air Pulpit; the fine woodwork inside the College buildings—those early three-scrolled linenfold panels and sixteenth-century oak carvings—all this medieval pageantry has a singular charm comparable only with a few other spots of unfading grace such as Schönbrunn or the slumbering Monplaisir in Peterhof of the Imperial era, or the Petit Trianon, lost in the emerald foliage of the Versailles gardens.

But it is not merely the physical setting—the tangible remains of the splendid Elizabethan epoch—that constitutes the irresistible attraction of this world-renowned temple of learning; there is also that atmosphere full of loquacious legend and historical gossip that in many a devious way ties the venerable College to our dull modernity. Even today—to give but one example—the visitor is reminded of a Stokesley, a queer fellow of Magdalen, who was accused by his crude contemporaries of having baptised a cat with a view to discovering some hid treasures; of these dreadful charges—presumably to everybody's satisfaction—he was unequivocally cleared, and in later years, the gentleman became not only the Bishop of London, but still more, a pious servant of God.

Altogether, Magdalen, with her gold and blue emblems, stands engirdled with queer customs and antiquated traditions—a depository of innumerable anecdotes which cling to her walls as firmly as her own shields and crests and escutcheons beset with the chaste lilies of Eton.

It was Magdalen, then, that put the finishing gloss to Wilde's education, and he emerged from Oxford into the busy traffic of life with the somewhat hazy title of "Art Critic and Professor of Æsthetics," as he is described in Foster's *Alumni Oxonienses.*

According to some writers, there dwelt in those days amidst the stately elegance of the old town a sinister spirit of corruption which converted "the finest school for the highest culture" into "the worst training ground for the lowest forms of debauchery."

It is also claimed that largely due to the neglect of the dons, unrestrained eroticism was permitted to flourish within the College walls, so that the students' minds automatically, as it were, became infested with morbid and filthy content.

Promiscuous reading of the classics may have had something to do with this condition, for Oxford students, sometimes much to their detriment, were permitted to mingle freely with the ancient writers. On this point the authority of Lord Alfred Douglas might properly be invoked:

> Why, he asks, are boys brought up to read the classic authors, including the *Eclogues* of Virgil, not excepting (as Byron says)
>
> . . . that horrid 'un
> Beginning with *formosum pastor Corydon?*

Why were we at Oxford taught to read Plato and to regard the *Symposium* as a magnificent work?

Undoubtedly, vice and sexual perversions of all kinds must have been practiced among the youthful Oxford inmates, and, perhaps, the wicked examples to which Oscar was exposed actually did contribute to the structuralization in him of certain genetic tendencies already there. The wholesale condemnation of Oxford, such as we find in some of Wilde's biographies, is, however, devoid of foundation, particularly if it is recalled that the early suggestions of moral turpitude were conveyed to him by his own parents, in the fold of his own family.

Among present-day psychiatrists, there is still much disagreement on the nature of sexual inversion. Krafft-Ebing, one of the greatest experts on the subject, and also August Forel, have steadily maintained that this anomaly is an innate psychosis which, while possible of suppression, latently persists even when its growth seems to have been definitely arrested. They attribute uranism to a peculiar psycho-physical condition in which the genital gland possesses all characteristics of one of the sexes whereas the brain has, to a great extent, those of the opposite sex. But this view has been challenged—and not without a measure of success—by another authority, Albert Moll, who denies the presumption of hereditary effemination among men or inborn viraginity among women.

On the other hand, the innocent layman must feel quite perplexed when he attempts to gain some light on the causes of sodomy from reading learned discourses by our modern psychoanalysts, Jung, for instance, with their misty speculations about the "non-projection of the soul image," where

> the unconsciousness of the *persona* results in its projection upon an object, more especially of the same sex, thus providing a foundation for many cases of . . . admitted homosexuality, and of father-transferences in men or mother-transferences in women.

Again, some alienists maintain that inverts are often tainted with the epileptoid stigma, while others, on the contrary, seek to explain the psychotic phenomenon of erotic perversions in general by metabolical troubles, thyroidal defects and derangements in the endocrine system. Verily, as Terence said: *Quot homines tot sententiæ!*

Without taking sides with any of these, and numerous other contentions, there are good reasons for stating that the problem of homosexuality distinctly belongs to the domain of medical science and not to the field of jurisprudence. Perversions of this kind, whether they be indulged in by either men or women, are conceived today as pathological disturbances as much as any other ailment of the body or soul. We are no longer content with the narrow and hypocritical Victorian attitude toward sexual digressions as manifestations of one's lack of decency. Nor can the enlightened mind of our age accept the penal codes with their rusty and obsolete maxims, some dating back to the good old days of Beccaria or the Nantes Edict—as safe guides for our notions on various psychic aberrations.

Considering that in some countries, notably in England, public opinion rather superstitiously continues to adhere to the medieval interpretation of sex relations, Laurence Housman deserves high commendation for this truthful statement:

> Always, so long as it stays remembered, the name of Oscar Wilde is likely to carry with it a shadowy implication of that pathological trouble which caused his downfall. And whatever else may be said for or against the life of promiscuous indulgence he appears to have led, his downfall did at least this great service to humanity that, by the sheer force of notoriety, it made "the unmentionable" mentionable.

Now, reverting to the ætiological aspect of Oscar's morbidity, there is this general observation to be made: the clear-cut Mendelian formula of inheritance which probably holds true in the vast kingdom of plants and among lower zoölogical species, is altogether inapplicable to the immensely complicated phenomena of human genetics where a slight twist in the neural system—some faintest irregularity in the structure of a synapse, or the atrophy of an axon—may produce unexpected and even unsuspected results. What, despite the brilliant investigations of the Bechterews, Pavlovs, Piérons and other great scientists of our times, do we actually know about the functioning of the brain; or the hidden springs in the framework of our emotions; or the relation between man's physiological fabric and the mysterious functions of his psyche? —Very candidly we should avow our utter ignorance of virtually every matter coming within the province of psychology, and more particularly, psychopathology. Nor should we acquiesce in the facile doctrine of the behaviourists, who claim to have solved all the riddles with which the intricate problems of character formation are fraught.

However, this much may be safely asserted: in every child's life, there is a somewhat protracted period during which sexual differentiation really does not exist, so that any of the embryonic urges of the carnal appetite registered amongst infants may be alternatively directed toward individuals now of this now of that sex. At this early age, then, the male and female biological principles dwell in a state of coalescence or physical equilibrium, and, accordingly, they are not yet ready to assume a crystallised form of well-defined behaviour with a set of more or less fixed reactions to heterosexual excitations of the normal pattern. It is precisely at this prepubertal stage that, under the influence of evil experiences, depraved habits take their root.

The "noble Speranza," possibly more than anyone else, was responsible for the effeminization of her second son, diverting his thoughts, undeveloped though they were, from the normal tracks of boyish psychology and "conditioning" his natural instincts in such a way that, in his mature years, they turned in a distinctly abnormal direction.

Furthermore, it is idle to deny that in most boarding schools where young men or girls are crowded together in common dormitories, homosexual leanings, if not actual practices, are sure to be found. In nine cases out of ten, these half-infantile frivolities and libertine temptations disappear with time, leaving no trace in one's psychic constitution. But where, as in the case of Wilde, the soil was ripe for the reception of any putrified idea or immoral conception, mere libidinous chatter, so widespread amongst college boys, sufficed to convert him to the corrupt habits of an Ulrich.

Long before Wilde had actually given himself to the frequentation of such haunts as Taylor's rooms in Little College Street, he evinced a series of minor temperamental traits, all of which were indicative of a potential, and, indeed, inevitable twist in the complex life of his inner self. For did he not from early childhood display strange repugnance for physical exertion of any kind? Had he not made himself conspicuous amongst his schoolmates by queer eccentricities in his attire? Is it not true that even in his youthful days he had been a victim of vain egocentricity? Did he not also take an hypertrophic interest in æstheticism, anæmically desisting from everything robust, virile and genuinely masculine? And, finally, had he not exhibited a curious taste for amorality, which, as a rule, is but the steppingstone to immorality?

Wilde acquired none of these characteristics at Oxford; they were all there when he traversed the threshold of Magdalen and installed himself next to the Kitchen Staircase, in those rooms on the first floor whence he was able to observe the Addison Walk, and the old Magdalen Bridge and the placid waters of Cherwell River.

CHAPTER VII

OSCAR'S POSE

IN A serene mood Wilde entered Oxford, that "home of lost causes and forsaken ideals and unpopular names and impossible loyalties," as Arnold once described it.

There he was on the verge of strikingly intriguing experiences fraught with countless novel revelations, pitched to intellectual romance and all set for fascinating journeys through those realms of fancy which he himself wove out of his dreams. Even as a college student, Oscar showed pronounced distaste for the platitudes of this life which, he claimed, were terribly deficient in form. As yet, however, his was an instinctive preference for the unique rather than a carefully framed philosophy of a blasé decadent bored by everything around him. For at that age, Wilde's mind was still oscillating hither and yon, uncertain of its course and dubious of its powers.

From Trinity he brought with him some acquaintance with English literature and an ardent admiration for ancient art; the luxury of half-knowledge and vague æsthetic yearnings; a critical sense and a highly receptive brain addicted to wit and indeed, to scholarly pursuit, but still too immature to have enabled him to devise any definite plan of action.

Everything about Oxford seemed to appeal to Wilde's imagination: those lovely Magdalen Walks with their delicate odour "of leaves and of grass and newly turned earth" when "the birds are singing for joy of the Spring's glad birth"; the grey walls of her colleges and churches garlanded with moss and adorned with green ivy; her silver mists, melting, as in Corot's undying landscapes, over the fragrant fields and pensive parks; the carefree atmosphere and aristocratic manners, and the whole tone of refinement so different from the crude Trinity genre and the Dublin bourgeois contentment.

For once in his earthly existence, Wilde felt happy and exalted as though he were at the gates of a Paradise into which, however, he was destined never to enter.

Strangely, this enthusiasm, instead of uplifting his soul to lofty heights of self-denying idealism, dragged it down to the level of queer affectation; it led him into the labyrinth of sophisticated speculations, out of which he knew not how to find his way back to the road of normal growth and natural advancement.

He found the first outlet for this confused mood when he started decorating his new dwelling with all sorts of handsome bibelots and artistic bagatelles. He occupied three rooms, of which two were sitting rooms connected by an arch. The ceilings were painted and he had hung on the panelled walls a whole array of fine engravings mostly representing fair houris in piquant *déshabillé*. But the *pièce de résistance* in his scenic suite was the notorious set of blue china about which numerous stories have been recounted and spread. Evidently, Oscar himself was quite proud of that collection, and on one occasion, he even exclaimed: "Oh, would that I could live up to my blue china."

Mr. Walter Hamilton in *The Æsthetic Movement in England* draws this picture of Oscar in his Oxford days:

> He was hospitable, and on Sunday nights after "Common Room" his rooms were generally the scene of conviviality, where undergraduates of all descriptions and tastes were to be met, drinking punch, or "B. and S.," with their cigars. . . . His chief amusement was riding, though he never used to hunt. He was generally to be met on the cricket-field, but never played himself; and he was a regular attendant at his college barge to see the May eight-oar races, but he never used to trust his massive form to a boat himself.

Recently, Mr. G. T. Atkinson, a classmate of Oscar's at Magdalen, gave in the *Cornhill Magazine* an accurate description of Wilde's physical appearance, which seems to match

Photograph reproduced through the courtesy of Robert H. Sherard

OSCAR WILDE

(1875)

perfectly the well-known Guggenheim photograph appearing in Sherard's *Story of an Unhappy Friendship:*

His hair was much too long, sometimes parted in the middle, sometimes at the side, and he tossed it off the face with much the same gesture that is used by the flapper of today. His face was colourless, "moonlike," with heavy eyes, and thick lips; he had a perpetual simper and a convulsive laugh. He swayed as he walked, and lolled when at table.

On the other hand, Sir Frank Benson, who also knew Wilde quite well, stresses the point that Wilde was by no means "a flabby æsthete" or "a weedy drawing room jester." It would seem that he was one of the most powerful men in the college, ready to defend himself and his furniture, of which he was proud. In *John o' London's Weekly,* Sir Frank recounts an episode when Oscar overwhelmed several of his college fellows who came one night to "rag him":

. . . Four intruders burst into their victim's room, the others following upstairs as spectators of the game. To the astonishment of the beholders, number one returned into their midst, propelled by a hefty boot-thrust down the stairs; the next received a punch in the wind that doubled him up on top of his companions below, a third form was lifted bodily and hurled onto the heads of the spectators. Then came the triumphant Wilde, carrying the biggest of the gang, like a baby, in his arms. He was about Wilde's size and weight, and hefty at that. But his struggles were useless, and he was borne by Wilde to his own rooms and buried by Wilde underneath a pile of the would-be ragger's fine furniture.

During another encounter of the same kind Oscar, however, got the worst of it.

Some eight healthy young Philistines [says Hamilton] waylaid the "blue china cove" while out walking, fell upon him, bound him with cords and dragged him up a hill, trailing him along the ground. He was much hurt and bruised, but he did not resist, for that was useless; nor did he protest with a single word. When at last they released him at the top of the hill, he simply flicked the dust off his coat, with the air of a Regency beau flipping the grains from the *tabatière* off his lace *jabot,* and looking at the prospect, said: "Yes, the view from this hill is really very charming."

Certainly, these incidents go to prove that Oscar was not wanting in either self-control or stamina. Sherard, too, maintains that Wilde, far from being an effeminate creature, was a man of action, full of physical courage which he displayed whenever the occasion arose.

However, it was at Oxford that Wilde first started practicing dandyism, from which he was unable to rid himself for almost the rest of his life. He meant to be different from his fellow men, and choosing the least laborious course, he adopted the facile way of focusing other people's attention on his egotistic self by acting conspicuously and assuming a rôle which never could have become genuinely his own. For he was fully conscious of the fact that a pose, no matter how cleverly displayed, is in vulgar discord with the ideal of beauty, which to him had always been fascinating.

There is little merit in the suggestion, made by some of Wilde's apologetic commentators, that his affectation and ostentatious conduct were wrought upon him "by the hazards of life," or "the folly of his contemporaries." Still less reason is there to maintain that Wilde was a faithful servant of "the splendid and sterile Dolores, our Lady of Pain."

To begin with, by the time Oscar had started his masquerading, there was nothing in his whole biography that would have even remotely justified his silly behaviour. It was not necessary for him to resort to the shallow tricks of an æsthetic juggler in order to attain the success to which, by reason of his talents, he would have been entitled anyway, and to win fame which would have naturally been his. Yet, the amorality which he inherited from Sir William and the vanity which, by contagious contact, he acquired from his mother, instigated in him the insatiable desire to achieve prominence overnight, even if it had to be purchased at the exorbitant price of notoriety.

Furthermore, though some critics have tried to make out of

our poet an anarchist and "apostle of the liberties of man," he was nothing of the kind: the Schiller complex, the Swinburnian preoccupation with the theme of ecstatic suffering and the Byronic sense of "universal grief" were altogether absent in Wilde, whose fundamental craving in life was self-gratification. He relished all mundane spices and niceties with the gluttonous appetite of a gourmet. His was a *bon vivant's* philosophy, sensuous and fleshly, cynical and selfish.

Endowed with sparkling wit and natural shrewdness, Wilde found it quite easy to attract the curiosity of the Magdalen undergraduates by his blue china and those paradoxical talks, in which, even at that youthful age, he was an unrivalled virtuoso. He seems also to have divined that, due to the influence of Swinburne, Pater and Ruskin, æstheticism and the cult of beauty were coming more or less into vogue.

Today, it is a *secret de polichinelle* that Oscar knew little about painting. However, at times, he endeavoured to convey to his unimaginative listeners the impression that he was seriously studying painting, although it is doubtful if he knew how to hold a brush or what to do with the palette.

Though Irish by birth, he suffered from a typically English malady known as "unrequited love for music." It is even said that he was bored by all philharmonic things, and like his own King in that delightful tale *The Remarkable Rocket,* he knew only two airs "and was never quite certain which he was playing." And yet, cleverly displaying the air of a learned expert, he would eloquently discuss Beethoven or Bach, delighting his half-educated auditors with the brilliancy of his epigrammatic style.

Innocent artifice of this kind tended to create for Oscar a reputation which he neither deserved nor really cared for. It was merely part of a well-planned game, a little ruse calculated to dupe his fellow freshmen. Once in a while, a vexing *lapsus linguæ* would occur in his discourses, similar to that, for example, recorded in his oft-quoted comment: "A splendid scarlet thing by Dvořák"; or the one cited in Mark Twain's humourous article *English as She is Taught,* where a schoolboy is said to have remarked that "Chaucer was the father of English pottery." But then, even renowned parliamentary speakers, as Mr. Lloyd George will probably admit, are not altogether blameless of such embarrassing errors.

It was also at Magdalen that Oscar began to indulge in the queer habit of dressing eccentrically in knee breeches and silk stockings, and of wearing fanciful neckties and similar insignia of an æsthete's creed.

Perhaps the best-known incident of Wilde's exhibitional practices is connected with the fancy dress affair which Mrs. George Morrell gave at Headington Hill Hall on May 1, 1878. Oscar seized upon this occasion to appear all dressed up as Prince Rupert with the needlepoint ruffle, a velvet yoke and silk Spanish puff sleeves. The success of his performance, at least among the Oxford snobs, seems to have been unique. But this prank should again be regarded as only one link in a long chain of carefully conceived manœuvrings which served as a sign of Wilde's determination to conquer the so-called smart sets of English society by purely feminine tricks. Indeed, it is only natural for a young and vain débutante to seek the applause of her audience by means of displaying a gorgeously deep-cut décolleté and a lot of rouge and other varnish on her fair features. And it is true that many a man has been greatly impressed, if not actually overpowered, by women bearing all the earmarks of having just emerged from the gentle folds of a *salon de beauté*. But for a young "six-footer" to resort to silk gowns, cosmetics and the charms of his velvety tenor as a device for attracting to himself the attention of an idle crowd is most abnormal. In the case of Wilde these powder-puff tactics prognosed a deeply rooted morbidity which, with time, sadly affected his scintillating mind.

CHAPTER VIII

THE GRECIAN ADVENTURE

THE spring of the year 1877,[1] perhaps, should be conceived as the breaking point in Wilde's *Sturm und Drang* period, for it was then that he proceeded, under the personal guidance of Mahaffy, on his eventful journey to Greece.

He went to that "land of lost gods and godlike men" via Genoa and Brindisi, and one morning he caught sight of the Peloponnesian coast embraced by the "sapphire-coloured" waves of the Ionian sea.

> Fair Greece! Sad relic of departed worth!
> Immortal, though no more; though fallen, great!

The educational significance of his pilgrimage to the Holy Land of Beauty can neither be doubted nor should it be underestimated. It was there, at the foot of the Acropolis, in close proximity to the glorious ruins of the Erechtheum and the Propylæa, on the enchanted banks of the Alpheus, that he imbibed for the first time in his young life the serene Homeric atmosphere, the undisturbed spirit of completeness which permeates the homogeneous structure of ancient Hellas. For Italy, beautiful and alluring as she may have revealed herself to him during his earlier Continental travels,[2] was after all an intricate combination of many successive civilisations; a battleground, indeed, of contending principles, conflicting aims and historical epochs, which though mechanically brought together and subjected to the process of nivelization, were never organically dissolved in the great retort of the Eternal City.

In fact, when in 1875, Wilde had visited Milan, Venice, Padua, Verona and Florence, he found himself confronted with a turbulent stream of contradictory impressions that left him in a maze from which he could recover only in a country such as Greece, in the world of golden pastoral, rustic charm and placid beatitude. It was only from Greece that he could receive his initiation into the mysteries of Attic workmanship with its keen appreciation of shape and form and style. And this "increased sense of the absolutely satisfying value" of art for art's sake later became the foundation of his own literary manner and his own poetic genius.

At first, inspired by the grandiose vision of Catholicism triumphant, and in his heart yearning for a spiritual communion with the Apostolic Church, Oscar had planned to go from Genoa straight to Rome. He had even confided his pious intention to Richard Harding, a young Oxford friend of his whom he used to call "Kitten." He wrote him:

> I start for Rome on Sunday: Mahaffy comes as far as Genoa with me; and I hope to see the golden dome of St. Peter's and the Eternal City by Tuesday night.
>
> This is an era in my life, a crisis—I wish I could look into the seeds of Time and see what is coming.
>
> I shall not forget you in Rome—and will burn a candle for you at the Shrine of Our Lady.

But Mahaffy, to whom he had also disclosed his mystic longings, is known to have met this avowal with the abrupt rebuttal:

> Stop this nonsense! Come with me to Greece. I am going to make an honest pagan out of you.

And thus, only a few days later, Oscar from Corfu sent to Kitten this brief but quite significant report:

> I never went to Rome at all! What a changeable fellow you must think me but Mahaffy my old tutor carried me off to Greece with him to see Mykenae and Athens—I am awfully ashamed of myself but I could not help it and will take Rome on my way back.

Like Venus emerging from the snow-white sea foam, Hellas appeared to Wilde as a miraculous revelation: his innate predilection for the æsthetic aspect of being found an eloquent affirmation in the whole fabric of Hellenism, where beauty and rhythm were the propelling motives of creative achievement. Not only in the stately elegance of a Doric column or the measured strains of the hexameter but even in the throes of agony, in the volcanic eruptions of human suffering, in the boundless misfortunes of a Laocoön, in the tragic fate of Prometheus and Œdipus, the Apollonian spirit—the invincible harmony, the flawless symmetry, the orderly Cosmos—prevail over the unruly Chaos of earthly things. In Greece, Wilde must have conceived one of his most cherished ideas that when the golden moments of joy fleet into the sombre hours of sadness, Art alone reminds one of Beauty, which is undying even in the face of all-engulfing sorrow and triumphant death.

Grecian culture also seemed to have borne out Wilde's dogmatic faith in the extrinsic virtue of form as contrasted with the intrinsic value of content.

Oscar's sojourn in Greece was taken up with serious work, with visits to museums, short journeys hither and yon to places of historical interest and with lengthy exegetic discourses of Mahaffy on the things observed by his little group.

It was a happy coincidence that Wilde should have had for his mentor so cultured a man as that Trinity scholar. He was the one who really laid the foundation of his pupil's devotion, disinterested and sincere, to the eternal truth of Hellenism. With all his faults, Mahaffy was endowed with a delicate instinct for the genius of classicism, and not only was he a connoisseur of Greek literature, but he also knew Greece more thoroughly than perhaps any foreigner before his days, or since. He rambled and roamed over her sacred soil with that flaming enthusiasm of which the commonplace tourist is sadly devoid. To him, that land was not merely a geographical locality, but a shrine full of superb reminiscences, unfading bloom and captivating magic.

Mahaffy's knowledge of Greece was indeed encyclopædic. With enviable ease and commanding credibility, he dwelt in his talks and writings on Ionic art and Hellenic mythology; on

Olympian games and the *mise en scène* of a Sophoclean play; on the subtle shades in the colouring and the delicate twists in the carving of some triglyph or metope adorning the frieze of an abandoned temple. To him, as he himself said, "all culture culminated in Greece—all Greece in Athens—all Athens in its Acropolis—all the Acropolis in the Parthenon." And there he stood, gazing with veneration upon all those ancient shrines and statues, which even Time, that pitiless rival of Beauty, was impotent to rob of their glory and grace.

But there was even more in Mahaffy's attitude toward Hellenism than a mere ambition to gather punctiliously and evaluate critically first-hand data on pagan Greece. No one reading his *Rambles and Studies* can fail to note that pure-minded idealism which in itself was distinctly Hellenic. His was a feeling of intimate oneness with the very air of Hellas, her lucid myths and astonishing gladness. Renan surely was right when he divined in the Hellene a deeply rooted instinct for the natural.

> A little nothing [he said] a tree, a flower, a lizard or a turtle, provoked in the Greek a *souvenir* of a thousand metamorphoses sung by their poets . . ., and pastorals, such as those of Theocritus, in that land were conceived as truth. For the Greek, Nature was the counsel of elegance, the mistress of straightforwardness and virtue.

In one of his dramatic idylls, Theocritus gave a remarkably graphic picture of Grecian everyday life—simple, undisturbed and unbroken. The fair ladies, Gorgo and Praxinœ, are shown there gaily twittering like two little birds "knowing neither toil nor care." Gladly they live, tormented by no Hamletian splits of consciousness; serenely they partake of the mundane feast; and calmly they retire to the realm of the silent shadows.

This also was the keynote of Mahaffy's naïve and trusting philosophy. Only a few among the moderns, very few, indeed, have succeeded in absorbing the spirit of Hellas as completely as that Dublin pilgrim. And these few were men of superlative taste, like Poushkin and Goethe and Keats.

Even in the debris of destruction, to which Greece has been

reduced by the barbarism of man, Mahaffy's searching eye detected, as in those seven Corinthian pillars, the solemn splendour of a civilisation whose influence upon our present system, though sometimes unnoticed, is lasting and real. Is it not because, as Merejkovsky suggested?—

> There is something austere and sternly divine in this desolation; yet nothing sad, no signs of that despondency or of that feeling of death which one experiences under the brick vaults of Nero's palace or in the Colosseum ruins. There—the dead grandeur of a shattered power; here—eternal and live beauty.

No doubt, in those days, Wilde earnestly meant to embrace the classical ideal in all its purity and fragrant freshness. And how could he have escaped the unique charm of Athens which C. E. Robinson so graphically described in his *Everyday Life in Ancient Greece?*

> Outside the city gates and lining the roadway are tombs, some bearing marble figures or scenes carved in bas-relief; others, commemorating the dead of a poorer class, with no more than a simple jar, yet as exquisite in shape as it is simple. Finally, towering above the roofs and buildings of the town itself, stands the majestic rock of the Acropolis, and on it, serene and dazzling in the pure, smokeless air, the marble columns and gabled roofs of Portico and Temples, a miracle of loveliness, perfect alike in finish and proportion, rich with coloured patterns of crimson and blue and purple, and here and there a gilded ornament which catches the sunlight and flashes its rays far out across the plain to the surrounding mountains or over the dancing waves of the sea.

Wilde perceived all this loveliness and grasped its profound cultural meaning, its immutable significance to the spiritual refinement of the human race. What he may have overlooked was the fact that the beauty of Greece was due not merely to her Art but in equal measure to Nature in whose bosom Art had taken birth. In his conception, the element of artifice in the creative effort of man always prevailed over the element of Nature; the sophisticated subtlety of Hellenic workmanship somehow appealed to him more directly than its rectilinear simplicity. Later, possibly converted to Paganism by the skeptic views of Mahaffy, and also swayed by Pater's sensual æstheticism, Wilde lost altogether that appreciation of chastity which was the essence of true Hellenism. And then a treacherous cleavage began to imperil Oscar's basic notions on art; his whole life outlook became tainted with discord and decadent negation which were so repugnant to the ancient Greeks.

What was the cause of this strange digression? Available biographies of Wilde do not attempt to solve this psychological problem. However, this must be remembered: Wilde's extensive acquaintance with antiquity was derived not solely from his personal contacts with Italy and Greece, but also from his assiduous labours in the field of those records, fragmentary though we find them, in which the poets and thinkers of that remote era have unfolded before us the panorama of a life so strikingly alien to our own. Oscar read them with much reverence, but with no discrimination—an Æschylean tragedy along with Petronius' *Satyricon;* some chiselled verses of Horace or an Aristotelian treatise on logic; and then a bit from Aristophanes, whose biting burlesques, *The Frogs,* for example, or *The Clouds,* much as they may gratify our sense of humour, and in spite of their inspired lyrical passages, are full of filthy language, obscene allusions and conspicuous eroticism.

Most assuredly, young men in colleges should not be tutored in the sentimental spirit of a mousseline *demoiselle,* and it is good and useful for them to acquire firsthand acquaintance with the immortal Greek and Latin masters. The difficult problem is for the teachers to make it clear to their undeveloped pupils that there is a cardinal distinction between Pagan and Christian ethics; and further, that a line of demarcation should be drawn between that in antiquity which was lofty, elevating and noble, and that which was vulgar, unworthy and mean.

Plato himself unmistakably sensed this contrast. There is a chapter in his *Feast* dedicated to the place of Aphrodite amidst the merry company of the Greek deities. It appears from this account that there were two mythological Aphrodites, who albeit identical in name were quite opposed to each other in their practice and interpretation of Love: the heavenly one, the goddess of tender amorous devotion, who had no mother and whose father Uranus was the mighty potentate of the Celestial Sphere; the other, one of later origin, the daughter of Zeus and Dione, commonly called "Pandemos" or the "popular," a vicious goddess indeed, the inspiratrix of the lowest forms of carnality and of sexual perversions of every kind.

Is it not possible that, because of the double amoral influence of Sir William and Lady Wilde, Oscar acquired from the classics the "pandemian" taste for lust which, according to Plato, is indulged in by "men of base temperament, whose love . . . is directed toward young boys rather than women," a predisposition generating debauchery of both mind and body?

Nor did the Olympian mythical lore, with its Bacchic hymns in honour of Joy and its feasts in glorification of Life, exhaust the contents of the Hellenic spirit. It had another aspect, a profoundly mystical vein which found its most complete expression in the Eleusinian rites where passion not divorced from its sublime pathos, and religion not stripped of its esoteric essence, produced one grand and full-sounding concord. In the flaming reveries of Dionysian orgasm, not Zeus, nor even Apollo, but Gemeter, or Demeter, the goddess of Earth, and Kore-Persephone, queen of the lower world, appeared as the focal deities, incarnating the everlasting antinomy between Life and Death.

Olympus, with all its charm and direct appeal to the mind of the Greek, the "pure artist," was at its best only a bit above the platitudes of shallow reality. But the myth of the two great goddesses, *megalai theai,* by some devious paths and through many an enigmatic route, linked blithe Hellas to dark Egypt with her hierophants and sacred temples, with her Isis and Osiris. And in this way perhaps the Greeks caught a glimpse of Atlantis, that strange land beyond the pillars of Hercules, where mankind, having lived through its golden age, is said to have solved the vexing problem of the universal libido by the anthropological miracle of the androgyne.

To this phase of the Hellenic culture which, if it were not

for St. Clement, the renegade Christian Father of Alexandria, would probably never have been revealed to the modern world, Wilde remained indifferent. Still, it was precisely the Greece of the *virgo paritura* (pregnant virgin), and of the Orphic tradition, which inherited the theurgic wisdom from both the West and the East, the occult initiations of Pythagoras and Brahma, Orpheus and Rama. This, then, is the vindication of Cicero's claim that the *telesterion,* and not the Parthenon, was the noblest achievement of ancient Greece.

Now, these nocturnal revelations of mystic Intuition, rather than the diurnal speculations of empiric Reason, inspired the Hellene, the inborn dialectician, to seek the ultimate synthesis of man's existence in that state of resurrected flesh merging with its antithesis—the inextinguishable psyche—which was vaguely conceived by Goethe when he said:

> Truly, he who has not guessed
> What the words mean: "die and be,"
> Will remain a sightless guest
> Midst this world of mystery.[3]

The time that Wilde spent in Greece, "those dear Hellenic hours," deepened and widened his mental diapason and equipped him with precious material for his future literary work. The Grecian excursion, above all, furnished him with a criterion of the beautiful, with an æsthetic gauge which enabled him to evaluate the merits of artistic achievement, to judge the measure and value of the creative effort not by any patented theory borrowed from some mediocre textbook on art, but by all the wonderful things which, as he perceived them in Greece, had become part of his own inner experience.

To the idle voyager, Greece might have meant little more than just another spot that had to be checked off in his Baedeker. But Wilde invested all the faculties of his alert mind in the scrutiny of those grand bagatelles which, centuries ago, were moulded, shaped, carved and painted by the refined imagination of the Greek artist. And every minute coil, every subdued shade, every soft curve that lends beauty to form were painfully sorted and scrupulously catalogued by Oscar. Thus when he spoke of the exquisite grace of a Tanagra statuette, he knew what he was talking about.

> Those [says Sherard] who ever proclaimed the man an impostor have been heard to say that of Tanagra's statuettes he knew no more than any man who has access to dictionary and encyclopædia. Now, during the many days that he spent in Athens with Professor Mahaffy and his friends, the museums at Athens were sedulously visited, and particular attention seems to have been paid to these statuettes, which in 1877, had only recently been unearthed in Tanagra in Bœotia. With what attention these little figures of terra cotta, often delicately modelled and richly coloured both in dress and limbs, were then studied, appears very clearly from Mahaffy's book.

Of course, Wilde's interest was not exclusively directed toward the tangible and visible fragments of "the glory that was Greece." He knew that, in addition to her material frame, to her archæological residues, her stone and plaster, there dwelt in that wonderland a flaming soul which had been caught in her myths and rites and cults, more lofty and enduring perhaps than the Acropolis itself. And he laboured with perseverance seeking to comprehend the eternal truth of Hellenic philosophy, which taught men the lesson of happiness, before which wisdom herself must bow.

Even if, as stated, he did not succeed in absorbing the full meaning of Hellenism, he acquired an enviable knowledge of the ancient world and he came near to divining the true character of those gods and goddesses who gracefully disported themselves on Olympus. He was almost on the verge of the "Great Secret" when, many years later, in *De Profundis,* he wrote these remarkable lines:

> For the Greek gods in spite of the white and red of their fair fleet limbs were not really what they appeared to be. The curved brow of Apollo was like the sun's disc over a hill at dawn, and his feet were as the wings of the morning, but he himself had been cruel to Marsyas and had made Niobe childless. In the steel shields of Athena's eyes there had been no pity for Arachne; the pomp and peacocks of Hera were all that

was really noble about her; and the Father of the Gods himself had been too fond of the daughters of men. The two most deeply suggestive figures of Greek mythology were, for religion, Demeter, an earth goddess, not one of the Olympians, and for art, Dionysos the son of a mortal woman to whom the moment of his birth had proved the moment of her death.

Well, these and many other deep thoughts were conceived by Wilde in those unclouded days when he went to Greece to learn from her the canons of Beauty. What he brought back with him from that enchanting land forever remained a treasured possession of his, which lent him courage to live through the humiliation of his trial and the sufferings wrought on him in the miserable cell at Reading Gaol.

CHAPTER IX.

ATHENS VERSUS ROME

IT MUST have seemed to Wilde that the shortest road from Athens to Oxford lay through Rome, and so, having completed his Grecian adventure, he went back to Italy, a country which also left unforgettable impressions in his heart. Like Goethe and Taine and Browning and Shelley and Keats, and many other weavers of dreams, he fell in love with the sunburnt Campagna, and the peaceful hillside by Genoa, and every valley from Florence to Rome. He took a fancy to those oleanders "robing the plains with scarlet," to the cyclamen "filling the meadows with purple." How happy he felt amidst the smiling verdure of the Borghese Gardens which, in his own comment, "are too lovely for words—for prose rather," "where each leaf is a note" and "the groves are symphonies."

There, by the tides of the Yellow Tiber, Wilde was living under the hypnosis of Roman Catholicism with its pomp and majesty, its militant spirit, solemn ritual and iron discipline.

On Italian soil he recognised more vividly than ever before the fact that, despite his Protestantism, the frigid philosophy of which never did appeal to his artistic sense, there slumbered within him, in the depths of his Irish soul, an ineradicable longing for the grandeur of the Western Church. After all, Portora, with its hopeless bigotry, could not dim in him the conviction that he was a true, if not really devout, Catholic, and at no time is he known to have had that contemptuous insensibility to Rome which Arnold observed in the average Englishman.

So far, little attention has been paid by biographers to Wilde's interest in Catholicism, and, inadvertently, to his aversion for Protestantism. That both feelings must have been strong in him clearly appears from an undated letter which he wrote from Dublin to Kitten. It was occasioned by the death of one of Oscar's uncles, whose will, he confessed, "was an unpleasant surprise like most wills."

> He leaves my Father's Hospital [wrote Oscar] about one thousand pounds, my brother two thousand pounds and me one hundred pounds on condition of my being a Protestant!
>
> He was a poor fellow bigotedly intolerant of the Catholics and seeing me on the brink struck me out of his will. It is a terrible disappointment to me; you see I suffer a good deal from my Romish leanings, in pocket and mind.
>
> My father had given him a share in my Fishing Lodge in Connemara, which of course ought to have reverted to me on his death, well even this I lose "if I become a Roman Catholic for five years"—which is very infamous.
>
> Fancy a man going before "God and the Eternal Silence" with his wretched Protestant prejudices and bigotry still clinging to him.

Nor is it generally known that even long before the wrath of Nemesis had crushed the poet's spirit, he had been seeking a "reunion" with Catholic circles, and that toward the end of his undergraduate term at Magdalen, possibly as a sequel to his Roman experience, he had interviews with certain priests in the Brompton Oratory of St. Philip.[1]

Many years later, when Wilde once more had visited the Eternal City, he wrote Ross these significant lines:

> I wish you could come out here; one is healed at Rome of every trouble. . . . I do nothing but see the Pope: I have already been blessed many times—once in the private Chapel of the Vatican. . . . My position is curious; I am not a Catholic; I am simply a violent Papist. No one could be more "black" than I am.

However, Wilde's thirst for religion, at least during that youthful period, should not be overrated, since there was in him no well of mystical insight, no genuine passion for any metaphysical revelations. With all his shining wit and sparkling brilliancy, he was devoid of the power of either potently moving any one, or being forcefully moved, by some "categorical imperative" or lofty ideal. In this, how different he was from Nietzsche with his sombre rovings through the Inferno of Negation, and his morbid love *"zum Fernsten,"* for the "distant," his proud ascent to the eagle heights of what, he claimed, was wisdom, and his voracious craving for the superman—the *homo sapiens*—of a yet unlived era; or the unruly and rebellious Dostoievsky, who, by his daring descent to the tenebrous depths of tragic contrasts, discovered the very source of man's everlasting discords; or Flaubert smitten with the Tantalean torture of desperate yearning for the impossible and the unreal.

Italy conveyed to Wilde something in the order of a Christian experience, but as between Olympus and Golgotha he was really unable to make any final choice:

> Helen [he said] took precedence of the Mater Dolorosa: the worship of sorrow gave place to the worship of beauty.

For a brief moment, his mind had been captivated by the magnificence of Latin Christianity: its majestic domes, worshipping frescos, pealing organs and thundering hymns—all this was so astonishing and new!

To what extent Oscar's fervour was derived from pure religious sentiment is a matter of conjecture, since he, like many other secret worshippers of Papacy—and with such Nicodemuses Purgatory must be full—was tempted not merely by its inflexible commandments and compromising pontifical practices but equally, perhaps more so, by its æsthetic aspect and artistic flavour. And many a pilgrim to the Western Mecca has been prompted to track some devious road to Rome, or tread some sunlit lane to Italy, for precisely the same motives which led Gogol, that martyr of Russian Orthodoxy, to seek refuge from his suffocating spleen amidst the marble folds of St. Peter's; or Ruskin, the convinced apologist of Anglicanism, to kneel humbly before the portal of St. Mark's and to revive, by the flame of his eloquence and the power of his pen, the still and silent stones of Venice.

It was Rome particularly that aroused in Wilde a whole gamut of reverent emotions which, displaying a freshman's diligence and a proselyte's zeal, he hastened to catalogue in rhymes at once exalted and sincere. Such, for instance, is his *Urbs Sacra Æterna,* a poem in which, with a feeling close to idolatry, Wilde touches upon the mighty theme of Papism:

> When was thy glory! when in search for power
> Thine eagles flew to greet the double sun,
> And all the Nations trembled at thy rod?—
> Nay, but thy glory tarried for this hour,
> When pilgrims kneel before the Holy One,
> The prisoned shepherd of the Church of God.

In *Easter Day,* again reverting to the splendour and fame of Christ's Vicar on Earth, he makes the opening lines sound a solemn chord:

> The silver trumpets rang across the Dome;
> The people knelt upon the ground with awe;
> And borne upon the necks of men I saw,
> Like some great God, the Holy Lord of Rome.

The same deeply religious mood pervades the sonnet composed at Genoa during Holy Week. Here is its impressive finale:

> Outside, the young boy-priest passed singing clear,
> "Jesus, the son of Mary, has been slain,
> O, come and fill his sepulchre with flowers."
> Ah, God, ah God! those dear Hellenic hours[2]
> Had drowned all memory of Thy bitter pain—
> The Cross, the Crown, the Soldiers, and the Spear.

All this was certainly more than mere coquetting with Catholicism. Oscar went to Italy prepared to embrace that simple faith which was glowing under the ashes of his travesties and pretentious sophistication. And yet the immortal shadows of *pagan* Rome and the subtle artistry of the Renaissance arrested the growth of a sentiment that might have prevented him from entering the forbidden realm of sensualism and carnal self-gratification.

Wilde could not help but discern the fact that in religion, as exemplified by the Roman Church, æstheticism strangely blends with asceticism; side by side with the undisturbed serenity of a Perugino or a Fra Angelico, there dwells the fierce fanaticism of a Savonarola, that unmitigated cruelty of which the "Holy" Inquisition is an unyielding symbol. And the all-forgiveness of those martyrs, saints and madonnas who in endless variations appear and reappear on the medieval tableaux, stands in hopeless contradiction with the sinister craving for persecution, the hatred of the sinner and an unquenchable passion for the suppression of the flesh. But to Wilde, the *flâneur,* the matter of the "flesh" was even in those days one of utmost importance, more important perhaps than that of the spirit. As he wrote once, "after the partridge comes the Pope." Self-restraint, still less moral coercion from without, to him never seemed either appealing or in fact justifiable, and he regarded the tempting suggestion that "not the fruit of experience but experience itself, is the end" as a vital motive and the highest maxim of human behaviour.

Heraclitus' conception of life as a perpetual flux of never-ceasing changes, in our age has assumed a dominant significance in that incredulous faith which regards "all things and principles of things as inconstant modes or fashions," a mere kaleidoscopic transformation of moods and tendencies and thoughts into a world of rhythmic urges, fascinating but vague like Mona Lisa's smile with its intriguing uncertainty of meaning and its subdued mystery of promise. Such was the credo expounded by Walter Pater, the learned Oxford don, whose judgment in matters of style Wilde implicitly trusted and for whom he felt a most enthusiastic admiration. He said once to Harris:

> Then there was Pater, Pater the classic, Pater the scholar, who had already written the greatest English prose; I think, a page or two of the greatest English prose in all literature. Pater meant everything to me. He taught me the highest form of art: the austerity of beauty. I came

to my full growth with Pater. . . . He . . . forced me always to do better than my best—an intense vivifying influence, the influence of Greek art at its supremest.

And referring to Pater's fascinating Essays, Wilde admitted that to him they became

the golden book of spirit and sense, the holy writ of beauty. . . . In certain things he stands almost alone. The age has produced wonderful prose style, turbid with individualism, and violent with excess of rhetoric. But in Mr. Pater . . . we find the union of personality with perfection. He has no rival in his own sphere and he has escaped disciples. And this, not because he has not been imitated, but because in art so fine as his there is something that, in its essence, is inimitable.

Substantially, Pater's was a doctrine akin to the Epicurean tenet; its moral justification was based upon the idea that we all are labouring and living under the eternal threat of a suspended death sentence, that Damocles' sword which is alluded to in Hugo's famous phrase: *"Les hommes sont tous condamnés à mort avec des sursis indéfinis."* Because of this tragic state Pater counselled his Oxford disciples to crowd into the narrow space of time accorded to one's earthly existence as many pleasurable pulsations as can be accumulated, absorbed and reintegrated in man's over-refined consciousness.

Christianity, however, even in its way of Martha, means abnegation and the humility of self-effacement—practices which never could have given satisfaction to a complex psychological product such as Wilde. Though "the Cross, the Crown, the Soldiers, and the Spear," for one brief moment stirred in him a feeling of inner responsibility derived from some high law of super-rational nature, the heathen sybaritism of the Cæsars was a condition to which the Irish poet was always aspiring.

In Wilde's estimate, Catholicism itself was far from immune to the delightful but seductive influences of classical antiquity. Indeed, has not the Holy See entered into an illegitimate liaison with Paganism by raising the Cross over the ancient temples from whose altars the frightened gods have fled—whither no one knows? And the Obelisk of St. Peter's?—has it not been removed from the Circus of Nero? And is it not true that what, in days past, used to be the Pantheon, has now been converted into the Chapel of Santa Maria Rotunda, where a glorious tomb is sheltered, on whose headstone "*Ille hic est Raphael*" is forever engraved? And last, has not the Vatican become the hospitable host of that Bathing Venus?

All barriers between Christ and Cæsar having fallen, the radiant pagan spirit reigns supreme, pervading every pore and penetrating every fibre of the new order which for so many a century dwelt in a state of ascetic isolation. Of this sudden metamorphosis, which marked the beginning of the epoch, Schuré says:

> Tritons and Nereids floating on wave-crests reappear along the seashore. Gardens surrounding private villas once more are invaded by Nymphs and Fauns. In village chapels and princely boudoirs alike, the distinction between Angels and Amors is altogether effaced. The Popes have their tables graced with silver Sirens serving as handles to crystal pitchers, while gold vases in the cardinals' homes are engirdled by vine-crowned Bacchantes. One might say that, swung by some formidable *élan,* the ancient world with its entire mythology has launched an assault upon the Christian world, and now fraternizes with its victim.[3]

Verily, then, ultramontane monotheism has given its sanction to urbane polytheism, the two merging in one, each becoming an organic part of the other. A synthesis as provocative as this must have seemed intriguing to the alert, curious and contriving intellect of Wilde.

Still more spontaneous was Wilde's response to the titanic work of the Renaissance, at once credulous and agnostic, Christian and heathen, a record full of nuance and insoluble antinomies. He may never have grasped the specialised pictorial technique and the intricate details distinguishing the various schools of painting; still less—the fundamentals of architectural style or the means by which the sculptor's chisel carves its superb creations, conveying plastic and living form to the amorphous blocks of dead marble. For, unlike Ruskin, who has given us a long line of learned discussions on "the warm hues of a sun-ray" and "hill anatomy" and "the truth of clouds," the author of *Salomé* was neither a technician nor a skilled specialist. But he did penetrate, perhaps more by instinct or intuition than by analytical test, into the beguiling mysteries of Poetry and Art. And to him the hidden essence of Leonardo's colour poems or the superb craftsmanship in Benvenuto's Perseus or the exquisite outline of the Pisan Tower against the azure background of the Italian sky were just as comprehensible, alluring and real as a choice Damascus blade with its gold incrustations, or the delicate aroma of a field flower, or some lovely fragment of Venetian glass.

Again, the Renaissance, as it has been conceived and interpreted by modern thinkers, is quite remote from any ecclesiastical stigma or ethical ideal. What is being treasured in all those canvases, bronzes and rhymes produced by the genial maestros of Italy's Golden Age is precisely that philosophy which soars above both Christianity and Deism of every kind; that ardent longing for the Beautiful, where perfection of style, rather than purity of content, is the ultimate aim of the artist. Nor was our poet's moral sense at all shocked by the proverbial vices of the Borgias or the sentimental sins of a Ludovico Sforza. As Wilde later remarked:

> To those who are preoccupied with the beauty of form, nothing else seems of much importance.

Having accepted these canons of reasoning, Wilde savoured in the legacy of the Renaissance only that which was coloured with the ecstatic revelations of men like Michelangelo, Titian and Botticelli, who, even under the guise of angelic piety, in fact were determined to express their own harmonies, their own exotic phantasms and fiery-coloured fancies. This was a proud challenge to the "frozen orthodoxy" of Catholic tradition, which at times may forgive the sinner but must always condemn the dreamer.

To be sure, in Rome, our poet did discover the Pope, but Italy, as a whole, had wrought upon Wilde a stormy symphony of heterogeneous impressions most of which had little bearing upon religion, with its stern dictates and uncompromising laws. Whether or not Wilde had really become a "violent Papist," he continued to adhere to his belief that there was more infallibility and infinitely more truth in the finesse of the artist's dream than in the unerring dogmas of the Church.

Athens and Rome made Wilde forget Oxford. He failed to return to England on time for his Autumn term, and the Magdalen dons imposed on him an exorbitant fine of forty-five pounds, which, however, was restored to him in the Spring of 1878, when, just before graduation, he took the famous Newdigate Prize for his *Ravenna.*

CHAPTER X

FIRST TINKLES OF THE LYRE

WILDE'S literary career began in 1875, while he was still at Oxford. In the November issue of that year, *The Dublin University Magazine* printed what is known as his earliest published poem, *Chorus of Cloud Maidens,* adapted from Aristophanes. Signed "Oscar O'F. Wills Wilde," it was marked "Magdalen College, Oxford." Here and there, the octosyllabic strophes mingle with double and decasyllabic lines, and the whole song is but an imperfect specimen of imitative versification.[1]

In his College days, Wilde made also several contributions to two other Dublin journals, *The Irish Monthly* and *Kottabos;* the latter at the time was edited by Robert Y. Tyrrell, Fellow of Trinity College.

One of Oscar's youthful stanzas, *The True Knowledge,* written in four-foot iamb, was printed in the September 1876 issue of *The Irish Monthly.* Several months later, these verses were followed by *Lotus Leaves,* a lyrical piece of somewhat hazy content. The stylistic merits of these two compositions are neither great nor indicative of the potent talent which, in years to follow, Wilde evinced in a long range of essays, fairy tales, novels and dramatic works.

Nor were Wilde's subsequent poems, *Threnodia,* adapted from the Greek, and *A Fragment from the Agamemnon of Æschylus,* in any sense more successful. The only significant point about these and many other of Wilde's juvenile poetic exercises is that they were all influenced by the grand patterns of Hellenic literature, for which, as we know, he had a real fondness.

The technique of Wilde's verses, which never did attain the heights of excellence, is quite crude in his immature experimentations: in virtually every strophe there is at least one bad flaw or metrical distortion. Even within the simple iambic frame, there are digressions into discordant metres which sadly interrupt the musical flow of his verses.[2]

Much more satisfactory, though far from perfect, is *Heu Miserande Puer,* a sonnet dedicated to the tomb of Keats which Wilde had visited in 1877, with his college friends Bouncer and Dunsline. Indeed,

> That happen'd early in the Spring—
> The grass was scarcely greening,

and the young poet was then living in a spell of ecstasy, deeply moved by the majesty and magic of the Eternal City. For an ardent lover of Keats, such as Oscar always professed to be, it was only natural to make a pilgrimage to the last resting place of him who ever dreamed of "wings to find out an immortality." The keynote of Wilde's poem was borrowed from the inscription on the headstone, which has become world famous:

> This grave contains all that was mortal of a young English poet, who on his deathbed, in the bitterness of his heart, desired these words to be engraven on his tombstone: *Here lies one whose name was writ in water.* February 24, 1821.

In words touching and sincere Wilde told the story of his emotions at the sight of that lonely tomb surrounded by the dreamy shadows of the old Protestant Cemetery at Rome of which Shelley said it made one "in love with death to think that one should be buried in so sweet a place."

> As I stood beside the mean grave of this divine boy, I thought of him as a Priest of Beauty slain before his time; and the vision of Guido's St. Sebastian came before my eyes as I saw him at Genoa, a lovely brown boy, with crisp, clustering hair and red lips, bound by his evil enemies to a tree, and, though pierced by arrows, raising his eyes with divine, impassioned gaze towards the Eternal Beauty of the opening heavens. And thus my thoughts shaped themselves to rhyme:
>
> Rid of the world's injustice, and his pain,
> He rests at last beneath God's veil of blue:
> Taken from life when life and love were new

The youngest of the martyrs here is lain,
Fair as Sebastian, and as early slain.
  No cypress shades his grave, no funeral yew,
  But gentle violets weeping with the dew
Weave on his bones an ever-blossoming chain.

O proudest heart that broke for misery!
  O sweetest lips since those of Mitylene!
    O poet-painter of our English land!
    Thy name was writ in water—it shall stand:
  And tears like mine will keep thy memory green,
As Isabella did her Basil tree.[3]

When Oscar had embarked upon a poetic career, he was indeed very young, mentally as well as physically. Although he had read much and studied diligently, his mental horizon was still but slightly above the average. His quick, appreciative and fertile brain with its vague cosmopolitan leanings was then feverishly seeking to solve the perplexing distinction between "the hexameter's sacred strains" and the frivolous melodies of the rondel, between Sophocles and Théophile Gautier.

Perhaps it is characteristic of the artistic temperament of Wilde that even at an early age he should have chosen from among all poetical modes of expression precisely the sonnet, which is of necessity confined to a constrained form. This preference seems to indicate that there dwelt in him a strange longing for the element of artifice in art, while the spontaneous and extemporaneous impulses, both so typical of a true creative gift, are rarely to be found in his poetical works.

Wilde's faculties of *littérateur* developed with no marked impetus, and his belletristic début, which was not epoch-making at all, took place when he had reached his twenty-second spring, that age at which Keats had already created his *Endymion,* Poushkin—his unfading *Ruslan and Ludmila,* and Schiller—the flaming *Robbers.* Besides, Wilde's budding literary urges seem to have been focused upon the formal rather than the inspirational aspects of poetry and art; on the gloss and technical finish rather than the ideational substance of his verses. This is why, as Hagemann suggested, so many of

Wilde's poems, though decorative, are chilly and strangely unconvincing.

Oscar himself graphically described these youthful moods of his as

> days of lyrical ardour and studious sonnet writing; days when one loved the exquisite intricacy and musical repetitions of the ballade and the villanelle with its linked long-drawn echoes and its curious completeness; days when one solemnly sought to discover the proper temper in which a triolet should be written; delightful days in which, I am glad to say, there was far more rhyme than reason.

Such, indeed, were Wilde's earliest lyrical speculations, his first pirouettes on the English Parnassus.

Fate conferred her first smile upon Oscar with the academic success of his *Ravenna*. It was a curious coincidence that the choice of topic for this college competition should have fallen on a town which, by mere chance, he had only recently visited on his way to Greece.

Sir Roger Newdigate, the founder of the prize, made the proviso that the competing poems should consist of not more than fifty lines on a subject devoted to "the study of the ancient Greek and Roman remains of Architecture, Sculpture and Painting." Subsequently, the original statute was hazardously modified: the verses were to be arranged in heroic couplets and the restriction as to length was waived.

So, then, it was Ravenna that was chosen a victim for the Oxford undergraduates' poetic zeal "not limited to fifty lines." But where the rank and file aspirant was confronted with the painful task of trying to stimulate his imagination by perusing some dull encyclopædia or dusty textbook, Wilde's tale could be happily enriched by the memory of many a delightful moment actually spent in Ravenna: he had seen "Yon lonely pillar, rising on the plain," where Gaston de Foix, "the prince of chivalry," "the bravest knight of France was slain"; he had watched with the beams of the morning sun, "that Holy City rising clear, crowned with her crown of towers"; and he had solemnly beheld "the grave where Dante rests from pain."

His mind had been vividly impressed by the beautifully

planned octagonal Church of San Vitale, which dates back to the remote age of "huge-limbed Theodoric, the Gothic king," who "prisoned now within a lordly tomb . . . sleeps after all his weary conquering."

In Oscar's time, Ravenna was, and in many respects still is, a most intriguing spot, abounding in historical relics and animated by architectural charm. There, the Cæsarian tradition strangely mingles with the Byzantine flavour; the reserved horizontal lines of the Roman Basilica blend in harmony with the splendour of glass mosaics and the iridescent motifs of Eastern ornamentation, reminding one now of Venice, that precious pearl of Adria, with her gold and azure of St. Mark's, and now of Santa Sophia with her exquisite gamut of towering domes.

Wilde recited his poem in the Sheldonian Theatre on the twenty-sixth day of June, 1878. The captivating manner in which he read his verses, the rare beauty of his voice, his handsome countenance, coupled with the excellence of some of the verses completed his triumph and proved him worthy of the Newdigate laurels. Assuming an air of indifference and horribly swaggering, Oscar pretended that he "did not care a bit" about his winning the contest. In fact, the next day after the Sheldonian exercises he did not go up to the Schools, saying "it was a bore"; but, of course, he was quite proud of his success, which also greatly delighted Lady Wilde.

However, *Ravenna,* too, after all, is hardly anything more than a pseudo-classical rhetoric composition, protracted and verbose, only here and there marked with sincere poetic verve. Such—to cite but one example—is the passage dealing with the description of nature:

> Full Spring it was—and by rich-flowering vines,
> Dark olive-groves and noble forest-pines
> I rode at will; the moist glad air was sweet,
> The white road rang beneath my horse's feet,
> And musing on Ravenna's ancient name,
> I watched the day till, marked with wounds of flame,
> The turquoise sky to burnished gold was turned.

There are other equally beautiful strophes in this poem, but its artificial tip-toe tone divulges a still inexperienced rhymer struggling to squeeze his lyric moods into the Procrustean bed of a formal iambic exercise. There is an abuse of legendary nomenclature, a whole array of Pans and Dians and Hylases, which—as Ransome remarked—converts Wilde's poem into "a rhymed dictionary of mythology." This epidemic of heathen names and terms is even more conspicuous in some of his later productions, such as *Charmides, Panthea,* and *The Burden of Itys*—a defect by no means unusual for poets in their prime.

But Wilde's assiduous invocation of all the Olympians signified not so much a lack of artistic tact as a sophisticated coquetry to which he intentionally resorted for the avowed purpose of impressing upon the public his elaborate acquaintance with those vanished deities of olden times. And some of his allegories and mythological hints, like the allusion to the mysterious "Euphorion" in *The New Helen,* are either altogether meaningless or sadly obscure.

A word about the construction of *Ravenna:* had the Fourth and Fifth Songs been simply omitted the piece would have been greatly improved as these long *obiter dicta* about Greece and the "wind-swept heights of lone Thermopylæ," and Lord Byron and the "Dryad-maid in girlish flight"—merely tend to detract one's attention from the leitmotiv of the poem.

There is in *Ravenna* a passage in which the poet, as it were, prophetically foreshadows his own ill-fate:

> Discrowned by man, deserted by the sea,
> Thou sleepest, rocked in lonely misery!
> No longer now upon thy swelling tide,
> Pine-forest like, thy myriad galleys ride!
> For where the brass-beaked ships were wont to float,
> The weary shepherd pipes his mournful note;
> And the white sheep are free to come and go
> Where Adria's purple waters used to flow.

Is this not a pathetic picture of Oscar's personal drama?—When, intoxicated with success, Oscar was reciting his poem, he was, without knowing it, telling the story of his own coming glory so mercilessly shattered by a tragic catastrophe.

He departed from Oxford with a B.A. degree and that *bagage d'idées,* or a wealth of learning, that had scarcely any commercial value. It was all theory, all dream, intangible assets of mental dexterity and literary skill—things that could not be easily traded over the City's prosaic counters. And the nebulous title of "Professor of Æsthetics and Art Critic," which he conferred upon himself, after all was not too powerful a weapon for the realisation of his bold scheme to conquer London, captivate England and dominate the World of Letters.

CHAPTER XI

A FOOTHOLD ON PARNASSUS

THE official triumph which Wilde scored at the Sheldonian was an event of considerable biographical importance, for it encouraged him in his purely poetical endeavours. From now on he could look with a measure of assurance to his literary future, and for two years following his graduation he turned his attention mostly to poetry, as yet paying but secondary heed to prose. Again, this preference for verse and rhyme is quite a normal trait in immature writers.

> When [Wilde tells us] I first had the privilege—and I count it a very high one—of meeting Mr. Walter Pater, he said to me, smiling, "Why do you always write poetry? Why do you not write prose?—Prose is so much more difficult!"

Precisely because "prose is so much more difficult," Oscar at first fervently pursued his lyrical hobby without attempting to contend with either De Quincey or Ruskin or Pater, although at a later stage he himself had become one of England's most ingenious essayists. But the early steps of his career were those of a determined lyricist. At varying intervals his poetical pieces appeared in English and Irish periodicals, including *The Burlington, The Month, World* and *Pan.*

Early in 1881, Wilde, after some hesitation, decided to publish a collection of his verses. The problem was not an easy one, since he had to defray the printing expenses out of his own pocket. However, in May of that year he managed to raise the necessary sum, and a few weeks thereafter an edition of *Poems* limited to only two hundred and fifty copies[1] was brought out by David Bogue. The volume was artistically printed on Dutch handmade paper, handsomely bound in parchment. On the fly-leaf of his manuscript, Wilde wrote:

Mes premiers vers sont d'un enfant,
Mes seconds d'un adolescent.

These truthful words have been often overlooked or purposely forgotten by his censors who went so far as to attribute to the young minstrel the ambition—of which he was quite innocent—of launching an entirely novel poetic movement. Far from claiming anything of the sort, Wilde publicly admitted his allegiance to the Pre-Raphaelites, who, according to him, owed their very existence to Keats, the founder of a school similar to that which Phidias originated in Greek art. Commenting on this point Wilde observed:

> Later, Burne-Jones in painting, and Morris, Rossetti and Swinburne in poetry, represented the fruit of which Keats was the blossom.

English critics, who traditionally have been suspicious of every new star ascending on the literary horizon, vehemently attacked Oscar's first book. *The Saturday Review* announced that his verses belonged to a class "which is the special terror of reviewers" and "in which one searches in vain for any personal touch of thought or music." The article concluded with a statement that "the book is not without traces of cleverness, but is marred everywhere by imitation, insincerity, and bad taste."

Punch, of course, was prompt to leap into the foreground with derogative insinuations against our poet and his "Swinburnian jargon":

> Mr. Lambert Streyke in *The Colonel* [thus runs the review] published a book of poems for the benefit of his followers, and his own—and Mr. Oscar Wilde has followed his example. The cover is consummate, the paper is distinctly precious, the binding is beautiful, and the type is utterly too. *Poems by Oscar Wilde,* that is the title of the book of the æsthetic singer, which comes to us arrayed in white vellum and gold. There is a certain amount of originality about the binding, but that is more than can be said for the inside. . . . This is a volume of echoes—

> it is Swinburne and water, while here and there we note that the author has been reminiscent of Mr. Rossetti and Mrs. Browning.

These lines demonstrate a lamentable lack of critical insight on the part of that comic sheet which subsequently made itself rather conspicuous in its relentless war against Æstheticism.

With good reason, Walter Hamilton has compared *Punch's* outbursts against Wilde with Christopher North's earlier attacks on Tennyson, attacks which the future Poet-Laureate met with this witty retort:

> You did late review my lays,
> Crusty Charivari;
> You did mingle blame and praise,
> Rusty Charivari.
> When I learnt from whom it came,
> I forgave you all the blame,
> Musty Charivari,
> I could *not* forgive the praise,
> Fusty Charivari.

The Zoilists unwittingly benefited Wilde in that they gave free, if not fair, publicity to his unpretentious début.

A much warmer reception was given to the *Poems* by the American press. *The New York Times,* for instance, wrote that

> in Wilde, England has a new poet, who, if not of the first order of power, is so true a poet underneath whatever eccentricity of conduct or cant of school that his further persecution in the press must be held contemptible. It will only be on a par with the infatuation some people have to vilify what is really best in their own country. Oscar Wilde need not have written but this one poem, *Ave Imperatrix,* to win him respectful hearing wherever people exist who are responsive to what is noble in literature.

Likewise, *The Century* (New York, 1881) acclaimed *Ave Imperatrix* as a piece of poetry which "is strong enough, simple enough, beautiful enough to delight an unsympathetic foreigner."

> How an Englishman [observed the reviewer] can read it without a

glow of pride and a sigh of sorrow is beyond comprehension. Mr. Wilde can comfort himself. *Ave Imperatrix* outweighs a hundred cartoons of *Punch.*

The ode to which both *The Century* and *The Times* have given so generous a praise is, however, by no means among the best in the collection: with all its merits, it is saturated with strained political pathos and social extremism that harmfully affect the literary value of the poem. To what extent Oscar's revolutionary propensities were really sincere is best seen from his interview with the San Francisco *Daily Examiner* (March, 1882), when in answer to a correspondent's question:

> Does the *Sonnet to Liberty* voice your political creed?

our poet candidly admitted that it did not, and added:

> No, that is not my political creed. I wrote that when I was younger. Perhaps something of the fire of youth prompted it.

Still, *Ave Imperatrix,* with its bombastic lines:

> Yet when this fiery web is spun,
> Her [England] watchmen shall decry from far
> The young Republic like a sun
> Rise from these crimson seas of war.

is but another way of displaying the Jacobite cap which so ostentatiously crowns his *Sonnet to Liberty.* So that, when sentimental writers of Kenilworth's stamp suggest that Wilde was "the messenger of the Rightful Stirring Up so that new eras be born out of the chaos of all social forms" or that "he was a man of tempestuous aspirations," one is not inclined to take their declarations too seriously. There was, of course, in Wilde an innate sense of intellectual freedom, a revulsion against conventional narrow-mindedness, and, possibly, a vague, or half-crystallised feeling of sympathy for what Dostoievsky called "the downtrodden and insulted." But he never deigned to go to the root of the ills and evils of our present social structure and he was quite earnest when he once uttered this phrase:

> If the poor only had profiles, there would be no difficulty in solving the problem of poverty.

Oscar's mutiny against society was a rather pacific affair, largely confined to matters of style or to the hideous manifestations of purely English bigotry. A convinced individualist, he preached in the field of personal conduct the physiocratic doctrine of *laissez-faire, laissez-passer* and the defiance of all laws seeking to restrain the artist's self-expression.

Like every genuinely lyrical collection, *Poems* contains a good deal of autobiographical data; inklings of the complex moods of the poet's inner world; simple love songs alongside the ingenious conjectures of a sophisticated mind; sighs and sorrows of a youthful heart mingled with mystic urges and repentant tears.

It seems that in those days Wilde sincerely yearned after inner betterment. The rust of agnosticism as yet had not touched his intellect with stains of tedium and decay. The image of Our Saviour stood out before his eyes like a fascinating vision, and in Him the poet placed all confidence and hope:

> Come down, O Christ, and help me! reach Thy hand,
> For I am drowning in a stormier sea
> Than Simon on Thy lake of Galilee:
> The wine of life is spilt upon the sand,
> My heart is as some famine-murdered land,
> Whence all good things have perished utterly,
> And well I know my soul in Hell must lie
> If I this night before God's throne should stand.
>
> "He sleeps perchance, or rideth to the chase,
> Like Baal, when his prophets howled that name
> From morn to noon on Carmel's smitten height."
> Nay, peace, I shall behold before the night,
> The feet of brass, the robe more white than flame,
> The wounded hands, the weary human face.

And, in *Rome Unvisited,* there are also lines burning with religious fervour, like these for instance:

O joy to see before I die
  The only God-anointed King,
  And hear the silver trumpets ring
A triumph as He passes by,

Or at the altar of the shrine
  Holds high the mystic sacrifice,
  And shows a God to human eyes
Beneath the veil of bread and wine.

Pondering over these early poems one experiences particular delight in the brief lyrical impromptus, which are of far greater literary import than the heavy discharges of poetic energy in works such as *Humanitad* and *Panthea* with their protracted horticultural discussions, or even *Charmides,* although there one finds verses full of inimitable grace and musical charm. The Shakespearean influence in this poem is, of course, obvious, but Ingleby was right when he said:

> Had Shakespeare never written *Venus and Adonis,* Wilde might have written *Charmides* but it would not have been the same poem. The difference between the true poet who has studied the great verse of bygone ages and the mere imitator is that one will produce a work of art enhanced by the suggestions derived from the contemplation of the highest conception of genius, whereas the other will outrun the constable and merely accentuate and burlesque the distinguishing characteristics of the work of others. In the case in point, whilst we note with pleasure and interest the points of resemblance between the poem and the models that its author has followed, we are conscious that what we are reading is a work of art in itself and that its intrinsic merits are enhanced by the points of resemblance and do not depend on them for their existence.

Still, all these verbose compositions reveal less graphically Oscar's tender nature than the gentle improvisations on the *Magdalen Walks;* or where, as in *La Fuite de la Lune,* he spins the delicate web of a nocturne; or in his vivid word·picture of awakening London with the sudden dramatic effect of that "pale woman all alone," caught in the gas lamp's flare "with lips of flame and heart of stone."

These evasive silhouettes, veiled, as it were, with a greyish mist like that which at once conceals and adorns Carrière's canvases, comprise a whole world of inner reserve and harmony and feeling, something that divulges a genuine though still budding talent. Verily, in these gems, as Baudelaire would have said:

Les parfums, les couleurs et les sons se répondent.

The loveliest perhaps in the whole booklet is the touching and mournful *Requiescat* written in memory of Isola, Wilde's little sister. This wee poem has become a classic, and with good reason it is regarded as one of the most treasured pieces in English poesy. Composed in a minor key, it is tremulous with sweet emotion:

Tread lightly, she is near
   Under the snow,
Speak gently, she can hear
   The daisies grow.

All her bright golden hair
   Tarnished with rust,
She that was young and fair
   Fallen to dust.

Lily-like, white as snow,
   She hardly knew
She was a woman, so
   Sweetly she grew.

Coffin-board, heavy stone,
   Lie on her breast,
I vex my heart alone:
   She is at rest.

Peace, peace, she cannot hear
   Lyre or sonnet,
All my life's buried here,
   Heap earth upon it.

Moody critics have tried to show that *Requiescat* is little more than an imitation of Hood's merciful *Bridge of Sighs:*

> One more Unfortunate
> Weary of breath,
> Rashly importunate,
> Gone to her death.
>
> Take her up tenderly,
> Lift her with care,
> Fashioned so slenderly,
> Young and so fair.

There is not much virtue in this suggestion: where Oscar strictly adheres to the four-line construction, Hood's strophes are arranged somewhat along the pattern of our present-day "free verses," varying from the conventional double couplet to stanzas comprised of five, six, seven and even nine lines which intentionally follow an irregular order of rhyming. Nor is it fair to draw parallels between *Requiescat,* a hymn to Innocence, to a darling child, fragrant and chaste as the lily of the valley, and Hood's plea in defence of a "fallen woman" stained with "muddy impurity." Besides, even if it were true that Wilde had been influenced by the *Bridge of Sighs,* this does not in the least rob *Requiescat* of its singular beauty.

A few more words about Wilde's imitative propensities: they are so clearly traceable both in his poetry and prose that in some quarters he has been accused of sheer plagiarism. It seems futile to deny the fact that not only in his early days, before he had become the *enfant terrible* of Mid-Victorian England, did Oscar borrow freely from many a literary source, English or French, but that even some of his later emulations were quite unceremonious and provoked stormy protests and outbursts of indignation. As a mere example we may cite his philippic *On the Massacre of the Christians in Bulgaria,* which is obviously a paraphrase of Milton's sonnet *On the Late Massacre in Piemont.* Arthur Ransome has made a chivalresque but rather ineffective attempt to exonerate our poet by setting forth the far-fetched hypothesis that in this poem Wilde was not really copying or flattering Milton but simply juxtaposing the "doubting faith of our days with the noble assurance of the Puritans," and that in this way he performed a clever act of criticism or of "exact appreciation."

We are not privileged to know precisely what Wilde may have had in his mind when appropriating now a suite of rhymes from Milton, now a passage from Pater, or some metrical construction of Gautier's. Ross made a good point when in refuting Wilde's alleged or real habit of literary pilfering, he said:

> To what extent an idea may be regarded as a perpetual gift, or whether it is ethically possible to retrieve an idea like an engagement ring, it is not for me to discuss.

As a matter of record, the history of literature and art in general is one continuous assimilative process of mutually permeating influences so that no artist ever is, or can be, altogether exempt from some stylistic, if not ideational, kinship with this contemporary or that predecessor. Wilde's remark, after all, is right:

> In art as in life the law of heredity holds good; *on est toujours fils de quelqu'un.*

Thus it always was and ever will be: a great work of art is produced; the public gets hold of it; it is talked about, admired, studied, scorned, doubted, criticised, and imperceptibly becomes an integral part of that material which is used in subsequent creations. Raphael would have been impossible without Perugino, Luini without Leonardo. But the practice of imitation goes even further: one branch of æsthetics is, in a measure, dependent upon all other ramifications of artistic endeavour. As Goethe has it:

> The actor should properly go to school to the sculptor and painter; for in order to represent a Greek hero, it is necessary for him to study carefully the antique sculptures . . . and to impress on his mind the natural grace of sitting, standing and walking. But the mere bodily

is not enough. He must also, by diligent study of the best ancient and modern authors, thoroughly cultivate his mind.

This, then, is the justification of all mirroring in art.

If one has to insist on the shortcomings in Wilde's youthful *Poems,* the over-emphasis of the personal element should be noted. Throughout the whole collection, the poet's ego figures altogether too prominently and too persistently; the subjective overshadows the objective, so that, to this first book of Wilde's his own words spoken about a certain woman critic are singularly applicable:

I remember being told in America that whenever Margaret Fuller wrote an essay upon Emerson, the printers had always to send out to borrow some additional capital "I's."

CHAPTER XII

VERA – A *FAUTE DE JEUNESSE*

THE eighteen-seventies in Russia were fraught with grave internal unrest and revolutionary excesses of the vilest kind. Terrorism against state officials was freely resorted to by young desperadoes whom Dostoievsky so ingeniously depicted in his *Possessed* and whose sad philosophy has been immortalised by Turgenev in the character of Bazarov, perhaps the weariest among all the Russian "useless heroes." This was an epoch when Nihilism, acclaimed by the rabble as the greatest social doctrine ever conceived by the human mind, threatened to create a condition of social vacuity which Hegel thus defined in his biting motto: "From nothing –through nothing–to nothing."

Alexander II, the most benevolent of all monarchs, past or living, who by one stroke of his pen had emancipated millions of serfs, granting them not merely personal freedom but lands as well, was subjected to perfidious persecution: attempts against his life followed one another in endless succession. But true to his ideals, this fearless knight carried on the noble and gigantic task of modernising, reforming and reconstructing Russia. Courageously and calmly he faced the rising tide of anarchy, ready to meet the challenge of the dark forces by another act of mercy, by that Magna Charta which was to bestow upon the Russian people the right to mould their own destinies. On the eve of that historical day, on March 1, 1881, the Czar-Liberator was assassinated in St. Petersburg.

The Western World, as usual, ignorant of the real state of affairs in Russia, derived its basic conceptions, or rather misconceptions, about the Eastern Empire from calumnies and hostile propagandist sources. Outsiders emphatically failed to grasp the magnitude and complexity of the dramatic events in that mysterious land.

The radical European intelligentsia brought up on the fiery pamphlets of Mazzini, on Lassalle's *Workers' Program* and the Marxian *Communist Manifesto,* was inclined to diagnose the Russian situation through the prism of incurable prejudice: Russia, they argued, is an autocratic country; the "bloody Romanoffs" are maintaining their rule by means of the knout; the people are longing for all sorts of parliamentary prerogatives and dreaming of nothing but a democratic republic. This, then, is the reason why they are so perseveringly hurling bombs at their oppressors.

These simplified ratiocinations are quite prevalent even in our age: today, when the enlightened Hollywood producer sets out to feature the reign of either Paul the First or Nicholas the Second—it matters not which—he proves utterly incapable of stretching his imagination beyond the stereotyped picture of the Czar brutally whipping his innocent subjects and spending his leisure hours revelling and feasting in the company of a whole cohort of vicious courtiers and half-naked Cleopatras.

Oscar Wilde, who had inherited from Speranza a good deal of her bombast, and thus far had acquired no knowledge of either current history or politics, envying perhaps the laurels of Calderón or Shakespeare, turned somewhat unexpectedly from "studious sonnet writing" to the difficult occupation of a historical dramatist. Had he chosen for his scenic début either Ireland or England or Greece, he might have succeeded halfway. But for some incomprehensible reason, of all the lands about which he knew nothing, he picked Russia, which to a determined Westerner, such as Oscar, was the least intelligible country, wrapped in a dense fog of misunderstanding and altogether outside the scope of anything he could have absorbed at Trinity or learned at Oxford.

The fruit of this unhappy liaison with Melpomene was *Vera,* a four-act melodrama or rather farce, with a prologue, outspokenly designed to ridicule "evil Czardom" and glorify the virtuous Nihilists—those *enfants dociles* who were here conceived as champions of blessed emancipation.

Better than any one else Wilde has explained the motive which prompted him to engage in the task of composing that play:

> I have tried in it [he wrote Marie Prescott] to express within the limits of art that Titan cry of the peoples for liberty, which in Europe of today is threatening thrones and making governments unstable from Spain to Russia, and from north to southern seas. But it is a play not of politics but of passion. It deals with no theories of government, but with men and women simply; the modern Nihilistic Russia, with all the terror of its tyranny and the marvel of its martyrdoms, is merely the fiery and fervent background in front of which the persons of my dream live and love. With this feeling was the play written, and with this aim should the play be acted.

To Wilde, with his highly emotional temperament, there was a strong temptation to gain the repute of a thoroughbred Whig and to earn the applause of the "gods." For surely, at the time, the theme was a modish one, while its treatment, the very hyperbole of Czarist corruption and Nihilist heroism, as artificially concocted in that piece, should have assured at least penny success to his bold undertaking. Alas, it proved a dismal failure.

Vera was to be staged in London at the Adelphi Theatre on December 17, 1881, with Mrs. Bernard Beere in the leading rôle. But at the eleventh hour the performance was cancelled, and the *World* printed an announcement to the effect that "considering the present state of political feeling in England, Mr. Oscar Wilde had decided on postponing, for a time, the production of his drama, *Vera.*" The real reason for this reverse has never been clearly ascertained, but it appears that the author was much more disappointed in the way the actors sought to render his play than in the play itself. Now, it was hardly fair to have put all the blame upon the rendition of *Vera* by the London cast, when the drama itself was but a mediocre, if not altogether flimsy, specimen of modern dramaturgy. No doubt, critics often had been severe toward Wilde, but their uncomplimentary innuendoes regarding *Vera* were fully justified.

Shortly after the play had been withdrawn from the Adelphi repertoire, *Punch* noted this incident in an article entitled *Impressions du Théâtre,* which reads in part:

> The production of Mr. Oscar Wilde's play *Vera* is deferred. Naturally, no one would expect a Veerer to be at all certain: it must be like a pretendedly infallible forecast, so weather-cocky. *Vera* is about Nihilism: this looks as if there were nothing to it.

The verdict "nothing to it" may be slightly harsh, but it is an incontestable fact that the specific gravity of Wilde's work is quite close to zero. A melodrama such as this should be full of live action, with swiftly developing plots of which the "star" is the storm center. Besides, as Ingleby suggested, "pure melodrama especially, despite a very general idea to the contrary, requires an acquaintance with . . . stage mechanism that is only obtainable after many years of practice."

But in those days Wilde knew nothing, not even the A. B.C., of stagecraft; he must have been labouring under the mistaken belief that because he had written a few excellent verses he would instantly manage to become a proficient playwright. Apparently, he had no idea that general literary ability is a thing quite apart from dramaturgy, for as Clayton Hamilton observed:

> Tennyson—the perfect poet; Browning—the master of the human mind; Stevenson—the teller of enchanting tales:—each of them failed when he tried to make a drama.

A "star system" production, unless it is a *Hamlet* or *Prometheus* or *Cyrano de Bergerac,* rarely makes a scenic success; it is bound to be a flat failure when, as in our play, the attention of the spectator is continually diverted from the leading part to the minor *dramatis personæ.* For one thing, *Vera's* technique is clumsy and sadly ineffective: Vera, Oscar's heroine, the solitary feminine rôle in the drama, is lost amidst a whole crowd of insignificant characters engaged in petty intrigues and utterly unimportant political wrangles.

Through the Prologue and the First Act, Vera's appearances are weak, being completely taken up with frenzied outbursts against "martial law" and similar "soapbox" topics. In the Second Act, Vera does not appear at all, and in her next scene, at the conspirators' headquarters, she reveals an outright hysterical constitution. In the beginning, she keeps monotonously moaning:

> Alexis! why are you not here?
> O, why? O, why, O, why? . . .

Weary lamentations, indeed! But suddenly she breaks forth with a protracted tirade about Liberty, the crucified and "mighty mother of eternal time." And she talks and talks, precisely like a mentally deranged woman:

> Ay, the spirit of Charlotte Corday beats in each petty vein, and nerves my woman's hand to strike as I have nerved my woman's heart to hate.

In passing, the logic of this outcry may well be questioned: to a "nihilist" of the Vera-Wilde pattern, there should be little attraction in fair Charlotte who slew Marat—but for Robespierre, the busiest and most tumultuous ringleader of the era of Terror.

Then the epilogue: here, "Enter Vera in a black coat" with a long dagger. She penetrates into the Palace, all set to assassinate the Czar. Unnoticed, she reaches the antechamber where the crowned ruler peacefully slumbers. Now at last his fate is in her hands. Now is her chance to "save Russia" by delivering the mortal blow. But contrary to all hopes of the tired audience, our maiden is accomplishing nothing of the kind: forgetting her duties of heroine, she begins to indulge in her rights as a woman. In a purely operatic fashion she proceeds to the footlights and recites there a lyrical monologue which is followed by a brief but live verbal exchange with the young Czar. The scene winds up with sweet kisses, and so forth.

"All's well that ends well": the loving pair are serene and happy. Yet relentless fate evidently is opposed to the tender passion of the two palpitating hearts, for when presently Vera hears her bushy-haired comrades cheer in the street below—"Long live the people!" she promptly stabs herself and dies, shouting to posterity, "I have saved Russia!" (The really vexing question is: *how* did Vera manage to stab herself, since only an instant before doing so, for precaution's sake, she had flung her dagger out of the window?)

The supporting characters—all those Kotemkins, Rouvaloffs, Michaels and *tutti quanti*—hardly deserve any mention at all: they are either insignificant marionettes, or dead mannequins, or poorly sketched caricatures, devoid of national flavour and psychological truth.

The *couleur locale,* as far as history is concerned, has been masterfully misinterpreted, if not deliberately distorted by Wilde. The whole play is dedicated to Nihilism, that is, a movement which originated on Russian soil in the 'sixties of the past century. Yet the Prologue is supposed to take place in 1795, that is during the reign of Catherine the Great, when there were in Russia neither Nihilists nor any other revolutionists. On the other hand, in the opening scene the Colonel utters this nonsensical sentence:

> You peasants are getting too saucy *since you ceased to be serfs,* and the knout is the best school for you to learn politics in.

With due respect to our Oxford graduate, one must challenge his chronology, for the Russian peasants ceased to be serfs, not in 1795, but in 1861. And then the plot itself, according to the author, develops in the year 1800. Still, in the Second Act, the Czar, in the course of his dialogue with one of the numerous Princes, whispers: "The Emperor Paul did it. The Empress Catherine . . . did it. Why shouldn't I?" As Oscar could have easily ascertained from any encyclopedia, in 1800, Paul the First was still alive and rather active as "The Autocrat of all the Russias."

Another piquant detail: the Czar, scolding one of his officers, says:

> . . . I banish you for your bad jokes. Bon Voyage, Messieurs! If you value your lives you will *catch the first train* for Paris.

The difficulty here is that in 1800, there were no trains, whether in Russia or elsewhere.

Only one more illustration: what could have suggested to our poet the bold idea that in Russia there has ever existed the "Order of the Iron Cross," to which the Czar alludes in one of his tedious dissertations? Obviously, Wilde must have confused the Hohenzollerns with the Romanoffs.

One could go on almost indefinitely cataloguing the unpardonably silly blunders which pervade this "historical" extravaganza. But today no one takes *Vera* seriously; the play rather should be regarded as a dramatic failure. After all, *humanum est errare.*

CHAPTER XIII

AMERICAN DÉBUT

WILDE left Oxford with a rather lean purse and with only limited opportunities to earn his bread and butter. His *Poems* brought but meagre financial returns. *Vera* could not be produced on the London stage. All this was embarrassing, and the future must have appeared gloomy to our poet.

However, His Majesty, almighty Chance, seemed to favour Oscar when, at the right moment, he stepped into his life with a graceful smile: in 1881, Gilbert and Sullivan's musical *amusette, Patience,* satirising æsthetes and æstheticism, was produced by Mr. D'Oyley Carte at the Standard Theatre on Broadway. It made an instantaneous hit which served as an indication that the American public might be interested in seeing on the lecture platform that man who was said to personify the principles of the new gospel.

At the suggestion of Colonel W. F. Morse, business manager of D'Oyley Carte, on September 30, 1881, the following cable was dispatched from New York to Oscar Wilde, who was then occupying rooms at 1, Ovington Square, London:

> Responsible agent asks me to enquire if you will consider offer he makes by letter for fifty readings beginning November 1. This is confidential. Answer.

On the next day Wilde sent this reply:

> Yes, if offer good.

All details of Wilde's first appearance in America were left in the hands of Morse.

At this point it might be well to refute a widely accepted

version that Wilde had undertaken his first journey to America with the hidden motive of advertising *Patience*. In the first place, there was no need for "boosting" the operetta, which enjoyed continued success. Besides, as Hamilton justly observed, Wilde was "scarcely the man to condescend to become an advertising medium for a play which professed to ridicule nearly everything he held sacred in art and poetry."

That Oscar entertained no illusions about *Patience* may be gathered from a statement which he made shortly after his arrival in New York. Referring to the performance of that piece on the London stage, he said:

> We attended at the opening night and had all manner of fun. I was not to be laughed out of my theory. I had arrived at what I sincerely believed to be the truth in these matters, and the praise or blame of the public was to me a matter of no importance whatever.

Far from trying to plead the cause of the musical comedy, Wilde, on the contrary, seems to have had in mind the vindication of æstheticism. The fear that Americans might confuse G. & S.'s "vegetable loves" with the "true representation of us," prompted him to appeal for public indulgence and to urge the audience assembled at Chickering Hall to grant him a bit of their "patience."

> You have listened [he remarked] to the charming music of Mr. Sullivan and the clever satire of Mr. Gilbert for three hundred nights, and I am sure, having given so much time to satire it is not asking too much to ask you to listen to the truth for one evening.

The immediate occasion for the acceptance of Colonel Morse's offer was indeed quite simple: to Wilde it was a unique opportunity to test and to capitalise his wonderful gift as a public speaker. He was fully awake to his exceptional command of English and the extraordinary beauty of his voice, coupled with a most attractive personality. Another thing: Oscar placed great hopes in the production of *Vera* in the States, and altogether, he regarded the American tour as a steppingstone to a literary career overflowing with success.

And so, without much hesitation, saying to himself: *"In hoc signo vinces,"* he courageously ducked into that overseas adventure from which he did emerge tempered and triumphant.

Wilde departed from England aboard the *Arizona* on Christmas Eve in the year of Our Lord, 1881. *Punch's* farewell message was framed rather humourously:

> Bon Voyage! When he gets there, may he say with Marshall MacMahon: *"J'y suis, j'y reste!"*

The boat reached New York on the evening of January 2, too late to pass Quarantine before sundown. Without a moment's delay, a whole detachment of American reporters—even in those days they enjoyed the reputation of being the most merciless creatures on earth—launched a frontal attack upon "the poet and apostle of English æstheticism." Perceiving, and, of course, relishing the element of sensationalism in Oscar's début, they gazed at him with intense curiosity, eager, like children who reach out for a pie, to stick their fingers into that tempting product of an exotic culture.

The *Tribune's* correspondent gave this vivid pen-portrait of the distinguished visitor:

> The most striking thing about the poet's appearance is his height, which is several inches over six feet, and the next thing to attract attention is his hair, which is of a dark brown colour, and falls down upon his shoulders. . . . When he laughs his lips part widely and show a shining row of upper teeth, which are superlatively white. The complexion instead of being of the rosy hue so common in Englishmen, is so utterly devoid of colour that it can only be said to resemble putty. His eyes are blue, or a light grey, and instead of being "dreamy," as some of his admirers have imagined them to be, they are bright and quick—not at all like those of one given to perpetual musings on the ineffably beautiful and true. Instead of having a small delicate hand, only fit to caress a lily, his fingers are long and when doubled up would form a fist that would hit a hard knock, should an occasion arise for the owner to descend to that kind of argument. . . . One of the peculiarities of his speech is that he accents almost at regular intervals without regard to the sense, perhaps as a result of an effort to be rhythmic in conversation as well as in verse.

Though assuming an air of nonchalance, Oscar apparently was only too glad to seize the opportunity to lay bare before the New World the mysteries of his Hellenic cult. He talked from the outset, overwhelming his interviewers by multiloquous monologues, which the *Herald* chronicler admitted he was unable to follow.

Quite extensively, and *molto vivace,* Wilde discussed art in poetry and dress, "the secret of life," the "correlation of all the arts," and similar obscure topics. But the point in all this ostensibly learned chit-chat would have been altogether missed by both the publicists and their public, were it not for the fact that even when he had nothing to say he knew how to say it charmingly. Overnight some of his smart sayings gained for him extraordinary notoriety and "put him on the map." Only one day after his landing, everybody knew that he was "disappointed in the tame Atlantic" and that "he had nothing to declare except his genius." Statements such as these were heartily enjoyed by the freak-loving Americans.[1]

Wilde's entry into Uncle Sam's dominions was a tumultuous, if not exactly a triumphant one. The pose which he skillfully displayed was novel; his tone, so typically English, was amusing; and the public, always avid for entertainment of any kind, seemed satisfied to be treated to the outlandish æstheticism about which they knew little and cared still less.

Much to Oscar's disappointment, Americans refused to take him seriously. His masquerading was distinctly ludicrous and his over-zealous dandyism—unequivocally distasteful. No matter how, at the time, one might have felt about Swinburne and Baudelaire, or Rossetti and the rest of the P. R. B.s, mannerism in dress was a poor argument in favour of the new school of thought.

In the eighties, still more than at present, the American people as a body had no instinct for either belles lettres—or art in general. Prosaic in their habits, provincial in their modes of thinking, they were utterly unable to draw a line of demarcation between Wilde—the poet, and Wilde—the clown. Despite his literary gifts and innate refinement, what could he have expected from a nation—if the term may be appropriately used in the case of the American melting, or rather mixing, pot—which only three decades before, with astounding solidarity, had condemned to oblivion its greatest poet, Edgar Allan Poe?

Thus, when Oscar appeared on the American horizon, he was at once taken as a joke, and the sort of publicity he received would have ruined the reputation of even Cæsar's wife. Take this little bit from *The New York Times:*

> . . . The feeling against this young man who has foolishly taken advantage of his chances as a successful poseur, is—among the best class of people here, and among the real literary class—a feeling of contempt. . . . It is rightly felt that chance notoriety, based upon the slightest possible claims, is not reputation. The honest literary man loves fame and dreads noise. . . . Mr. Wilde has signally posted himself as an "æsthetic sham," and it is his own fault if writers and men who respect themselves take him at his own counting.

Not less derogatory was *The Tribune* in its denunciation of poor Oscar:

> Wherever he has appeared some new way of enhancing the public's enjoyment has been invented. College students in the University towns found in him a perfectly justifiable object for their ridicule. Quack doctors hit upon his favourite sunflower as a means of advertising their own nostrums. . . . In the free and untrammelled West, tradespeople utilized his form as a means of advertisement, and if Mr. Wilde took up a newspaper there, he very likely saw himself, dressed in his special garb, standing at the head of an announcement by a clothing dealer that "Wild Oscar, the Ass-thete, buys his clothes of our establishment."

And the "panegyric" winds up with the moral:

> We did not need Mr. Wilde's visit to teach the old truth that he who dresses to attract attention confesses that he can hope to attract it in no other way.

Now, we all know what the æsthetic garb looked like. Quite recently, *The Saturday Evening Post*[2] reprinted a full-length portrait of Wilde from a well-known photograph taken by

Sarony in 1882: he appeared there in his habitual costume consisting of a short velvet camisole, silk knee-breeches, silk stockings and slippers adorned by grosgrain bows. The genteel, studied and pensive expression on his face probably accounts for the silly inscription appearing under the picture, "Oscar Wilde grieved at the sale of Keats' Letters" which, however, were auctioned off in London some three years later.

Circus tactics adopted by the Irish wit proved all the more unfortunate as his lectures, for those who did take the trouble to listen to them, were full of meaning and lacked neither eloquence nor erudition.

Another decidedly adverse factor that contributed much toward the ridicule of Wilde's name was the would-be "smart women" of America. Had these charming creatures been less gushing, or a bit more shy of sensational and hopelessly trivial fads; had they only left that victim of their temperaments to paddle his own canoe through the treacherous rapids of conflicting publicity, he would probably have discarded his guise of a professional æsthete before the people had grasped it as a pretext for identifying him not so much with the poet's mantle, as with the jester's cap. For he was too shrewd a man to have insisted upon his tomfoolery had he been given straightforward and unmistakable evidence that society had no use for his silk hosiery, long hair, sunflowers and all the rest of his paraphernalia.

But it so happened that almost immediately upon his landing in New York he found himself surrounded by a whole bevy of American sirens. On their part there was a great onrush to lionize him recklessly and hysterically, with the result that their extravagant receptions became a welcome subject for idle town gossip.

Rather amusingly, Oscar summarized his first experiences in the American metropolis in a letter of January 15, 1882, to Norman Forbes Robertson, an English friend of his:

> I go to Philadelphia tomorrow. Great success here—nothing like it since Dickens, they tell me. I am torn in bits by Society. Immense receptions—wonderful dinners—crowds wait for my carriage—I have a

gloved hand and an ivory cane and they cheer. Girls very lovely, men simple and intellectual. Rooms are hung with white lilies for me everywhere. I have a "Boy" at intervals—also two secretaries, one to write my autograph and answer the hundreds of letters that come begging for it. Another, whose hair is brown, to send locks of his own hair to the young ladies who write asking for mine—he is rapidly becoming bald—also a black servant—who is my slave: in a free country one cannot live without a slave—rather like a Christy minstrel—except that he knows no riddles—also a carriage and a black tiger who is like a little monkey. I give sittings to artists—and generally behave as I always have behaved—dreadfully.

Now, these first "successes" were liable to turn Oscar's head, leading him to believe that a cleverly conceived pose was all that was needed to convert his lecture tour into a victorious march through the vales and dales of the New World.

The signal for a long series of Wilde festivities came from Mrs. A. A. Hayes, when she gave in the poet's honour a gorgeous reception in her mansion at East Twenty-fifth Street. The suite of Japanese rooms furnished pleasant surroundings for the herald of the "new departure." His more fastidious followers expressed regret that there were no Greek porticos and Doric columns, "with open spaces looking towards the blue Ægean," and nearby the Venus of Milo or a chaste Diana, to furnish the necessary background.

On this occasion, the Irish minstrel wore a tightly buttoned Prince Albert coat and held a pair of pastel-shade gloves in his hand. At once he became the idol of the harmlessly insane but worthy ladies who adhesively clustered about him.

During the formal phase of the reception he was forced to stand in the middle of the parlour. Back of him was placed a gigantic Nippon umbrella decorated with grotesque figures of gaily coloured paper. After a while the guest of honour was permitted to leave his platform. The privilege of free locomotion having been restored to him, he started seeking refuge in some remote corner, but in this he failed, for, to use *The World's* version, wherever he moved, the crowd followed with evil-bred curiosity, making faint excuses over the punch bowl to see him quaff his tea.

OSCAR WILDE

(1882)

In all justice to our hero, he received these attentions with an air of calm unconsciousness and no symptoms of a superiority complex.

Mrs. Hayes's afternoon reception was succeeded by an equally fashionable entertainment given by Mrs. John Bigelow. Next came a supper at Mrs. John Mack's Fifth Avenue residence whither Wilde was abducted immediately after his Chickering Hall lecture. A galaxy of "American beauties," including "Aunt Fanny" Barrow, Mrs. Judge Field, Mrs. John Lillie and Miss Annie Stephens, attended the feast. The male celebrities, notably President F. A. P. Barnard, Commissioner McLean and General McMahon, were in a sad minority. The valiant hostess, an intimate friend of Lady Wilde's, exerted her efforts to please Oscar whose first professional appearance in New York had just created a sensation.

The queer character of some of these affairs can be gathered from a description by Anne de Brémont of a dinner party which had been arranged *ad majorem gloriam* of our poet by a former pupil of Sir William, somewhere in the vicinity of Madison Square. Let the Countess tell her story:

> About twenty guests sat down at the great round table in the handsome dining-room, full of the mysterious glow of softly subdued lights and fragrant with the perfume of costly flowers, where the mirrors at either end of the room reflected the sumptuous table covered with a cloth of white satin, over which were thickly strewn loose red roses. White tall crystal vases supported exquisite white lilies: the display of the famous sunflower being a privilege accorded only to Oscar Wilde as the guest of honour.
>
> The company was entirely composed of ladies well-known for their beauty and wit in the society of Boston and New York; many had donned æsthetic robes of charming design that were evidently a delight to the eye of Oscar Wilde, for his glance roamed from one to the other of his fair followers with increasing pleasure in his smile of approval.
>
> He was himself, naturally, the centre of attraction at that very æsthetic dinner. His splendid youth and manly bearing lent a certain charm to the strange costume in which he masqueraded. He shone to far greater and better advantage amid these surroundings than he did on the lecture platform. There was a dignity and graciousness in his

manner that blinded one to his eccentric appearance. . . . He sat, or rather posed, in a large, high-backed, carved chair, while, directly opposite to him, the host occupied a chair of more modest dimensions. The two prettiest women of the company were seated on the right and left of the guest of honour. . . . One of these favoured women wore an æsthetic costume of pale green satin, relieved by chains of shimmering pearls, while the other was really dazzling in a gown of yellow velvet, also of æsthetic design, with a massive necklace of topaz set in diamonds and a Greek coiffure bound with bands of topaz and diamonds.

To the modern mind this spectacle appears not only unbelievably eccentric, but trashy in the extreme. The banalities which on that evening Oscar is alleged to have uttered certainly add little to the glory of his wit or the depth of his wisdom. For instance, this one:

> What is the soul? It is the essence of perfect beauty. I would inhale the soul of beauty as I do the fragrance of this perfect rose—and die upon it if need be!

Or this:

> America reminds me of one of Edgar Allan Poe's exquisite poems because it is full of belles!

This was the signal for a riotous *coup de grâce:*

"Behold the tribute of the belles!" cried one of the "enthused" women, grasping the roses which lay on the table before her, and casting them toward their fondling.

> The others quickly followed her example. Roses rained upon him from every side. And I am sure there was not a thorn in all that shower of roses, to judge from the smile that illumined his face as he bowed under our fragrant ovation.

As Lermontov said once:

> All this would truly be amusing
> If, alas, it weren't so sad.[3]

The silliness of these extravagant shows inevitably branded Wilde with a stigma, profaning the movement which he purported to represent.

Occasionally, he seemed to have deliberately disregarded the sacred commandments of the social code, a fact which in the Anglo-Saxon world, from time immemorial, has been regarded as an unpardonable sin. Some of his blunders, the one, for example, he made in Baltimore, provoked severe public censure.

The *faux pas* occurred on January 19, 1882, when Oscar was invited to a party at the imposing mansion of Mr. and Mrs. Charles Carroll. On that day, Wilde was first expected to attend a lecture by one Archibald Forbes, and the reception was to take place afterwards. Meanwhile, the house of the prominent hosts had been magnificently decorated; and it is said that every florist in town was depleted of his stock of sunflowers and lilies. Not until eight in the evening did Mrs. Carroll learn, much to her horror, that her distinguished guest, having had an altercation with the lecturer on the train from Philadelphia, had refused to get off at Baltimore and proceeded to Washington. It was too late to call off the invitations, and thus several hundred people in full dress gathered for the ultra-formal *rendez-vous*. When the truth became known, the ladies who later were to have entertained the poet, taking advantage of their feminine privilege, promptly changed their minds and cancelled the engagements on the spot.

The scandal was still fresh and much discussed when Baltimore society was again shocked by the news that to a courteous invitation from the Wednesday Club, Wilde had replied by a letter in which, according to *The Tribune,* he stated that "he charged $300.00 a night for his presence at entertainments not held in private houses."

Episodes like these were apt to create ill-feeling toward the English visitor. No matter how ingenious or witty his lectures and table talks may have been, American society could not forgive him the snobbish bearing and chilly indifference which at times he displayed in contacts with those very people whom he hoped to convert to æstheticism and whose support in the cause of Beauty he sought to enlist.

CHAPTER XIV

ON THE LECTURE PLATFORM

WILDE made his first public appearance in New York on January 9, 1882, only a week after his landing. Chickering Hall, which had been chosen for his opening lecture, was filled to capacity with a select crowd of men and women, well over one thousand, all pretending to belong to the "Four hundred."[1] The newspapers printed long accounts of the notable event, paying particular attention, not so much to the "English Renaissance of Art" which was the topic of the discourse, as to Oscar's long hair, short breeches and silk stockings.

The prevailing mood of the audience was one of sheer curiosity. It was felt that "Mr. Wilde was worth *seeing,*" though "no sunflower nor yet a lily dangled from his buttonhole," and much to everybody's surprise, the coat "looked as though it had been made for the wearer and not as a mere piece of decorative drapery."

However, aside from the eccentricity of the poet's attire, both the lecture and the lecturer produced upon the house a rather favourable impression. Even the more fastidious were captivated by his masterful delivery, and some of the press notices were, indeed, highly gratifying. *The World's* critic, for one, came out with a warm endorsement of the whole performance. This is what he said:

> A subject as evasive as beauty, for beauty was the real subject of the lecture, is difficult to grasp with logic. Not analysis, not description was the method of treatment, but revelation. . . . Long melodious sentences, seldom involved, always clear, unfolded his meaning as graceful curves reveal a beautiful figure. A vocabulary as wide as Swinburne's and well nigh as musical, modelled on that rich and flowing prose which is as marvelous as Swinburne's verses—how could such a style be dull?

> . . . Almost gorgeous at times, his language never quite ran away with him, but was always equal to the clear expression of the most subtle fancy. The best parts of the lecture were its clear glimpses of a rare appreciation of artistic literary work from Homer to William Morris.

As we now compare the thesis on *The Rise of Historical Criticism,* which, in 1879, Wilde wrote for the Chancellor's English Essay Prize at Oxford, with the substance of his Chickering Hall oration, it seems that, during the brief interlude of less than three years, his mental power had doubled in strength and width: while the losing paper was only a banal composition of studious demyship, the Renaissance talk strikes one with its philological excellence and wealth of information on world literature and European art.

When, for instance, Oscar expounds the credo of the artist, whose conception of all things genuinely beautiful and inherently real crystallises into a grand dream of colour and feeling and sound, his style is so perfect that the most captious critics would hardly dare to challenge it:

> The artist is indeed the child of his own age, but the present will not be to him a whit more real than the past, for, like the philosopher of the Platonic vision, the poet is the spectator of all time and all existence. For him no form is obsolete, no subject out of date; rather, whatever of life and passion the world has known, in desert of Judæa or in Arcadian valley, by the rivers of Troy or the rivers of Damascus, in the crowded and hideous streets of a modern city or by the pleasant ways of Camelot—all lies before him like an open scroll, all is still instinct with beautiful life. He will take of it what is salutary for his own spirit, no more; choosing some facts and rejecting others with the calm artistic control of one who is in possession of the secret of beauty.

And again, the language which he uses to explain one's feeling of gladness at the sight of some precious relic of inimitable craftsmanship is full of fragrant purity, feminine charm and manly vigour. Is not this a classic specimen of English prose?—

> You have most of you seen . . . that great masterpiece of Rubens which hangs in the gallery of Brussels, that swift and wonderful pag-

eant of horse and rider arrested in its most exquisite and fiery moment when the winds are caught in crimson banner and the air lit by the gleam of armour and the flash of plume. Well, that is joy in art, though that golden hillside be trodden by the wounded feet of Christ and it is for the death of the Son of Man that that gorgeous cavalcade is passing.

Or, where he defines the harmonious nature of poetic meditation, his prose, like Turgenev's *Song of Triumphant Love,* resolves itself into cadenced periods, graceful in their delineation and fascinating in their build. Says Wilde:

> . . . the joy of poetry comes never from the subject but from an inventive handling of rhythmical language, from what Keats called the "sensuous life of verse." The element of song in the singing, accompanied by the profound joy of motion, is so sweet that, while the incomplete lives of ordinary men bring no healing power with them, the thorn-crown of the poet will blossom into roses for our pleasure . . . and when the poet's heart breaks it will break in music.

Now we know that much of what was set forth in that discourse on the Mid-Victorian artistic revival was inspired primarily by Pater—a fact which Edward Bock conclusively proved in his monographic study *Walter Pater's Einfluss ueber Oscar Wilde.* Added to this was Ruskin's pre-eminent influence, which his Magdalen disciple never sought to deny. Of his great indebtedness to the English moralist he was, in fact, quite proud. Talking once to a New York reporter, he declared:

> Very many of my theories are, if I may say so, Ruskin's theories developed.

And, only a few months later, pondering over Ruskin's place in the cultural movement of Europe, he spoke these affectionate words:

> Master indeed of the knowledge of all noble living and of the wisdom of all spiritual things will he be to us ever, seeing that it was he who by the magic of his presence and the music of his lips taught us at Oxford that enthusiasm for beauty which is the secret of Hellenism, and that desire for creation which is the secret of life, and filled some of us,

at least, with the lofty and passionate ambition to go forth into far and fair lands with some message for the nations and some mission for the world. . . .

But the point to note here is that as early as 1882, Wilde's æsthetic theories had reached a state of complete structuralisation. To these ideas he continued to adhere throughout his entire literary career; whatever else, in subsequent years, he may have written about art and artists, be it in that peerless *Envoi* to Rennell Rodd's *Rose-Leaf and Apple-Leaf,* or in his eloquent defence of Mr. Wainewright's strange addiction to "pen, pencil and poison," or even in *Dorian Gray*—came merely as an elaboration of those basic tenets which he had conceived during his strolls along the silent Magdalen Walks or in the hours of his meditations under the majestic vaults of St. Peter's and amid the marble ruins of Greece.

A carefree amateur, Wilde was not in the least concerned with the nature of rhythmic emotion or any metaphysical principle underlying art. He felt that, quite apart from the interpretation which philosophy may give to the varied manifestations of Beauty, it has some elusive refinement, intrinsically its own, a value which, though evanescent as a dream and evasive as the melting lights and shadows of an evening sky, is lasting and real, an excellence of form which expresses itself now in the divine harmonies of a Chopin nocturne or in the sweet music of Shelley's rhymes, now in the colour symphonies of a Murillo or in the graceful silhouette of a Gothic cathedral, now in some mighty cast of Donatello or in the bewitching marble visions of Phidias and Canova.

It is doubtful whether the public took much interest in the theoretical concepts which Wilde may have been expounding at the time. What they cared for rather was his charming personality. His eloquence was unusual and convincing; his wit spontaneous and amusing; his manners different and intriguing. And all these combined assured wide-spread attention to his sojourn on the American Continent.

He toured the States with varied success. Praise and blame,

eulogies and denunciations followed one another in zig-zag succession. Unruly fun seekers, students mostly, made plans to "guy" him in several towns. One outstanding incident of this sort was staged by the Harvard boys.

On the evening of January 31, 1882, the Boston Music Hall, where Oscar appeared to give his talk, was densely filled. The audience was largely composed of idlers who went there to see what promised to be a comical show. The two front rows in the orchestra were occupied by some sixty Cambridge roughnecks arrayed in "æsthetic" costumes: in dress coats, knee-breeches and extravagantly green cravats. They all wore lilies and carried huge sunflowers.

The lecture was repeatedly interrupted by ill-timed thunderous applause so that finally the poet was compelled to make a long pause before his noisy listeners regained their senses and silence enabled him to proceed. On that occasion he showed such perfect self-control, Irish dignity and disarming courtesy that the trouble-makers were compelled to acknowledge their defeat.

The Boston Evening Transcript printed an excellent write-up of this exhibition of Yankee "culchaw."

> Boston is certainly indebted to Oscar Wilde for one thing—the thorough-going chastening of the superabounding spirits of the Harvard freshmen. It will be some time, we think, before a Boston assemblage is again invaded by a body of college youths, massed as such, to take possession of the meeting. . . . Whether in his first off-hand observation, or in the pointed remarks scattered through his address, or in the story he told of the Oxford boys and Mr. Ruskin, nothing could have been more gracious, more dignified, more gentle and sweet, and yet more crushing, than the lecturer's whole demeanour to them, and its influence upon the great audience was very striking. . . . Mr. Wilde achieved a real triumph, and it was by right of conquest, by force of being a *gentleman* in the truest sense of the word. His nobility not only obliged *him*—it obliged his would-be mockers—to good behaviour. He crowned his triumph, and he heaped coals of fire upon those curly and wiggy heads, when he, with simplicity and evident sincerity, made them an offer of a statue of a Greek athlete to stand in their gymnasium, and

May 12 '82

My dear Norman —

I am so delighted you are coming over. I will see that you have some pleasant houses in Boston to go to. I hope I will be there. You and I will sit and drink boy in our room and watch the large posters of our names — I am now six feet high — (my name on the placards —) prettier it is true in those

Letter from Oscar Wilde to Norman Forbes-Robertson from Montreal (1882)

primary colours against
which I pass my life
protesting – but still it
is fame – and anything
is better than virtuous
obscurity even though one's
name is in alternate
colours of albert blue
and magenta and six
feet high –

This is my view of

present from the Windsor
Hotel Montreal. I feel
I have not lived in
vain — my second lecture
at New York was a
brilliant success — I
lectured at Wallack's
theatre in the
afternoon — not an
empty seat — and
I have greatly
improved in speaking
and in gesture — I

am really quite
clever – at
times – I was
really congratulated
Tomorrow night
I lecture Lorne
on Dadoes et
Others.

A nice
friend of his has
just called – Murray
Balfour – friend of
Millais

Oscar

he said he should esteem it an honour if they would accept it. This really seemed to stun the boys, for they even forgot to recognize the offer with applause. It was a lovely though sad sight, to see those dear silly youths go out of the Music Hall in slow procession, hanging their heads meekly, and trying to avoid observation, followed by faint expressions of favour from their friends, but also with some hisses. A lady near us said, "How mortified I should be if a son of mine were among them!" We think that everyone must feel about it very much as we do, and that those who came to scoff, if they did not exactly remain to pray, at least, left the Music Hall with feelings of cordial liking, and perhaps, to their own surprise, of respect for Oscar Wilde.

In spite of this Boston success the students at New Haven, owing probably to the traditional rivalry between Harvard and Yale, only one night later engineered on their part a silly demonstration against Wilde.

The episode was thus described in *The Times:*

Oscar Wilde lectured in Peck's Opera House this evening to an audience of twelve hundred people, including two hundred Yale students, most of whom were in the galleries. . . . A mammoth sunflower fan was displayed in one of the front seats before Mr. Wilde began, but this was suppressed at the suggestion of an attendant. The students frequently applauded passages which called for no notice whatsoever.

Once more, Wilde met the challenge by simply complimenting the youngsters upon Yale's victories in the field and on the river. But he also told them that athletics should not be their sole ambition. This warning must have sounded, to at least some of the demonstrants, like a most impious suggestion.

A similar outburst of discourtesy, accompanied by whistles and cat-calls, took place at the Brooklyn Academy of Music, where, on February 3, Oscar was speaking on the English Renaissance. The gist of this lively affair was summed up in a headline of one of the New York papers, "The Anti-Æsthetic Ruffians . . . Crushed by Display of Æsthetic Contempt."

Having thoroughly explored the Atlantic Coast, Wilde proceeded to Pittsburgh, Chicago, Omaha, Denver, Salt Lake City and California, also visiting Canada and Nova Scotia.

On returning to New York, Oscar met with additional annoyance; he fell into the hands of professional sharpers, and was cheated out of a substantial sum of money. Embarrassing though this lesson may have proved, it did interrupt the monotony of the lecture epidemic and was partly responsible for the miniature essay *On American Card Games,* including poker, which, in the poet's own words, "like most of the distinctly national products of America, seems to have been imported from abroad." Elaborating upon so grave a subject, with subtle humour, he told the story of a Kentucky sage who, desiring to give his sons a solemn advice "for their future guidance in life," had them summoned to his deathbed and spoke these words:

> "Boys, when you go down the river to Orleens jest you beware of a game called Yucker, where the jack takes the ace;—it's unchristian!" After which warning he lay back and died in peace.

It must also have been in the course of his association with the New York "bunco steerers" that our Irish globetrotter grasped the full flavour of the old saying that "there are only thirty-eight good stories in existence, of which thirty-seven cannot be told before ladies."

Altogether, the vicissitudes, both pleasant and disturbing, of this eventful trip throughout the Western Hemisphere gave Wilde much valuable and, in some ways, unique experience. He cleverly capitalised it, first, in those perfectly charming *Impressions of America,* and later, in the comedies which marked the climax of his popularity in England.

Here it may be noted that if Americans did not take Oscar ever so seriously, he reciprocated by refusing to treat America in earnest; so much so that he even chose to adopt a moody semi-Byronic attitude toward Niagara on the main ground that "every American bride is taken there, and the sight of this stupendous waterfall must be one of the earliest, if not the keenest, disappointments in American married life."

And, in addition to Niagara, there was much in the New World that must have appealed immensely to Oscar's sense of humour—pre-eminently its distinct local atmosphere and that "one hundred per cent" American "style" which, for instance, he observed in St. Joseph, Missouri.

Outside my window [he wrote to Robertson] about a quarter of a mile to the west there stands a little yellow house, with a green paling, and a crowd of people pulling it all down. It is the house of the great trainrobber and murderer Jesse James who was shot by his pal last week, and the people are relic hunters.

They sold his dust-bin and foot-scraper yesterday by public auction, his door-knocker is to be offered for sale this afternoon, the reserve price being about the income of an English Bishop; the citizens of Kansas have telegraphed to an agent here to secure his coal-scuttle at all hazards and at any cost and his favourite chromo-lithograph was disposed of at a price which in Europe only an authentic Titian can command, or an undoubted masterpiece. The Americans are certainly great hero worshippers, and always take their heroes from the criminal classes.

[Author's Collection]

Another amusing experience of his American tour Oscar recorded in a letter to Mrs. Bernard Beere, who many years later took the part of Mrs. Arbuthnot in *A Woman of No Importance* at the Haymarket Theatre.

My dear Bernie [he wrote her], I have lectured to the Mormons—the Opera House at Salt Lake is an enormous affair about the size of Covent Garden, and holds with ease 14 families. They sit like this

and very, very ugly. The President, a nice old man, sat with 5 wives in the stage box. I visited him in the afternoon and saw a charming daughter of his.[2]

It appears that San Francisco gave Wilde a grand welcome with a colourful display of traditional Western hospitality:

There were 4000 people waiting at the Depot to see me—Open carriages—Four horses—An audience at my lecture of the most cultivated people in "Frisco"—charming folk. I lecture again here tonight, also twice next week—as you see I am really appreciated—by the cultured classes—the railway have offered me a special train and private car to go down the coast to Los Angeles, a sort of Naples here—and I am feted and entertained to my heart's content.[3]

Equally sarcastic, though quite good-natured, were Wilde's comments on Leadville, that "richest city in the world" which "has also got the reputation of being the roughest," since "every man carries a revolver."

> I was told [Wilde added] that if I went there they would be sure to shoot me or my traveling manager. I wrote and told them that nothing they could do to my traveling manager would intimidate me.

After weighing all the pros and cons of the proposed journey, Oscar finally decided to go to that famous town. And what enormous enjoyment he derived from his association with the "people"!

> My night with the miners at Leadville [he relates] was most exciting—down in the mine; I opened a new shaft called "the Oscar," in Governor Tabor's "matchless mine,"—I had hoped that the miners in their simple artless way would have given me shares in it, but in their childlike frankness they did not, but when they saw that I could smoke a long cigar, and drink a cocktail without winking, they called me in their simple language "a bully boy with no glass eye," spontaneous and artless praise far better in its unstudied frankness than the laboured and pompous panegyric of the literary critics.

In that flourishing Colorado community he delivered a lecture on the "Ethics of Art" and Benvenuto Cellini, with whose stormy biography the miners seemed much delighted.

One thing in America that surely did genuinely gratify Oscar's finicky taste were the American girls, those "charming little oases of pretty unreasonableness in the vast desert of practical commonsense."

CHAPTER XV

L'ENVOI

WHILE still "on the road," desperately engaged in the "apostolic task" of trying to sell æstheticism to the hard-boiled Yankees, our Irish Beau Brummel composed a most admirable literary *morceau*—the *Envoi* to Rennell Rodd's *Rose-Leaf and Apple-Leaf*. This delightful prelude is practically forgotten by our generation, and nearly every one of the so-called "Complete Works" of Wilde has sadly ignored it.

Only two years after Oscar had won the Newdigate Prize with his *Ravenna,* James Rennell Rodd, then a demy at Oxford, triumphed in that contest with a poem on Sir Walter Raleigh.

In 1881, Rodd published in London a collection of lyrics which originally appeared under the title *Songs of the South.* He sent Wilde a presentation copy, inscribing on the fly-leaf four lines in Italian verse which Mason justly characterised as prophetic:

Al tuo martirio cupida e feroce
Questa turba cui parli accorrera
Ti vertammo a veder sulla tua croce
Tulli, e nessuro ti campiagnera.

For verily martyrdom did befall Wilde, and curious crowds gathered to see him crucified on the cross of public contempt, and no one showed pity for him. When this came to pass, he could have recalled the words of the Gospel:

> I was a stranger, and ye took me not in: naked, and ye clothed me not: sick, and in prison, and ye visited me not.

Some months later, the *Songs* were reprinted in Philadelphia under the supervision of Wilde, who gave the collection a sonorous though somewhat pretentious title—*Rose-Leaf and Apple-Leaf*. It was Wilde's preface, his *Envoi,* rather than the "leaves" themselves, that established Rodd's literary reputation.

The suggestion that the American issue was published without the author's knowledge must be discarded once and forever in view of the letter which, on October 6, 1882, Mr. Rodd addressed to Stoddart, his overseas publisher. Among other things, he said there:

> I had not till lately seen the little edition—which is charming. I have seen no *édition de luxe* in England to compare with it. . . . I have to thank you for the great care and delicacy with which this little book has been published.

The tone of the writing clearly demonstrates Rodd's familiarity with the fact of the Philadelphia publication, although it is true that he had taken no part in its revision and editing.

In a somewhat unceremonious manner, Wilde took full advantage of the *carte blanche* which, with regard to this American edition, he must have received from his young college friend. First of all, two pieces, *Lucciole* and *Maidenhair,* included in the *Songs,* were omitted from the collection, while nine new poems were added to it, most probably without Rodd's consent. But, of course, much more disturbing was the vain self-dedication which Oscar preposterously caused to be printed in that dainty little volume:

TO
OSCAR WILDE
"HEART'S BROTHER"—
THESE FEW SONGS AND MANY SONGS TO COME.

No wonder Rodd took exception to this manifestation of sentimental friendship. Nor did he try to conceal his indignation. Again writing to Stoddart, he stated:

> There is one thing in it that has annoyed me excessively, and had I had proof I should not have allowed it to stand. The dedication is too effusive. I have written to Mr. Wilde on this score, but if he does not

write to you, I must ask you as a personal favour to see to it. I want to have it removed from all copies that go out for the future.

So it was on this ground, and not, as Sherard would have us believe, because of "the lamentable style" in which the book was produced that Rodd felt himself aggrieved by Oscar Wilde.

However, disregarding these petty personal misunderstandings, it must be admitted that in respect to its general appearance and bibliophilic qualities, the book is a perfect gem, which Hamilton relishingly described thus:

> The printed matter occupies one side only of a thin transparent sheet of hand-made parchment paper, interleaved with pale apple-green, the delicate tint of which shows through the printed page in a manner most grateful to the reader's eyes. The illustrations are of a decidedly Japanese type and the outer case is of white vellum.

Martin Birnbaum, in his *Fragments and Memories,* recorded some details concerning the get-up of this edition. He said:

> Few people know that the curious paper on which that book is printed was originally intended for early paper currency, and was found in an old Philadelphia warehouse, where it had been stored since the revolution. Some of the emblems scattered through the book were engraved on wood, sketched by the distinguished pioneer in American art, James Edward Kelly. The most interesting picture is the one, on the title page, of the seal of a ring given to Wilde by his mother.

With the *Envoi* itself, Rodd seems to have been unfavourably impressed, principally because he found himself identified with much that he disapproved. And yet, this undeniably is one of the most beautiful things Wilde ever wrote. His essay, spoken of as "a poem in prose" composed "in praise of a poem," is something in the order of an æsthetic manifesto: he frames there his credo with an *élan* and inspiration which are at once convincing and sincere, carefully avoiding those twisted paradoxes which often made his Victorian contemporaries laugh, but rarely made them think.

Like that lecture on the English Renaissance, the *Envoi* is pre-eminently an eclectic production, a combination of theories and principles which in part were borrowed from Ruskin and the Pre-Raphaelite school. But in some respects it reveals the influence of the classic *Critique of Judgment,* where Kant, reverting to the old Aristotelian theory, has set forth the view that the beautiful is an autonomous concept distinct from any considerations of either rational or utilitarian order. In the world of logical and psychological phenomena, fine art, then, occupies an independent place, while the æsthetic emotion stands in a class by itself, merging with neither the ethical nor the ratiocinative functions of our mind.

Again in this essay, as in many other of his works, Wilde submissively accepted Pater's authority, almost paraphrasing him. Here is one curious coincidence:

SAYS PATER:

All art constantly aspires towards the condition of music. For while in all other kinds of art it is possible to distinguish the matter from the form, and the understanding can always make this distinction, yet it is the constant effort of art to obliterate it.[1]

SAYS WILDE:

For music is the art in which form and matter are always one . . . and it is to this condition that all the other arts are constantly aspiring.

And here is another example:

SAYS PATER:

Not the fruit of experience but experience itself is the end.

SAYS WILDE:

He [the artist] will not acquiesce in that facile orthodoxy . . . searching for experience itself, and not the fruit of experience.

Pater also speaks in his paper on Winckelmann of the "many-headed gods of the East" and "the orientalised many-breasted Diana of Ephesus," while in Oscar's *Envoi* we find these words:

> The metaphysical mind of Asia may create for itself the monstrous and many-breasted idol. . . .

and so forth.

L'Envoi attempts to set no specific "norm of beauty," as Hogarth would have said, for every genuinely sublime expression of imaginative thought, no matter what its inner tenor may be, to Wilde, is equally precious. Gauged by some ethical precept or social theory, every creative effort seems to him "quite useless," since its sole function is to generate within one a sense of delight derived from the absolutely satisfying standard of perfect workmanship. In this, once more, he virtually repeats Pater's salient maxim that art comes to us "frankly to give nothing but the highest quality" to our moments, as they pass, "and simply for these moments' sake."

Further, Wilde stresses the point that in the domain of æsthetics, not the artist's motives, or his "pathetic intentions," but the accomplished result only is of true significance and determining import.

> Nor [says he], in looking at a work of art, should we be dreaming of what it symbolises but rather loving it for what it is. Indeed, the transcendental spirit is alien to the spirit of art. . . . Nor, in its primary aspect, has a painting, for instance, any more spiritual message or meaning for us than a blue tile from the wall of Damascus, or a Hitzen vase. It is a beautifully-coloured surface, nothing more, and affects us by no suggestion stolen from philosophy, no pathos pilfered from literature, no feeling filched from a poet, but by its own incommunicable artistic essence—by that selection of truth which we call style, and that relation of values which is the draughtsmanship of painting . . . the arabesque of the design, the splendour of the colour, for these things are enough to stir the most divine and remote of the chords which make music in our soul. . . .

To Wilde, one's reaction to all things fascinating and beautiful constitutes the mystical substratum of art criticism which is but another ramification of art itself. Thus he combines the analytical faculty of the mind, its discreet tendencies and heterogeneous ideas, with the concrete mediums of artistic expression—the golden tongue in which the poet sings; the colours that are caught in the web of the painter's canvas; the bronze and marble which melt under the sculptor's chisel; the cadenced sounds that flow in music's fairy lane—briefly, the whole fabric that goes to mould the material frame of art.

These two links of the æsthetic structure, though symbolising the primordial discord or cosmological dualism—life and death, body and spirit, matter and thought—indeed, are inseparable; and their very unity, or ensuing synthesis, is the major premise of every form of creative achievement where a mere ideal, a vague mirage, an evanescent dream, is projected into the sphere of physical things and tangible reality. Though, as Wilde claims, art should be judged by its results always, and by its inspiring motives never, to the initiated, the artist's "holy of holies" inevitably reveals itself in his creation, unfolding the mysterious record of some strange experience which determines the unaccountable manner in which he chooses to externalize his vision.

When approached from this angle, a book of poems, such as Rodd's, is no longer to be treated as a mere collection of graceful though somewhat chilly verses, but becomes a means by which the inner life of the poet, with its cherished hopes and subdued urges, is conveyed to the reader. And *Rose-Leaf* does contain many a line where, through the fanciful vignettes of metrical design, there suddenly breaks a mood of exclusive intimacy—some feeling of infinite sadness—which, for a few moments only, lifts the veil hiding the poet's *sui generis* "I." Such, for instance, are the opening stanzas *In Chartres Cathedral:*

> Through yonder windows stained and old
> Four level rays of red and gold
> Strike down the twilight dim,
> Four lifted heads are aureoled
> Of the sculptured cherubim,
> And soft like sounds on faint winds blown
> Of voices dying far away,
> The organ's dreamy undertone,
> The murmur while they pray;
> And I sit here alone, alone,—
> And have no word to say;
> Cling closer shadows, darker yet,
> And heart be happy to forget.

Turning from his æsthetic code to the songs and rhymes of his friend, Wilde draws this magnificent picture:

> . . . One might weave these disconnected poems, these stray and scattered threads, into one fiery-coloured strand of life, noting first a boy's mere gladness of being young, with all its simple joy in field and flower, in sunlight and in song; and then the bitterness of sudden sorrow at the ending by death of one of the brief and beautiful friendships of one's youth, with all those unanswered longings and questionings unsatisfied by which we vex, so uselessly, the marble face of death; the artistic contrast between the discontented incompleteness of the spirit and the complete perfection of the style that expresses it . . . and then the birth of Love, and all the wonder and fear and the perilous delight of one on whose boyish brows the little wings of love have beaten for the first time; and the love songs, so dainty and delicate, little swallow flights of music, and full of such fragrance and freedom that they might all be sung in the open air and across the moving water; and then autumn, coming with its quireless woods and odorous decay and ruined loveliness, Love lying dead; and the sense of the mere pity of it.

The syntactic peculiarities of the *Envoi* are quite apparent: deliberately, Wilde constructs his sentences in a manner boldly challenging the classical tradition according to which style, to be considered perfect, must be concise, avoiding as much as possible incidental prepositions and interpolated phrases. This rule of terse verbal economy has been strictly adhered to by all great masters of prose from Cæsar to Walter Scott. Theirs, indeed, are mathematical formulæ to which not a single symbol should be added, and from which not a single figure can be deducted.

But in his professed capacity of a *jeune guerrier du drapeau romantique,* Wilde makes, with studied intent, a grand display of his linguistic resources: he stages scintillating fireworks of sudden metaphors, choice epithets and unexpected allusions, spinning the delicate threads of his fugitive thoughts into a striking fabric of impressive images. Take this passage:

> Such a poem as *The Sea King's Grave,* with all its majesty of melody, as sonorous and as strong as the sea by whose pine-fringed shores it was thus nobly conceived and nobly fashioned; or the little poem that fol-

lows it, whose cunning workmanship, wrought with such an artistic sense of limitation, one might liken to the rare chasing of the mirror that is its motive, or *In a Church,* pale flower of one of those exquisite moments when all things except the moment itself seem so curiously real, and when the old memories of forgotten days are touched and made tender, and the familiar place grows fervent and solemn suddenly with a vision of the undying beauty of the gods that died; or the scene in *Chartres Cathedral,* sombre silence brooding on vault and arch, silent people kneeling on the dust of the desolate pavement as the young priest lifts Lord Christ's body in a crystal star, and then the sudden beams of scarlet light that break through the blazoned window and smite on the carven screen, and sudden organ peals of mighty music rolling and echoing from choir to canopy, and from spire to shaft, and over all the clear, glad voice of a singing boy, affecting one as a thing over-sweet, and striking just the right artistic keynote for one's emotions; or *At Lanuvium,* through the music of whose line one seems to hear again the murmur of the Mantuan bees straying down from their own green valleys and inland streams to find what honeyed amber the sea flowers might be hiding; or the poem written *In the Coliseum,* which gives one the same artistic joy that one gets watching a handicraftsman at his work, a goldsmith hammering out his gold into those thin plates as delicate as the petals of a yellow rose, or drawing it out into the long wires like tangled sunbeams, so perfect and precious in the mere handling of it; or the little lyric interludes that break in here and there like the singing of a thrush, and are as swift and as sure as the beating of a bird's wing, as light and bright as the apple-blossoms that flutter fitfully down to the orchard grass after a spring shower and look the lovelier for the rain's tears lying on their dainty veinings of pink and pearl; or the sonnets—for Mr. Rodd is one of those *qui sonnent le sonnet,* as the Ronsardists used to say—that one called *On the Border Hills,* with its fiery wonder of imagination and the strange beauty of its eighth line; or the one which tells of the sorrow of the great king for the little dead child—well, all these poems aim, as I said, at producing a purely artistic effect, and have the rare and exquisite quality that belongs to work of that kind; and I feel that the entire subordination in our æsthetic movement of all merely emotional and intellectual motives to the vital informing poetic principle is the surest sign of our strength.

In this impetuous and effervescent paean, every stern law

of English grammar, every ossified commandment of academic tradition, every rule of conventional etiquette, is shattered and broken, whilst the foaming words, like racing waves in a turbulent sea, overtake one another in leaps and bounds. When moulding these lines, Wilde was well aware of the fact that he had discovered a novel track of literary adventure which he called "the beautiful architecture of a long sentence, which is the fine flower of prose writing." This he expressly stated in a remarkable and hitherto unpublished letter to Sherard (now in the author's collection) which he wrote some time in May, 1883:

HÔTEL VOLTAIRE,
QUAI VOLTAIRE,
Wednesday.

My dear Robert,

I send you the volume of the true poet, and the false friend: there are some new things in it, Chartres Cathedral, and the Viking's Grave, which have much beauty in them, the latter particularly and the *Envoi* I hope you will like: the rhythmical value of prose has never yet been fully tested, I hope to do some more work in that "genre" as soon as I have sung my Sphynx to sleep, and found a trisyllabic rhyme for catafalque.

Ever affectionately yours,
OSCAR WILDE

Sworn critics of the old school might raise all sorts of objections to this vagrant mode of writing, but then they would have to extend their grudge far beyond Wilde's *Envoi.* Would they forget D'Annunzio or Banville? Or Ruskin himself who, despite his veneration of the *verbum humanum* as the nearest emblem of Divine Thought, contributed to the treasury of the English tongue wayward passages full of pathos and passion such as this one, where he meditates over the wondrous workings of Nature:

Every one of those broad spaces she would linger over in protracted delight, teaching you fresh lessons in every hair's-breadth of it, and pouring her fulness of invention into it, until the mind lost itself in following her,—now fringing the dark edge of the shadow with a tufted line of level forest—now losing it for an instant in a breath of mist—

then breaking it with the white gleaming angle of a narrow brook—then dwelling upon it again in a gentle, mounded, melting undulation, over the other side of which she would carry you down into a dusty space of soft, crowded light, with the hedges, and the paths, and the sprinkled cottages and the scattered trees mixed up and mingled together in one beautiful, delicate, impenetrable mystery—sparkling and melting, and passing away into the sky, without one line of distinctness, or one instant of vacancy.

Here, the affinity of the two styles—Ruskin's and Wilde's—is obvious.

An ardent admirer of Attic culture, and a standard-bearer of the New Hellenism, Wilde took little pains to apply to his own manner of writing that rectangular and rectilinear grace which is the real virtue of Grecian art. Its cold symmetry and inherent sense of measure, to him, were qualities of a theoretical rather than practical value, and though he would profess a keen appreciation of the inimitable simplicity embodied in some marble frieze adorning an Ionic temple, or in its slender grooved columns, yet his pen would be wandering and roaming along the enchanted banks and devious by-ways of nebulous romanticism.

The unadorned rhythms of Homer's lyre or the noble chastity of Theocritus and his younger Alexandrian contemporaries may have given Wilde a purely intellectual satisfaction, but emotionally he was never able to condense his style to that unaffected restraint which characterises the ancient poets:

> Would that my father had taught me
> the craft of a keeper of sheep,
> For so in the shade of an elm tree,
> or under the rocks on the steep,
> Piping on reeds I had sat; and had
> lulled my sorrow to sleep.[2]

Instead, Wilde felt fascinated by ornamentation, by abundance in colour and movement and sound—as in Rubens' gigantic compositions crowned with luscious garlands of human bodies; or in the glamorous pageantry of hues on Titian's

Hotel Voltaire.

Quai Voltaire

Wednesday.

My Dear Robert,

I send you the volume of the true poet, and the false friend. There are some new things in it, Chartres Cathedral, and the Vikings Chant, which have much beauty in them, the latter particularly and the "Envoi" I hope you will like: the rhythmical value of prose has never yet been fully tested, I hope to do some more work in that genre, as soon as I have sung my Sphinx to sleep, and found a trisyllabic rhyme to catafalque.

Ever affectionately yours

Oscar Wilde

LETTER FROM OSCAR WILDE TO ROBERT H. SHERARD

(*Author's Collection*)

iridescent palette; or Hugo's rhythmical storms—in every form of artistic ambrosia and every mode of Epicurean excess. This tendency is reflected in many of his mature works—in the sinful entreaties of Salomé, in the seductive promises of Myrrhina, in the beautiful description of the Infanta's birthday robe and in the incense-laden atmosphere permeating the sad story of Dorian Gray. Everywhere we find the stigma of rhetorical bravura, a desire to "paint the lily" and "to throw a perfume on the violet." Was it not because Wilde, as Mr. Chislett suggested, "sacrificed his life for sensationalism . . . for false Hellenism, false Romanticism, false Individualism?"

Much as Wilde prided himself on being "a lord of language," it was on rare occasions only, as in the last few sentences of his *Envoi,* that he succeeded in attaining a style altogether free from hyperbolic flourish and intentionally exaggerated accumulation of chromatic material. These lines are indeed flawless:

> We were staying once, he and I, at Amboise, that little village with its grey slate roofs and steep streets and gaunt, grim gateway, where the quiet cottages nestle like white pigeons into the sombre clefts of the great bastioned rock, and the stately Renaissance houses stand silent and apart—very desolate now, but with some memory of the old days still lingering about the delicately-twisted pillars, and the carved doorways with their grotesque animals, and laughing masks, and quaint heraldic devices, all reminding one of a people who could not think life real till they had made it fantastic. And above the village, and beyond the bend of the river, we used to go in the afternoon and sketch from one of the big barges that bring the wine in autumn and the wood in winter down to the sea, or lie in the long grass and make plans *pour la gloire, et pour ennuyer les Philistins,* or wander along the low, sedgy banks, "matching our reeds in sportive rivalry," as comrades used in the old Sicilian days; and the land was an ordinary land enough, and bare too when one thought of Italy, and how the oleanders were robing the hillsides by Genoa in scarlet, and the cyclamen filling with its purple every valley from Florence to Rome; for there was not much real beauty, perhaps, in it, only long, white dusty roads and straight rows of formal poplars, but now and then some little breaking gleam of broken light would lend to the grey field and the silent barn

a secret and a mystery that were hardly their own, would transfigure for one exquisite moment the peasants passing down through the vineyard, or the shepherd watching on the hill, would tip the willow with silver, and touch the river into gold; and the wonder of the effect, with the strange simplicity of the material, always seemed to me to be a little like the quality of these the verses of my friend.

Even though Mr. Rodd, at the time, may have been displeased with the *Envoi,* it is a moot question whether he himself could have written a more eloquent or more elegant preface to his own poems. And this, at least, is clear: as a poet, the author of the "leaves" has long sunk into the great gulf of oblivion, and tracelessly his rhymes have died away.

But the *Envoi* continues to live and remains one of the sweetest flowers in the fragrant wreath of English imaginative literature. For in these lines, Wilde gave us a glimpse of a solemn vision whose light, streaming through the magic crystal of his lordly language, enables one to perceive Art in its two facets, now appearing as the Beauty of Truth, and now as the Truth of Beauty.

CHAPTER XVI

ON THE QUAI VOLTAIRE

AFTER the American lecture tour had come to an end, there was nothing else for Oscar to do but to go home. And so, without much drum-beating, almost incognito, on December 27, 1882,[1] he sailed from New York for Liverpool.

Much as Wilde may have been amused by the New World, he had been living there in a state of intoxication with social success as signified by lavish entertainments and floods of adulation. But now the romance was over and once more he was brought face to face with the cold reality of haughty and hypocritical London, and still with not much money in his purse. The contrast was "too awful," as Wilde used to say, for he could not help sadly missing "the slave," "the tiger," the two secretaries, the luxurious suites in fashionable American hotels and the brilliant receptions staged in his honour. But, above all, he must painfully have felt the loss of that milieu where he was the centre, the lion, the idol, the worshipped hero of the occasion.

Over there, the pose he had adopted and the rôle he had been diligently performing seemed more or less legitimate, if not exactly ingenuous. Not so in England: by the time he had returned to London, the æsthetic guise, the white lily, the golden sunflower, the knee-breeches and the long hair were utterly discredited, and it would have been quite disgraceful for our poet to persist in his masquerading. So he promptly discarded his fancy garb, assuming a conventional appearance. Nor was it difficult for him to embrace the plain rules of the bourgeois etiquette and the easy ethics of the modish salons.

Notwithstanding *Punch's* giggles about the æsthetes in general and Oscar in particular, English society showed itself tolerant toward him, and the few weeks which he spent in London in January and February, 1883, were all taken up with tea parties, premieres, *vernissages,* and those dinner engagements about which he remarked once that they were really quite delightful since "the clever people never listen and the stupid people never talk." Everybody lent him a curious ear, perhaps because the English have traditionally been fond of hearing a little innocent gossip about their American cousins, and always enjoyed being told that they have everything in common with them "except, of course, the language."

Still, the flimsy attentions and petty social niceties which Mayfair extended to Mr. Wilde were but a weak parody compared with the tumultuous ovations which marked his triumphant journey all the way from New York to San Francisco. In America, indeed, it was "fame," whereas England offered but little more than "virtuous obscurity" to a poet painfully struggling for his laurels.

Altogether, after the vicissitudes of the American adventure, London was a poor place for Wilde to take his *Nachkur.* And it occurred to him that "gay Paree" was the spot where life somehow is more complacent and one is permitted to forget oneself without necessarily being forgotten by the cliques *en vogue.* Oscar was very familiar with the charmingly light and easy-going atmosphere of the French capital with its coquettish grisettes and the *Bohème* of its *Rive-gauche* inhabited by a whole crowd of *littérateurs* and artistic stars of various magnitudes. For an innate wit like Oscar, that city of classic calembours and idle blague must have held a strong attraction. Because, innerly at least, he did acknowledge his great debt to French literature, it was not surprising that he should have craved to meet and mingle with those men from whom he had borrowed so much both in style and ideas. As yet the hard-earned American dollars had not been entirely expended, and so one day Oscar packed his bag and proceeded across the Channel.

In Paris he engaged rooms on the second floor in the Hôtel Voltaire on the Quai Voltaire, which perhaps is the most romantic section of *Vieux Paris* and one that Alphonse Daudet described as "the writer's true quarter." When Wilde was once complimented upon the fine view over the Seine from his apartment, he made this foppish remark:

> Oh, that is altogether immaterial, except to the innkeeper, who, of course, charges it in the bill. A gentleman never looks out of the window.

Mr. Sherard, who had met Wilde for the first time in February 1883, has given a most interesting account of the young poet's manner of living in Paris:

> In the daytime [says this author] when he was at work, he dressed in a white dressing-gown fashioned after the monkish cowl that Balzac used to wear at his writing-table. At that time he was modelling himself on Balzac. Besides the dressing-gown, he had acquired an ivory cane with a head of turquoises . . . which was a replica of the famous walking-stick which Honoré de Balzac used to carry when love had transformed the recluse into a fop. . . .
>
> But he was not borrowing from the master these foibles of toilette alone. I think that at that time he was striving in earnest to school himself into labour and production. He was sated with social success, and had fixed a high ambition to carve out for himself a great place in English letters, the place which he surely might have won had adversity come to him much earlier and in a different form. He had inspired himself with that passage in *La Cousine Bette* in which Balzac declares that constant labour is the law of art as it is the law of life . . . and points to the fact that all great artists have been unresting workers such as Voltaire in his study and Canova in his studio. . . .
>
> Amongst the books strewed about the room . . . were biographies of Balzac, books of the gossipy class, full of personalia, "Balzac in Slippers," and so forth—text-books with which to study a part. . . . On the mantelpiece was a photogravure of that picture by Puvis de Chavannes which shows the nude, meagre, nut-breasted form of a young girl sitting up on her unravelled shroud. . . .

For a while, as though by inertia, Oscar continued, with only trifling modifications, to indulge in some of his old æsthete habits. As in the good old days, he clung to his fur coats, which French gentlemen never wear. His ties were still deliberately knotted in a quasi-bohemian nonchalant fashion and their carefully preconceived insouciance was designed to betray in him what is known as "the artistic nature."

Oscar also paid undue attention to his hairdress. But instead of displaying the flowing locks which were so intensely admired by many an American houri and so loudly talked of in the States, he adopted a queer caplike style, finished off by a tightly curled fringe descending low on his forehead. Discussing this important topic with a reporter, Wilde told the following story:

> I got a hairdresser—and French hairdressers are artists—to come with me to the Louvre, and I showed him the young emperor's bust. He cut my hair after the fashion he saw there, as nearly as he could. I afterwards found that the bust represented Nero, one of the worst behaved young men in the world, and yet a man of strong artistic passion. I thought it just suited my case.

But Wilde soon discovered, most probably to his disappointment, that his "Neronian coiffure," *"la canne de Monsieur Balzac"* and the eccentric cravat produced little impression upon the literary Paris whose recognition he had set out to win. For French men of letters, with a few exceptions, are quite natural in the exercise of their profession and remarkably free from mannerism of any kind. Like Bourget or Zola or Balzac himself, they are, and always were, hard workers, concerned more with mental than physical culture. And even Baudelaire, with all his digressions from normalcy and obviously psychotic mentality, was never known to have been an *habitué* of beauty parlours.

There was no difficulty for Wilde, the author of *Poems* and the entertaining *causeur,* to find his way into Parisian artistic circles.

The literary pleiad then comprised many illustrious names and glorious reputations. Though a very old man, Victor Hugo was still there; his mind was dimmed by fatigue and the burden of his declining years, but, in his honorable retirement, he was universally esteemed, perhaps more as a famous relic than as a living emblem of the romantic tradition. Close to him stood Edmond de Goncourt, who occupied the second place amongst the celebrities of that epoch. Mallarmé, Jean Richepin, Emile Zola and Alphonse Daudet had already firmly enthroned themselves on the French Parnassus, whilst Henri de Régnier and Paul Bourget were regarded as the two rising stars. And then there were others—the satellites such as Henri Becque, Parodi, Vacquerie, and also Théodore de Banville, that "delicate acrobat" of rhyme and sparkling balladist of the nineteenth century, who exercised so marked an influence upon Swinburne's style.

Oscar decided not to wait for the mountain to come to Mohammed. So, just as soon as he had settled down at his Quai Voltaire apartment, he started distributing autographed copies of his *Poems* among the many "choice and master spirits" of the French literary ant-hill, penning in his fine handwriting personal letters full of complimentary phrases and flattering allusions. The reaction was, as ever, polite, spontaneous and, on the whole, quite favourable.

In this way, Mohammed approached the Mountain.

Now that the doors of the literati had been thrown open, it was up to Wilde to accomplish the final conquest. His French, though not flawless, was extraordinarily good, more so for a man of English education. His manners were charming, his voice alluring, his mind cultured, his wit epigrammatic and his whole disposition even and kindly. But did Wilde really succeed in his task? The answer must be in the negative, for as Hagemann put it:

> *Im ganzen, machte Wilde in Paris nicht die Figur wie zu Hause.*[2]

To be sure, the quick and appreciative Frenchmen gave Oscar credit for his innate talent. Always a little *bavards* themselves, they were genuinely amused by his exuberant *bavardage.* Some of his stories made them laugh; some of his remarks made them think. But somehow his genius, sterling yet volatile, did not appeal to the precise, systematic, cold and reserved mentality of his Latin colleagues. It was a difficult problem to win over those practical *petits bourgeois* to a cause as nebulous as that which Wilde came to champion on the picturesque banks of the Seine. Charles Grolleau gave us an inkling of the embarrassments with which at times Oscar had to contend:

> In the house of Victor Hugo, seeing that he must wait to let the veteran sleep out his nap while others among the guests slumbered also, he made up his mind to astonish them. He succeeded, but at what cost! Although he was a verse writer, most sincerely devoted to poetry and art, and one of the most emotional and sensitive and tender-hearted among modern wielders of the pen, he succeeded in gaining only a reputation for artificiality.

In the opinion of the French, Wilde was rather an admirable punster, an animated reciter of prepense paradoxes, than a true poet, and even those among them who were able to speak and read English could hardly have grasped the refined beauty of his chiselled rhymes.

Take Goncourt. In his voluminous diary, on May 5, 1883, we find this entry:

> Dined with the poet Oscar Wilde. This poet who tells the most improbable stories, gives us an amusing picture of a town in Texas, with its population of convicts. . . . He tells us of the hall of the Casino which, as it is the biggest room in the place, is used for the Assize-Court, and here they hang criminals on the stage after the performance. He told us that he had seen there a man who had been hanged to the scenery uprights while the audience fired their revolvers at him from their seats. . . . In those places, it would appear that the theatrical managers look out for real criminals to play the parts of criminals, and when *Macbeth* is to be staged and a person is wanted for the rôle of Lady Macbeth, offers are made to a woman who had been convicted for poisoning and who had been released from serving her sentence.

And so forth! . . . Obviously Monsieur de Goncourt failed to catch the humourous spirit of the anecdote about "the great train robber and murderer, Jesse James," which Oscar told in one of his letters to Robertson.[3]

Verlaine was another disappointment: though Wilde admired his poetry, the repulsive physical appearance of that "child with the head of Socrates" made him shiver at the very reminiscence of their first and last meeting at the Café François Premier, where poor Paul in sad solitude used to sip his absinthe. For ugliness and deformity of every kind filled Wilde with nothing but horror, and he was quite serious when he said on one occasion that "it is better to be beautiful than to be good, but it is better to be good than to be ugly."

Nor was Wilde more successful with Alphonse Daudet, who apparently objected to the young poet's pronounced artificiality and somewhat *pétri de vanité* tone of conversation. To the Frenchman, the exhibition of this superiority complex was altogether distasteful. Clever a psychologist as Daudet might have been, he could never rid himself of that first feeling of distrust which the Irish dandy created in his mind. This is probably why Daudet, upon hearing the news of Wilde's conviction, uttered words of which any enlightened person should forever be ashamed. Referring to England, where he happened to be at the time, he said: "This is a fine country. I admire a country where justice is administered as it is here, as is shown by today's verdict and sentence."

True, when at times Wilde would start speaking—as he did once at the house of Victor Hugo—on English poetry and poets, the improvised audiences could not help but capitulate to the keen critical sense revealed in those fugitive remarks and the sincerity which he evinced on such occasions. One of the writers of those days, after having heard him "perform" in a fashionable salon, thus summed up his impression:

> It seems that heretofore we did not even suspect that words could be so bewitching. He intoxicated us with his lyricism. His speech sounded like a hymn. Passionately and tensely we were listening to him. This Englishman who, at first, appeared to us as a mere snobbish *poseur,*—now started creating before us, with exquisite simplicity, the greatest ode mankind has ever heard. Many among us were deeply moved and wept . . . and don't forget: this happened in a drawing room and he was talking as people are supposed to talk in a drawing room.

However, the Wilde genre of soliloquy could scarcely have been appreciated by most Parisians, those ardent admirers of the fine art of conversation. They dislike being subjected to the tedious procedure of listening to protracted monologues, no matter how subtle. What they enjoy above all is a free interplay of wits; clever repartee flying back and forth like a ping-pong ball; the lively exchange of extemporaneous *bon mots;* the graceful sport of word-fencing, where the smartest of the two rivals succeeds when, with a courteous smile, he can utter the classic *"touché."*

Thus, although the French were divided in their attitude toward Wilde, his geniality, the exhilarating hedonism of his disposition, his unusual brain power, won for him recognition in Paris, such as has never before or since been accorded to any foreign writer, with the possible exception of Turgenev and Adam Mickiewicz. It is doubtful if in any of the salons he was welcomed *à bras ouverts.* Yet he was invited to every artistic affair of importance staged by every prominent writer and every ambitious hostess. Painters and poets, dramatists and actors, alike, were gratified by his presence, though some of them must have been a little bored by the incessant fireworks of his inverted sayings.

Another thing: Oscar was already twenty-nine when he was gleaming in Paris. Everybody there remembered his recent statement to the United States Customs that "he had nothing to declare but his genius." However, as a matter of fact, there was little he could produce in support of his claim to immortality except the handsomely bound volume of his *Poems.* This, then, was the real reason why Oscar's Parisian début was less triumphal than he might have hoped for at the time. Good a beginner as he undoubtedly was, the credit side of his balance sheet revealed only a few assets of admitted weight, whilst his eloquence, the velvet of his tenor and the turquoises in his cane were looked upon by the skeptical Parisians as entries of a dubious character, something like those "good will" items which adorn the accounts of many a shaky commercial establishment.

Of course, Wilde met in Paris practically every one worth meeting, including such men as de Nitis, Dégas, Picasso, Sargent and Coquelin, but his *intimus* seems to have been Paul Bourget. Both men were often seen dining at Foyot's opposite the Luxembourg, or at some place like the Café D'Orsay. To what extent, however, the French novelist's appreciation of Wilde was genuinely sincere is a debatable question, for it is known that when dishonour descended upon the English poet, Bourget gave little evidence of any devotion to his former literary companion.

It seems that the only real friendship which Wilde contracted in Paris was the one with Robert Sherard, whose disinterested and noble feelings for the fallen idol will go down in history as a fine example of what, in human relations, affection and cordiality should mean.

Long after Wilde had died in misery and oblivion, Sherard's able pen continued unceasingly to exonerate the memory of his friend, defending him against the insidious and malignant lies and libels, the scandalous stories which the international literary *canaille* has been studiously spreading about that ill-fated genius. It is largely due to Sherard's valiant efforts that the real Oscar Wilde with all his faults and sins, but also with all his chivalrous traits and virtues, is beginning to emerge out of the sea of mud in which he had been drowned by the wrath of his open enemies and the treason of his false friends.

It appears that Sherard at once took a sincere liking to Wilde. Day after day, they would be meeting, mostly at the Hôtel Voltaire, for only once did Oscar deign to call at Sherard's humble apartment in a remote section of Passy. As an excuse for his desistance Oscar gave this reason:

> Passy is a dreadful place to go to. It is so far off that one's cabman keeps getting off his box to ask for something on account of his *pourboire.*

In his memoirs, Sherard repeatedly reverts to Wilde's tender-heartedness and his veneration for poor Speranza. But the thing which more than anything else impressed him in Oscar's character was his sincere tolerance toward his enemies. Says Sherard:

> During his career he was often attacked and ridiculed, but I never heard him speak of those who had sought to cause him pain except in condonation. He never had one bitter word for the many friends who betrayed him. This admirable quality reached to heroism in his tragic days. In the abyss into which he was plunged, never once did a word of recrimination pass his lips. He sought to devolve on no one any fragment of his responsibility, he blamed no one for the horror of his fate, he essayed in nowise to lessen the crushing fardel of his infamy, by shifting onto other shoulders any portion of its burden.

Such, indeed, was Oscar Wilde, not only in the grim cell of Reading Gaol but likewise during his Parisian days when he was all happiness, all smiles and sunshine, a virtuoso animated by the glorious feeling of mental vigour and the anticipation of approaching success.

CHAPTER XVII

THE DUCHESS OF PADUA
THE SPHINX

BUT Paris for Wilde was not merely a playground. Though caught in the whirl of social affairs and lavish entertainments, silently he continued his creative work. It is true that during those few happy months in France he revealed no symptoms of literary profusion: after all, *The Duchess of Padua,* a five-act tragedy in blank verse, and *The Sphinx* are the only two works commonly attributed to Oscar's Parisian period. Yet even this contention should be accepted with grave reservations.

In the first place, *The Duchess* was originally conceived by Wilde in 1882, while he was still lecturing in the States. Stuart Mason, in his *Bibliography,* reproduces the text of a "rough draft" of Oscar's agreement with Hamilton Griffith, which reads:

> NEW YORK
>
> Memoranda of agreement entered into this day between Oscar Wilde of the First part and Hamilton Griffith of the 2nd part Oscar Wilde agrees to write for Miss Mary Anderson a first class Five act tragedy to be completed on or before March 1st 1883. . . .
>
> Done this day of 1st part
> A.D. 1882 2nd part

For the most part, then, the play must have been written either in New York or in London before Wilde had settled on Quai Voltaire.

The erroneous opinion—which is also maintained by Sherard—that *The Duchess* was "made in France" is largely based upon the remark appearing on the title page of the first privately printed edition: "Written in Paris in the XIX Century." But on the last page, Wilde himself gave the exact date of the completion of the manuscript as "March 15, 1883, A.D.," that is, only shortly after his arrival in Paris. This seems to corroborate Sir Johnston Forbes Robertson's story that he and his brother Norman had heard Oscar read *The Duchess* at 13 Salisbury Street, Strand, where in January, 1883, following his return to England from America, he had been sharing rooms with Frank Miles, the artist. Also, in the authorised edition of the play which, in 1905, was brought out by Wyman-Fogg Company of Boston, Robert Ross, Wilde's literary executor, made the comment that *The Duchess of Padua* was begun in 1882 and finished in March, 1883.[1]

As to *The Sphinx,* it is certain that Wilde did work on it in Paris: one has merely to read his hitherto unpublished letter to Sherard, reproduced here on page 119. But it is doubtful whether he had either started or could have finished it there. The poet himself seems to allude to his own age when he says in the opening of the poem:

> I have hardly seen
> *Some twenty summers* cast their green
> for Autumn's gaudy liveries. . . .

Was this merely poetic license?—Knowing, as we do, Wilde's typically feminine weakness for concealing his true age, it might be suggested that in this case, too, he had deliberately sought to mislead the reader. But Charles Ricketts, who illustrated the poem, contends that it "was written at Oxford." He probably means that the early draft of *The Sphinx* dates back to Oscar's days at Magdalen. This view has been also expressed by R. Thurston Hopkins in his *Oscar Wilde, A Study of the Man and His Work.*[2] Yet, the faceting and chiselling of that amazing poem, the tedious occupation of "putting in" and "taking out" commas, or matching trisyllabic rhymes for "catafalque" and "Mandragores," must have absorbed—with intervals, of course—many months, if not several years. It is significant that Ricketts himself, commenting upon the first printing of *The Sphinx,* which appeared only in 1894,[3] has revealed the fact that, even when reading the proof, Wilde was still contemplating various changes in his manuscript, and that he then was trying "to make it longer."

As a matter of convenience, however, both *The Duchess* and *The Sphinx* may be discussed at this point.

Compared with *Vera,* the *Duchess* is a genuine masterpiece. But viewed objectively and *in abstracto,* it is a mediocre melodrama and not a tragedy at all. No wonder Wilde, only a few days before his death, said to Ross: "*The Duchess of Padua* . . . is . . . unworthy of me."

The three principal characters in the play—Simone Gesso, the Duke of Padua; Beatrice, his wife, and Guido Ferranti, the *jeune premier*—are conspicuously divested of every ethical standard. Of the three, the Duke is the most cynical. His moral code is fully expressed in that advice which he so generously bestows upon young Guido:

> . . . be not over-scrupulous; clean hands
> With nothing in them make a sorry show.
> If you would have the lion's share of life
> You must wear the fox's skin; Oh, it will fit you;
> It is a coat which fitteth every man,
> (The fat, the lean, the tall man, and the short,
> Whoever makes that coat, boy, is a tailor
> That never lacks a customer.)

And he admits, with pride, that failure is the only crime which he has not committed.

The theme of amorality is less conspicuous in both Ferranti and the Duchess. But their acts, their common drama, are again the outgrowth of a moral insensibility, and hence, their behaviour, like that of lower animals, is governed by blind instinct and incoherent impulse.

The stage technique of the *Duchess* is inexperienced and clumsy; in parts the play is much too long, which painfully affects its dynamic qualities. The Elizabethan device of introducing comic relief in the development of a tragic plot is trivial and overwrought. Take this dialogue:

Duke
Come hither, fellow! What is your name?

First Citizen
Dominick, Sir.

Duke
A good name! Why were you called Dominick?

First Citizen
Marry, because I was born on Saint George's day.

Duke
A good reason! here is a ducat for you! Will you not cry for me God save the Duke!

First Citizen
God save the Duke!

Duke
Nay! louder, fellow, louder.

First Citizen (a little louder)
God save the Duke!

Duke
More lustily, fellow, put more heart in it! Here is another ducat for you.

First Citizen (enthusiastically)
God save the Duke!

Duke
Why, gentlemen, this simple fellow's love touches me much.

One more example from the fourth act:

Third Citizen
What think you of this young man who stuck the knife into the Duke?

Second Citizen
Why, that he is a well-behaved, and a well-meaning, and a well-favoured lad, and yet wicked in that he killed the Duke.

Third Citizen
'Twas the first time he did it: maybe the law will not be hard on him, as he did not do it before.

The audience is supposed to enjoy heartily these flat and vulgar jokes, which remind one of the silly mimes that used to be performed on street corners in decadent Rome. Yet, even in that remote epoch of debased tastes, there was a saying, *"mimi solis inhonestis et adulteris placent."*

As a philological composition, *The Duchess,* on the whole, is but a weak paraphrase of various Shakespearean texts. For instance, the opening dialogue of Guido and Moranzone is almost a replica of the ghost scene in the first act of *Hamlet.* The character of the Duke, of whom Wilde seeks to make a perfect villain, is admittedly fashioned after *Richard the Third.* Again, where Guido reveals the secret of his affection for Beatrice, Wilde liberally borrows from the love duet in the second act of *Romeo and Juliet,* while Moranzone's theme of revenge and murder is yet another way of expressing Lady Macbeth's bloody dream in the famous passage—"We fail! But screw your courage to the sticking place and we'll not fail."

Some of Shakespeare's classic phrases: "But your news is not new"; or "I am more an antique Roman than a Dane"; or "A father killed, a mother stained"; or "Words, words, words," etcetera, anæmically and annoyingly reappear in *The Duchess.* It is unimaginative mimeography and not creative inspiration—the production of a studious copyist rather than of a genuine poet.

Whereas in *Hamlet* or in *Romeo and Juliet,* we are faced with masterful and mighty psychological dramas divulging Shakespeare's magnificent understanding of the human soul, its sufferings and sins, its hopes and oscillations, Oscar gives us cold and rectangular schematic outlines marked with no spontaneous impetuosity, heartfelt sorrow, raging storms or penetrating fervour. To him, at that stage of his mental life, the immensely complicated world of emotional phenomena was still a closed book.

A few years later, in an article on Russian novelists, Wilde spoke with great admiration of Dostoievsky's clairvoyant faculty, his "fierce intensity of passion and concentration of impulse," and "his power of dealing with the deepest mysteries of psychology and the most hidden springs of life, and a realism that is pitiless in its fidelity and terrible because it is true." Yet realism of this kind was quite alien to Wilde, something altogether beyond his gifts as an artist. His early works evince a distinct lack of Rembrandtesque nuances in the treatment of psychological themes, complete absence of melodious transitions from tone to tone, from state to state, from mood to mood. Now, for example, Guido in *The Duchess*, with his many shifting attitudes and twinkling tempers, is an imperfect psychological type in that the kaleidoscopic changes in his conduct are altogether devoid of inner cohesion. There is nothing in either Guido himself or in the plot to justify the continual swinging of the pendulum from action to inaction. In the same way, the Duchess' bombastic announcement of her love for the young Ferranti comes like a lightning bolt out of a clear sky. When she suddenly utters these words:

> Guido, though all the morning stars could sing,
> They could not tell the measure of my love.
> I love you, Guido—

the reader does not exactly know how to react to this amorous outburst. Indeed, from the little Wilde has thus far told us about the Duchess, one might be suspecting her—dreadful suspicion though it be—of being the virtuous, perhaps a bit sentimental and unimaginative housewife of an imbecile Duke. Yet, suddenly she leaps to the footlights like some Messaline or Cleopatra, tempting that innocent child Guido to commit adultery with her.

Why, she does more: in a purely Macbethian fashion, she proceeds to butcher the sleeping Duke and, while the poor creature is still groaning on his deathbed, the Duchess carrying the blood-stained knife steps into the chamber and triumphantly announces to her lover: "I have just killed him!" And she entreats the boy:

> Kiss me upon the mouth and I will tell you.
> You will not kiss me now?—Well, you will kiss me
> When I have told you how I killed the Duke.

The youthful hero feels dreadfully embarrassed, and wresting the dagger from the Duchess, he shrinks from her in horror and starts running.

At this moment the electrician behind the slip stages "a flash of lightning followed by a peal of thunder." Then, to the amazement of the audience, Beatrice in the wink of an eye makes up her mind to punish her unresponsive sweetheart, and she orders the guard to seize him as the alleged murderer of Simone Gesso, the Duke of Padua.

Verily, *The Duchess* is unworthy of Oscar's reputation as an artist, and this he fully recognised himself when, in 1898, he wrote Ross: "*The Duchess* is unfit for publication—the only one of my works that comes under that category." Thus, Mary Anderson's refusal to appear in the play, disappointing though this may have proved to our poet, bears evidence of her innate taste.

How different *The Sphinx!*—From the standpoint of sheer prosodic technique, it is among the finest productions of Wilde's inverted genius. Of course, the poem is not a monolithic whole such as *The Ballad of Reading Gaol* or the miniature chef d'œuvre *The Harlot's House:* rather it is a long string of disconnected images and visions hemmed into one frame of a perfect and carefully selected style; a dream where dispassionate reasoning, profound learning and fiery imagination appear at once as contestant and contributory elements.

All his life, Wilde seems to have been haunted by the mystery of the Sphinx. The earliest allusion to this Egyptian symbol appears in *The Grave of Shelley* (1877):

> Surely, some old-world *Sphinx* lurks darkly hid,
> Grim warden of the pleasaunce of the dead.

On May 25, 1887, *The World* published Wilde's story *Lady Alroy,* the title of which he subsequently changed to *The Sphinx without a Secret.* And in *The Happy Prince* (1888), we read these lines:

> He told him of the *Sphinx* who is as old as the world itself, and lives in the desert, and knows everything. . . .

Only one year later, in *The Decay of Lying,* Wilde returned to his *idée fixe:*

> The solid, stolid British intellect lies in the desert sands like the *Sphinx* in Flaubert's marvellous tale.

Even that light and graceful comedy, *A Woman of No Importance* (1894), contains a word about the mistress of Thebes:

> Women are *Sphinxes* without secrets.

And so forth.

Much like the scholarly *Tentation de Saint Antoine,* Wilde's poem can neither be intelligently read nor fully comprehended without the use of a bulky encyclopædia: archæology and numismatics, mineralogy and architecture, zoölogy and botany, the Apocalypse and the Prophets, are all crowded by the artist's fancy into one hymn to the Eternal, Silent and Unknown. Ancient myths and long-forgotten legends, theurgic rites and occult revelations—the strange and vanished world of Babylon and the Bible—is once more brought to life and fascinatingly revived in these sonorous lines where burning passion is tempered by frigid reason and stern reason is disturbed by leaping passion. As Ransome puts it: "In a firm lava-like verse, the Sphinx's paramours are stiffened to a *bas-relief.* The river-horse, the griffon, the hawk-faced god, the mighty limbs of Ammon are formed into a frieze of revelling."

The Sphinx embraces and reflects widely divergent literary and artistic influences which blend here in startling harmonies, as in the splashes, whirls and bursts of *Prometheus,* that mighty tone poem of Scriabin. There is no plot, no tale, no fable woven into these sombre and fantastic strophes—nothing but quests and queries hurled at the Sphinx by a restless, oscillating and dissatisfied mind; interrogations to which there is no answer, or one as hopeless as Poe's croaking "Nevermore."

Who knows, *The Raven* may have suggested to Wilde the psychological plan for his poem, with its strange intrusion of the "exquisite grotesque half-woman and half-animal" which, like Poe's ominous bird, serves as the central device for the realisation of the poetic concept. The Raven and the Sphinx both symbolise the fixed and dreadful immobility of a nightmare hanging over the troubled souls of these poets.

Both Poe and Wilde seek to banish the obsessional idea:

> Leave no black plume as a token of that lie thy soul hath spoken!
> Leave my loneliness unbroken!—quit the bust above my door!
> Take thy beak from out my heart, and take thy form from off my door!
> Quoth the Raven, "Nevermore."

This is Poe. And Wilde, in turn, implores his ghostly guest to fade away and leave his "loneliness unbroken."

> Away! The sulphur-coloured stars are hurrying through the Western gate!
> Away! Or it may be too late to climb their silent silver cars!

Wilde's revulsion against the frightful monster becomes all the more emphatic as he realises its sinister and sinful nature. In a state of delirious fury, like Ivan Karamazov in that famous scene with the Devil, our poet exclaims:

> Get home, you loathesome mystery! Hideous animal, get hence!
> You wake in me each bestial sense, you make me what I would not be!

The Raven and the Sphinx are both tongueless phantoms that "creep through the curtain of the night" into the innermost of man's obscure ego, and there they coil up like some venomous serpent which contaminates and deadens a faithless heart. And in both poems, the concluding chords sound a note of utter despair.

Says Poe:

> And the Raven, never flitting, still is sitting, still is sitting,
> On the pallid bust of Pallas just above my chamber door;
> And his eyes have all the seeming of a demon's that is dreaming,
> And the lamp-light o'er him streaming throws his shadow on the floor:
> And my soul from out that shadow that lies floating on the floor
> Shall be lifted—nevermore!

To which Wilde echoes:

> False Sphinx! False Sphinx! By reedy Styx, old Charon, leaning on his oar,
> Waits for my coin. Go thou before, and leave me to my crucifix,
> Whose pallid burden, sick with pain, watches the world with wearied eyes,
> And weeps for every soul that dies, and weeps for every soul in vain!

Comparable as the two poems are, both as regard inner construction and outward architectonics or rythmical build, the ideational gulf between them is quite evident. The theme of *The Raven* is something like Chopin's *Marche Funèbre* or Mozart's *Requiem:* it is music of boundless "sorrow for the lost Lenore,"

> For the rare and radiant maiden whom the angels name Lenore—
> Nameless here for evermore.

It is the song of a bleeding heart lamenting over some irreparable harm, a heart that can find no rest or consolation, like that one in the beautiful lines from *Harmonie du Soir:*

> *Le violon frémit comme un cœur qu'on afflige,*
> *Un cœur tendre, qui hait le néant vaste et noir!*
> *Le ciel est triste et beau comme un grand reposoir,*
> *Le soleil s'est noyé dans son sang qui se fige.*

And *The Raven* stands out as one of the purest, though saddest, melodies ever composed in world poetry.

Not so *The Sphinx*—a dream unholy and unwholesome, sensual and destructive to the point of psychotic aberration.

Here, then, enters Baudelaire.

Like "poisonous plants that on corruption live" he stimulated in Wilde, by the mere magic of his rhymes, the dangerous thought that "there is immortality in sin,"—a theme which is fully developed in his delightful essay on Mr. Wainewright. Such lyrical chants as *Sed non Satiata,* or *Le Serpent qui Danse,* or *Femmes Damnées,* or *Le Vin*—well, virtually each one of those sinister and impure meditations—must have accentuated Wilde's inherent and morbid curiosity for the things deviating from the monotonous and, as some would have it, hopelessly virtuous patterns of everyday normalcy.

Now, *The Sphinx* is full of allusions to sexual perversions of every conceivable form. It is an orgy of moral decadence, a long hallucination of "mad passions in the senseless stone," the product of an exotic and obscene imagination that moulds visions evoked by vice and evil, sadism and necrophilia, animalism and masochistic delusions. As in some corybantic *danse macabre,* the young slave with his pomegranate mouth, the torpid crocodile, the giant lizards, the Gryphons with their metal flanks, the blue-faced ape of Huros and the gilt-scaled dragons, those hideous paramours, which, in monstrous combinations, come to tempt the langorous, immobile Sphinx, voluptuously stroking her curving claws of yellow ivory, her agate breasts and heavy velvet paws, "with fearful heads and fearful flame to breed new wonders from her womb—" all these ideational malformations verily belong to the dark realms of some Matisse, or Dali or Picasso—those prophets and practitioners of our modern neurotic cults.

Still, here and there, amidst all these impious reveries of an ill-directed mind, the eye suddenly catches the fading silhouette of some religious vision—a strange antithesis, suggesting the thought that Wilde's soul, as in a schizophrenic split, was divided into two distinct selves which dwelt there in a state of constant combat, seeking to unite in some as yet undivined synthesis.

But as years passed by, the content of his brilliant intellect became increasingly polluted with sexual obsessions of the saddest kind, until the memory of God and Good vanished and faded from his arid heart.

CHAPTER XVIII

A FRIENDSHIP BROKEN

"THE happy days in Aranjuez are coming to an end." This phrase of Schiller's might have come to the mind of Wilde when he was leaving France in the summer of 1883. With his American dollars merrily spent in Paris and with no income from Ireland to depend upon, he was by no means faced with that condition which the French call *embarras de choix*. There was hardly anything else for him to to do but to go back thither whence he had started his conquest of the world literary citadel. By that time Oscar had won for himself a literary reputation, not a first-class reputation perhaps, but still one that could not be ignored. He was now determined to make the most of it, particularly as every other opportunity seemed non-existent.

Wilde knew that in London it would be a stubborn fight amidst unresponsive and unimaginative Victorians interested in literary matters not at all, and striving for nothing but material gain. He was also aware of the fact that the humbug of his Oxonian pose would henceforth be of no avail. Something different had to be invented. But under the circumstances, what could he have devised other than *work, work* and more *work?* It is all to Wilde's credit that despite a natural predisposition for the idle atmosphere of fashionable salons where he reigned supreme, he did not sink to the shallow level of a professional loafer or a featherweight dilettante.

So, shortly upon his return to London in June, 1883, Wilde went to see Colonel Morse, who was then acting there as the representative of an American publishing house. It was decided to have a lecture tour arranged for the poet throughout England and Scotland.

Among the first addresses delivered by Wilde during that

season was the one at Princes' Hall, Piccadilly, on his *Personal Impressions of America. The London World* gave an excellent summary of the performance, marking "an undercurrent of Irish fun" and the curiously amusing fashion of presenting vivid sketches "of the men and women, and mountains, and rivers, and theatres, and teacups, and magnolias, and moons, and girls,"—all the things which he had observed on the other side of the "disappointing Atlantic."

The Queen spoke of the lecture as "paradoxical, audacious, abounding in good stories well told, in picturesque description, often humourously nonsensical, with plenty of original information."

In the course of that year, Wilde had delivered with varied success upward of sixty-five addresses in all parts of the United Kingdom, and it was then that he prepared a new lecture on *The Value of Art in Modern Life.*

A lady from one of the provincial towns thus summed up the impression made upon her by the lecturer:

> I can remember him as though I had seen him yesterday. My mother was delighted with his appearance; she often afterward spoke of his hair and his hands and his tie—oh! his tie, how it impressed us all. For my part, though I was only a girl then, I felt he was saying things which nobody present could understand, and it seemed to me at times as though he knew it also. I felt it was a pity he should have had to come here at all, for I suppose it was necessity that drove him on to the lecture platform. Many of the things he said have remained familiar to my mind ever since. I never see a big curtain-pole without thinking of what he said about the sins of the upholsterer, and I know that I never drink a cup of tea at a railway refreshment room without remembering how he described the cup out of which he drank his coffee at the hotel in San Francisco, where he contrasted the crockery of the Chinese in the Chinese quarter of that city with the domestic vessels used by the Europeans. It was a real distress to me to sit in that lecture-room, looking at this wonderful youth, and listening to his profound and beautiful words, while the rest of the audience were either gazing with dismay or surprise, or showing how bored they were. The room was not half full, to begin with, and during the whole course of the lecture people kept getting up and going out. But he

seemed quite indifferent to the mood of his audience; his manner, if I may use the term in such a condition, was quite businesslike. It was as if he was saying to himself, "I am here to say certain things, and I shall go on speaking until I have said them." He began speaking the moment he came on the stage, and when he had said his last word he walked off as if anxious to catch a train and get away from us all.

Possibly the most responsible of all the lectures given by Wilde in England was his talk before the art students of the Royal Academy at their Club in Golden Square, Westminster.

Magdalen College did develop in Wilde a taste for literature and a vague appreciation of art; but, after all, at Oxford, as elsewhere, he indulged in dilettantism even though of a highly cultured order. Yet here he was confronted with the immediate task of delivering an address to a group of men eager to learn something practical that would help them in their craft and would tend to improve their canvases.

Prudently, he turned for advice to James Abbott McNeill Whistler who, he was sure, was better qualified than any other artist to give counsel on the technique of painting.

In those days Whistler and Wilde saw much of each other. They used to dine frequently at the Café Royal, and G. Renier tells us that a bottle of *Château des Mille Secousses,* a claret discovered by the famous painter, was consumed on those occasions. Temporarily, there prevailed between the two a feeling of sincere friendship.

Wilde seems to have been greatly impressed by Whistler's æsthetic credo. The idea, for instance, that men of genius, in proud isolation, stand aloof from the rest of humanity, and that they are, so to speak, moulded of a different clay, immensely appealed to Oscar's self-glorification and his own sense of superiority.

On the other hand, Whistler ardently preached the paradoxical doctrine that Art is the mistress of Life, every manifestation of our daily existence being subordinate to the creative impulses of the artist. This, too, was something Wilde himself strongly stressed in his writings.

Finally, he was an enthusiastic admirer of Whistler's profound understanding of the "ins" and "outs" of the pictorial *métier,* which to an amateur such as Wilde always seems somewhat imposing.

In Whistler's view, the layman was not supposed to pass any judgment upon matters relating to art. On one occasion, he expressed this conviction to Humphry Ward, critic of *The London Times:*

> My dear fellow, you must never say that this painting's good or that bad. Never! Good and bad are not terms to be used by you; but say, "I like this and I dislike that" and you'll be within your right. And, now, come and have a whiskey. You're sure to like that.

Wilde, who, according to Frank Harris, was present at this conversation, was carried away by Whistler's witty fling, and exclaimed: "I wish I had said that." To which the painter at once rejoined: "You will, Oscar, you will!"

When Whistler started tutoring Wilde preparatory to his Royal Academy début, he imparted to the young Oxonian a few rather general and quite loose ideas from that artistic catechism which, at the time, was *en vogue* among the London Bohemian sets. Thus flimsily equipped, Wilde ascended the public platform on June 30, 1883.

His was a brilliant talk on art in its broad outlines, on Phidias and the Parthenon, Euripides and Æschylus, on Gothic architecture and early Renaissance which, he asserted, stood in astounding contrast to our modern civilisation stripped of beauty.

The lecture touched upon a theme that was somewhat foreign to Wilde's own credo: contrary to the stereotyped academic contention that Beauty can be discovered only if her ideal is theoretically defined, Wilde proclaimed that "nothing is more dangerous to the young artist than any conception of ideal beauty," which either leads him into "weak prettiness" or "lifeless abstraction."

Again and again he emphasised the point that æsthetic philosophy should not be divorced from the tangible world which the artist seeks to mirror in his creations. Neither science nor history can serve as a proper foundation for artistic inspiration, while archæology, he said, "is merely a science of making excuses for bad art." It is life, then, life in all its multicoloured glory, variety and fragrance, that should be regarded as a vast reservoir whence the motives of the beautiful should be drawn and then recreated and reincarnated in picture, statue and rhyme. What a significant admission on the part of a man of Wilde's leanings! The fastidious taste for the artificial rather than the genuinely artistic, for a moment at least, capitulated to the everlasting truth of Nature which is the ultimate symbol of Life itself. Wilde, who steadily maintained that "the proper school in which to learn Art is not Life but Art," and who, only recently, had been speaking of "a departure, definite, different and decisive" from the teachings of Ruskin, here unexpectedly drew nearer than ever before, or at any time since, to the Ruskinian thesis of the inescapable subservience of the humble achievements of art to the glorious reality conceived in the work of the Creator of all things. For it was Ruskin who, in *Modern Painters,* comparing the might of Nature with the weakness of Art, wrote these lines:

> . . . There is no climate, no place, and scarcely an hour, in which nature does not exhibit colour which no mortal effort can imitate or approach. For all our artificial pigments are, even when seen under the same circumstances, dead and lightless beside her living colour; the green of a growing leaf, the scarlet of a fresh flower, no art nor expedient can reach. . . .

Now, it was typical of Wilde to heap together in his works—whether essays, novels or lectures—most contradictory principles and antinomical doctrines. After his graceful *révérence* to Ruskin, he turned rashly to Whistler whose very name was hideous to the author of *The Crown of Wild Olives:* one has only to read his philippics in *Fors Clavigera,* where contemptuously speaking of Whistler's "ill-educated conceit" that "so nearly approached the aspect of wilful imposture," Ruskin gave vent to his indignation:

> I have seen and heard much of cockney impudence before now,

but never expected to hear a coxcomb ask two hundred guineas for flinging a pot of paint in the public's face.

For Wilde's purposes, however, Whistler was just as good as Ruskin, and, among other things, he told the students that appearance is, in fact, a matter of effect merely, and it is with the effects of nature that they had to deal, not with the real condition of the object. "What you, as painters, have to paint," he remarked, "is not things as they are but *things as they are not.*" Would not Ruskin have fainted on hearing this awful heresy which undoubtedly bore the stamp of the Whistler doctrine?—But what did all this matter to Wilde?—He had to make out his case *quand même,* and he cheerfully came forth with another Whistlerian theorem:

Do not wait [he counseled his audience] for life to be picturesque but try and see life under picturesque conditions. These conditions you can create for yourselves in your studio, for they are merely conditions of light. In nature, you must wait for them, watch for them, choose them; and, if you wait and watch, come they will.

This was but an echo of a thought which the painter must have suggested, and which afterwards he so delightfully included in his own *Ten o'Clock* lecture:

And when the evening mist clothes the riverside with poetry, as with a veil, and the poor buildings lose themselves in the dim sky, and the tall chimneys become campanile, and the whole city hangs in the heavens, and fairy-land is before us—then the wayfarer hastens home; the working man and the cultured one, the wise man and the one of pleasure, cease to understand, as they have ceased to see, and Nature, who, for once, has sung in tune, sings her exquisite song to the artist alone, her son and her master—her son in that he loves her, her master in that he knows her.

Boldly deviating from the conventional conception of ancient Hellas as a land where the ideal of Beauty found its fullest and most perfect expression, Wilde declared that the Greeks were *not* an artistic people and that they had no appreciation of art because they were not appreciative of their artists. This paradox which, again, was essentially Whistlerian, stood in direct conflict with Winckelmann's, Goethe's and Mahaffy's interpretation of the Grecian spirit with that incommunicable sense "for the consummate modeling of divine and human forms" which led Hegel to characterise the sculptors and philosophers and poets of the age of Pericles "as ideal artists . . . cast each in one flawless mould; works of art, which stand before us as an immortal presentment of the gods. . . ."

And *pour la bonne bouche,* Wilde concluded his sermon with a grand eulogy of Whistler himself:

> Now, having seen what makes the artist, and what the artist makes, who is the artist? There is a man living amongst us who unites in himself all qualities of the noblest art, whose work is a joy for all time, who is himself a master of all time. That man is Whistler.

Altogether, this lecture may be regarded as an ingenious concoction of carefully prepared witticisms, epigrammatic statements, inverted thoughts and pleasing *bon mots,* whose specific gravity, however, was, indeed, insignificant.

From a biographical viewpoint, the Golden Square performance would have been quite unimportant were it not for the fact that it led to a somewhat dramatic rift between the two Dioscuri. The occasion was furnished by Whistler's *Ten o'Clock.* In his discourse he used virtually the same material with which he had previously provided Oscar, accusing the latter of parrotism. Wilde attended the event, and next morning, on February 21, 1885, there appeared in the *Pall Mall Gazette,* over his full signature, a long review wherein he gave a rather sarcastic account of the artist's new venture.

Wilde's *Rengaines* being altogether unknown, or at least forgotten by the reading public, it seems appropriate to give here somewhat lengthy excerpts from his article:

> Last night at Prince's Hall, Mr. Whistler made his first public appearance as a lecturer on Art, and spoke for more than an hour with really marvellous eloquence on the absolute uselessness of all lectures of the kind. . . .
>
> . . . Mr. Whistler was relentless, and with charming ease, and much grace of manner, explained to the public that the only thing they

should cultivate was ugliness, and that on their permanent stupidity rested all the hope of art in the future. The scene was in every way delightful; he stood there, a miniature Mephistopheles, mocking the majority! He was like a brilliant surgeon lecturing to a class composed of subjects destined ultimately for dissection, and solemnly assuring them how valuable to science their maladies were and how absolutely uninteresting the slightest symptoms of health on their part would be. . . . Nothing could have exceeded their enthusiasm when they were told by Mr. Whistler that no matter how vulgar their dresses were, or how hideous their surroundings at home, still it was possible that a great painter, if there was such a thing, could, by contemplating them in the twilight, and half closing his eyes, see them under really picturesque conditions which they were not to attempt to understand, much less dare to enjoy. . . .

Of course, with regard to the value of beautiful surroundings, I entirely differ from Mr. Whistler. An artist is not an isolated fact, he is the resultant of a certain *milieu* and a certain entourage, and he can no more be born of a nation that is devoid of any sense of beauty than a fig can grow from a thorn or a rose blossom from a thistle. That an artist will find beauty in ugliness, *le beau dans l'horrible,* is now a commonplace of the schools, the argot of the atelier, but I strongly deny that charming people should be condemned to live with magenta ottomans and Albert-blue curtains in their rooms in order that some painter may observe the side-lights on the one, and the values of the other. . . .

For there are not many arts but one art, namely: poem, picture, and Parthenon, sonnet and statue—all are in their essence the same, and he who knows one, knows all. But the poet is the supreme artist, and the real musician besides, and is lord over all life and all arts. . . .

However, I would not enjoy anybody else's lectures unless in a few points I disagreed with them, and Mr. Whistler's lecture last night was, like everything he does, a masterpiece. Not merely for its clever satire and amusing jests will it be remembered, but for the pure and perfect beauty of many of its passages—passages delivered with an earnestness which seemed to amaze those who looked on Mr. Whistler as a master of persiflage only, and had not known him, as we do, as a master of painting also. For that he is indeed one of the greatest masters of painting, is my opinion. And I may add that in this opinion Mr. Whistler himself entirely concurs.

No wonder Whistler took strong exception to the contents and tone of these remarks on his *Ten o'Clock*. There ensued an exchange of letters in which the painter and the poet mutually insulted each other. Over a period of several years both sides exhibited much *finesse d'esprit*, but also much bitterness, lack of tact and utter disregard for literary manners. Wilde adopted, in his reviews and literary notes, the fashion of publicly pricking his ex-friend's amour-propre. Thus, in one of Oscar's "laborious disquisitions" on things of little importance, there is this allusion: "Mr. Whistler always spelt art, and we believe still spells it, with a capital 'I'. . . . His brilliant wit, caustic satire, and his amusing epigrams, or, perhaps we should say, epitaphs, on his contemporaries, made his views on art as delightful as they are misleading, and as fascinating as they were unsound." But not content with such half-innocent persiflage, our poet arrogantly accused Whistler of having attacked him "with both venom and vulgarity" and he concluded his denunciation with the statement that

> It is a trouble for any gentleman to notice the lucubrations of so ill-bred and ignorant a person as Mr. Whistler. . . .

The painter, in his rejoinder, called Oscar "the all-pervading plagiarist" who should have been included in the list of culprits and should have been made "to pick oakum, as he has hitherto picked brains—and pockets." He also declared that Wilde knew nothing about art and that, generally, he was an ignoramus.

> What [wrote Whistler] has Oscar in common with art? Except that he dines at our table and picks from our platters the plums for the pudding he peddles in the Provinces. Oscar—the amiable, irresponsible, esurient Oscar—with no more sense of a picture than the fit of a coat, has the courage of the opinions—of others!

Thus ended the friendship between two illustrious men, of whom one at least was lavishly endowed with "the gentle gift of making enemies." Fortunately for both, this episode is *en route* to oblivion.

CHAPTER XIX

THE TIES OF HYMEN

THE summer of 1883 held out little promise to Wilde in England. The season was a dead one; the lectures brought but meagre income, while in the way of literary productions he had nothing to offer save his booklet of poems which, by that time, had lost the charm of novelty. In addition, *Vera* proved a complete fiasco, notwithstanding the fact that in Oscar's own opinion it was a genuine masterpiece on which he had placed most fervent hopes. Even at the time of his first arrival in New York in January, 1882, speaking to the reporters of *The Herald* and *The World,* he had high-flyingly declared:

> I have come here with the intention of producing upon the American stage a play which I have written, and which I have been unable to produce in London. It is extremely desirable that it should be produced with a cast of actors who shall be thoroughly able to present the piece with all the force of its original inception.

And with a great deal of self-conceit, he explained that his play was not produced in London because he "could not get a cast fitted for its presentation."

In America, Wilde was fortunate to find in the person of Marie Prescott an exceptionally gifted actress, and he was very much satisfied with her selections for the cast—George Boniface for the rôle of the Czar, Edward Lamb for the Prime Minister and John De Gez for the part of Count Rouvaloff. In fact, he wrote her:

> I have to thank you for the list of your company which you have sent me; and congratulate you, as well as myself, on the names of the many well-known and tried actors which I see it includes.

Everything seemed to justify Wilde's optimism. In high spirits in August, 1883, he again crossed the Atlantic, and on his arrival in New York he personally superintended the last rehearsals of his drama. Finally, on August 20, the great day of the *première* had come. Although, owing to the hot summer season, the cream of society had deserted New York, the Union Square Theatre was well attended and the galleries were jammed. The audience was by no means over-critical; at first, there was even a tendency to receive the play more or less enthusiastically.

With all this, *Vera* fell down flatly, and by the end of the performance there was much jeering at the melodramatic and conspicuously unrealistic sentimentality of the heroine.

With the possible exception of *The New York Mirror,* the press was unanimous in its condemnation of the play both on the ground of its technical errors and the incompetent treatment of the would-be historical theme:

> A foolish, highly peppered story of love, intrigue and politics . . . it was little better than a fizzle [wrote *The Tribune*].
>
> It is long-drawn dramatic rot, a series of disconnected essays and sickening rant, with a coarse and common kind of cleverness [seconded *The Herald*].

Anna de Brémont had tried to explain the dead failure of *Vera* by the low cultural level of those who came to see the play. But even she, who had been present at the first night, was compelled to admit that

> at all events the play proved a summer bubble that burst after floating a week in the uncongenial atmosphere of Union Square. It was [she added] a bitter disappointment to Oscar Wilde and to those of his friends who had taken the trouble to forego the delights of their seaside cottages and brave the torrid heat of an August night to assist at his success.

The defeat of Oscar as dramatist on the American Continent made his position in England all the more difficult. His re-entry into London early in September was by no means a triumphant one. Chuckling over his set-back, dear old *Punch* cheerfully greeted our poor playwright with a little stinging humoresque dedicated to "Vera Bad."

> Will the Æsthetic give us some more *Impressions du Théâtre?*—If so he will probably have something to tell of "my Soul's dread weariness" and not very much to say in favour of "my freedom and my life Republican."

Thus, Wilde's early experience must have convinced him that neither playwriting nor poetry was a paying proposition. It was at this point in his career that Fate brought him to Dublin where he became engaged to Miss Constance Mary Lloyd, daughter of Horace Lloyd, Q.C.

Nothing definite is known regarding the origin of that romance. Wilde's biographers—even those who knew him intimately—keep mute on the episode which was destined to play such an important part in his life. One looks in vain for any facts concerning Oscar's matrimonial adventure. Ingleby, Ransome, Carl Hagemann and O'Sullivan have all emphatically failed to solve the riddle of that strange union. Nor does Mason's unique *Bibliography* shed any light on the matter, and even Sherard, both in his *Life of Oscar Wilde* and *The Story of an Unhappy Friendship,* has confined himself to a laconic statement that in November, 1883, Oscar, having returned from Dublin to London, told him about the forthcoming nuptials. But when did Wilde first meet Constance? When did he start courting her? What were the motives that prompted him to propose? When did Constance take a fancy to the poet? What were their relations prior to the engagement?—All these questions remain unanswered.

In his usual venomous manner, Harris sought to reduce this *page d'amour* to a purely mercenary scheme. "Suddenly," he says, "Wilde cut the knot and married . . . Miss Constance Lloyd, a lady without any particular qualities or beauty whom he met in Dublin on a lecture tour. Miss Lloyd had a few hundreds a year of her own, just enough to keep the wolf from the door."

First of all, to what extent can the contention be sustained that Constance was "a lady without any particular qualities or beauty?"—Sherard, for one, challenges Harris's assertion with disdain, on his own part invariably calling her "gentle and beautiful." This she certainly looks in the picture which accompanies an article, "Mrs. Oscar Wilde at Home" in *To-Day* of November 24, 1894. She appears there in a calm and pensive mood, full of poise. Her principal attraction must have been her eyes and also that lovely, ruddy brown hair which served as a frame for her delicately shaped, and in no sense banal, features. Constance made the same impression upon Comtesse Anna de Brémont, who has dwelt in some detail upon her appearance. This is her pen-portrait of Mrs. Wilde:

> As I write [meditates our Comtesse], a vision of her sweet face and graceful personality seems to arise in the vista of the past. A face whose loveliness was derived more from the expression and exquisite colouring than from any claim to the regular lines that constitute beauty. Sympathy, sensitiveness and shyness were expressed in that charming womanly face, and revealed a character intensely feminine. . . . It was a feminine soul that gazed forth from the windows of her clear, thoughtful eyes, a pathetic soul that lent a shade of sadness to her brightest moods. Yes, Constance Wilde was a thoroughly womanly woman.

And then, if she hadn't been blessed with a touch of captivating charm, Wilde, with his exquisite taste, surely would not have selected her as an "artistic *poseuse*" and the living incarnation of his own theories of beauty in dress. His æsthetic tact would not have permitted him to entrust to a homely creature the painfully difficult rôle of a model exhibiting now an ancient Greek, now some early Venetian or a similarly stylish costume. To wear successfully a Hellenic tunic or a Pompadour gown, a woman must be elegantly formed.

So much for the outward attributes of Constance. As regards the dowry, it is difficult to believe that Miss Lloyd's "few hundreds a year of her own" were the only bait that lured Wilde into the trap of wedlock. Money considerations, indeed, may have played some part in Oscar's decision to marry her;

CONSTANCE WILDE

but apart from his own feelings, Wilde was convinced that in Constance he would find a deeply devoted wife and companion. How passionately she was enamoured of her future mate is fully revealed in this piteous letter which she wrote him probably some time in the winter of 1883:

> My darling Love, I am sorry I was so silly: you take all my strength away, I have no power to do anything but just love you when you are with me. . . . Every day that I see you, every moment you are with me, I worship you more, my whole life is yours to do as you will with it, such a poor gift to offer up to you, but yet all I have and so you will not despise it. . . . Do believe that I love you most passionately with all the strength of my heart and mind: anything that you asked me to do, I would, in order to convince you and make you happy.
>
> When I have you for my husband, I will hold you fast with chains of love and devotion so that you will never leave me, or love any-one as long as I can love & comfort you.

(After all, Oscar may have been right when he said that "women spoil every romance by trying to make it last forever.")

Still, at that time, Oscar himself was infatuated with his fiancée. On this point, one should recall Sherard's story of the Wildes' honeymoon sojourn in Paris, where he had first met Mrs. Wilde:

> They were staying in some very pleasant rooms on one of the higher stories of the Hotel de Wagram, in the Rue de Rivoli, and a beautiful pair they made. The lovely young wife seemed supremely happy. There was bright sunlight, as one only sees it in Paris, on the Tuileries without, yet the room where I first met her was just as gladsome. It was full of flowers and youth and laughter. I felt that my morose forebodings at the time that I first heard of the engagement were more than stultified; and as we walked out together, Oscar Wilde told me that marriage was indeed wonderful. We were passing through the Marché St. Honoré at the time, and here he stopped and rifled a flower-stall of its loveliest blossoms, and sent them, with a word of love on his card, to the bride whom he had quitted but a moment before.

It does seem clear that Oscar's engagement to Constance

was pre-eminently, if not altogether, a matter of mutual love, at once disinterested and sincere. Hence, Harris's disparaging suggestion that Wilde had married Miss Lloyd merely for the purpose of keeping the wolf from his door falls of its own accord. Even the bitterest enemies of the poet have never accused him of being a gigolo or a mercenary schemer. And as a matter of record, Wilde's marriage hardly improved his financial position. It did enable him to lease a four-story red-brick, comfortable, though not at all luxurious, house in peaceful Tite Street—in the very heart of London's artistic quarter, just within a stone's throw of Shelley's and Keats's houses, Sargent's studio, Whistler's home, and many other equally famous abodes adjacent to the charming Cheyne walk along the Chelsea Embankment. Illustrious and comforting as these surroundings were, they did not in the least help to solve Wilde's monetary problems. And the poet himself told the amusing story of how Constance's old grandfather, John Horatio Lloyd, "lying on what threatened to be his deathbed, no sooner had joined the hands of the young couple and given them his blessing, than, for very joy of the occasion, he suddenly blossomed out into new health and vigour." Only much later, when the venerable gentleman, after much effort, finally passed on, did Mrs. Wilde come into possession of a more or less substantial estate.

Altogether, then, one might well discard Harris's falsehoods and insinuations. As Mr. Robert Lynd has justly observed: "Harris's *Life and Confessions of Oscar Wilde,* if read in the future at all, will be read as fiction and not as fact."

On May 29, 1884, the marriage of Oscar and Constance was solemnised in London at the small Paddington Parish Church of St. James, in Sussex Gardens. The bridegroom's "rank or profession" is described in the Church records as that of a "Gentleman," residing at 9 Charles Street, Grosvenor Square. Curiously, his age was given there as "28," when, in fact, he was almost thirty. The register further shows that the bride was twenty-six and that she was then residing at 100 Lancaster Gate.

The ceremony was performed by Reverend Doctor Walter

Abbott, the Vicar, in the presence of both Lady Wilde and her son William. It is said that at the Church door, just before the wedding, this jocular telegram was handed to Oscar Wilde:

> Fear I may not reach you in time for ceremony—don't wait.

The message was from James McNeill Whistler.

Though the marriage service was meant to be a rather informal affair, and only a few invitations had been sent out, the Church was crowded with curiosity-seekers.

The private character of the occasion did not prevent Wilde from giving the ceremony the somewhat distasteful flavour of an æsthetic spectacle. For one thing, the bride's wedding gown, fashioned in a quasi-Venetian style, and the dresses of the bridesmaids, were ostentatious and most elaborately designed. From a newspaper description of these garments we learn:

> The bride's rich creamy satin dress was of a delicate cowslip tint; the bodice, cut square and somewhat low in front, was finished with a high Medici collar; the ample sleeves were puffed; the skirt, made plain, was gathered by a silver girdle of beautiful workmanship, the gift of Mr. Oscar Wilde; the veil of saffron-coloured Indian silk gauze was embroidered with pearls and worn in Marie Stuart fashion; a thick wreath of myrtle leaves, through which gleamed a few white blossoms, crowned her fair frizzed hair; the dress was ornamented with clusters of myrtle leaves; the large bouquet had as much green in it as white. The six bridesmaids were cousins of the bride. Two dainty little figures, that seemed to have stepped out of a picture by Sir Joshua Reynolds, led the way. They were dressed in quaintly-made gowns of Surah silk, the colour of a ripe gooseberry; large pale yellow sashes round their waists; the skirts falling in straight folds to the ankles displaying small bronze, high-heeled shoes. Large red and yellow feathers shaded the damsels' golden hair; amber necklaces, long yellow gloves, a cluster of yellow roses at their throats, a bouquet of white lilies in their hands, completed the attire of the tiny bridesmaids. The four elder bridesmaids wore skirts of the same red Surah silk, with over-dresses of pale blue *mousseline de laine,* the bodices made long and pointed; high crowned hats trimmed with cream-coloured feathers and red knots of ribbon, lilies in their hands, amber necklaces and

yellow roses at their throats made up a sufficiently picturesque *ensemble*. One of the ladies present wore what was described as a "very æsthetic costume." It was composed of "an underdress of rich red silk with a sleeveless smock of red plush, a hat of white lace trimmed with clusters of red roses under the brim and round the crown."

Surely, this ornamental display of modiste craftsmanship must have been suggested by Oscar himself. How could he have missed so exceptional an opportunity to stage a little masquerade?—This was only the beginning of a long "comedy of errors" which he imprudently wrought upon Constance, in whom he had hoped to combine the loyalty of a wife and the virtues of a mother with the pretentious pose of a mannequin.

After the Church services, only near relatives were asked to meet at the bride's house. The brief notice of the occurrence in *The London World* reads in part:

> There is only this much to be recorded about it; that the bride, accompanied by her six pretty bridesmaids, looked charming; that Oscar bore himself with calm dignity, and that all most intimately concerned in the affair seemed thoroughly pleased. The happy little group of *intimes* saw them off at Charing Cross.

And, speaking of British wives taken with routine monotony to Paris on their *voyages de noce*, one wonders how much more or how much less dangerous these journeys are than the young American brides' traditional pilgrimages to Niagara.

CHAPTER XX

THE HOUSE BEAUTIFUL

FORTUNATELY, like everything else in the world, honeymoons do not last forever.

Having returned to London, the Wildes set down to the task of arranging their "house beautiful." The available accounts, scattered and fragmentary, of their home in Tite Street are insufficient to reconstruct a vivid and minutely accurate picture of the place where the couple built their nest. This much, however, we know. The decoration of the entire apartment was executed under the personal supervision of Mr. Whistler, and it was probably owing to his influence that there was hardly anything in the rooms suggestive of the *manière esthétique* with its silly sunflower, peacock and lily emblems. The general colour scheme was distinctly Whistlerian; discarding all conspicuous effects, the artist deliberately resorted to those subdued and melting hues that comfort the eye and never lose the charm of softness and repose.

The study on the top floor was in white with scarlet furniture, while the small library downstairs, where Oscar did most of his writing, using Carlyle's writing table as his desk, was an ingenious *arrangement*—not in "grey and black," but in buttercup yellow and lacquer red. The walls were hung with beautiful pictures, among others—a Monticelli, a Japanese painting of children at play and a drawing by Simeon Solomon. Behind the poet's armchair a red stand supported a cast of the bust of Hermes by Praxiteles. In the drawing room, of which Wilde was justly proud, the main attraction was the ceiling, said to have been designed by Whistler himself. A lover of beautiful things, Oscar managed to assemble there a large number of curious bibelots, fine pictures and precious books which reflected naturally the host's own cultural leanings and the refined taste which his wife must have possessed. A contemporary of theirs has given us some further details of that distinguished salon:

> Rare engravings and etchings form a deep frieze along two sides of the drawing-room, stand out on a dull gold background, and the only touches of bright colour in the apartment are lent by two splendid Japanese feathers let into the ceiling, while, above the white, carved mantelpiece, a gilt-copper *bas-relief*, by Donaghue, makes living Mr. Oscar Wilde's fine verses, *Requiescat*. To most of Mrs. Oscar Wilde's visitors not the least interesting work of art in this characteristic sitting-room is a quaint harmony in greys and browns, purporting to be a portrait of the master of the house as a youth; this painting was a wedding present from Mr. Harper Pennington, the American artist, and is much prized by the wife of the original. Even apart from this picture, Mrs. Wilde can boast of an exceptionally choice gallery of contemporary art. Close to a number of studies of Venice, presented by Mr. Whistler himself, hangs an exquisite pen-and-ink illustration by Walter Crane. An etching of Bastien Le Page's portrait of Sarah Bernhardt contains in the margin a few kindly words written in English by the great *tragédienne*.

Perhaps the loveliest spot in the Wildes' home was the quaint dining room in which, according to Comtesse de Brémont, everything was carried out in a decorative scheme of white, harmonising with delicate tints of blue and yellow. The Chippendale chairs, all painted cream-white, were upholstered in white plush to match. The smoking lounge on the first floor, furnished with Turkish divans and beset with all sorts of Moorish bagatelles, was arranged in a strictly Oriental style. A correspondent of *The Boston Evening Transcript* who had visited the Wildes' house in Tite Street observed that Oscar's sanctum was a veritable chaos of piled books, slippers, pipes, cigarettes and manuscripts, and it seems that, like most writers, our host "had made war on the dust-pan and brush, so that the servants had to watch for their chance when he was at the club or at a tea party."

It was often asserted that Oscar exercised a dominating

influence upon his wife. In a measure this was probably the case, but, at the same time, he let her have her own way in everything that concerned their joint abode and its outward appearance. On matters of interior decoration, Mrs. Wilde had very definite ideas which did not necessarily correspond with those of Wilde himself. In an interview with a correspondent of *To-Day,* Constance gave an account of her conception of what a "house beautiful" should be. It is noteworthy that her taste was one of marked simplicity, as opposed to the skittish eccentricities or garish profusion blemishing the works of some recognised masters.

> One of the most effective effects in house decoration can be obtained by leaving, say, the sitting-room, pure cream or white, with, perhaps, a dado of six or seven feet from the ground. In an apartment of this kind, ample colouring and variety will be introduced by the furniture, engravings, and carpet; in fact, but for the trouble of keeping white walls in London clean, I do not think there can be anything prettier and more practical than this mode of decoration, for it is both uncommon and easy to carry out.

Mrs. Wilde appears to have been opposed to the fashion of heaping up conflicting styles in order to make a house look "different," and she cleverly observed that "of late, people, in their wish to decorate their homes, have blended various periods, colourings, and designs, each perhaps beautiful in itself, but producing an unfortunate effect when placed in juxtaposition." It was her belief that living quarters must reflect the personality of their owner and not that of the upholsterer. And even on the somewhat banal subject of flowers, she revealed views which were distinctly her own. She said, for instance, that "it is possible to have too many flowers in a room, and I think that scattering cut blossoms on a table cloth is both a foolish and a cruel custom, for long before dinner is over the poor things begin to look painfully parched and thirsty for want of water. A few delicate flowers in plain glass vases produce a prettier effect than a great number of nosegays."

Anna de Brémont has accused Mrs. Wilde of "lack of the

literary instinct." Yet this contention is hardly just: inanimate things, in their very silence, sometimes appear as eloquent witnesses that shed true light on the intimate traits of one's personality. In the case of Mrs. Wilde, her autograph-book, that plain little volume encased in a cover she had made herself, bears evidence of the fact that she had a keen appreciation of culture and of those talented men and women who visited her Tite Street home throughout the years of her married life. That unique booklet became, as it were, a meeting-place for all the celebrities of the late Victorian era. Artists and poets and statesmen and actors were all represented there—George Watts, England's greatest ideographist, and Ellen Terry, his wife, whilom the queen of the London stage; dreamers like Swinburne and Robert Browning side by side with John Bright and Arthur James Balfour; Sargent and Ruskin shaking hands with Henry Irving and Mark Twain.

If Constance Wilde had been utterly devoid of the literary propensity she would surely not have collected with so much care and reverence the dicta and signatures of the illustrious persons with whom fate had brought her in contact.

Furthermore, people are inclined to forget Constance's contribution to Wilde's fame as an epigrammatist and wit. Biographers rarely, if ever, mention the fact that the world-renowned *Oscariana,* which helped so much to popularise the poet's name, was the fruit of Mrs. Wilde's appreciative labour. Of course, she was not endowed with a literary genius equal to that of her husband; her own literary articles, like the one in the *Woman's World* on "Children's Dress," may be of mediocre import, but on the whole it seems that she was an admirable counterpart to a great man of letters and learning such as Wilde.

As one looks back to that period in Oscar's career which immediately followed his marriage, it becomes clear that the event produced in him, at least in the beginning, an almost incredible change; it cured him of that Oxonian claptrap which, for a while, made him a laughing stock on both sides of the Atlantic. His whole outlook seems radically to have

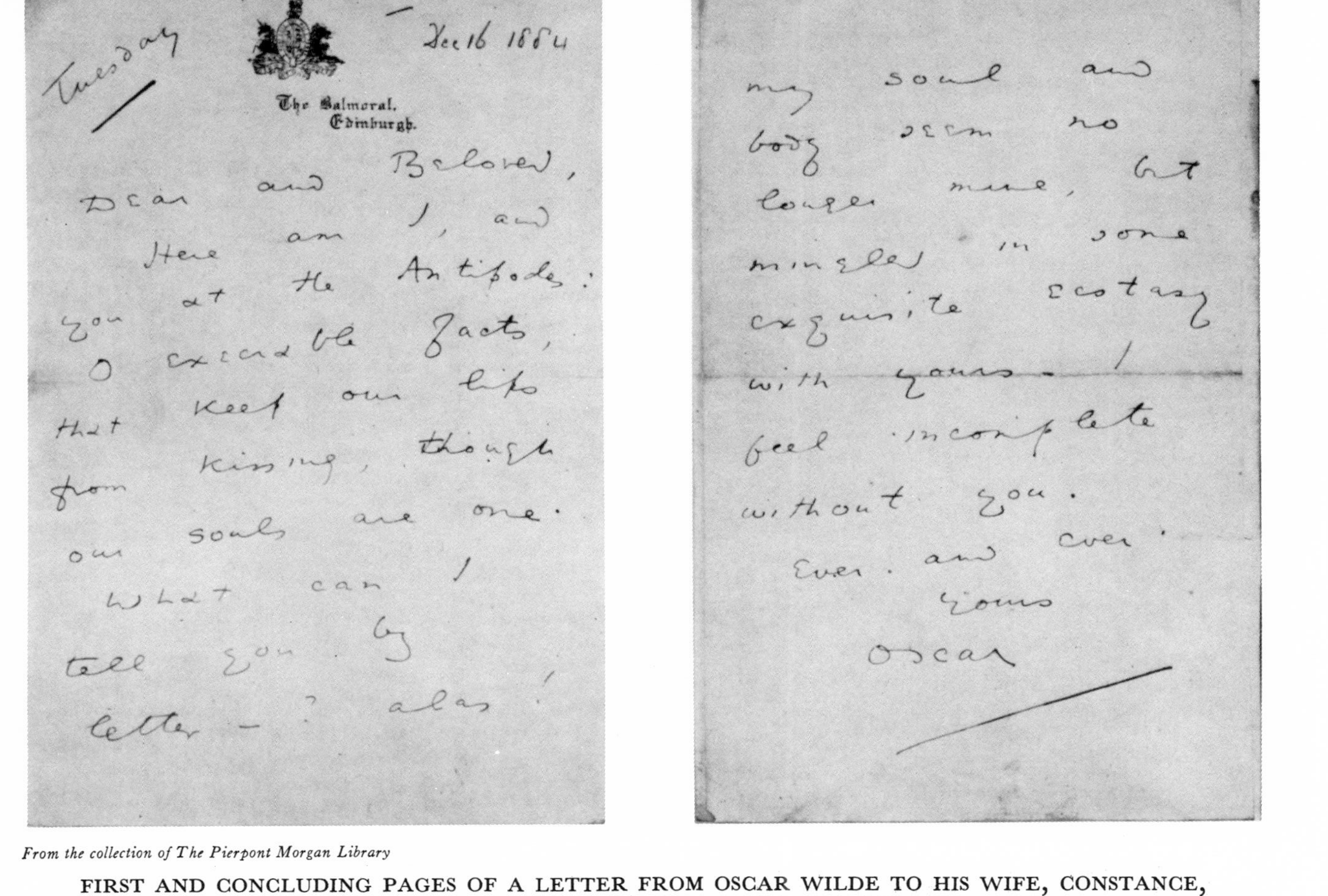

Tuesday — Dec 16 1884

The Balmoral, Edinburgh.

Dear and Beloved,
Here am I, and you at the Antipodes: O execrable facts, that keep our lips from kissing, though our souls are one.
What can I tell you by letter — ? alas!

my soul and body seem no longer mine, but mingled in some exquisite ecstasy with yours. I feel incomplete without you.
Ever and ever yours
Oscar

From the collection of The Pierpont Morgan Library

FIRST AND CONCLUDING PAGES OF A LETTER FROM OSCAR WILDE TO HIS WIFE, CONSTANCE, DECEMBER 16, 1884. (*This letter is reproduced in full on page 383*)

changed. Affectation no longer tainted his demeanor, and though retaining his epicurean tastes, he learned the secret of relishing the sane and simple pleasures. On this point we have some interesting comments by Mr. W. B. Maxwell. Referring to that period of Wilde's career, Mr. Maxwell says:

> He was fond of delicate food served to him in beautiful rooms, with a soft cushioned chair to sit on. Yet he could devour rough and ready fare even in the uncomfortable circumstances of an out-of-door picnic with equal appetite. It greatly pleased him to hear a good joke, but in default he would laugh heartily at a bad one. Again, we were charmed by his total difference from the Oscar Wilde of public repute. I remember that in regard to this he told us that of course he had never walked down Piccadilly with a lily in his hand. "Any one could have done that," he said in mock pride. "The great and difficult thing was what *I* achieved—to make the whole world believe I had done it." And he laughed. His laugh was explosive, joyous, spreading a contagion of mirth.

His habits became more dignified. The novel position of a *pater familias* conferred upon him a sense of responsibility. The necessity itself of providing support for his wife, whom he dearly loved,[1] and for his two little sons, Cyril and Vyvyan, whom he also adored, compelled Oscar to seek steady employment. Having assumed marital responsibilities, he could no longer flit hither and yon, from flower to flower, gleaning the joys of life and reaping the applause of cosmopolitan audiences. The saying that nothing succeeds like success may be true in the New World, but in Europe, particularly in England, work, hard and systematic labour, is the prerequisite for success. Although in the old romantic days, it may have been possible for a Lord Byron to "awake one morning" and "find himself famous," the commercial spirit of the Victorian reign made all such miracles inconceivable. Our poet must instinctively have felt that the thorny path of industry and perseverance—which Balzac in France and Dickens in England once patiently trod—was the only sure road to the beacon of fame.

Deliberately choosing the difficult part of a "Pegasus in the plough," Wilde entered the field of journalism, which he wholeheartedly loathed. Certainly, the idea of joining the crowded ranks of mediocre press toilers could not have pleased him, but then his was a case of *force majeure,* and so, courageously discarding, for the time being, his higher ambitions, he gave up his finicky Chelsean habits and started working for several London newspapers and magazines, among them the *Pall Mall Gazette* (1884), *The Dramatic Review* (1885) and *The Nineteenth Century* (1885).

Some of Wilde's articles, particularly on Shakespearean plays performed at Oxford in the Lyceum Theatre as well as on other English stages, revealed his extraordinary knowledge of the Elizabethan repertoire. The sketch, *Shakespeare and Stage Costume,* which originally appeared in the May 1885 issue of *The Nineteenth Century,* was later reprinted under the title *The Truth of Masks* in his *Intentions.*

Oscar's rather uneventful career was suddenly interrupted in June, 1887, when he received the flattering offer from Messrs. Cassell & Co. to become editor of *The Woman's World,* a one-shilling monthly which was designed to cater to the whims of the *femmes recherchées* of London society. Oscar's reputation as an art critic and connoisseur of interior decoration, embroidery, women's fashions and kindred subjects led the publishers to believe that in the long run their venture would prove a financial success. If they failed in their expectations, it was primarily because the magazine was too narrow in its scope and never could have had a circulation large enough to assure adequate returns to its owners. After all, even in a city like London, the number of persons willing to waste their time on feminine frippery must, of necessity, be limited.

Perhaps in those days, Wilde's own importance from the "social register" standpoint was still too slight; of course, in artistic circles his name was widely known, but the uppish *beau monde* neither then nor since regarded him as their equal. For some reason or other he was never able to efface the dividing line between himself and those who, by right of birth or otherwise, belonged to the English aristocracy. Vincent O'Sullivan, who had ample occasion to study Wilde's complex personality, has cleverly summarised the traits that probably prevented his friend from capturing the Mayfair stronghold. This is what he tells:

> To whatever class Wilde considered he belonged, it may be said that he was by no means what is known as the "English-gentleman" type. He was perhaps something better; but that certainly he was not. He had good manners, was scarcely ever rude, admirably good-natured. But he had something about him of that excessive look seen in the pictures of men put on advertisements of health foods, and cigarettes and automobiles. From the English-gentleman point of view there was something a little wrong with him everywhere—in his appearance, and his clothes, and his manners. He never looked well-dressed; he looked "dressed up."

The fact is that when Wilde became editor of *The Woman's World* he was still struggling for public recognition. Witty and sparkling as some of his reviews were, they remained more or less unnoticed by that reading public to which they pre-eminently were addressed.

On the whole, Oscar did better as an editor than most poets would have done had they been transplanted into the dull surroundings of Ludgate Hill. The task, no doubt, was a tedious one—a daily routine of perusing a lot of literary trash, correcting galley sheets and interviewing impetuous authors whose manuscripts had been rejected.

The editorial office of *The Woman's World* seemed to Wilde something like a reformatory where he was subjected to a rigid discipline that became all the more annoying as the house made it an inviolable rule that none of the employees, including the editor himself, should be allowed to smoke during business hours. Oscar, who used to puff cigarettes incessantly, must have felt painfully that puritanic restriction. Besides, he had to observe office hours, and, to one of the Apollonian cast who maintained that "punctuality is the thief of time," promptness must have been inherently repulsive. Nevertheless, he went about his prosaic labours with laudable conscientiousness, sparing no effort to place his periodical on the journalistic map of England. For a man of a profession as elusive as that of an æsthete, he showed an executive ability which was really remarkable. Only one year after he had been associated with *The Woman's World,* the public and the press began to show their appreciation of the general tone and appearance which he succeeded in giving to that monthly. *The Times* gave it high commendation and stated that the magazine "written by women, for women and about women" had taken "a high place" among contemporary periodicals.

Wilde went to great pains to draw into the funnel of *The Woman's World* every talent within his reach, and he finally did manage to secure the good will and co-operation of some of the noted personages of those days, Arthur Symons, Lady Sandhurst, Princess Christian, Marie Corelli and Queen Elizabeth of Rumania, who wrote under the pen-name of "Carmen Sylva." He was also after Sarah Bernhardt, whose name, he knew, would have greatly appealed to the womenfolk of England and, unhesitatingly, he addressed to her this charming, but long-forgotten, epistle:

My dear Sarah: You have seen by now, no doubt, the first two numbers of the paper I am editing. I ordered that they be sent to you with the editor's compliments. And the editor has been waiting to hear how you liked them. Our friend Mr. William Rossetti lent me the drawing by his brother Dante Gabriel, of his sister the poetess, to have copied for one of the frontispieces. . . . My paper is, and shall be as long as I occupy the office of its editor, a medium for the expression of the intellectual woman of today. . . . I want to ask you for several articles. Anything on the stage, by you, would be acceptable. So would a chapter or two of your rose-coloured reminiscences. You might call one of your articles "The History of My Tea-Gown," or "The Evolution of the Sarah Bernhardt Tea-Gown." I would be happy to put them into English for you, of course, and know that you will not disappoint me. I want to make capital of the tea-gown in an early issue. Could you not write an article for me on your American travels, with your impressions of the American people? I should very much like to have this from your pen. If you do not care to write it, would you have any objection to my writing it and printing it under your name? The paper *must* live up to its name and be written by women. But you will write it of course. My readers would not relish or even tolerate, I am afraid, any actual glorification of the Americans, so they should not be treated as civilised altogether. English people are far more interested in American barbarism than they are in American civilisation, anyhow.

When they sight Sandy Hook they look to their rifles and ammunition, and after dining once at Delmonico's they start off for Montana and the Yellowstone Park. . . .

You know better than I about their French; put that in. Your opening line might be "Columbus discovered America once and then left the Country in peace. But the Americans once discovered France and have kept on discovering it ever since. Never having learnt English, they set out to learn French. They explain their unending visits to our land, saying that they come over to finish their educations, and we have to tolerate people who are so fascinatingly unreasonable as to attempt to finish in a foreign land what they never had the courage to begin in their own!" I shall hope to have an answer about this within a few days. Do let me count upon you, not because it is respectable, or for any other such unworthy and tedious reason, but because I am so truly

Your friend,
OSCAR WILDE

Notwithstanding this eloquent plea, the "Divine Sarah" never did send Oscar her tea-gown sonata.[2]

Each issue of *The Woman's World* contained at least one article by the editor himself—a quasi-critical *mélange* on current artistic tittle-tattle. Full of genuinely Irish humour, these sketches ran under the unpretentious caption, *Literary and Other Notes*. Some of the witticisms scattered throughout the columns have reappeared in Oscar's later works, notably in *Dorian Gray* and his four comedies.

Though at times in straitened circumstances and even compelled to patronise the pawnbroker, Oscar managed to have his clothes ordered from the best Old Bond Street tailors. Dressed as a dandy, with a carnation or orchid in his buttonhole, he used to appear every morning in La Belle Sauvage Yard, devoting long hours to his editorial duties.

Some writers have suggested that Wilde even seemed to enjoy the dignity of his office. But it is difficult to believe that a man of his mental refinement, with all the laurels and public applause conferred upon him by his Yankee admirers, should have sincerely savoured press-work of this routine kind. To think only of the countless trivial topics, fribbling trifles and silly scrabble he had to deal with in those years of journalistic apprenticeship! The titles alone, of his impromptus in *The Woman's World* and other periodicals, do seem appalling. Let us mention these few: *French Cookery for Ladies, Are Servants a Failure? Modern Embroidery, Typewriting and Shorthand for Women, A Whirlwind in Petticoats, Chronicling the Fashions, Fancy Dress for Children,* and so forth. Poor Oscar! We can easily imagine the Newdigate prize winner, the classical scholar and "professor of æsthetics," sitting there at his dusty desk concocting with the earnestness of a Hegel some learned dissertation on the "monstrous fashion" of mercilessly lacing up a decorous English girl into a "fifteen-inch corset" for the worthy purpose of laying the foundation of "a real Spanish figure." No wonder he emerged from his experience as a gazetteer with a profound contempt for gazetteerage—for that crowd of men whom he described as his "vile gutter friends from Fleet Street." True, while he was still slaving in the newspaper mills, he occasionally spoke of journalism with a note of indulgence. When, for example, his brother William became connected with *The Daily Telegraph,* Oscar once remarked: "There is a great fascination in journalism. It is so quick, so swift. When Willy goes to a Duchess's ball, he slips out before midnight, is away for an hour or two, returns, and as he is driving home in the morning, can buy the paper containing a full account of the party which he had just left." But one is inclined to suspect that remarks of this kind were simply concessions or forced compliments to Her Majesty the Press—all the more so as, through his entire subsequent career, he deliberately challenged the journalistic profession, using at times a language which was distinctly insulting, as in his notorious outburst against reporters in *The Soul of Man,* where he accused them of having "nailed their ears to the keyhole" in search of cheap sensationalism and vicious scandal.

When the crash came, and Wilde was suddenly stamped into the mud of social contempt, English journalists, with touching unanimity, kicked back at him, and showered their dull and bigoted attacks upon the dishonoured man.

The Woman's World experience is of some biographical import: the long list of notes, articles, essays and sketches written by Wilde for that magazine divulges the queer fact that they all monotonously deal with feminine, if not exactly effeminate, subjects, which to a normal man are, or at least should be, of neither interest nor value. Most assuredly, a mentally balanced male should not be focusing his brain-power on things properly belonging to a vanity case or a lady's mesh bag. Like the earlier oddity of dress, Wilde's morbid curiosity regarding lipstick topics was an unmistakable symptom of that sexual anomaly which affected the emotional tone of his whole conduct and made him the victim of his essentially psychotic nature.

CHAPTER XXI.

THE VICTORIAN IDEALIST

TIME and again, critics have told us that Wilde was a man who *passa sa vie à se parler,* which may be true to the extent that of all the talkers of modern times, he was perhaps the most captivating and sparkling. In his admirable Victorian peep-show, Mr. E. Benson gave a classic account of Oscar as a *raconteur.* Here, in part, is what he says:

> . . . it seemed almost right that any vain excess or extravagance should be condoned in so lavish a maker of mirth who talked as he could talk. It was no wonder that his brilliance should dazzle and intoxicate himself as well as his listeners. . . . Like Vivian in his *Decay of Lying,* he was prepared to prove anything. He loved a string of jewelled phrases in his spoken word as well as in his writing, and if possibly they sometimes sounded like a recollection of Walter Pater, as perhaps they were, who cared so long as the Pied Piper continued to flute? How like was his talk to the play of a sunlit fountain! It rose in the air constantly changing its shape, but always with the hue of the rainbow on it, and almost before you could realise the outline of this jet or of that, it had vanished and another sparkled where it had been, so that you could hardly remember even the moment afterwards, what exactly it was that had enchanted you. . . . Behind the brilliance of his talk, behind and infinitely more charming than his poses, in those days before his bitter ruin came on him, was an extraordinarily amiable and sunny spirit which wished well to every one, and the sense of that gave him a charm that many of those who distrusted him and found him sinister were unable long to resist.

Fully aware of this boon conferred upon him by benevolent nature, Oscar used and even abused it for the purpose of self-advertisement and as a means of gaining both social prestige and literary fame. "Language," says Lynd, "was a vice with him. He took to it as a man might to drink. He was addicted rather than devoted to language." Among all the deities, the Queen of Mirth, to him, was perhaps the most pleasing. A born toast-master, Wilde loved the gay mise en scène of the fashionable London dinner, of which he was the natural center. His studied impromptus were applauded and memorised by those who had little, if anything, to learn or to remember. But if Hughes Rebell was right in saying that "the jokes of a wit seldom survive the speaker," it is equally true that the life of table talk, no matter how clever, rarely extends beyond the fleeting hour spent at a banquet table.

There is no question that Wilde was at his best not in the written but in the spoken word. As a sheer conversationalist he had no rival. With an air of insouciance he could go on uttering tuneful trifles—many of which indeed were about nothing. But then Renier remarked that "the one pure English element in Oscar's talk was his masterly handling of nonsense."

The method of stunty paradox and inverted proverb which lay at the bottom of Wilde's *succès de salon* was quite typical of his intellect, keen-witted but pointedly artificial. This note of ostentation pervaded not only his conversation but also most of his writings, so that by-and-by he acquired the reputation of being a standard-bearer of stylistic mannerism, and hardly anything more than that.

Still, in the many-faceted personality of Wilde there was one aspect which his English interpreters have almost utterly overlooked, or deliberately neglected—his idealism. Strangely, that trait dwelt in him side by side with the snobbish attitudes of a *flâneur* and the farcical habits of a dandy. Unmistakable signs of idealism may be traced in some of his poetical meditations—technically perhaps not his best, but pure and sincere—in *Madonna Mia,* for example, or in that lovely but sad piece *Impression du Matin,* or in *The Grave of Shelley.*

At times, as in *Vera,* that unselfish impulse of pity for the mere fanatic of anarchy who, in Chesterton's definition, is at once a nuisance to humanity and an honour to human nature assumed with him an attitude neither profound nor convincing; it was something in the nature of a moody grudge against the imperfections of our social order. But, fortunately, politics were altogether outside the range of his intellectual grasp. And it was Oscar's earnest conviction that the only difference between a Radical and a Tory lay in the fact that the former has never dined and the latter has never thought. Due to some insurgent instinct, perhaps imparted to him by his exalted mother, he developed idiosyncrasies of which he was proud in his days "republican." It did seem to him both modish and pleasing to advocate revolutions, or at least an immediate "revaluation of all values." Even when he reached a ripe age, he fatally erred whenever he ventured to touch upon political subjects.

Writers of "leftist" orientation have made it a point to play up the importance of Wilde's *Soul of Man under Socialism.* However, praiseworthy as this essay may be from the viewpoint of literary style, as an economic treatise it is a weak, almost childish bit of reasoning. And when a Wilde eulogist, like John Powys, earnestly assures us that *The Soul of Man* is "perhaps the wisest and most eloquent revolutionary tract ever written," he expresses an opinion that is by no means flattering to our present-day pink and red pamphleteers.

H. G. Wells once remarked that Wilde's essay on socialism is little more than a candid exposé of the feelings which most artists today are experiencing toward "the ugly congestions of our contemporary civilisation," "the prolific futile production of gawky, ill-mannered, jostling new things" and "the shabby profit-seeking that ousts beauty from life and poisons every enterprise of man."

The Soul of Man is tainted with much immature romanticism, and like Lamennais' impetuous *Paroles d'un Croyant,* it should be treated rather as a poem in prose than a learned discourse on the grave problems with which mankind finds itself confronted. The principal thesis in Oscar's work, namely that socialism is the surest method of attaining "the most intense mode of individualism," today sounds silly. Even an incurably enthusiastic disciple of Marx would venture to make no such claim, while individualism, to an orthodox Leninite, is an atavistic superstition, a thing that must be destroyed and uprooted before the collectivistic El Dorado can be attained. Indeed, how can political, economic and intellectual regimentation, upon which socialism is necessarily predicated, tend to encourage freedom of self-expression in art?—Is it not a palpable fallacy to mistake this kind of all-pervading and omnipotent dictatorship with what Wilde called the "New Hellenism"?

There is something pathetic about the ignorance displayed by our poet in his analysis of the machine evils resulting from capitalism as distinguished from the alleged advantages which mechanics will bestow upon the human race under socialism. He says, for instance:

> At present machinery competes against man. Under proper conditions machinery will serve man. There is no doubt at all that this is the future of machinery, and just as trees grow while the country gentleman is asleep, so while humanity will be amusing itself, or enjoying cultivated pleasures which—and not labour—is the aim of man—or making beautiful things, or reading beautiful things, or simply contemplating the world with admiration and delight, machinery will be doing all the necessary and unpleasant work. . . . On mechanical slavery, on the slavery of the machine, the future of the world depends.

Thus he goes on in a loose way, page after page, meditating about the happy morrow when all work will be done away with and men will find their millennium in a condition of general idleness. Presently, Oscar himself begins to surmise that he is only building castles in the air. But even this discovery does not embarrass him; with typically Irish ingenuity he turns around and seeks to find his way out of the impasse by resorting to one of his innumerable paradoxes:

> Is this Utopia? [he exclaims]. A map of the world that does not include Utopia is not worth even glancing at, for it leaves out the one country at which humanity is always landing.

Well, for all that, *The Soul of Man* is a generous appeal to the better side of man, an ardent plea for the improvement of the living standards of the toiling masses. Despite the many blots and flaws with which the book is fraught, there is in it a note of disarming sincerity, and one feels that Wilde, *malgré lui,* is deeply moved by sympathy for the humiliating suffering, shameful misery and boundless despair that dwell in the Boweries and Whitechapels of our modern Babylons.

In those days, Wilde still spoke with haughty disdain of those places in the world, notably Russia, where "even now . . . the message of Christ was necessary and where perfection could be realised only by pain." He was then incapable of appreciating the bottomless depth of Dostoievsky's genius. But here and there, *The Soul of Man* evinces in its author a touching tenderness, a compassion for Silent Grief that is deeper than the depths of the sea, and one suddenly captures a glimpse into that other phase of his sophisticated nature which found a more complete, more delicate expression in his Tales and in *De Profundis,* that tragic avowal of an erring heart.

Thus, Wilde appears in *The Soul of Man* not as an economist or a political thinker—for that he never was and never could have been—but as a determined individualist, like Nietzsche or Ibsen; a passionate idealist who raises the banner of revolt against the suffocating imbecility and puritanic lip-service of the human herd which self-conceitedly acquiesces in the gilded glory of democratic commercialism. Here, Wilde deliberately relinquishes his boyish bravado; he throws aside the mask of a London dandy, and proclaims a social credo that must evoke a responsive echo in the troubled souls of those who labour and are heavy laden.

While Oscar was still struggling to free himself from the clutches of journalism, he began writing those fairy tales which have long taken their place with some of the most treasured achievements in the field of belles-lettres.

It has become commonplace to compare *The House of Pomegranates,* as well as *The Happy Prince,* now with the *Kinder- und Hausmärchen,* now with Andersen's *Eventyr,* for verily in Wilde's beautiful legends, as in those conceived by the ingenious Dane and the Grimm brothers, there is a reverent tribute to the simple virtues and a humility which through centuries have carried a direct message to the young. Yet when Wilde was contemplating his Tales he did not start with an idea which had to be clothed in some fixed form, but, as he remarked in a letter to Thomas Hutchinson, "I . . . began with a form and strove to make it beautiful enough to have many secrets and many answers." Nor did he have a preconceived desire necessarily to cater to puerile mentality. This he frankly admitted in one of his letters to *The Pall Mall Gazette*.

> In building this House of Pomegranates I had about as much intention of pleasing the British child as I had of pleasing the British public.

He addresses himself to children of all ages, to the unripe and the adult alike, "to those who have kept the childlike faculties of wonder and joy and who find in simplicity a subtle strangeness." Intuition must have taught him that mystery fascinates not only those who seek to discover it by curiously peeping through the curtain of their future, but those, too, who have lost the secret of life in the mist of their own past. Accordingly, he asserted that even if children are fond of Andersen, "his true admirers . . . are to be found not in the nursery but on Parnassus."

With remarkable unanimity have Russian and German critics acclaimed Wilde's Tales as his masterpieces, equalled in style only by *The Picture of Dorian Gray* and certain immortal passages in *De Profundis*. However, among Anglo-Saxons, there seems to be a great deal of uncertainty as to the artistic value of these pearls of Wilde's creative genius. Arthur Ransome, for example, disparagingly speaks of the poet as "amusing himself with fairy tales," and intimates that he wrote them "as an experiment, to show . . . that he could have been Hans Andersen if he had liked." And Ingleby, who has the greatest admiration for Wilde as a poet, heaves a sigh of regret over the concluding paragraphs in *The Happy Prince*. "I wish," he says, "that the last sentences . . . could be erased." What are they?—

"Bring me the two most precious things in the city," said God to one of His Angels; and the Angel brought Him the leaden heart and the dead bird.

"You have rightly chosen," said God, "for in my Garden of Paradise this little bird shall sing forevermore, and in my City of Gold the Happy Prince shall praise Me."

Now, these lines are not only perfect from the standpoint of literary power, but, as a crowning touch to the poem, they make a most effective finale, full of inner meaning and ethical pathos. It is difficult to understand why so experienced a critic as Ingleby should have wished that these words had been deleted. On the other hand, Pater, to whom Wilde had sent a copy of *The Happy Prince* (1888), gave high praise to the Tales. This is what he wrote:

I am confined to my room with gout, but have been consoling myself with *The Happy Prince,* and feel it would be ungrateful not to send a line to tell you how delightful I have found him and his companions. I hardly know whether to admire more the wise wit of *The Remarkable Rocket,* or the beauty and tenderness of *The Selfish Giant:* the latter certainly is perfect in its kind. Your genuine "little poems in prose," those at the top of pages 10 and 14, for instance, are gems, and the whole, too brief, book abounds with delicate touches and pure English.

In fact, the rhythmical qualities of Wilde's prose attained in several of these marvel tales a height of excellence which in English literature has hardly ever been surpassed.

No wonder Justin McCarthy, himself a gifted poet, dedicated to Wilde an enthusiastic poem, *The Happy Prince,* with its touching last stanza:

Long have I lingered an enchanted guest
  In the green garden of your fairy tales;
  Yet for my thanks my fancy falters, fails—
I love them all, but love, indeed, the best
The red rose blossom of the Song-bird's breast.

Analyzing the style of the *House of Pomegranates,* Mr. Turquet-Milnes observed that Wilde was influenced by the Baudelairian ideal of a "poetical prose" which adapts itself easily to the lyrical movements of the soul and the most delicate modulations of "nameless reveries."

On the whole, the reaction of the British press to both collections was quite favourable. A fine criticism of *The Happy Prince* appeared in *The Saturday Review* (October 21, 1888). In the opinion of that paper, Wilde's genre, peculiarly his own, was full of appeal to those who, whatever their age, were true lovers of fairy stories and regarded them as the most delightful form of romance. Again, *The Athenæum* drew a laudatory comparison between Wilde and Andersen, justly noting, however, the element of contemporary satire which, to be sure, differentiates the English poet from an ordinary fable teller. But, according to the reviewer, that touch of quaint humour "was so delicately introduced that the illusion was not destroyed and a child would delight in the Tales without being worried or troubled by their application."

Imbued with Hellenic paganism, Wilde, as we know, though frequently dwelling upon the subject of Papism, seldom gave serious thought to the religious problem. Official churchdom irritated and bored him. But, strangely, Jesus, as the living incarnation of a lofty *idéal,* always attracted his imagination, perhaps as a *contrepoids* to his self-centered and mundane philosophy. Although he made no attempt in the fairy tales to compromise with Christianity, he told his lovely stories in a true Christian spirit. By prominently introducing in them the eternal theme of Christ, he struck a note that was sure to make every child's heart quiver. And it is significant that in Wilde's wonderland, Christ is invariably found mingling with the young, whose minds have not yet been affected by the deadly toxin of modern scepticism. It is through them that God's truth is revealed to the world, and the adults, with their false wisdom and frozen hearts, are made somehow to bow to the chaste simplictiy of the babes.

The Bishop refuses to crown the Young King when he appears at the great portal of the cathedral in a humble attire with only a circlet of wild briar set on his head.

> . . . I praise thee not for this that thou hast done [the Bishop admonished the lad] but I bid thee ride back to the Palace and make thy face glad and put on the raiment that beseemeth a king, and with a crown of gold I will crown thee, and the sceptre of pearl will I place in thy hand. . . . The burden of this world is too great for one man to bear, and the world's sorrow too heavy for one heart to suffer.

But the face of the Young King flushed with anger, for he knew that there was no truth, no virtue, in these frigid words, and he strode past the Bishop, and climbed up the steps of the altar to the image of Christ. Then the miracle happened:

> He stood before the image of Christ, and on his right hand and on his left were the marvellous vessels of gold, the chalice with the yellow wine and the vial with the holy oil. He knelt before the image of Christ, and the candles burned brightly by the jewelled shrine, and the smoke of the incense curled in thin blue wreaths through the dome. He bowed his head in prayer and the priests in their stiff copes crept away from the altar. . . .
>
> And lo! through the painted windows came the sunlight streaming upon him, and the sunbeams wove round him a tissued robe that was fairer than the robe that had been fashioned for his pleasure. The dead staff blossomed, and bare lilies that were whiter than pearls. The dry thorn blossomed and bare roses that were redder than rubies. Whiter than fine pearls were the lilies, and their stems were of bright silver. Redder than male rubies were the roses, and their leaves were of beaten gold. . . .
>
> He stood there in a king's raiment, and the Glory of God filled the place, and the saints in their carven niches seemed to move. In the fair raiment of a king he stood before them, and the organ pealed out its music, and the trumpeters blew upon their trumpets, and the singing boys sang.
>
> And the people fell upon their knees in awe, and the nobles sheathed their swords and did homage, and the Bishop's face grew pale, and his hands trembled. "A greater than I hath crowned thee," he cried, and he knelt before him.

Christ also triumphs over that Selfish Giant whose heart melted as he once beheld in his frost-bitten garden a little boy whom he had never seen before. Other children were afraid of the morose Goliath and used to run away from him, but this darling child suddenly stretched out his arms to him, flung them around his neck and tenderly embraced him. Then the boy vanished. But never thereafter could the Giant forget his little friend, and he longed for him and often used to say, "How I would like to see him!" Years passed by, and the Giant grew old and feeble; but no longer did he frighten the children, and every afternoon, when school was over, they came and played in his garden. Nor did he, as in days past, hate the Winter, "for he knew that it was merely the Spring asleep, and that the flowers were resting." One morning he awoke and suddenly his eye caught a marvellous sight:

> In the farthest corner of the garden was a tree quite covered with lovely white blossoms. Its branches were all golden, and silver fruit hung down from them and underneath it stood the little boy he had loved.

In great joy, the Giant ran out into the garden, but when he came quite close to the child and saw his hands and little feet bearing the print of nails, he grew angry and cried:

> "Who hath dared to wound thee?—Tell me that I may take my big sword and slay him"—
>
> "Nay!" answered the child; "but these are the wounds of love."
>
> "Who art thou?" said the Giant, and a strange awe fell on him, and he knelt before the little child.
>
> And the child smiled on the Giant, and said to him, "You let me play once in your garden, today you shall come with me to my garden, which is Paradise."
>
> And when the children ran in that afternoon, they found the Giant lying dead under the tree, all covered with white blossoms.

These carved Biblical sentences are marked with a naïveté that even the humblest mind is able to comprehend. But few poets have reached in their creations the same level of beauteous simplicity. *The Selfish Giant* may be compared only with such masterpieces of world literature as that story of little Dombey's death, or the pages dedicated to Dora's last hours, in

David Copperfield, or Dostoievsky's heart-breaking vision of *Christ's Christmas Tree.*

In Wilde's conception, Christ is above all a symbol of suffering. It is for this reason that the theme of "sorrow that endureth forever," like the mournful sighs in Tchaikovsky's *Pathétique,* pervades and colours most of Wilde's Tales. In them, for the first time, he recognised the element of grief as a universal condition that is just as real as man's intense longing for happiness. But while joy is essentially selfish, suffering is altruistic and ennobling; it creates new moral values and awakes consciousness to that high Law which the human mind is unable to test and which it should never seek to challenge. In this new conception, love itself emerges from pain and is born of compassion.—It is precisely to this kind of emotion that *The Nightingale and the Rose* is dedicated.

The Nightingale, "the true lover" in the tale, overhears the lamentations of a young student whose beloved promised to dance with him at the Prince's ball if he would bring her a red rose. But there is no red rose in his garden. In an impulse of self-sacrifice, the little bird decides to make a crimson rose by pressing her heart against the sharp thorn of a rose tree; out of the magic of her music, out of the stains of her blood and the silver threads of the moon, the red rose must be fashioned. So, when the moon shone in the heavens, the Nightingale flew to the rose tree and set her heart against the thorn. "All night long she sang with her heart against the thorn, and the cold crystal moon leaned down and listened." All night long she sang of the birth of Love in the heart of a boy, and of the rise of passion in the soul of man, and of Love that is stronger than Death, "of the Love that dies not in the tomb." Deeper and deeper went the thorn into her breast and her life blood ebbed away from her. But as her blood dripped on the pale rose, the tender petals became touched with delicate pink "like the flush in the face of the bridegroom when he kisses the lips of the bride." And when the thorn touched the little bird's heart and a fierce pang of pain shot through her suffering body, the rose suddenly grew crimson as a red ruby, "crimson like the rose of the eastern sky." The trills of the dying Nightingale were so enchanting that—

> the white Moon heard it, and she forgot the dawn, and lingered on in the sky. The red rose heard it, and it trembled all over with ecstasy, and opened its petals to the cold morning air. Echo bore it to her purple cavern in the hills, and woke the sleeping shepherds from their dreams. It floated through the reeds of the river, and they carried its message to the sea.

The Young Fisherman loses his Soul because he committed the mortal sin of falling in love with the only daughter of the Sea King, the little Mermaid whom he had once caught in his net. "So beautiful was she that when the Young Fisherman saw her he was filled with wonder, he put out his hand and drew the net close to him, and leaning over the side, he clasped her in his arms."

> Her hair was as a wet fleece of gold, and each separate hair as a thread of fine gold in a cup of glass. Her body was as white ivory, and her tail was of silver and pearl. Silver and pearl was her tail, and the green weeds of the sea coiled round it; and like sea-shells were her ears, and her lips were like sea-coral.

So great was his love for the Mermaid that he banished his soul. And even when one day a great cry of mourning reached him from the sea, "and the black waves came hurrying to the shore bearing with them a burden that was whiter than silver"; and when he saw the surf take the body of his beloved from the waves, and when the foam took it from the surf and the shore received it—even then the bewitched lover could not part with his dream. Here again, the tears of woe and the sobs of despair give birth to a miracle. For when "the sea came nearer, and sought to cover" the Fisherman with its waves, "and when he knew that the end was at hand, he kissed with mad lips the cold lips of the Mermaid, and the heart that was within him brake. And as through the fullness of his love his heart did break, the Soul found an entrance and entered in, and was one with him even as before."

Now, in all these beautiful Tales, where Suffering makes its appearance; or great Sorrow creeps through "the sunless lanes of Poverty"; or Love breaks a palpitating heart; or grim Death throws his shadow upon a blossoming life—Beauty, by the splendour of her scintillating light, miraculously transforms the discords of the human drama into a melody as sweet as that which is born when angels touch the silver strings of some celestial harp. The poet has finally discovered a lasting æsthetic value in things which heretofore seemed indifferent to him because, in his judgment, they lay outside the realm of creative inspiration.

CHAPTER XXII

MR. W. H.

IT IS curious how often men of letters who in their prime are possessed with a sort of *furor poeticus,* after a time definitely desert the poets' ranks for the sake of sober prose. Wouldn't a survey of such metamorphoses be a fascinating study for college undergraduates?

Wilde's record in this respect was quite typical: he, too, began his literary career as a composer of sonorous and pleasing verses in which, however, as he himself admitted, "there was more rhyme than reason"; yet, as he grew older, he seemed to have lost all taste for poetry, and though there is nothing that would justify the contention that he ever regarded his early poems as callow productions, the fact remains that upon reaching maturity he took no further interest in that delightful occupation which Browning aptly called "the unlocking of hearts with sonnet keys." Except for the *Sphinx,* a poem first conceived at Oxford, and *The Harlot's House,* which appeared in the *Dramatic Review* in 1885, Wilde, after his marriage, virtually abandoned the lyre, and only many years later, in *The Ballad of Reading Gaol,* did he turn once more to the poetic mode of expression.

By creating *L'Envoi,* Oscar proved to his own satisfaction that he could master prose in a most artistic manner. The years of journalistic toil confirmed him in that belief, while the public reaction to *The Happy Prince* finally determined the future course of his literary work. From that time on, he gave himself entirely to prose. It is in this field that he scored his greatest triumphs, and it is through *Dorian Gray,* the Fairy Tales, *Intentions, The Portrait of Mr. W. H.,* and *De Profundis* that he won his battle for world fame.

After his successful début with *The Happy Prince,* Wilde at once turned to *The Portrait of Mr. W. H.,* which was published in the July 1889 number of *Blackwood's Edinburgh Magazine.* Though written in the style of an ordinary story, it is "a learned thesis, masquerading as fiction," an ingenious essay in which our poet made a daring attempt to discover the identity of the person who had ostensibly inspired Shakespeare to compose his famous *Sonnets.*

To the best of our present-day knowledge, these sonnets were written in, or rather before, the year 1598, when Francis Meres made a direct reference to them in his *Palladis Tamia.* However, they were first published in book form in 1609, by one Thomas Thorpe, and it was he, and not Shakespeare, who prefixed the following dedication:

To the onlie begetter of
these insuing Sonnets
Mr. W. H., all happinesse
and that eternitie
promised
by
our ever-living poet
wisheth
the well-wishing
adventurer in
setting
forth
T. T.

Amateurs of literary crossword puzzles have long and futilely sought to solve the "W. H." enigma. The still accepted theory is that the *Sonnets* were dedicated to Henry Wriothesley, Earl of Southampton, while the other three *dramatis personæ* are Shakespeare himself, the friend of Henry Wriothesley; George Chapman, the rival poet; and finally, Mary Fytton, "the dark lady," one of Queen Elizabeth's maids of honour, with whom both Shakespeare and his titled patron were supposed to be in love.

Others have suggested that Shakespeare's youthful friend was no one else than William Herbert, Earl of Pembroke. The latter version, however, has been ably refuted by Wilde. He pointed out that Lord Pembroke, who was born in 1580, did not come to London till he was eighteen years of age, whereas, from the text of Sonnet CIV, it appears that Shakespeare's acquaintance with, if not friendship for, W. H. must have begun in 1594, or, at the latest, in 1595. Here are the corroborating lines:

> To me, fair friend, you never can be old,
> For as you were when first your eye I ey'd,
> Such seems your beauty still. *Three* winters cold
> Have from the forests shook *three* summers' pride,
> *Three* beauteous springs to yellow autumn turn'd
> In process of the seasons have I seen,
> *Three* April perfumes in *three* hot Junes burn'd,
> Since first I saw you fresh, which yet are green.

Now, it was not Wilde, but Malone and Tyrwhitt who some one hundred and fifty years ago first suggested that the mysterious initials *W. H.* in the dedication stood for "*W*ill *H*ughes." The conjecture was based upon a clever *jeu de mots* in the CXXXV pun sonnet, beginning with

> Whoever hath her wish, thou hast thy *Will*. . . .

and in Sonnet XX:

> An eye more bright than theirs, less false in rolling,
> Gilding the object whereupon it gazeth;
> A man in *hue,* all *hues* in his controlling,
> Which steals men's eyes and women's souls amazeth,

with its last couplet:

> But since she prick'd thee out for women's pleasure,
> Mine be thy love, and thy love's *use* their treasure.

Thus, there was nothing original in Wilde's interpretation, but what he did add to Malone's theory was that legend of his own creation, which transformed Will Hughes into a young actor for whom Shakespeare allegedly created the characters of Imogen, the daughter of Cymbeline, Viola, Rosalind, Portia, Desdemona, Juliet, and perhaps that of Cleopatra herself.

In support of this contention, he cited six stanzas from Sonnet XVIII:

> But thy eternal summer shall not fade,
> Nor lose possession of that fair thou ow'st,
> Nor shall death brag thou wander'st in his shade,
> *When in eternal lines to time thou grow'st;*
> So long as men can breathe, or eyes can see,
> So long lives this, and this gives life to thee.

Of course, today, as in the time of Wilde, no one would venture to assert that his Will Hughes hypothesis has solved "the sonnet mystery." Still, the delightful style in which the story is told; the profound Shakespearean exegesis; the erudition, wit and mental refinement which adorn the essay, make *The Portrait of Mr. W. H.,* as Wilde once remarked, "one of his early masterpieces" which in English imaginative literature remains almost unmatched. One may well recall Mr. Clifford Smyth's words that

> under the transforming touch of Wilde's fancy it becomes a real flesh-and-blood story, a rare chronicle that brings to life again the stage and those who peopled it with the bravest shapes that ever sprang from the mighty cauldron of the human imagination, in those far-off, greatest days of Merrie England.

Innocent though the theme of Wilde's sketch may appear to our way of thinking, nevertheless it is indicative of the poet's mental leanings in the late 'eighties. For certainly there was something more in Oscar's speculations than a mere ambition to solve a literary riddle by unmasking the wonderful features of Mr. W. H. Throughout the narrative, one detects an erotic undertone, a scarcely concealed desire to glorify the strange passion for the young man whose physical beauty, we are told, was such "that it became the very corner-stone of Shakespeare's art; the very source of Shakespeare's inspirations; the very incarnation of Shakespeare's dreams." In painting the portrait of his hero, Wilde brings into play the choicest and most gorgeous colours from the palette of his perverted intellect:

> I could almost fancy [he recounts] that I saw him standing in the shadow of my room, so well had Shakespeare drawn him, with his golden hair, his tender flower-like grace, his dreamy deep-sunken eyes, his delicate mobile limbs, and his white lily hands. His very name fascinated me. Willie Hughes! Willie Hughes! How musically it sounded! Yes; who else but he could have been the master-mistress of Shakespeare's passion, the lord of his love to whom he was bound in vassalage, the delicate minion of pleasure, the rose of the whole world, the herald of the spring, decked in the proud livery of youth, the lovely boy whom it was sweet music to hear, and whose beauty was the very raiment of Shakespeare's heart, as it was the keystone of his dramatic power?

Wilde concludes this glorious tirade with a plea that Shakespeare be forgiven for his sin, "if such it was," and when he quotes these lines from the Sonnet "of noble score" (CXXI)

> No, I am that I am, and they that level
> At my abuses reckon up their own:
> I may be straight, though they themselves be bevel;
> By their rank thoughts my deeds must not be shown . . .

we can visualise Wilde himself contemptuously throwing his glove in the face of his pharisaical compatriots and insolently telling them:

> All men are bad, and in their badness reign.

The Portrait of Mr. W. H. was never published in England in book form, for fear perhaps that "the English public would have to read Shakespeare's Sonnets."

The unleavened Victorian mind was thoroughly shocked by the impious suggestion that the king of English literature could have composed those passionate verses to a person of his own sex.

Renier once read an English book in which the accusation of abnormal sexual tendencies in Shakespeare was dismissed with the curt remark that, having been a great poet, he, therefore, was too noble to have been guilty of this offense. This, indeed, is characteristic of the Anglo-Saxon mentality, which in matters of sex and ethics is susceptible to no canons of reason and to no demonstration of historical proof.

CHAPTER XXIII

A CHALLENGE TO VICTORIANISM

FOR once Frank Harris told the truth when he asserted that *The Portrait of Mr. W. H.* did Oscar incalculable injury, since the paper did leave a stigma on Wilde's reputation, giving his enemies "the very weapon they wanted, and they used it unscrupulously and untiringly with the fierce delight of hatred." But what did Wilde care?—He knew that he had succeeded in creating a storm of discussion, and nothing else really mattered. Certainly, he was quite indifferent as to what people said so long as they talked about him and he was the center of public attention.

The very notoriety which *Mr. W. H.* had given Oscar encouraged his self-assurance, and in this frame of mind he published only a year later, in *Lippincott's Magazine* (July, 1890), *The Picture of Dorian Gray.* However beautiful, the novel never was, and never will be, treated as a classic work of English fiction, if for no other reason than because the theme of love and the element of conventional romance are absent from the provocative story.

Particularly on British soil, Wilde could attain no appreciable measure of moral prestige; deliberately and with youthful fanfaronade he challenged tradition, that holy of holies of England, which, more than any other country, is attached to the rites and rituals of its past. The secret of the astounding popularity of Dickens lay in that his genius, philosophy, feelings, tastes, manners, even his prejudices, were in perfect accord with those of England herself. Notwithstanding his "revolt" or rather reformist passion, Dickens, even like Lord Henry in Wilde's novel, could have said about himself: "I don't desire to change anything in England, except the weather." The characters which he had created—the Pickwicks and Pecksniffs, the Copperfields and Twists—all were unhesitatingly recognised by the Victorians as an integral part of themselves, of their national life. But Wilde started by proclaiming himself an iconoclast and intellectual rebel. To him, the firmly established and highly treasured modes of England's daily routine were unbearable, and he went to great lengths so to inform his readers.

Undoubtedly, in that attitude, as in his earlier æsthetic pose, there was a good deal of cynical exhibitionism and calculated ostentation, which, to his compatriots, was all the more irritating. They were utterly unable to understand, and still less to forgive, any normal person for wishing to be different from them; and inasmuch as they were profoundly satisfied with themselves, with their bigoted morality and middle-class comfort, they bitterly resented the unceremonious manner in which our poet told them that he neither admired nor even respected their ideals. It must be also remembered that the Victorians of Wilde's epoch, perhaps more than the Elizabethans, were thoroughly convinced of their superiority to the rest of mankind, and in relation to the non-English they maintained an attitude of polite contempt like that of the Dutch skipper in Multatuli's anecdote who, while watching a foreign girl performing stunts in the water, remarked, "Of course, all those foreigners can swim. They've got to wash continually because they are so dirty."

Not content with being a British subject, Oscar strove to become a citizen of the world. But to the Anglo-Saxon, the cosmopolitan mind is, and always has been, an enigma full of most mischievous potentialities, an amoral phenomenon mortifying by reason of its heterodoxy from his own parochial standards.

Among other things that, imprudently perhaps, Wilde dared to touch upon in *Dorian Gray* was the subject of sex, which, in the Victorian age, was considered a mortal sin. While on the Continent, especially in Germany and France, perversions of every kind, for decades, have been freely pictured and discussed in fiction—suffice it to mention Gautier's *Mademoiselle de Maupin,* Linkeus' *The Mother,* Balzac's *La Fille aux Yeux d'Or,* Wedekind's *The Awakening of Spring* and Dostoievsky's *Brothers Karamazov*—public opinion in England even in our day vigorously suppresses the theme of uranism and kindred manifestations of sexual morbidity.

No one viewing Wilde's novel objectively can really call it immoral. Indeed, only a narrow man like Edward Carson, defence attorney for the Marquis of Queensberry, could have perceived anything æsthetically, or even ethically, "improper" in the scene of the meeting between Dorian and Basil Hallward, the artist. When the learned counsel triumphantly read into the record several passages from a dialogue in the ninth chapter where Basil describes his admiration for "Prince Charming," his model, he must have been earnestly convinced that he had scored a great legal point. But, today, one is almost inclined to disbelieve that arguments such as these could have had any probative weight or evidential force in a civilised court of justice. These are the lines which particularly incensed Carson:

> Dorian, from the moment I met you, your personality had the most extraordinary influence over me. I was dominated, soul, brain and power, by you. You became to me the visible incarnation of that unseen ideal whose memory haunts us artists like an exquisite dream. I worshipped you. I grew jealous of every one to whom you spoke. I wanted to have you all to myself. I was only happy when I was with you. When you were away from me, you were still present in my art. Of course, I never let you know anything about this. It would have been impossible. You would not have understood it. I hardly understood it myself. I only knew that I had seen perfection face to face, and that the world had become wonderful to my eyes—too wonderful perhaps, for in such mad worships there is peril, the peril of losing them; no less than the peril of keeping them. . . .

Far from containing anything of a pornographic nature, Basil's "confession" merely reveals the passionate longing of a Pygmalion for the still beauty of form. But then, to a pathologically virtuous mid-Victorian of the Carson type, the ancient legend of Galatea probably seemed to have been inspired by some dreadful necrophilic aberration.

There were of course other reasons why *Dorian Gray* set those honest English philistines in revolt against its author. Above all, there was that natural aversion of hypocrites to him who tears the masks off their faces. The English were aware of the fact that London, like any other great metropolis, was full of vice, but they would not permit any one, least so a prominent writer, to admit that condition in a public utterance. When Oscar started describing the red-light districts of London, their loathsome dens and crude violence of disordered life; when he divulged the shameful secret of a civilisation that breeds wretched misery and ghastly evil side by side with fabulous wealth and the pretentious dignity of the pulpit, he at once infringed upon the most sacred convention of English pietism. And it was not so much *what* he had told, as *how* he told it, that drove his countrymen into a state of rage.

Breaking all commandments of Ruskinian æsthetics, Wilde, with obvious intent to *épater le bourgeois,* proclaimed amorality as the *sine qua non* of all true art. He went further and declared that "all Art is immoral." The very insolence with which he remarked: "I never take any notice of what common people say, and I never interfere with what charming people do" was insulting to those hypocritical men and women whose whole lives were spent in listening to and propagating gossip, and whose meddling with other people's morals was conceived as the loftiest means of practising Christian morality.

Though there was nothing, from the point of view of Victorian society, intrinsically wrong about depicting sin in a novel, the way Wilde did it, his evident interest in the course of unnatural iniquity, his whole approach to the sinner—all this was something the English would not tolerate. They would have been quite ready, if not actually pleased, to peep with a sort of peccant curiosity into the ill-doings of the hero; clandestinely, deep in their hearts, they might even have savoured the spicy flavour of crime, on condition, however, that the author sound a note of unequivocal disapproval of all the bad things he ventured to recount in his story, and it goes without saying that, with the fall of the curtain, vice should be punished and virtue made triumphant. But there was Wilde, with his charming and mirthful smile, initiating his audience in a perfectly nonchalant manner into the strange fascination of "beautiful sins," which, he said, like beautiful things, were "the privilege of the rich!"

In fact, the whole book was a challenge to the Victorian golden mean, and so it was received by the public. In some quarters, it was even insinuated that the story should be "coerced and suppressed by a Tory Government" in the interest of morality. Oscar could easily have shown that the teachings of his book violated no precepts of decency and no rules of literary decorum. He might also have set forth the argument that the harsh but just law of retribution was fully vindicated by the tragic death of his hero. Instead, the poet defended himself by merely stating that art and ethics have nothing in common and that vice and virtue are to the artist merely materials for his creative speculations.

The very tone, haughty and disparaging, of Wilde's rebuttals to the campaign of slander engineered by the English press added fuel to the fire. For instance, in answer to a charge which was made by *The St. James's Gazette* that the novel was nothing but a means of self-advertising, he wrote:

> I think I may say without vanity—though I do not wish to appear to run vanity down—that of all men in England, I am the one who requires least advertisement. I am tired to death of being advertised. I feel no thrill when I see my name in a paper. The chronicler does not interest me any more. I wrote this book entirely for my own pleasure and it gave me very great pleasure to write it. Whether it becomes popular or not is a matter of absolute indifference to me. I am afraid, sir, that the real advertisement is your cleverly written articles. The English public, as a mass, takes no interest in a work of art until it is told that the work in question is immoral. . . .

And in one of the subsequent letters to the same newspaper,

Wilde, referring to the relation between ethics and art, declared:

> It is this Puritanism to which your critic has given expression that is always marring the artistic instinct of the English. So far from encouraging it, you should set yourself against it, and should try to teach your critics to recognise the essential difference between Art and Life. . . . To Art belong all things that are, and all things that are not, and even the editor of a London paper has no right to restrain the freedom of Art in the selection of subject-matter. . . . In conclusion, sir, let me ask you not to force on me this continued correspondence by daily attacks. It is a trouble and a nuisance. As you assailed me first, I have a right to the last word. Let that last word be the present letter, and leave my book, I beg you, to the immortality it deserves.

When the hundred-mouthed goddess began whispering about Wilde's suspicious friendship for a handsome lad by the name of John *Gray,* she disseminated at once the idle rumour that he was the real hero of the novel. In refutation of this calumny it would have been enough for the poet to point out that *Dorian Gray* had been written and printed *before* he had ever met his eponymous friend. Wilde did nothing of the kind. On the contrary, braving public opinion, he alluded to John Gray, often half-seriously, as his "Dorian" or his "Prince Charming."

Promptly after the publication of the novel, *Punch* attacked the story by labelling it as Wilde's "Wildest and Oscarest work" —"poisonous!—Yes!" and tainted with "loathly leprous distilment," a characterisation which must have filled the heart of every Mrs. Grundy in the United Kingdom with pious indignation. *To-Day,* a middle-class paper edited by Jerome Jerome, hastened to declare the novel "corrupt"; a critic in *The Scots Observer,* hiding his identity under the pseudonym "Thersites," stated that *Dorian* was fit only "for the Criminal Investigation Department," and suggested that if Wilde could write for none but "outlawed noblemen and perverted telegraph-boys," the sooner he took up "tailoring (or some other decent trade)" the better it would be "for his own reputation and the public morals." In full accord with these reviews,

The Daily Chronicle, whose editorial opinions were regarded as a sort of last word by the liberal bourgeoisie of those days, pronounced the verdict "guilty" and described the story "as a tale spawned from the leprous literature of the French *décadents*—a poisoned book, the atmosphere of which is heavy with mephitic odours of moral and spiritual putrefaction." So that when the academic archons of *The Athenæum* denounced *The Picture* as "unmanly, sickening, vicious (though not exactly what is called 'improper'), and tedious," they were simply echoing an opinion which was more or less general amongst the poet's contemporaries.

Strictly considered, *Dorian Gray* is not a novel at all, for lack of inner cohesion and a carefully conceived plan. It may also be argued that for a work of pure fiction it contains too much of that didacticism which more properly belongs to an essay than to a *roman psychologique*. But all the same, it is an outstanding piece of imaginative literature.

No doubt, the plot was suggested not only by Balzac's *Peau de Chagrin* and Huysmans' *A Rebours,* but also, in a measure at least, by Poe's *The Oval Portrait* and *William Wilson*. However, the true genesis of *Dorian Gray* was revealed by Mr. Basil Ward, the artist, in his preface to one of the later editions of the novel in book form. From this source we learn that, in the year 1884, Oscar frequently visited Mr. Ward's studio, and it so happened that one of his sitters at the time was a young man of such unusual beauty that his friends had nicknamed him "The Radiant Youth."

> Each afternoon Wilde watched the work advance, enchanting everybody meanwhile with brilliant talk, until at last the portrait was finished and its original had gone his way. "What a pity, sighed Wilde, that such a glorious creature should ever grow old."—"Yes, it is indeed, answered Mr. Ward, how delightful it would be if 'Dorian' could remain exactly as he is, while the portrait aged and withered in his stead. I wish it might be so!"

In this anecdote, we find the kernel of the intrigue of Oscar's sensational novel which, in R. Thurston Hopkins' opinion, "stands on a pinnacle peculiar to itself and unapproachable." Incidentally, it might be noted that the name of one of the three principal characters in Wilde's story is *Basil* Hall-*Ward* who painted the picture of Dorian—"the radiant youth."

There is hardly anything essentially new in the theme of a double life such as young Gray leads after his soul has been deflowered by Lord Henry's cynical philosophy; yet there is an exquisite cunningness in the handling of this medico-legal subject, which is adroitly interwoven with supernatural incidents somewhat after Poe's fashion. Besides, Wilde has given here, as he did later in his comedies, a fine example of his unique mastery of dialogue, full of movement, provocative wit and epigrammatic surprise. Altogether, the style of the novel is admirable, while some of its passages, like the one describing Basil's studio in the opening chapter; or the scene of Dorian's chat with Lady Henry in the little library at her house in Mayfair—should be included in every anthology of English prose. As to the aphorisms scattered through the pages of the novel, many of which reappear in Wilde's comedies, they are, in Ingleby's estimation, "as biting as a *Saturday Review* article, in the old days." Indeed, *Dorian Gray* abounds in such pithy remarks as "she is still *décollettée,* and when she is in a very smart gown she looks like an *édition de luxe* of a bad French novel"; or the one referring to the same frail dame, "when her third husband died, her hair turned quite golden from grief." All these are typical *Oscariana*—light and superficial, effervescent and inimitable, as Oscar himself was. Even the flaws tarnishing the book are conspicuously Wilde's own. He had, as stated, a natural *penchant* for ornamentalism, or that wasteful excess which tempts artists of Oscar's type "to gild refined gold." There is, for instance, a prodigality of detail in the endless list of embroideries and tapestries, those "crocus-coloured robes of Athena," Nero's huge velariums, and the curious table napkins "wrought for the Priest of the Sun" which, the poet tells us, "performed the office of frescoes in the chill rooms of the Northern nations." Why should it have been necessary to crowd into the frame of a story monotonous allusions to all those heavy woven textiles and kindred requisites of theatrical decoration? And yet Oscar faithfully, word for word, copied them into the *Picture* from his own review of Lefebure's *History of Embroidery and Lace.*

The same tendency is manifest in the catalogue of the precious stones in Dorian's collection.

> He [Dorian] would often spend a whole day settling and resettling in their cases the various stones that he had collected, such as the olive-green *chrysoberyl* that turns red by lamp-light, the *cymophane* with its wire-like line of silver, the pistachio-coloured *peridot,* the rose-pink and wine-yellow *topazes, carbuncles* of fiery scarlet with tremulous four-rayed stars, flame-red *cinnamon*-stones, orange and violet *spinels,* and *amethysts* with the alternate layers of *ruby* and *sapphire.* He loved the red-gold of the *sunstone,* and the *moonstone's* pearly whiteness, and the broken rainbow of the milky *opal.* He procured from Amsterdam three *emeralds* of extraordinary size . . . and had a *turquoise de la vieille roche* that was the envy of all the connoisseurs.

What a riot of colours, what a profusion of mineralogical nomenclature! Still, this was Wilde's trusted method of delineation, his peculiar genre, to which he resorted with equal delight in *The Birthday of The Infanta,* when he meditates upon the flowers in the dreamy gardens of the Royal Palace, and in *Salomé,* where he describes the priceless treasures of the Tetrarch of Judæa, and in *La Sainte Courtisane,* when she seeks to lure Honorius into the net of her feminine charms by depicting to him the amazing opulence of her chamber.

As a study of dual personality, the character of Dorian has considerable psychiatric interest; his is a classic case of split consciousness, as in Stevenson's adventurous story about Doctor Jekyll and Mr. Hyde, the two embodying in their conjunction one man in whom "the law of his members" is in a state of constant war with "the law of his mind." Only, the Jekyll, or "would do good," phase in Wilde's hero is almost non-existent. Lord Henry–that sneering and jeering Mephistopheles–having imparted to his disciple all the commandments of the religion of amorality, assumed over him a peculiar, verily hypnotic, control which caused an utter disintegration of Dorian's volitional mechanisms. He was fully aware of that perplexing subjugation to his friend.

I wish now, he exclaimed once, I had not told you about Sybil Vane.

You could not have helped telling me, Dorian. All through your life you will tell me everything you do.

Yes, Harry, I believe that is true. *I cannot help telling you things. You have a curious influence over me. If I ever did a crime, I would come and confess it to you. You would understand me.*

And before committing suicide, he comes close to confessing his murder to Lord Henry.

Thus, Dorian's behaviour reminds one of the obscure states of, so-called, post-epileptic automatism when all sorts of acts, even most violent crimes, are performed under the sway of some mysterious compulsion.

In substance, then, the psychic drama of Dorian is not predicated upon any inner conflict of two polar emotions, as in Goethe's Faust—"*Zwei Seelen leben—ach! in meiner Brust*"; or as in the much-discussed case of a talented but mentally deranged Russian novelist, Gleb Ivánovich Ouspensky, who, in his delirious paroxysms, imagined that the righteous "Gleb" was being tortured by his vicious demon "Ivánovich." The malady of Wilde's London Ganymede is that of a person whose "Gleb" has been totally annihilated, leaving "Ivánovich" free to drag his victim down the crooked path of man's ghastly underworld.

CHAPTER XXIV

OSCAR'S INTENTIONS

NO SOONER had the turmoil caused by Mr. Dorian Gray died down when Wilde once more stirred English literary circles. This time, however, he was brought into the limelight of public opinion not by a work of fiction, but by a group of essays which he had gathered together under the title of *Intentions.* Three of these brilliant sketches, *The Decay of Lying, The Critic as Artist* and *The Truth of Masks,* originally appeared in *The Nineteenth Century,* whilst *Pen, Pencil and Poison* was reprinted from *The Fortnightly Review.*[1]

Notwithstanding all the ethical objections on the part of English Philistia to *Dorian Gray,* that novel created for Wilde a literary reputation which heretofore he did not have; from now on, though still masquerading as a philosopher of paradoxes, he came to be regarded as a master of scholarly prose and a writer of provocative fiction. Hesitatingly, perhaps, the public began to realise that he could no longer be treated merely as a producer of amusing trifles.

Intentions was taken seriously even in those quarters where people were still inclined to treat Wilde as a joke, and all in all, it brought him a step closer to the gate of fame.

Of course, the frivolous style in which the essays are written —those cadenced sentences, delicately touched with affectation; the astute allusions to the ancient gods, legends and myths; the well-turned maxims which add a peculiar spice to the dialogue—all this was somewhat irritating to the arid intellects of the stiff English middle class. Voicing their unresponsive mood, *Athenæum* harshly condemned the book and accused Wilde of having deliberately resorted to tricks "of the smart advertiser in order to attract attention to his wares." The thing that aroused the greatest indignation of that ossified journal was Wilde's literary manner at once "tiresome," "ridiculous" and "mechanical."

> The form of language [we read there] in which he chooses to conceal his thoughts is easily described. His method is this: he takes some well established truth, something in which the wisdom of centuries and the wit of the greatest men have concurred, and asserts the contrary; then he whittles his assertion down, and when at his best arrives at the point which might have been reached by starting at the other end.

However, cultured men of letters—among others Richard Le Gallienne—sensed in these sketches something of a prelude to Wilde's overwhelming success.

The usually reserved and skeptical *Speaker* gave *Intentions* a most favourable write-up:

> A book like this with its curious convolutions of sentiment, its intricacies of mood and manner, its masquerade of disguises, cannot possibly receive adequate notice in the space of a brief review. Mr. Wilde is always suggestive; he is interesting even when he is provoking. At his best . . . when he is most himself—an artist in epigram—he can be admirable even when his eloquence reminds us of the eloquent writing of others. He is conscious of the charm of graceful echoes, and is always original in his quotations . . . over and over again he proves to us the truth of masks. . . .

In America, too, the essays were received with a great deal of enthusiasm, arousing public interest in Wilde's picturesque personality. As an instance, these significant lines may be quoted from an article in *The Photographic American Review:*

> We owe more to Oscar Wilde than any laudation can ever repay. . . . He is one of the cleverest men who ever touched our shores. . . . We have not, as a nation, come to the recognition of the value of this man to us. The paltry dollars he heaped into his pockets . . . were of no comparison in value with the impulse he gave us toward beauty, form, combination of colour, elevation of ideal, the sharpening of the critical faculty, the refining of personal taste, the opening up of new

views in decoration. . . . And now, after poems and novels, he again, in clever satire, in the reversal of ideas, in the charm of literary style which is fascinating to the cultivated, presents new thoughts in new ways in the volume just issued.

In this critical *ensemble* Wilde gave an exhaustive exposé of his æsthetical views. Essentially, they did not differ from those set forth in his Chickering Hall lecture on the English Renaissance, and in the *Envoi.* In *Intentions* there is a bit of everything: the subtle spirit of the Renaissance which Pater so delicately divined in the creations of Leonardo, and those of the school of Giorgione; that fresh aroma which, like a gentle breeze, blows from every page of Ruskin's hymns to Beauty and Truth; the same intense thirst for wresting the secrets of style which Winckelmann evinced in his studies of Greek coins and marbles and gems; the same romanticism that gave birth to the odes and sonnets of Keats; and also, that same pagan agnosticism which inspired Renan to compose his famous *Prière sur l'Acropole,* when he kneeled down before the marble Goddess of Beauty and worshippingly murmured:

The gods pass just as men do, and it would not be good if they were eternal. The faith in them, which one had, should never become a chain. One is freed from it when it has been reverently rolled into the purple shroud in which the dead gods slumber.[2]

In these ingenious essays, Wilde reveals his fundamental characteristic of "an artist in attitudes" to whom "a truth in art is that whose contradictory is also true." He dwells with equal freedom, eloquence, humour and delight on Plato and Browning, Turner and Florentine majolica, Shakespeare and Japanese painting—mingling all those wonderful subjects, schools, theories, ideas and aspirations which, he felt, somehow belong to the same age, to one and the same kingdom over which Beauty reigns supreme.

As Richard Le Gallienne said in his review for *The Academy,*[3] "Mr. Wilde's delight in words for their own sake is quite Rabelaisian. He loves to speak them in heaps, like a child bathing its hands in rich, many-coloured beads."

Undeniably, the most important portion of *Intentions* is the one dedicated to *The Critic as Artist*. On the Continent, criticism has always been acknowledged as a legitimate form of literary expression. In France, for instance, or in Russia, it would have been unthinkable to question the rôle of a Sainte-Beuve or a Bielinsky in the building of the artistic traditions and æsthetic beliefs from which subsequent generations borrowed their own ideals, their enlarged and enriched conceptions of style, harmony and form.

Not so in England. The reading public there has never taken much heed of what this or that critic said about a book of poems or some work of creative inspiration. Who knows but what Macaulay may have been partly responsible for this disregard of critique as an independent department of belles-lettres, since he earnestly, though quite erroneously, maintained that the critical and poetic faculties are not only distinct, but almost incompatible. Hence, art criticism of any kind necessarily loses its *raison d'être*. In his excellent *Essays on Art*, Mr. Clutton-Brock very justly observed:

> The only kind of critic taken seriously in England is the art critic; and he is taken seriously as an expert, that is to say, as one who will tell us not what he has found in a work of art, but who produced it. No one wants to know whether a certain picture is good or bad. The question is: Was it painted by Romney?

Which means that, in the estimation of the English, the judgment of the critic has always been valued not for the soundness of his æsthetic opinions, but as a matter of business with which not the spectator or reader, but the shopkeeper and professional art dealer, are primarily concerned.

Some while ago, *The Times* printed an article by Sir Thomas Jackson, where he said that if people would only rely upon their own judgment, the profession of art critic would be brought to an end. And he even recklessly suggested:

> Were all art criticism made *penal* for ten years, lovers of art would learn to think for themselves and a truer appreciation of art than the

commercial one would result, with the greatest benefit both to art and to artists.

Now, this humbug is an offshoot of England's customary misunderstanding of the true function of art criticism. The English still stubbornly cling to the obsolete and time-worn aphorism, *"la critique est aisée–l'art est difficile"*; they continue to suspect in every critic the symptoms of that malady which Mr. E. W. Cook has defined as "the itch of phrase-making," and they simply refuse to give thought to the fact that the critic, like any other artist, should be judged by the thing he has produced and the manner in which he was able to express himself.

Men of Sir Thomas' mentality have often advanced the argument that the critic's appreciation of art can be of no import whatever, since he is not an artist. But if there were any truth in this assertion, one might as well contend that art itself is of no value to any one except the artist, and to him only who happens to practice the same kind of craft, so that sculpture would be of no concern to any one but sculptors, or painting to any one but painters, and so forth.

Wilde's position in the matter was simply this: he was convinced that it is neither necessary nor wise to draw a line of demarcation between the artist and the critic, and also, that art and criticism must stand or fall together. That an artist of necessity must be a critic is commonplace, for the creative process is pre-eminently one of æsthetic selection and critical evaluation–selection of the theme which the master intends to use in some future creation, and an evaluation of both the means and techniques required for the realisation of his ideal.

But to what extent can the critic be conceived of as an artist? –To this Wilde answers:

> It [criticism] works with materials, and puts them into a form that is at once new and delightful. What more can one say of poetry? Indeed, I would call criticism a creation within a creation. For just as great artists, from Homer and Æschylus down to Shakespeare and Keats, did not go directly to life for their subject-matter, but sought

for it in myth and legend and ancient tale, so the critic deals with materials that others, as it were, purified for him and to which imaginative form and colour have been already added. Nay, more, I would say that the highest Criticism, being the purest form of personal expression, is in its way more creative than creation . . . and is, in fact, its own reason for existing, and as the Greeks would put it, in itself, and to itself, an end.

In this sense, criticism is essentially an imaginative act, a mental operation which does not confine itself to the weary speculations of dry scholasticism, but one that creates altogether new values, æsthetical experiences and sensations which did not exist before. Thus conceived, criticism of art becomes an art of criticism.

When [says Wilde] Rubinstein plays to us the *Sonata Appassionata* . . . he gives us not merely Beethoven, but also himself. . . . Beethoven reinterpreted through a rich artistic nature, and made vivid and wonderful to us by a new and intense personality.

And just as Gautier has told us that painting is not an art of imitation or copying external things, but rather a delicate gift of representing on canvas the picture which the painter carries in himself and which he translates into the tongue of colours, peculiarly his own, so Wilde insists that a critic should be guided in his work by those creative urges—"*ce trouble et cette inquiétude sublimes*"[4]—which in a real artist give birth to the foreknowledge of the beautiful, and the intense longing for the exquisite and unique.

The true critic, then, far from being a person who "thinks by proxy and talks by rote," should be endowed with a rich temperament susceptible to Beauty in its variegated manifestations. This faculty, though it be innate, must be studiously cultivated by some form of refined environment. In support of this view Wilde cites Plato, who invariably stressed the necessity of bringing up Greek lads in the midst of fair sights and melodious sounds, "so that the beauty of material things may prepare their souls for the reception of the Beauty that is spiritual." It is only by means of this purified instinct that criticism may attain its creative level, a sort of Ariadne thread through the maze of scattered ideas and disconnected facts in one way or other related to the universal phenomenon of Art. It is also the inspired critic, and he alone, who can unerringly divine the distinction between gold and gilt, between genuine Beauty and its countless falsifications.

Such, briefly, is Wilde's interpretation of the part criticism is called to perform in the domain of creative achievement. He gave the modern critics "a new creed and a new charter," which, as Ransome says, made them free

> to do all they have ever attempted, to track the secret stream of inspiration to its source, to work out alike the melody and counterpoint of art, to discover its principles, to enjoy its examples, to paint portraits, to talk with their sitters, to enounce ideas, to catch the fleeting sunlight and shadow of impression.

Today, unconsciously perhaps, critics in all lands are learning their craft from those rules and canons which Wilde has so cleverly framed in his æsthetic code.

If, from a literary angle, *The Critic as Artist* is the best and most suggestive essay in *Intentions,* undeniably the most curious from a biographical point of view is *Pen, Pencil and Poison.* This psychological memoir, or "study in green" as Wilde somewhat pretentiously named it, is dedicated to Thomas Griffith Wainewright, "not merely a poet and a painter, but also a forger of no mean . . . capabilities, and . . . a secret poisoner almost without rival in this or any age."[5] Certainly, Wilde was fully justified in his assertion that "the fact of a man being a poisoner is nothing against his prose," and it is neither surprising nor wrong, that he should have chosen for the subject of his essay a character essentially vicious, though quite susceptible at once to the beauty of art and to the art of beauty. The thing, however, which strikes one in this charming account is the intellectual affinity between Wainewright and Wilde himself—almost a family likeness, revealing in the latter the same morbid taste for sin that drove the former into the abyss of moral insanity. The parallelism of the manifest leanings and concealed longings in both men, is indeed, remarkable; they both were "amateurs of beautiful things and dilettantes of things delightful"; they were both determined adherents to that æsthetic creed which savours with equal fascination "Greek gems, and Persian carpets . . . and book-bindings, and early editions, and wide-margined proofs"; both Wainewright and Wilde conceived of Life as an art; and both "had that curious love of green, which in individuals is always a sign of subtle artistic temperament, and in nations is said to denote a laxity, if not a decadence of morals"; both took a strange interest in matters of decoration and dress; and Wainewright's library, much as Wilde's own, was filled with rare etchings, dainty bibelots and quaint bric-a-brac belonging to every age, and every conceivable school of art.

The views of Wainewright as an art critic are a faithful replica of Wilde's doctrine.

> . . . He concerned himself primarily with the complex impressions produced by a work of art. . . . He cared nothing for abstract discussions on the nature of the Beautiful, and the historical method . . . but he never lost sight of the great truth that Art's first appeal is neither to the intellect nor to the emotions, but purely to the artistic temperament, and he more than once points out that this temperament, this "taste" as he calls it, being unconsciously guided and made perfect by frequent contact with the best work, becomes in the end a form of right judgment.

In that article, as though foreboding his own fate, Oscar dwelt in some detail upon Wainewright's trial at the Old Bailey, where he was indicted for forging a certain power of attorney with intent to defraud the Bank of England. There were five charges against the prisoner, who, having pleaded guilty on two minor ones, was sentenced by the Recorder "to transportation for life."

With no veiled sympathy, Wilde described his hero's experiences at Newgate Gaol. He quoted with particular delight Wainewright's repartee to the agent of an insurance company who visited him in prison one afternoon and, thinking he would improve the occasion, pointed out that "after all, crime was a bad speculation."

> I have been determined through life [rebutted the forger] to hold the position of a gentleman. I have always done so. I do so still. It is the custom of this place that each of the inmates of a cell shall take his morning's turn of sweeping it out. I occupy a cell with a brick-layer and a sweep, but they never offer me the broom!

In Wainewright, cynicism was as deeply imbedded as in Wilde himself, and some of Wainewright's crimes, like Wilde's sins, may have been committed "for a caprice, or to quicken some hidden sense of power, or for no reason" at all. It was just that basic indifference to every form of moral restraint that led Wilde to proclaim a maxim which had become his life rule: "The only way to get rid of temptation is to yield to it." Even like his ingenious biographer, Wainewright could have said about himself: "I grew careless of the lives of others. I took pleasure where it pleased me, and passed on"; and both, having tasted of the cup of Circe, lost their "upright shape," "and downward fell into a grovelling swine."

CHAPTER XXV

GENIUS AND INSANITY

IN ONE of his essays, Charles Lamb made the optimistic yet erroneous assertion that "the great wits . . . will ever be found to be the sanest writers." That genius and insanity can well reside within one and the same bodily frame has been copiously demonstrated by Lombroso. One has only to recall the names of Schumann, Nietzsche, Baudelaire, Gogol, Maupassant, Ampère, Gounod, Carlo Dolci and Rousseau, to become convinced that most brilliant creative work in every field of human endeavour—poetry, physics, philosophy, music, painting, mathematics—can be, and actually has been, performed by hopelessly deranged minds. It was Schopenhauer, himself a victim of the *délire des grandeurs,* who wrote:

> People of genius are not only unpleasant in practical life, but weak in moral sense, and wicked.

And elsewhere:

> Genius is closer to madness than to ordinary intelligence. . . . The lives of men of genius show how often, like lunatics, they are in a state of continuous agitation.

Wilde cannot be accused of ever having had any liking for Puritan ideals or any leanings toward asceticism. Still, up to the crucial year of 1886, there was nothing in either his literary work or personal conduct that could have been correctly classified as vicious and immoral. Of course, ever since boyhood, he had been indulging in eccentricities of every kind—in dress and manner, in hobbies and style—which clearly divulged a hysterical twist in his intellectual make-up, a digression from normalcy that could not have been due to the dreadful venereal disease which, according to Sherard, Oscar had contracted in his Oxford days.[1]

If there be any foundation in the hypothesis of Hopkins that *The Sphinx* was first conceived at Magdalen, then the earliest symptoms of the pollution of Wilde's mind may be traced back to his college period. Even so, that was but a momentary flash of aberration. The manifestations of the psychosis became apparent much later when, on the one hand, he had broken off normal marital relations with his wife, while, on the other, he had been initiated by one of his closest friends into the vice of homosexuality. Coincidentally with these sad events, there developed in Wilde an abnormal interest in crime, and a perverted longing for sin, mingled with that kind of empty pride which tempted Lord Henry to seek what Flaubert called *la gloire du démoralisateur*. This sickly idea seems to have passed through three distinct stages in its growth: in *Lord Arthur Savile's Crime*[2] it assumed the form of a delightful humouresque, in which, however, the maniacal element was already graphically revealed. The next phase was marked by a more intense passion for the hazardous adventures that go with "beautiful sins" and the insidious undermining of all moral foundations. Of this precarious mental disposition, *Pen, Pencil and Poison, The Portrait of Mr. W. H.* and *Dorian Gray* bear strong evidence. Finally, in *Salomé,* with its voluptuous leitmotiv and sadistic frenzy, the structuralisation of the obsession reached its culminating point.

The same psychopathological process found its reflection in Oscar's personal conduct: in 1886, he was still Constance's faithful and kindly husband; suddenly, he turned to sodomy; his habits acquired a stigma of vulgarism; his attitude toward society became arrogant and reckless; the Wainewright philosophy, which up to that time was but a hidden complex, now invaded his consciousness; self-adoration reached the point of megalomania; all the carnal instincts, running amuck, rushed to his head; alcohol, to use Sherard's phrase, "had whipped the sleeping fiend into activity," and the whole clinical picture of Oscar Wilde in the 'nineties is one of conspicuous madness.

During the trial of his libel action against the Marquis of Queensberry, many scandalous episodes in Wilde's behaviour came to light, and in the course of the cross-examination, one after another his illicit liaisons with young men of homosexual reputation were made public. It was proved beyond doubt that Oscar had been leading a life of debauchery not only in London, but also in Paris and Cairo. Frequenting shameful dens, he associated with youths who, in no sense, could have been regarded as his equals. In a short time, he had become a victim of those depraved habits from which he was never able to rid himself.

Not only did his mind become affected by that unnatural passion, but even his physical appearance had undergone a marked change, which has been noted by most of his biographers. Comtesse de Brémont, who, after an interval of several years, met him at a dinner party early in the 'nineties, gave this interesting account:

> He was my vis-à-vis at the table. I was completely taken by surprise and somewhat embarrassed. . . . At first I thought my eyes had played me a trick, that it was not Oscar Wilde I saw, but someone with a very striking, yet unpleasant resemblance to him, someone older and more blasé than Oscar Wilde could possibly have become . . . since I had last seen him in Tite Street. . . . I could not see or feel his soul in the half-veiled gaze of those expressionless eyes under the lids that seemed heavy with the inexpressible weariness of boredom. . . . He seemed to have that sort of intellectual indigestion that comes of a surfeit of success or a surfeit of money.

Referring to the same period, another friend of Oscar's made the following observation:

> He was now utterly contemptuous of criticism and would listen to no counsel. He was gross, too. The rich food and wine seemed to ooze out of him and his manner was defiant, hard.

A similar picture of the dreadful metamorphosis was drawn by Sherard:

> I dined with him [Wilde] at Tite Street; for once there was no

pleasure, but distress rather, in the occasion. He looked bloated. His face seemed to have lost its spiritual beauty, and was oozing with material prosperity. . . . There is an American slang phrase which exactly describes the impression which he produced upon me. He seemed to be suffering from a swollen head. . . . He exuded unctuous prosperity and reminded me of a Roman emperor of the decadence, Vitellius, indeed, rather than Heliogabalus.[3]

It is only natural that a life of unbridled lust should have left upon Wilde a hideous impress like that which Dorian perceived in the once beautiful features of his own portrait. Almighty Fate turned the smile of success into a mocking grimace—ugly and repulsive as that on some of Leonardo's immortal grotesques.

The ten years that preceded the catastrophe of the trial were marked by an ever-increasing disequilibrium of Oscar's intellectual faculties, by a growing discord between his extraverted mind and his introverted will. Indeed, through all this period we see him in a state of constant inner unrest, staging that "flight into reality" which, in Freudian language, signifies a sort of wish-fulfillment where longed-for situations that have been deliberately repressed are unconsciously revived and reanimated.

Head forward, Oscar plunged into the sea of mundane pleasures, seeking "to cure the soul by means of the senses, and the senses by means of the soul." This maxim coined by Lord Henry Wotton was the medicine that Wilde started administering to himself. Not that the conception of "right" and "wrong" had been altogether effaced in him, but he simply ceased to care anything about ethics of any kind, and only the terrible prison experience made him conscious of the fact that sin always does speed on wings while repentance lingeringly limps on crutches.

In those days, two morbid impulsions—vanity and intemperance—working in sinister union, drove Wilde to his ultimate ruin. The demon of vanity urged him to turn out literary works with hysterical speed, one after another, in an almost uninterrupted succession, so that he might be talked of, advertised, gossiped about and lionised. The mere notoriety which he had acquired in the early 'eighties no longer satisfied him; now he craved for fame and thunderous applause, for glamourous triumphs and glittering success. He continued to play the rôle of one who to all intents and purposes is indifferent to other people's opinions. But, in fact, as Stuart Pratt Sherman suggested, "he dressed, posed, talked and sinned for the public, and he won the public because he kept it incessantly in a state of wonder, delight and amusement," contributing "by his vices no less than by his virtues to the precious sum of life's interests."

During these agitated years he exhibited a marvelous productivity—*The Happy Prince, Dorian Gray, Lord Savile's Crime, Intentions, The House of Pomegranates, The Soul of Man, The Sphinx, The Portrait of Mr. W. H., Salomé,* the four comedies—all these creations of unequal poetic merit, uneven craftsmanship and conflicting tendencies, like lava in a volcanic eruption, were hurled into the whirlpool of public acclaim.

With each new belletristic feat, the hue and cry around the name of Wilde grew stronger and more vociferous; and every added outburst of publicity made the condition of his hypertrophied self-assurance more menacing and drew him nearer and nearer to the tragic dénouement.

On the other hand, the demon of carnal intemperance wickedly incited him to indulge in the forbidden things which he began to practice with an insolence that was at once silly and unbearable, particularly on English soil, where vice, to be tolerated at all, has to be carefully concealed under the cloak of hypocrisy.

The seductive aromas of the flowers of evil and vice, amidst which Wilde dwelt in his reveries and dreams; the perversions and sins on which he kept pondering in his essays and fiction—exercised upon him the same effect that hashish has upon a habitual smoker.

It is likely that, in his intellectual rovings, he was constantly deceived by many a false notion about Hellenism as it had revealed itself to him in the works of those Greek philosophers and poets who have openly defended, if not actually glorified, the theory of androcentrism with its inevitable complement in the form of homosexuality. In an endeavour to justify his mania, Wilde may even have thought of Goethe—that great pagan of modern times—who said once that virile love, or what he called *"Knabenliebe,"* was as old as mankind itself. Then, again, there was a firm belief among the decadents of the eighteen nineties that all epochs of splendid artistic achievement—the golden age of Pericles in Greece, the Augustan era in Rome, the Renaissance in Italy, the reign of Louis XIII in France—have been identified with a widespread addiction to both uranism and tribadism. And thus, most probably, Wilde became convinced that sexual immorality, far from being a vulgar thing, or a repulsive psychosis, was a sign of æsthetic distinction to which every true artist should aspire.

The unwholesome fumes of all these ideas turned his head, and finally he was simply compelled to seek in physical orgasm an equivalent of his erotic phantasms.

> What the paradox was to me in the sphere of thought [Wilde said about himself] perversity became to me in the sphere of passion.

On more than one occasion George Bernard Shaw has shown prejudice toward his talented compatriot. But there is much truth in the statement that at least during this precarious period of his life Wilde seems to have said to himself: "I will love nobody; I will be utterly selfish, and I will be not merely a rascal but a monster, and yet you shall forgive me everything." When he had reached this degree of mental derangement his doom became inevitable, and in his lucid intervals he might even have surmised that, with terrific speed, he was being flung by some unknown force into a dark abyss whence there was no comeback to the gayly lit stage of life.

CHAPTER XXVI

THE KNIGHT OF SALOMÉ

AMIDST the nightmare of these sinister ideas, Wilde created his *Salomé*. He wrote it in French and brought it out in Paris at his own expense through the *Librairie de l'Art Indépendant.*

It is of no great import whether the play was really written for Sarah Bernhardt or whether, as Henri Mazel of the *Mercure de France* was inclined to believe, it was spontaneously conceived after witnessing a performance at the *Moulin Rouge,* where Wilde happened to see a Roumanian girl dance on her hands, as in the tale of Flaubert. Most probably there is a grain of truth in both versions. But whatever his point of departure may have been, it is the theme of the drama and its marvellous handling that are of prime interest to the modern reader.

Of course, it is generally known that the plot of *Salomé* is based upon St. Mark's (VI, 21–29) and St. Matthew's (XIV, 6–12) accounts of the beheading of John the Baptist. Wilde must have sensed that the Biblical story, as it was told by the two evangelists, contained great dramatic possibilities. Still, the terse and chaste scriptural phraseology, at best, could only have been taken as a mise-en-scène for the expression of that exotic vision which for some reason began to tempt Wilde's morbid mind. And so he turned to other sources, to inspiration of a different order.

No doubt, Flaubert's *L'Hérodias* was the first to attract his attention. There, the legend of *Salomé* was told in a fascinating style with a profuse abundance of picturesque detail and a keen insight into the spirit of the Asiatic Orient. This was the very thing Wilde needed for the incarnation of his own dream. In accepting this influence, our poet, with remarkable artistic tact, reminted, remoulded and reframed the material furnished to him by Flaubert; by eliminating all unnecessary accessories, he condensed the plot, intensified its dynamic *élan* and brought the climax to a swift and powerful finale.

In fact, some critics have greatly exaggerated the rôle of *L'Hérodias* as a formative factor in the creation of *Salomé*. In Flaubert's recital, the amorous theme is altogether absent; Wilde, on the contrary, makes love, or passion rather, the subject matter of the play, from which everything else is derived: the Young Syrian is bewitched by the beautiful Princess of Judæa; Herod Antipas burns with a perverse yearning for his step-daughter, and she in turn blasphemously craves for Iokanaan. From the storm of these discordant passions Wilde's tragedy is born.

L'Hérodias is a sedate narrative, perturbed by no sharp conflicts or suddenly precipitated crises. The remote past emerges from these pages not like a fiery coloured strand of life, but as a stately and silent haut-relief on the frieze of some ancient palace. On the other hand, *Salomé* is a blasting furnace of irreconcilable contrasts, impetuous collisions and perilous temptations.

Flaubert ignores the concept of the inevitable, whereas, in Wilde's treatment, blind Fate, as in Beethoven's *Fifth Symphony,* knocks ominously at the door of the human abode.

—Oh! something terrible will happen [says the Page of Herodias].

—Some misfortune may occur [echoes The Young Syrian].

—I hear in the Palace the beating of the wings of the Angel of Death [prophesies Iokanaan].

—Ah! I have slipped! I have slipped in blood! It is an ill omen— [exclaims Herod].

And foreboding the impending catastrophe, he murmurs, "Surely some terrible thing will befall." Here, inexorable Nemesis is omnipresent; she follows the steps of mortals and shatters their lives under her heavy blows.

In his *L'Hérodias,* Flaubert is a sober realist. Wilde, in his *Salomé,* is a fervent mystic: to him there is a curious accord between external phenomena and the inner world of man's soul. *Salomé* is a moon-drama. The Phœnician goddess, Astarte, the "queen of Heaven with crescent horns," appears as the symbol of Passion, leaving in her wake Folly, Destruction and Death. The *dramatis personæ* behold the Moon through the prism of their individual moods: to the young Page she seems like a dead woman rising from the tomb and seeking to cover herself with a shroud; to Salomé she is "a little silver flower," cold and chaste, full of virginal loveliness and fragrance; and Herod, whose mind is dimmed by voluptuous reveries about the Princess, compares the Moon to a mad woman who is seeking for lovers:

> She's naked too . . . the clouds are seeking to clothe her nakedness but she will not let them. She reels through the clouds like a drunken woman. . . . I am sure she's looking for lovers.

And the fate of the heroine is strangely linked to the migrations of Astarte through the sombre planes of the sky, for when, in a sadistic trance, tasting the blood of the prophet, Salomé whispers in the concluding scene: "Ah! I have kissed thy mouth, Iokanaan," a moonbeam falls suddenly on her and covers her with its dead light as though auguring the tragic moment when the soldiers will rush forward and crush beneath their shields Salomé, daughter of Herodias, Princess of Judæa.

Although Wilde preserved in his drama the Oriental frame, borrowing from Flaubert a few of his archæological data, happily, the play is free from all boring details of a *couleur locale.* Thereby, the work acquires the breadth of a profoundly human drama with its surging passion of the flesh and its disturbing quests of the spirit limited by no ethnographical boundaries and confined to no particular historical epoch. The things he depicts there are morbid and mortifying, but they are pathetic and eternal, and real despite the mysticism in which they are enveiled.

In the matter of style, the dominating influence in the execution of *Salomé* was that of Maeterlinck, whose lyrical poems, philosophical meditations, and, particularly, symbolic dramas, provoked in the late 'eighties and 'nineties live discussion amongst the European literati. Octave Mirbeau's enthusiastic review of *La Princesse Maleine* made the name of the Flemish poet famous overnight. Next came the powerful one-act drama *The Blind* (1890), which created a new era in modern dramaturgy by devising an altogether novel stage technique sometimes spoken of as "static theatre." The scenic effect in plays of this kind is achieved by a delicate delineation of the slow changes taking place in the psychic picture as reflected in a given dramatic situation. The rich and riotous hues of life are not permitted to divert one's attention from the airy watercolour sketch of the symbol "in which the visible world is no longer a reality, and the unseen world—no longer a dream." And the whole is a graceful symphony woven from musical pauses, soothing undertones, soft modulations and pensive intervals.

In 1891, Maeterlinck wrote his *Les Sept Princesses,* a drama which is quite characteristic of the ideas forming the basis of the new symbolism. Wilde, who was then conceiving the plan of his *Salomé,* must have concluded that the style and rhythmical properties of Maeterlinck's play could be admirably adapted to his Biblical drama. The thing which most appealed to Wilde's æsthetic sense in *The Seven Princesses* was its rigid verbal economy, the strange effect of those short and chiselled sentences recurring over and over again in accordance with strict contrapuntal rules, like the *dux* in a fugue. As an illustration of the syntactic principle underlying the metrical arrangement in Maeterlinck's text, the following lines from the dialogue between Marcellus and the Queen may be cited:

LA REINE

Non, non, ce ne sont pas (a) *des larmes,* mon enfant. . . . Ce n'est pas la même chose que (a) *des larmes* . . . (b) *Il n'est rien arrivé.* . . . (b) *Il n'est rien arrivé.* . . .

LE PRINCE

(c)
Ou sont mes *sept cousines?*

LA REINE

(d)
Ici, ici; attention, attention . . . n'en parlons pas trop haut; *elles*
(d)
dorment encore; il ne faut pas parler *de ceux qui dorment.* . . .

LE PRINCE

(d) (c)
Elles dorment? . . . Est-ce qu'elles vivent encore toutes *les sept?* . . .

LA REINE

(d)
Oui, oui, oui; prenez garde, prenez garde. . . . *Elles dorment ici;*
(d)
elles dorment toujours. . . .

LE PRINCE

(d)
Elles dorment toujours? . . . Quoi? quoi? quoi?—Est-ce que? . . .
(c) (c)
toutes les sept! . . . *toutes les sept!* . . .

LA REINE

Oh; oh! oh! qu'avez-vous pensé! . . . qu'avez-vous osé penser, Marcellus, Marcellus! Prenez garde![1]

The combination of the italicised words may be expressed in this formula:

a+a; b+b or 2a+2b
c+d; d+c or 1c+2d+1c
c+c; d+d or 2c+2d
d+c; c+d or 1d+2c+1d

We find an almost identical arrangement, for instance, in Wilde's dialogue between Herod and Herodias:

HÉRODE

(a)
. . . N'est-ce pas qu'il y a *du vent?*

HÉRODIAS

(a)
Mais non. Il n'y a pas *de vent.*

HÉRODE

(a) (b)
Mais si, il y a *du vent.* . . . Et *j'entends* dans l'air quelque chose
(c) (c)
comme un battement d'ailes, comme un battement d'ailes gigantesques. Ne l'entendez-vous pas?

HÉRODIAS

(b)
Je *n'entends* rien.

HÉRODE

(b)
Je *ne l'entends* plus moi-même. Mais je l'ai entendu. C'était le
(a) (b)
vent sans doute. C'est passé. Mais non, *je l'entends* encore. Ne l'enten-
(c)
dez-vous pas? C'est tout à fait *comme un battement d'ailes.*[2]

Thus, Wilde's indebtedness to Maeterlinck can hardly be doubted; but here, too, what Wilde did was not mechanical imitation, but rather artistic adaptation of a fixed metrical method to a strikingly different dramatic pattern. In his very plagiarism, our poet was always original and always true to himself.

Why did Wilde write his drama in French?—If the play was conceived for Madame Bernhardt, naturally, it had to be put into her native tongue, for her knowledge of English was rather limited. On the other hand, when the "divine Sarah" was rehearsing her part at the Palace Theatre, Wilde, in an interview, gave the following explanation:

> My idea was simply this: I have one instrument that I can command, and that is the English language. There was another instrument to which I had listened all my life, and I wanted once to touch this new instrument to see whether I could make any beautiful things out of it. . . . Of course there are modes of expression that a French man of letters would not have used, but they give a certain relief or colour to the play. A great deal of the curious effects that Maeterlinck pro-

duces comes from the fact that he, a Flamand by race, writes in an alien language. The same thing is true of Rossetti who, though he wrote in English, was essentially Latin in temperament.

It is well known that Wilde's original version was retouched by Marcel Schwob, Mr. Merrill, Retté, and, finally, by Pierre Louÿs himself, to whom the play was dedicated and who, in turn, sent to its author as a token of appreciation, a charming *sonnet-libertin.*[3]

Even though Oscar's syntax may indeed in some respects deviate from that prescribed by the wise *Académie,* nevertheless, that a non-Frenchman could have written so exquisite a drama in French is a unique feat in the history of belles-lettres. With good reason Sarah Bernhardt, upon hearing Wilde reading his *Salomé,* exclaimed:

Mais c'est héraldique; on dirait une fresque.

And then she added:

Le mot doit tomber comme une perle sur un disque de cristal; pas de mouvements rapides, des gestes stylisés.[4]

Lord Alfred Douglas was wholly justified in saying that

the French is as much Mr. Wilde's own as is the psychological motive of the play, it is perfect in scholarship, but it takes a form new in French literature. It is a daring experiment and a complete success.[5]

The moment it became known that *Salomé* was to be produced on a London stage, the censor at once leaped to the rescue of English morality by prohibiting the play. Wilde was greatly irked at this rebuke and he said to a representative of one of the dailies:

I shall publish *Salomé.* No one has the right to interfere with me, and no one shall interfere with me. The people who are injured are the actors; the art that is vilified is the art of acting. I hold that this is as fine as any other art, and to refuse it the right to treat great and noble subjects is an insult to the stage. The action of the Censorship in England is odious and ridiculous. What can be said of a body that forbids

Massenet's *Hérodiade,* Gounod's *La Reine de Saba,* Rubinstein's *Judas Maccabæus,* and allows *Divorçons*[6] to be played on any stage? The artistic treatment of moral and elevating subjects is discouraged, while a free course is given to the representation of disgusting and revolting subjects.

The thing which evidently incensed the poet more than anything else was the fact that the theatrical profession remained quite apathetic to the banishment of poor *Salomé.* Commenting on this point, he wrote to William Rothenstein:

> . . . All arts are free in England, except the actor's art; it is held by the Censor that the stage degrades and that the actors desecrate fine subjects—so the Censor prohibits not the publication of *Salomé,* but its production: yet, not one single actor has protested against this insult to the stage—not even Irving, who is always prating about the art of the actor—this shows how few actors are artists.

Burning with indignation, Wilde even threatened to renounce his English citizenship:

> If [he declared] the Censor refuses *Salomé* I shall leave England, and settle in France; where I shall take out letters of naturalization. I will not consent to call myself citizen of a country that shows such narrowness in its artistic judgment.

Thus, Oscar was quite earnest when he wrote the following letter to a member of the *Gaulois* staff in Paris:

> Sir—My resolution is deliberately taken. Since it is impossible to have a work of art performed in England, I shall transfer myself to another fatherland, of which I have long ago been enamoured. There is only one Paris, *voyez-vous,* and Paris is France. It is the abode of artists; nay, it is *la ville artiste.* I adore Paris. I also adore your language. To me there are only two languages in the world: French and Greek. Here [in London] people are essentially anti-artistic and narrow-minded. Now the ostracism of *Salomé* will give you a fair notion of what people here consider venal and indecorous.
>
> To put on the stage any person or persons connected with the Bible is impossible. On these grounds the Censorship has prohibited Saint-Saëns' *Samson et Dalila.* . . . Racine's superb tragedy of *Athalie* cannot

be performed on an English stage. Really, one hardly knows whether the measure is the more hateful or ridiculous. . . .

I am not at present an Englishman. I am an Irishman, which is by no means the same thing. . . . There is a great deal of hypocrisy in England, which you in France very justly find fault with. The typical Briton is Tartuffe seated in his shop behind the counter. There are numerous exceptions, but they only prove the rule.

Wilde's French "intentions" promptly became a live topic of London gossip. Bernard Partridge drew a clever caricature, picturing Oscar in the heavy field uniform of a *poilu* with the manuscript of *Salomé* sticking out of his knapsack. Mr. William Watson, taking advantage of the occasion, composed for *The Spectator* a brief satirical lament:

And wilt thou, Oscar, from us flee,
And must we, henceforth, wholly sever?
Shall thy laborious *jeux d'esprit*
Sadden our lives no more for ever?

The matter, after all, proved less serious than it may have appeared at the time, for Oscar did not sever diplomatic relations with the Court of St. James's and, happily for the Empire, he did not enlist in the French army. Moreover, in 1894, *Salomé* was translated into English by Douglas and was published in London by Messrs. Elkin Mathews and John Lane.[7] Considering the stiffness of the English tongue and the poverty of its chromatic resources, it must be admitted that Lord Alfred had splendidly succeeded in his difficult task.

The illustrations for the English edition were executed by Aubrey Beardsley. They are well known and need not be discussed here. This point, however, should be noted: in his art Beardsley was always a cynic; his lack of reverence and extraordinarily keen penetration into the depths of evil, coupled with a corrupt taste for sin, have become proverbial. Now, his "phallic symbolism"—to use Mr. Holbrook Jackson's term—which is conspicuously reflected in the sketches for *Salomé,* did not escape the attention of the Victorian prudes. In their indignant reception of Wilde's tone drama the "peacock skirt," the "stomach dance" and "the dancer's reward" played an important rôle, although these drawings, to which Wilde himself disparagingly referred as "naughty scribbles of a precocious schoolboy," do not in the least interpret the spirit of the play. What really happened was that the perversions of Beardsley's brush were all too readily, and in some cases intentionally, mistaken for the wickedness of Oscar's pen.

Upon its publication, *Salomé* was greeted with sharper abuse than any other of Oscar's previous works, and as Ross said, "it was consigned to the usual irrevocable oblivion." The press spared no effort to advertise its irritation, and Wilde's treatment of the Bible story was almost unanimously declared blasphemous.

In the opinion of *The London Times,* for instance, Wilde's drama was nothing but "an arrangement in blood and ferocity, morbid, bizarre, repulsive and very offensive in its adaptation of scriptural phraseology to situations the reverse of sacred."

Of course, occasionally there appeared sympathetic reviews, among which that of Henry Norman in *The Illustrated London News* should be particularly mentioned. But journalists of the conventional type told the public, with the solemnity of a Sunday-school teacher, that *Salomé* was a thoroughly bad and very wicked play, unhealthy and un-English, and that it should be condemned by all true Christians who, according to Lord Alfred's witty diagnosis, were suffering in those days "from that most appalling and wide-spread of diseases which takes the form of a morbid desire for health."

CHAPTER XXVII

OSCAR WILDE AND LORD ALFRED DOUGLAS

THE trial at the Old Bailey in April, 1895, was not the beginning, but the end, of Wilde's *débâcle*. Much as his reputation by that time may have been surrounded "by a vague fog of obscurity already sufficiently repulsive" and "covered by inventions even more dreadful," he would most probably have completed his earthly career without adding to the laurels of an artist the thorny crown of a martyr if chance had not played one of its nasty tricks on him just at the moment when he was about to score a final and perhaps unprecedented triumph.

No doubt, Oscar, early in the 'nineties, had been frequently seen in bad company, amongst male degenerates and homosexual youths. He openly entertained them in well-known London cafés, journeyed with them to beaches, gave them little souvenirs and wrote silly letters to several of them. From time to time, scandalous stories leaked out uncovering shocking details about "wilde" parties—like that which he gave on one occasion in a restaurant in Soho—which connected him with a monstrous orgy of some sort. Therefore, it is quite conceivable that he was closely watched by the authorities and that his name was listed among those twenty thousand men who, according to the official records of those days, made up the ranks of the glorious army of London pederasts. Any one familiar with Scotland Yard tactics will agree that moral offences of the kind in which Oscar was indulging are rarely prosecuted by the police. Nor has the English public ever viewed with favour court proceedings threatening the disclosure of a vice which is known to have been blossoming among the English *jeunesse dorée* during the latter half of the past century.

Even Wilde's *affichage,* his arrogant defiance of all the conventions of Victorian etiquette, would probably have led to no serious consequences if he had confined his amours to bell-boys, under-butlers and grooms. Unfortunately, however, there occurred in the life of our poet an event which proved fatal to him.

One day in the summer of 1891, Lionel Johnson, an eccentric poet, called on Lord Alfred Bruce Douglas at the house of his mother Dowager Lady Queensberry, 18 Cadogan Place, and took him to see Wilde in Tite Street. This was the first act of one of the most memorable dramas in modern literary annals.

Oscar was then thirty-six. By that time, he had grown heavy and plump. Though still fond of Constance, he was often impatient with her and she began to bore him. Much as he loved his children, the rôle of a happy father no longer amused him. Intoxicated with literary fame and the glamour of publicity, encouraged by large earnings and unable or unwilling to resist his perverse habits, he gradually drifted away from home. He used to spend long hours in fashionable clubs and modish restaurants, entertaining lavishly and leading, generally, the life of a perfect dandy amidst the envious applause of the pornographic pleiad who, in the guise of "new Hedonists," were strenuously, though quite unsuccessfully, seeking to secure for themselves a place, even if it were only a dug-out, on the English Parnassus.

Lord Alfred Douglas, son of John Sholto Douglas, eighth Marquis of Queensberry, was only twenty-one when he first met Wilde. He was then in his third year at Magdalen College. Harris described him as "girlishly pretty, with the beauty of youth, high colouring and fair skin." Appended to *The Autobiography of Lord Alfred Douglas* there are several pictures of him: at the age of five he was a most wonderful child with an angel face looking out from a frame of curling golden hair. In another photograph, he is shown in academic attire, wearing his mortarboard. He appears there as a handsome youth, though with only ordinary features.

When Douglas was twenty, he wrote a passionate and unusually fine poem, *Autumn Days,* which was printed in *The Oxford Magazine.* Referring to that early period of his, he recounts:

> My outlook in life at that time was largely sporting and convivial, though I had my intellectual and artistic side. . . . In addition to a real love of literature, and especially of poetry, I had also a passion for music. Although I had, by the time I got to Oxford, lost all belief in religion, I scarcely missed a day in attending the evening service in Magdalen Chapel. The celebrated choir which was and is, I believe, the finest in the world . . . was a lure which I could not resist.

Neglected by the Marquis ever since childhood, Lord Alfred was brought up by his mother to admire beauty, purity and truth, and he had "a natural taste for the best in everything." But the years he spent in school at Winchester turned him, as he puts it himself, into "a finished young blackguard, ripe for any kind of wickedness." Above all, he acquired the facile and superficial philosophy which teaches the gospel of self-gratification and denies the existence of any such thing as "sins of the flesh"; hence, he was thoroughly satisfied with that empty existence which, again to use his own words, was "a constant succession of amusement, sport, luxury and pleasure." No wonder he grew up with the conviction, which is concisely expressed in one of his sonnets, that he

> . . . was of the world's top, born to bask
> In its preferment where the augurs sit,
> And where the Devil's grace, to counterfeit,
> Is all the tribute that the augurs ask.

Besides, as he himself said, Winchester had completely destroyed his moral sense and "after much repugnance and resistance" he had learned "to do what everybody else did" in that school. Such, briefly, was Lord Alfred Douglas when he was introduced by Johnson to our Irish wit.

The first meeting seems to have been rather uneventful. A laconic account of it given in the *Autobiography* reads:

> We had tea in his [Wilde's] little writing-room facing the street on the ground floor, and, before I left, Oscar took me upstairs to the drawing-room and introduced me to his wife.

But apparently the youthful aristocrat produced a profound impression upon Wilde, who first of all must have been drawn by the lad's personal beauty. On the other hand, there is probably some truth in the statement of Frank Harris that

> Oscar . . . was enormously affected . . . by Lord Alfred Douglas' name and position: he was a snob as only an English artist can be a snob; he loved titular distinctions; and Douglas is one of the few great names in British history with the gilding of romance about it. No doubt Oscar talked better than his best because he was talking to Lord Alfred Douglas. To the last the mere name rolled on his tongue gave him extraordinary pleasure. Besides, the boy admired him, hung upon his lips with his soul in his eyes; showed, too, rare intelligence in his appreciation, confessed that he himself wrote verses and loved letters passionately. Could more be desired than perfection perfected?

Wilde had steadily maintained that youth is not only a blessing but perhaps the rarest of all arts, to which Nature always reveals her latest wonders. His own golden season had already waned: the wear and tear of Time had left a shadowy impress upon his once attractive features. Slowly, drop by drop, the poison of ennui was dripping into his fastidious brain, and, occasionally at least, he must have felt that nothing but a great romance, a loving contact with the springtide of life, could galvanise his senescent heart. And suddenly destiny had placed him face to face with an extraordinary specimen of the human race, fascinating and young, breathing with enthusiasm and grace, a "Hyacinthus," whose very being was a symbol of "the quick and vital pulse of joyous youth leaping and laughing," with "the frank and fearless freedom of wave and wind waking into fire life's burnt-out ashes."

What a contrast to that vulgar Cockney boy with the rosy

cheeks and his hair plastered down in a lovelock on his forehead whom Harris swears he had met once in Oscar's company at the Café Royal!

On his side, Lord Alfred was greatly flattered by the persistent attentions Wilde, the charmer and thc marvellous conversationalist, started paying to him.

> From the day I first met Oscar Wilde [says Douglas] . . . he made up to me in every possible way. He was continually asking me to dine or lunch with him and sending me letters, notes and telegrams. . . .

The affiliation with this famous man, to Douglas, must have seemed an intellectual treat which he highly treasured. In his preface to Sherard's latest book, he spoke these significant words:

> . . . I will say of him [Wilde] that even if he had never written a line of prose or poetry, he would still be the most wonderful man I ever met, and is so far beyond the ordinary "good talker" that I have never been able to discover anyone who was in the same class with him or even remotely approached it.

In those long past days, Lord Alfred's pagan mood was vastly strengthened by Oscar's ingeniously reasoned but seductive philosophy of amorality. The cynical gospel which Lord Henry, *alias* Wilde, went on eloquently preaching to Douglas must have sounded like an echo of his own inner voice, and he let himself be enticed by the whole range of deceitful ideas that form the quintessence of modern decadence. But despite the attraction which Wilde and Lord Alfred felt for each other, there was a certain difference between them, thus defined by the latter:

> . . . I was at that time a frank and natural pagan, and he was a man who believed in sin and yet deliberately committed it, thereby obtaining a doubly perverse pleasure. I was a boy and he was a blasé . . . who had immense experience of life.

A passionate friendship developed between the two men, and soon they became inseparable. With unusual courage,

Photograph reproduced through the courtesy of Robert H. Sherard

LORD ALFRED DOUGLAS AND OSCAR WILDE

(1893)

Lord Alfred himself has told the world about his relations with Wilde; he did not care to conceal the fact that these were not devoid of a sensual element.

> These familiarities [says Lord Alfred] were rare, but they did occur spasmodically. They began about nine months after I first met Oscar Wilde, as the result of a long, patient and strenuous siege on his part. They were completely discontinued about six months before the final catastrophe, and were never resumed after he came out of prison. Wilde always claimed that his love for me was ideal and spiritual. I once, after he came out of prison, in the course of a somewhat acrimonious discussion, brought up against him that this was not strictly the case, and that there had been another side to it. He said: "Oh, it was so little that, and then only by accident, essentially it was always reaching up towards the ideal, and in the end it became utterly ideal." Honestly, I believe he thought this to be true and meant what he said. In any case I am perfectly certain that his love for me, such as it really was before he went to prison, was the nearest he ever got to a pure and spiritual love.

Now, this is all that can or may appropriately be told about a matter that should never have been dragged out into the forum of public debate, and one which in no country, other than England, with the possible exception of the United States, would have been permitted to serve as a weapon for the vilification of a great poet and a man of genius.

Apparently, Constance, up to the very day of the fatal trial, entertained no suspicions as to the nature of her husband's friendship for Lord Alfred, from whom we have this specific statement:

> I was always on the best of terms with Mrs. Wilde. I liked her and she liked me. She told me, about a year after I first met her, that she liked me better than any of Oscar's other friends. She frequently came to my mother's house and was present at a dance which my mother gave during the first year of my acquaintance with her husband. After the *débâcle* I never saw her again, and I do not doubt that Ross and others succeeded in poisoning her mind against me, but up to the very last day of our acquaintance we were the best of friends.

Repeating the cheap insinuations made by Ross in a letter to André Gide of March 21, 1910, Frank Harris, in his *Life and Confessions,* has desperately sought to prove that Lord Alfred was the sole cause of Oscar's ruin. This is all rubbish, of course, since at the time Wilde himself was in a state of psychotic self-assurance, deliberately defying public opinion and exposing himself to grave accusations most of which unfortunately were true. Furthermore, it was Queensberry who, gripped by reckless frenzy, started persecuting both Lord Alfred and Oscar Wilde. To have implicated his own child in a formidable scandal was sheer insanity on the part of the old Marquis. He was surely right in objecting to this unnatural friendship, but nothing could have justified his incessant growls at Oscar and, still less, his insulting attitude toward Lord Alfred. If the real aim of Queensberry was to "save" the reputation of his son, he should have known that Lord Alfred was the last person in the world to be bullied into, or frightened off, doing anything. But courtesy and tact—alas!—were not among the virtues of that dangerous, spiteful and combative creature who, indeed, was nothing but "a mass of self-conceit." Living a notoriously immoral life, and subjecting his wife to all sorts of brutalities, the Marquis, who never took more than the very slightest and most perfunctory interest in the doings of his children—how could he have hoped that mere abuse would cow Alfred into obedience and make him turn against Wilde?

The picture of the Marquis which Douglas paints is really appalling:

> My father [he says] was a mad man, and his mania was to persecute my mother. My mother was and is an angel and a saint, who has never done a wrong thing or thought a wrong thought in her life. When my father was dying she went to him, and in a lucid interval that came to him before death he expressed his contrition, but right up to the time of his final illness, he continued to persecute her.

This was the kind of man who, driven by folly, had ventured to assume moral authority over an ambitious and self-centered youth such as Lord Alfred then was. It is amusing to note that

Queensberry himself, having once accidentally met Wilde at lunch and listened to his conversation, wrote a letter to his son saying that he wished to retract all he had said about the poet, whom he considered "a charming fellow and very clever," "perfectly all right," "besides being a man of genius and a most delightful and amusing talker." This natural gift of "conquest over strangers," which Wilde possessed in a high degree, has been recorded by a number of persons who had known him, and was also recently stressed by W. B. Maxwell in his most entertaining autobiography *Time Gathered.*

However, this was but a temporary concession on the part of the Marquis and only two months later he renewed his attacks against Oscar and this, in turn, threw Alfred into open revolt against his father. Let Douglas tell us his own story:

> One day I got another letter from my father repeating his old accusations against Wilde, and requiring me, once for all, to give an undertaking, on my word of honour, not to see him or associate with him. Failing this, my father told me that he would stop my allowance. I wrote back an angry letter, in which I said that I declined to do anything of the kind. I reminded my father of his neglect, and said that I did not consider that he had any right to interfere in my life, and I told him that if he was "mean enough" to stop my allowance he could go ahead and do it, which he promptly did. I am not justifying my conduct; I am merely relating the facts. No doubt it would have been far better for me if I had obeyed my father. On the other hand, I am entitled to say (and in this I am supported by my mother and also by my uncle, my father's now sole surviving brother, the Very Reverend Canon Lord Archibald Douglas, who is a Catholic priest) that the main responsibility for the trouble must rest with my father.

The aggressive tactics of the Marquis during the first stage of this family row and his violent temper are further graphically described in the *Autobiography:*

> He [Queensberry] had repeatedly threatened to thrash me if he found me in Wilde's company, and he went round to all the restaurants we frequented and "warned" the managers and *maîtres d'hôtel* that he intended to assault both Wilde and myself if he "caught us together"

on their premises. When I heard this I made a point of going regularly with Wilde to these very restaurants. I wrote more than once to my father and told him that on such and such a day, at such and such an hour, he would find us in such and such a restaurant, and I invited him to come round and "see what happened" to him if he started any of his "ruffianly tricks."

At last, after Lord Alfred had received from the Marquis a most insulting letter, he sent him this "celebrated telegram":

What a funny little man you are.

The kind of epistles Queensberry was then addressing to his son may be perceived from the following exhibit which was read into the record during the first trial at the Old Bailey.

You Miserable Creature,—

I received your telegram by post from Carter's, and have requested them not to forward any more, but just to tear any up, as I did yours, without reading it, directly I was aware from whom it came. You must be flush of money to waste it on such rubbish. . . . If you are my son, it is only confirming proof to me, if I needed any, how right I was to face every horror and misery I have done rather than run the risk of bringing more creatures into the world like yourself, and that was the entire and only reason of my breaking with your mother as a wife, so intensely was I dissatisfied with her as the mother of you children, and particularly yourself, whom, when quite a baby, I cried over you the bitterest tears a man ever shed, that I had brought such a creature into the world, and unwittingly had committed such a crime. If you are not my son, and in this christian country with these hypocrites 'tis a wise father who knows his own child, and no wonder on the principles they intermarry on, but to be forewarned is to be forearmed. No wonder you have fallen a prey to this horrible brute. I am only sorry for you as a human creature. You must gang your ain gait. Well, it would be rather a satisfaction to me, because the crime then is not to me. . . .

Not content with slandering his own son, the Marquis launched an extensive whispering campaign against Wilde, indulging in all sorts of venomous suggestions with regard to his character and behaviour. Naturally, the poet was fully aware of the intrigue, but there was positively nothing he could do to suppress the rumours—false and true—which were spreading all over London about his private life.

In June, 1894, Queensberry, accompanied by an unknown individual—possibly a private detective or bodyguard—called on Wilde at his house. Both men were received in the library: Oscar walked over to the fireplace, while the Marquis stood by the window. Presently, in a most arrogant tone, he said to Wilde: "Sit down," to which his host promptly replied: "I do not allow any one to talk like that to me in my house or elsewhere. I suppose you have come to apologise for the statement you made about my wife and myself in letters you wrote to your son. I should have the right to prosecute you for writing such a letter."—"The letter was privileged," rebutted Lord Queensberry, "as it was written to my own son. . . . You were both kicked out of the Savoy Hotel at a moment's notice for your disgusting conduct." The argument grew hotter and hotter. When the Marquis started threatening Wilde with physical violence, the poet lost his temper and said: "I do not know what Queensberry's rules are, but the Oscar Wilde rule is to shoot at sight." He then called a servant and gave the following order: "This is the Marquis of Queensberry, the most infamous brute in London. You are never to allow him to enter my house again."

Meanwhile, the friendship between Wilde and Douglas continued unabated. In the course of the years which elapsed between their first meeting and our poet's conviction in 1895, they saw much of each other. On several occasions, they stayed together in country places near and around London, but in every single case Mrs. Wilde accompanied her husband. It was during that period that Wilde wrote his masterful plays, *A Woman of No Importance, An Ideal Husband* and *The Importance of Being Earnest,* perhaps some of the best and most amusing comedies that have ever been written in the English tongue and produced on the English stage.

The two friends also travelled together abroad, visiting

Paris, Algiers and Florence. A few words should be said about their sojourn at Algiers, which was chosen by André Gide as a pretext for his despicable lies in *Si le Grain ne Meurt*. Mr. Sherard has ably and convincingly exposed the malicious fabrications printed in that pornographic book. The scandalous story was later repeated with rococo embellishments by H. J. Renier in his sketchy account of Oscar Wilde. In answer to a challenge by Sherard, Mr. Gide sent a post card, facsimile of which is given here below.

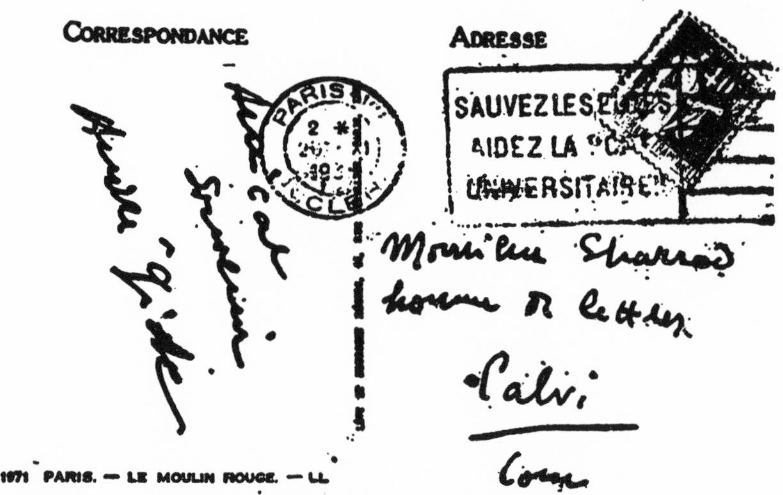

The above is a facsimile of André Gide's answer to the challenge thrown down to him in R. H. Sherard's pamphlet on the Algiers incident, in which he is accused of lying.

The "amical souvenir" addressed to "Monsieur Sherard, homme de lettres," may well be characterized as an example of classical insolence quite typical, however, of the trends in our contemporary journalistic deontology.

Gide's tale is not going to be repeated here. We might mention in passing that it refers to an alleged homosexual adventure in the Arab café near Boulevard Gambetta, in which Wilde; Gide; *"le petit musicien"* Mohammed, "celui de Bosy," (according to Gide's venomous *obiter dictum*) ; and a native darabukka player were the principal *dramatis personæ*. The whole obscene episode is conspicuously a piece of cheap sensationalism. Lord Alfred, to whose attention "the Algiers incident" had been called by Sherard, wrote this splendid letter:

35, Fourth Avenue,
Hove, Sussex.
May 25, 1933.

Dear Sherard,

André Gide's story about Oscar and myself in *Si le Grain ne Meurt* is a mass of lies and misrepresentations. When I first read the book (long after it was written) I hesitated what action to take about it, because I knew that a libel action in France would be a farce. As you know, there is nothing in France which corresponds to our own laws of libel. In England, a man who is libelled can get thousands of pounds in damages, or he can get the libeller sent to prison. In France, the libeller is condemned in the Police Correctionnelle to some paltry fine, probably 200 francs! If Gide had been an Englishman, I could have taken criminal proceedings against him and he would certainly have been sent to prison, probably for the maximum two years.

As you say, if I had gone to Paris and blown his brains out, no jury in the world (least of all a French jury) would have convicted me. But being a Catholic, it was not possible for me even to think of doing this. So on the whole, after much consideration, I decided to do nothing and to refrain from stirring up the mud or advertising Gide's filthy book.

I had several years of fighting against Ross, Harris and others, involving frightful mental strain and a ruinous expenditure, and I felt that I simply had neither the means nor the energy to start a new campaign in a foreign country. So I contented myself with writing my Autobiography and leaving the literary world to judge me by my own written words. Gide's confessions about his own disgusting conduct and the whole record of this dull, fifth-rate writer (this "egoist without an ego" as Oscar called him) whose success amongst stupid and corrupt people depends entirely on his revolting pornography, are, I believe, quite sufficient to discredit his contemptible lies about two poets.

Even if everything he said were true (instead of being a clumsy fabrication of lies founded on a small substratum of truth) he would stand convicted on his own evidence of being a despicable cad and a treacherous scoundrel who makes money by abusing the confidence of friends who trusted him. So on the whole, I prefer to leave him to the judgment of decent people, now and after my death.

Yours sincerely,
Alfred Douglas.

P.S.—I suggest that you print this letter in your book.

But Ross, who, according to Lord Alfred, had earned the enviable title of "the High Priest of all the sodomites in London," cheerfully conferred his benediction upon Gide's foul inventions, when he addressed to him these lines:

I am delighted that you have reprinted your brilliant Souvenirs of Oscar Wilde. I have told many friends, since your study appeared first in *l'Ermitage,* that it was not only the best account of Oscar Wilde at the different stages of his career, but the only true and accurate impression of him that I have ever read. . . .

Many and grave as Wilde's sins may have been, they were not half so many and not nearly so infamous as the petty scribes of the international literary *canaille* sought to make them appear. No poet, probably, has ever been libelled so maliciously and persistently, and with more impunity too, than Oscar Wilde, who remarked that one has to be careful in choosing his enemies, which, of course, is true. But he seemed to have underrated the danger of being careless in the selection of one's own friends. He was giddy-headed when it came to making social contacts and most indiscriminate in picking his confidants, and they were the first to betray him when disgrace fell upon him and when the affiliation with him could no longer serve their mercenary purposes. Men like Gide and Harris and Ross used to flatter Wilde and profess their ardent admiration for him. Yet they are the ones who have inscribed in the literary annals the vilest lies about the dead poet. Indeed, Wilde was right: "Every great man nowadays has his disciples, and it is always Judas who writes the biography."

CHAPTER XXVIII

THE TRIUMPH

WHEN in August, 1883, in Union Square, *The Nihilists* were routed not by the "brutal Czarist police," but by a peaceful crowd of theatrical "fans," who could have dreamed that Wilde would ever achieve fame as a dramatist?—Nor was there much more promise in *The Duchess of Padua,* which, despite a half-acknowledged and doubtful academic success, shared the fate of *Vera,* her plebeian predecessor; both, thoroughly forgotten, lie buried under the ashes of literary discard.

This dual experience, far from discouraging our poet, had taught him a good lesson. First of all, it made him aware of the fact that dramatic art and flimsy political didacticism are altogether incompatible. Further, he became convinced that sheer melodrama, whether in the guise of an anarchist plot, or plumed with all the paraphernalia of romantic mediævalism, will stand neither the test of criticism nor the patience of a modern audience. The fiasco of his first dramaturgic experiments also prompted him to undertake a serious study of stage technique—meaning all those natural rules and artful stratagems, jointly evolved by dramatist, actor and *régisseur,* without which dramaturgy would long since have degenerated into mere buffoonery or into a crude affair of spoken words and accompanying gestures along the lines of some vulgar Roman mime.

During the tedious years of his journalistic career Wilde had ample opportunity to explore the complex life of the theatrical organism, and some of his observations in this field proved so ingenious and so penetrating that they have since become the cornerstone of the new theatre and of the modern drama. Long before the advent of Max Reinhardt, Stanislavsky, Meyerholdt and Craig, our poet grasped the fundamental fact, now universally recognised, that a dramatic production, to be really effective, and not a mere *succès de tapisserie,* must seek to exploit every device of artistic craftsmanship, every form of creative thought. According to this revised conception, the theatre, instead of confining itself to one art only, should grow into an institution of all the arts, where literary expression and pure design and colour and melody and lighting may be brought to blend in a glorious synthesis. Some of these ideas, with particular emphasis upon the inner relation between landscape and costume, or between colour-scheme and archæology, as applied to stage-setting, were ably expounded by Wilde in *The Truth of Masks.*

His passion for classicism and his extraordinary mastery of dialogue enabled him to overcome the defects which marred the construction and mechanics of his earlier plays. With his unerring artistic instinct, he divined the hidden moods and the then yet uncrystallised trends of public taste in matters relating to the theatre and its function. He sensed the aversion of his contemporaries to the heavyweight performances of the old-fashioned playwright. Even in *Salomé,* Wilde managed to escape the traditional conventions of the ponderous stage-setting. Now, in his four comedies which followed one another in swift succession, Wilde created an inimitable genre of his own, amusing and light, epigrammatic and sparkling, full of life and delicate persiflage, mirroring English society in its Upper Ten stratum. He knew the London *beau monde,* its proscenium as well as its coulisse, and he satirised it with admirable finesse and good-natured humour, drawing his characters "with the pen of knowledge dipped in the ink of experience." He studied his milieu not as an outsider curiously peeping through the key-hole into a brilliantly crowded ballroom somewhere in Carlton House Terrace, but as a habitué who had lived all his life among those aristocratic snobs who hated to be suspected of being educated for fear it would put them "almost on a level with the commercial classes."

Ingleby guessed the secret of the instantaneous success of Wilde's comedies when he said:

> He gave us the *tone* of Society as it has never before been given. He was at home in it. . . . The company who came to his great parties were at least *vraisemblables,* beings who conducted themselves as if they really might have been there.

A great deal of capital has been made out of the contention that the style of Wilde's comedies is derived from all sorts of patterns not only belonging to different epochs, but even representing obviously heterogeneous dramaturgical tendencies. Yet, here, once more, our poet was only true to himself, to his innate eclecticism in thought and taste. No doubt, it is true that Aristophanes and Congreve, Shakespeare and Molière, Sheridan and Beaumarchais—to mention but these few—left their peculiar impress upon Wilde's scenic conceptions and schemes. But the fact itself that his inspiration is traceable to so many divergent sources shows that his indebtedness to any one of them could not be great. He may have recalled, as in that hand-bag episode in *The Importance of Being Earnest,* some dusty fragment from Menander; or he may have drawn upon Aristophanes for his cynicism; or upon Shakespeare for inner truth in some dramatic situation—for Wilde knew that pretense, though legitimate on the stage of the world, is unbearable in the world of the stage. Again, to him, there was nothing objectionable in filching from Sardou some emotional note that would suddenly, amidst the whirl of sprightly badinage and the flurry of delightful paradoxes, deeply move the audience with sympathy for some character behind the footlights; or, in "borrowing" a brilliant *bon mot* from *Love for Love.* Who can tell?—Oscar may have been guilty of all that, and yet what he did achieve was a thing pre-eminently his own with a mark of individuality that can neither be effaced nor still less duplicated. Critics' poohs over the senility of his well-tried plots and the exaggerations in their treatment are long forgotten, and Wilde, the Ibsen of modern comedy, stands universally recognised as one of the most glorious virtuosos of stagecraft.

When, on the memorable night of February 20, 1892, Sir George Alexander presented at the St. James's Theatre the première of *Lady Windermere's Fan,* the comedy, which Wilde himself described as "one of the modern drawing-room plays with pink lampshades," at once became a trump card in his hand.

The reviews were not particularly generous and, on the whole, the author was more scorned than praised. Above all, he was gravely reprimanded for his "exquisite impertinence" in coming forward at the end, pressing between his daintily gloved fingers a still burning and half-smoked cigarette, to commend his own play of which he said, "I am sure, ladies and gentlemen, you estimate its merits almost as highly as I do myself."

Mr. Clement Scott, then the dean of English critics, came out in *Players* with a protracted and acrimonious philippic, not so much against that comedy of manners as against Oscar's own manners. To this respectable journalist, the cigarette incident must have proved a severe shock. "People of birth and breeding, he exclaimed with virtuous indignation, don't do such things." And he went on with his sermon:

> It is possible he [Wilde] may have said to himself, "I will show you, and prove to you, to what an extent bad manners are not only recognised, but endorsed in this wholly free and unrestricted age. I will do on the stage of a public theatre what I should not dare to do at a mass meeting in the Park. I will uncover my head in the presence of refined women, but I refuse to put down my cigarette. The working man may put out his pipe when he spouts, but my cigarette is too 'precious' for destruction. I will show no humility, and I will stand unrebuked. I will take greater liberties with the public than any author who has ever preceded me in history. And I will retire scatheless. The society that allows boys to puff cigarette smoke in the faces of ladies in the theatre corridors will condone the originality of a smoking author on the stage." This may be the form of Mr. Oscar Wilde's curious

cynicism. He may say, "I will test this question of manners, and show that they are not nowadays recognised."

The sensational sally before the curtain was reported even in the American press, and *The Boston Transcript* rather judiciously observed that puffing a cigarette into the very face of the audience was just the thing Wilde loved to do, because it was breaking all rules of what in common parlance is called politeness, and was therefore "most unconventional."

Some of the leading London dailies, particularly *The Times,* could not resist the temptation of challenging even the purely stylistic merits of romantic *Lady Windermere.* Recalling perhaps Sainte-Beuve's phrase that *"l'écueil particulier du genre romantique, c'est le faux,"*[1] the reporter of that gazette accused Wilde of having produced a play at once unreal and insincere in which the *faux* appeared "in all its beauty."

But even some of the bitterest enemies of everything that bore the stamp of "Oscarism" were compelled to confess that the play was an extraordinary *pièce de théâtre* which carried one along from start to finish without boring for a single moment.

> It is a distinguishing note of Mr. Wilde [said *The Spectator*] that he has condescended to leave his business, and has written a workmanlike play as well as a good comedy. . . . A unique specimen in our day —as far as we know—absolutely unique—of the comedy of fine life and manners.

The critic of *The Speaker* remarked:

> If we have had more sparkling dialogue on the stage in the present generation, I have not heard it. . . . It breaks long-established laws of the theatre; makes, as M. Renan would say, a change in old customs, with light-hearted indifference. . . . The man or woman who does not chuckle with delight at the good things which abound in *Lady Windermere's Fan* should consult a physician at once: delay would be dangerous.

Utterly disregarding newspaper comment, whether favourable or adverse, all London was soon to rush to see Oscar's

Lady Windermere and his other plays. The public knew that these comedies were amusing; that they were interlaced with irresistible humour; that in those paradoxes, there was, behind the *jeu-de-mots,* a genuine *jeu-d'esprit.* And even if the average suburban playgoer "with two-pen'orth of brains" missed the subtlety of this or that amongst Wilde's mental agilities—and George Bernard Shaw in his review of *An Ideal Husband* told us that its three best epigrams would forever remain secrets between Mr. Wilde and a few chosen spirits—it mattered little. For, after all, what the public in those days craved was diversion; they were tired of their own seriousness and their everlasting fogs; they were avid for the light and charming frivolity with which that impertinent Irishman attacked every citadel of English convention, and they did not mind a bit being laughed at because, just as he was fully convinced of his superiority, these Late Victorians felt quite immune to outside criticism of any kind. Besides, Wilde had been blessed with the charm of that engaging frankness which made even his most mordant utterances sound inoffensive.

The reaction of the public to *Lady Windermere's Fan* made the critics far more tolerant if not actually enthusiastic, and the tone of their reviews eventually underwent a marked change. Oscar's second comedy, *A Woman of No Importance,* with all its irresponsible nonsense and touching pathos, was received by the press in a manner which is rarely accorded to a playwright in England. Shortly after Mr. Herbert Beerbohm Tree produced it at The Haymarket Theatre (April 19, 1893), the traditionally querulous *Times* affixed its *imprimatur* by declaring that "the play is fresh in idea and execution and is written moreover with a literary polish too rare on the English stage," while Mr. William Archer printed in *The World* a really flattering resumé of Wilde's comedy:

It is not his wit, then, and still less his knack of paradox-twisting, that makes me claim for him a place apart among living dramatists. It is the keenness of his intellect, the individuality of his point of view, the excellence of his verbal style, and above all, the genuinely dramatic quality of his inspirations. I do not hesitate to call the scene between

Lord Illingworth and Mrs. Arbuthnot at the end of the second act . . . the most virile and intelligent—yes, I mean it, the most intelligent piece of English dramatic writing of our day.

But the greatest applause was undoubtedly won by the third of Oscar's comedies, *The Importance of Being Earnest,* which was produced by Sir George Alexander on February 14, 1895, at the St. James's Theatre. Ada Leverson, who had seen Wilde on the evening of the first performance of that piece, noted in her *Memoirs* that he then appeared "at the zenith of his careless, genial career, beaming and filled with that *euphoria* that was curiously characteristic of him when he was not in actual grief or pain."

The play is neither a comedy of humours nor a comedy of manners; it is an extravaganza, a spirited pizzicato of sparkling dialogue, full of fun, with no discordant note of seriousness or melodramatic pretense; a light farce pure and simple. It is intentionally irrational, all burlesque in the treatment of both the characters and the subject.

The swiftness with which Wilde manages to capture his audience is really astounding: no sooner is the curtain raised than the hearts of the spectators begin to leap with joy. What could be more delightful in the way of an overture to this "bubble of fancy" or jocular exploit of Wilde's genius than that opening scene in Algernon's luxurious flat in Half Moon Street where the host and Lane, his manservant, are exchanging views on the grave topic of cucumber sandwiches and champagne?—First, we see Lane alone on the stage arranging tea, while the sound of a piano is heard from the adjoining room. An instant later, the music ceases, Algernon enters and then this dialogue starts the farcical ball rolling:

Algernon. Did you hear what I was playing, Lane?
Lane. I didn't think it polite to listen, sir.
Algernon. I'm sorry for that, for your sake. I don't play accurately—anyone can play accurately—but I play with wonderful expression. As far as the piano is concerned, sentiment is my forte. I keep science for Life.

Lane. Yes, sir.

Algernon. And, speaking of the science of Life, have you got the cucumber sandwiches cut for Lady Bracknell?

Lane. Yes, sir. (Hands them on a salver.)

Algernon. (Inspects them, takes two, and sits down on the sofa.) Oh! . . . by the way, Lane, I see from your book that on Thursday night, when Lord Shoreman and Mr. Worthing were dining with me, eight bottles of champagne are entered as having been consumed.

Lane. Yes, sir; eight bottles and a pint.

Algernon. Why is it that at a bachelor's establishment the servants invariably drink the champagne? I ask merely for information.

Lane. I attribute it to the superior quality of the wine, sir. I have often observed that in married households the champagne is rarely of a first-rate brand.

Algernon. Good heavens! Is marriage as demoralising as that?

Lane. I believe it *is* a very pleasant state, sir. I have had very little experience of it myself up to the present. I have only been married once. That was in consequence of a misunderstanding between myself and a young person.

Algernon. (Languidly). I don't know that I am much interested in your family life, Lane.

Lane. No, sir; it is not a very interesting subject. I never think of it myself.

And thus the ball rolls on as though chased by the velvet paw of a graceful kitten, whimsically and lightly bouncing from one scene to another, from one comic situation to the next, down to the concluding kiss, that *gros baiser* which Jack bestows upon Gwendolen—and the ensemble is an uninterrupted "Bumburying" of charmingly disarming insouciance. The atmosphere of the play is permeated with invincible hilarity where only the trivial things are treated seriously. And behind all this laugh and mirth and giggle, as a background for the airy *amusette,* is the cheerful and debonaire spirit of the dramatist himself with his conviction of "the importance of being Oscar," the applauded demigod of the comedial stage.

The Times attributed the overwhelming success of the play to the fact that "it sets a keynote of extravagance which, being taken up by the actors, is speedily communicated to the house, and the result is a harmonious whole which is not unlikely to entertain the public . . . for many months to come."

Mr. A. B. Walkley, who, under no circumstance, could have been suspected of any enthusiasm for Wilde's literary genre, commenting in *The Speaker* upon that comedy, said that the very fusion of the rational and absurd, the masterful combination of these two contrasting motifs, accounts for the continual outbursts of laughter that shake the audience. "Whatever its cause," he added, "it is to my mind the most delightful form of laughter."

Nor was the glorious fate of the play marred in the least by the silly appearance of the old sinner Queensberry at the box office on the first night with a bunch of carrots in his hand which he proposed to throw at Wilde; the Marquis having been refused admission, the whole incident came to naught.

All in all, *The Importance of Being Earnest* stands out as one of the most admirable comedies of the nineteenth century, "a superb and original piece of stage mastery," as John Drinkwater calls it. No wonder it had eighty-six consecutive performances—each a happy and unforgettable event to the London theatre-going crowds. No wonder the play was again received by the Londoners with the greatest enthusiasm when, in November, 1909, having been revived at the same theatre, it had a run to the end of September of the next year!

With all this, the most excellent among Wilde's plays is not *The Importance of Being Earnest,* but *An Ideal Husband:* it has a touch of dramatic earnestness which is not to be found in his earlier plays. The five principal characters in this last comedy—Sir Robert Chiltern, a paragon of "the seven deadly virtues"; Lord Goring, the *enfant gâté* of English aristocracy; Mrs. Cheveley, the convinced blackmailer and accomplished thief; Lady Chiltern, the ideal wife of "an ideal husband," and her daughter Mabel with that "fascinating tyranny of youth and astonishing courage of innocence"—they are all chiselled not only with a fine knowledge of stage technique, but also—and this is far more important—with a keen understanding of the human soul. There is nothing artificial, nothing of a *deus ex machina* in the sure and uninterrupted development of the plot which, it may be observed in parenthesis, was borrowed from Sardou's *Dora.* The cynical ultimatum which Mrs. Cheveley serves upon Sir Robert is but a logical outgrowth of his own shady past. This is a perfect setting for the ensuing psychological imbroglios which hold the audience in a state of unbroken tension. The third act, where Lord Goring outwits Mrs. Cheveley, in that masterful bracelet scene, brilliantly reveals Wilde's great power as a dramatist. Unlike his other plays, in which there is much flippancy and loose bavardage, here every word is significant, every sentence bears the stamp of genuine realism and is fully vindicated by the whole gamut of circumstances woven into the texture of the multifaceted intrigue.

Sir Robert's drama is that of a man who has attained success, wealth, fame, public esteem and happiness in his family life at the expense of one dishonourable act—the sale of a State secret; so long as this infamous stain remains hidden from the world, his reputation seems solid and safe, yet, in reality, it is a reputation built on sand: the threat of being found out is always there, and being there, it becomes a source of constant, though carefully concealed, inner fear which perhaps accounts for his nervous temperament and tired look. Chiltern is conscious of the fact that the most treasured of his earthly possessions—his wife's affection for him—was fraudulently exacted from her because he has never had the courage to confess to her his Suez Canal swindle. And he is also convinced that should Lady Chiltern ever discover his disgrace, her tender feeling for him would instantly turn into one of contempt, if not hatred. His whole nature revolts against the degrading offer of the adventuress which she terms "an amicable agreement," but the dread of the foulness of the public placard, the horror of losing his wife, compels him, despite his poise and pride of "an English gentleman," to yield to Mrs. Cheveley when he is suddenly struck by the truth of her pointed remark that no man is rich enough to buy back his past. Of these conflicting psychic states Wilde draws a most impressive picture.

Some of Oscar's intimate friends have observed in him something similar to Chiltern's inner agitation: Wilde, too, had shameful things to conceal from his contemporaries, and subconsciously, perhaps, he must have been dreading the approach of a cruel and terrible disaster which would expose him to public contempt and "a long farewell to all his greatness," to a fatal mischief that would shatter his career and rob him of his laurels. "I knew," he said once to Gide, whom he met in Paris after his release from Reading Gaol,—"I knew a catastrophe would come. This one or that one. I expected it. It had to end like that." On another occasion, conversing with O'Sullivan, he made this remark: "It is what we fear that happens to us." This was a feeling that must have weighed heavily upon his mind. Who knows?—It might have been the presentiment of his own impending ruin that enabled him to paint in the character of Chiltern, a strikingly vivid psychological type. Only, in Sir Robert's case, the storm clouds of a seemingly unavoidable scandal had been dispelled by the benign breeze of Wilde's creative power.

Altogether, the four plays proved an overwhelming success. Each one of them brought Wilde substantial returns, and during the early part of 1895, on the eve of the catastrophe, two of his comedies—*The Importance of Being Earnest* and *An Ideal Husband*—were simultaneously performed at St. James's and the Royal Theatre, respectively. For London this was, indeed, a rather unusual spectacle. At the same time, *An Ideal Husband* was scoring tumultuous triumphs at the Lyceum Theatre in New York.

Ah, at last the golden gate of Fame had been thrown open before Oscar, and there he stood, a proud Polycrates—

auf seines Daches Zinnen,
Er schaute mit vergnügten Sinnen
Auf das beherrschte Samos hin.

Yes, by the sorcery of his genius, which was his better self, he had at last been given a chance to dominate a hitherto resentful and uncongenial public; he had conquered—or he thought he had—an indifferent and matter-of-fact world; he made it laugh and he also made the London crowds pay dearly for the moments of hilarity which they got out of his wonderful plays. Now he was rich and all set to indulge in the luxury of a sybarite and the fastidious habits of an accomplished dandy.

Poor Oscar! Despite his instinctive apprehension, did he forebode what was coming? Did he suspect that, just as he was reaching out for the crown of glory, "Someone in Gray," as Andreev named merciless Fate, treacherously lay in wait for him, ready to strike the fatal blow that plunged him into "long years of outrage, calumny and wrong"?

CHAPTER XXIX.

A FATAL *FAUX PAS*

ON FEBRUARY 28, 1895, shortly after his return to London from Algiers, Wilde drove up in the afternoon to the Albemarle Club, of which he was a member. Sidney Wright, the hall porter, presented him there with an envelope addressed: "Oscar Wilde, Esq."; it contained a visiting card on which these words were written:

To Oscar Wilde posing as a so*m*domite.

The servant explained that on February 18th, while he was on duty, Lord Queensberry had called at the Club, and having, in his presence, jotted down the insulting sentence on the card, left the instruction that it be handed to Wilde.

Astonished at such an extraordinary breach of social etiquette, Wright considered it of sufficient importance to record the date and exact hour when the incriminating document had been left with him, and, with what Renier terms "English *savoir faire,*" he placed it in an envelope. This simple gesture of the "uniformed proletarian" might have saved the situation if Oscar, on his own part, had torn up the card, for it would have left the ill-bred Marquis at the very point whence he had started his offensive. In a state of great excitement, Wilde at once proceeded to the Hotel Avondale, Piccadilly, and from there sent Ross this prophetic S.O.S. message:

Dearest Robbie,

Since I saw you something has happened—Bosie's father has left a card at my Club with hideous words on it. I don't see anything now but a criminal prosecution—my whole life seems ruined by this man. The tower of ivory is assailed by the foul thing.—On the sand—is my life spilt. I don't know what to do. If you could come here at 11:30, please do so to-night. I mar your life by trespassing ever on your love and kindness. I have asked Bosie to come tomorrow.

Without even discussing the matter with Lord Alfred—which certainly would have been the logical thing to do—Oscar, induced by Ross, went the next morning to consult Mr. Charles Octavius Humphreys, senior partner in the solicitors' firm, C. O. Humphreys, Son and Kershaw. This was the first *faux pas* in a long series of blunders that Wilde made in his ill-fated attempt to appeal to society "for help and protection," and which he himself in *De Profundis* described as "the one disgraceful, unpardonable and to all time contemptible action" of his life.

A man of highest integrity and a most charming gentleman, Mr. Humphreys had no experience whatsoever in criminal matters; and he knew nothing about Wilde's private life nor could he have anticipated the insurmountable difficulties which a libel action of this peculiar kind would inevitably entail.

For some time, Lord Alfred Douglas had been urging Oscar to institute legal proceedings against the old Marquis. But it was always understood between the two friends that any such action would be handled by Sir George Lewis, a personal friend of Oscar's, and a man of reputed wisdom. When Douglas, upon returning to London from Biskra, learned that Wilde had chosen Humphreys as his solicitor, he exclaimed, "Why on earth didn't you go to George Lewis?" But then it was too late, because Wilde himself had already applied at the Police Court for a warrant for Queensberry's arrest on a charge of the publication of a libelous statement.

Referring to the matter of the selection of legal counsel, Lord Alfred says:

I certainly had always advised Oscar to fight my father, but I was not impervious to reason, and if old George Lewis had assured Wilde that he had no chance, and was cutting his own throat and playing into my father's hands, I would probably have been convinced; and in any case I had no power (though both Harris and his friend,

Bernard Shaw, . . . seem to assume that at the age of twenty-four I was entirely responsible for everything that Wilde did or did not do) to make Oscar Wilde disregard the advice of his solicitors.

However, in ordinary circumstances the wrong choice of an attorney would merely have placed Wilde at a certain technical disadvantage without necessarily ruining his whole future. The real calamity was brought about by Wilde himself, by his preposterous behaviour as a client: when Humphreys asked him the plain question, whether or not there was any truth in Queensberry's libel, Wilde unhesitatingly declared that there was none, upon which Humphreys remarked: "You should succeed." But if, then and there, Wilde had confessed to the learned counsel that he had not only been conspicuously *"posing,"* but steadily *acting*, as a "sodomite," Mr. Humphreys most certainly would have thrown the Marquis's card in the fire and would have told Oscar not to make a fool of himself. Many months later, in *De Profundis*, Wilde recalled with nauseous feelings his interviews with Mr. Humphreys.

> What is loathsome to me [he wrote] is the memory of interminable visits paid by me to the solicitor H——, when in the ghastly glare of a bleak room I would sit with serious face telling serious lies to a bald man till I really groaned and yawned with ennui.

Of course, it was sheer insanity on Wilde's part to have deliberately deceived his own attorney, thus leading him into a hopeless impasse. For it is almost a truism to say that it was Oscar's prime duty to lay all his cards before Mr. Humphreys, or at a later stage—before Sir Edward Clarke—who appeared as his counsel at the Old Bailey trial. Indeed, how was it possible for those lawyers to frame any opinion of the case, when they had before them an equation whose quantities were all X's?

On March 2, 1895, the case against Queensberry was opened by Mr. Humphreys at the Marlborough Street Police Court. Sir George Lewis, whose services the Marquis had meanwhile retained, appeared for the defence. Mr. Robert Milnes Newton presided.

The proceedings were strictly formal. Sidney Wright briefly told his story. Inspector Greet deposed that he had arrested the defendant at Carter's Hotel in Albemarle Street and that, when charged at the Police Station, he made no reply. At this point, Sir George intervened and, addressing the magistrate, stated:

> I do not wish this case to be adjourned without it being known that there is nothing against the honour of Lord Queensberry,

to which Mr. Newton remarked: "You mean to say that you have a perfect answer to the charge."

The case was adjourned for a week, and the Marquis was released on bail in the sum of £500, which Mr. William Tyser, a London merchant, had promptly offered.

On Saturday, March 9, the hearing at the Marlborough Street Police Court was resumed. From the time the Court opened, there was a constant stream of persons seeking admission. Many well-known people endeavoured to obtain seats on the bench, but the available space was soon taken up and refusals became general. No one was admitted till 11:30 A.M., and then there was a tremendous rush "even for standing room."

Mr. Edward H. Carson, Q. C., who now represented the Marquis of Queensberry, was the first counsel to put in an appearance, Sir George Lewis having ceased to act for the defendant. Oscar Wilde, accompanied by Lord Alfred Douglas and Lord Douglas of Hawick, sons of the Marquis, drove up in a carriage with a pair of horses.

From the very start, it became apparent that the defence had virtually no evidence against Wilde except a few letters he had written to Lord Alfred, and which had been stolen from him by a man named Allen, who thereupon handed them to a solicitor, Abrahams. This distinguished servant of Themis tried to get Wilde to buy them, under the threat that they would be made public. The poet emphatically rejected that blackmailer's offer and indignantly replied: "I hope the letters will be published."

Mr. Newton having ruled out cross-examination on the ground that it might lead to quasi-justification, which was not admissible in the lower court, the hearing proceeded without any particular excitement.

When counsel for the prosecution had closed his case, the magistrate uttered the stereotyped sentence:

> John Douglas, having heard the evidence, now is the time to make an answer to the charge. You need not say anything unless you please; but recollect that whatever you do say will be taken down in writing and may be given in evidence against you at your trial. What have you to say?

The Marquis replied:

> I have simply, your worship, to say this. I wrote that card with the intention of bringing matters to a head, having been unable to meet Mr. Wilde otherwise, and to save my son, and I abide by what I wrote.

The magistrate then ruled:

> You are committed for trial, and the same bail will be allowed you as before.

Such, in short, was the prologue to the drama which wrought disgrace and ruin upon one of England's most famous men of letters.

Now that the Marquis had pleaded justification, it became imperative for him to unearth such evidence as would prove the truth of his accusations. This was at once a difficult and a distasteful task in which Queensberry was greatly assisted by Charles Brookfield, the actor and author of *The Poet and the Puppets,* a travesty suggested by *Lady Windermere's Fan;* a private detective, Littlechild; and a whole company of professional blackmailers. At first, they seemed to have made but little headway until Littlechild happened to run into a prostitute who told him that business was very bad owing to the influence of Oscar Wilde.

> When he questioned her further [recounts Renier] she gave him an address where he could find all he wanted to know. At the address indicated the detective found a correspondence bureau where young

homosexuals collected letters, and a number of documents were discovered connecting some of these young men with Oscar Wilde. A whole chain of evidence was thus established, and it became possible to reconstruct much of that side of Wilde's life which he had thought would remain forever hidden from the world.

The address which Renier makes reference to was probably 13 Little College Street, where, at the time, Alfred Taylor was living. This is how Charles Parker, Sidney Mavor and Alfred Wood were dragged into the court room at the Old Bailey and into the subsequent proceedings against Wilde.

As the date set for the Queensberry trial drew nearer, Sir Edward Clarke, counsel for the prosecution, must have discovered that the Marquis was not only determined to push the fight to a triumphant finish, but that he had also succeeded in collecting a whole battery of facts which made his position almost impregnable.

On Friday, March 31, 1895, Wilde and Douglas had spent a whole day at Humphrey's office going over Queensberry's plea of justification which, according to Sherard (on the authority of Sir Edward Clarke), gave a full list of witnesses who were to be called for the defence, with the charges it was proposed to establish against Oscar.

Taking this statement for granted, it seems that counsel for the defence, in the light of all the sad news he had by then learned, was guilty of an unpardonable mistake in failing to put Lord Alfred in the witness-box. This would have been the one thing that might have saved Wilde, or at least gravely prejudiced, in the eyes of the jury, the reputation of the Marquis.

Here is what Lord Alfred himself wrote to Frank Harris on April 30, 1925:

> The main point was to show that his [Queensberry's] pretended solicitude for his son and his alleged desire to "save" him were nothing but a hypocritical pretense, and that his real object was to do, what in effect he succeeded in doing, ruin his son and finally break the heart of his martyred wife. I knew then, instinctively, that if I got into the witness-box I could carry a jury with me. I have proved it since over

and over again. I told Clarke that if he did not put me in the witness-box we might as well throw up the case at once. He said, "Make your mind at rest, Lord Alfred, I agree with everything you say. My idea of the way to conduct this case is to launch out at the outset with a deadly atack on Lord Queensberry for his conduct to his family, of which we have ample proof in his letters to you and to your grandfather, Mr. Alfred Montgomery, supplemented by your own evidence." I said, "Yes, but will you promise faithfully to put me in the box?" He replied, "I promise you I will; you shall go into the box immediately after my opening speech. . . ."

However, for some incomprehensible reason, Sir Edward broke his promise and did not call Lord Alfred as his witness. For this blunder no one but counsel himself could have been blamed.

On Wednesday, April 3, at the Old Bailey, before Mr. Justice Henn Collins, the trial of the Marquis of Queensberry was begun. In spite—or perhaps because—of the peculiarities of the case, and the "saucy" nature of the evidence which was to be revealed in the course of the trial, the courtroom was densely crowded, but no ladies were present.

Sir Edward Clarke, in opening the case, reiterated in detail the story of Queensberry's visiting card and went into a long and incredibly weak eulogy of his client's literary and artistic achievements. Imprudently, he made several ineffective allusions to *The Picture of Dorian Gray* and also to *Phrases and Philosophies for the Use of the Young,* a group of epigrams which, it may be recalled, was published in the December 1894 issue of *The Chameleon.* Sir Edward made no attack upon the Marquis except that, amusingly and with a touch of good-natured humour, he told the jury about the vegetable incident on the first night of *The Importance of Being Earnest,* which provoked merry laughter in the courtroom.

Nor did Sir Edward give any account of Lord Queensberry's immoral behaviour and his brutal attitude toward his wife, the mother of Lord Alfred. What a wealth of first-class incriminating material was wastefully thrown overboard by the learned counsel! How easy it would have been for him to tear from Queensberry's face the hypocritical mask of the saviour of his son! Could he not have told the jury the scandalous story of Queensberry's divorce? And why did Sir Edward keep silence on the insane persecution by the Marquis of his sons Drumlanrig, Percy and Alfred? Why did he conceal the fact that the Marquis was a rabid atheist, who had actually been ejected from the House of Lords because of his refusal to take the usual oath, which he characterised as "Christian tomfoolery"? Why was not the fact brought out that practically everybody connected by blood relationship with the Marquis wholeheartedly detested him?—This line of prosecution would immediately have put Queensberry on the defensive and it would have given Sir Edward the initiative, that prerequisite of successful strategy. Instead, he started quibbling about literary episodes which were altogether irrelevant to the cardinal issues of the case.

These anæmic tactics, from the beginning, made it psychologically difficult to call Lord Alfred to testify on Wilde's behalf. There was no foundation laid for any such testimony as a hounded and insulted son might have given against a neglectful and cruel father. Besides, Clarke's apathy left Carson free to launch a formidable offensive against Wilde, both the man and the artist.

In this historical tournament between two Oxonians and Irish gentlemen, Carson had a definite advantage over Wilde: like the latter, he was a man of high culture, an excellent scholar and a sincere admirer of the grand legacies of Athens and Rome; but, as Marjoribanks justly observed, "rarely has a classical education of the same kind produced two more contrasting types than Edward Carson and Oscar Wilde. The simplicity, the naked relevancy, the austerity behind all the best classical art and literature, had burned itself into the deep and receptive soul of the toiling student, while the child of genius was seduced by the by-paths, sickly and corrupt, which steeply decline from the heights of purity and the classical citadel." Wilde, with his artistic temperament, had no experience in practical matters. Carson, on the contrary, was all *terre à terre:* he was a "dogged politician," a remarkably clever, if not actually great, jurist, a relentless advocate and a sharp logician. His mind was thoroughly disciplined, his manners were reserved and dignified like those of a Roman patrician. He knew his court audience; he had the Queensberry case at the tip of his slim and delicately shaped fingers, and altogether he stood on firm ground.

True, Wilde possessed poetic talent which had been denied to Carson, yet, the Muse was hardly a welcome guest in the grim rooms of the Old Bailey, and the fact that Wilde was skilled in the art of "ringing sonnets" and composing rondelles made him no less vulnerable to the stings and blows of a merciless and cold-blooded "cross."

Now the two men—Wilde and Carson—stood facing each other—one, a conceited dandy, intoxicated by the glaring success of his literary achievements, bubbling over with captivating wit and biting satire; the other—a slow-moving and cautious lawyer, clad in the armour of unbending logic. They stood facing each other, ready to cross rapiers, both as confident in themselves "as is the falcon's flight." In an effort to outface the hazards of a criminal prosecution, so thoughtlessly started against the old Marquis, Wilde, that morning, appeared beaming and almost cocksure of his victory. But was he conscious of the truth, which he himself later so emphatically proclaimed, that "all trials are trials for one's life, just as all sentences are sentences of death"?

The first part of Carson's cross-examination was largely devoted to literary matters. Here Wilde was at his best: his answers were full of Attic piquancy, and the impression which he produced upon the jurors was distinctly a favourable one. Carson tried hard and unsuccessfully to implicate the witness in the story of the publication of "The Priest and the Acolyte" in *The Chameleon.* With obvious intent to create prejudice against Wilde, a long passage was recited from that filthy novelette, and counsel then asked the prosecutor if he approved of the words read into the record. "I think them disgusting, perfect twaddle"—was the answer.

Nor did Carson get very far with the *Phrases and Philosophies for the Use of the Young*. When, for instance, on having quoted Oscar's well-known epigram, "Wickedness is a myth invented by good people to account for the curious attractiveness of others," he asked him: "You think that true?"—"I rarely think that anything I write is true," was the poet's clever repartee. Again, Carson accomplished nothing by referring to Wilde's other paradoxes such as, "If one tells the truth, one is sure, sooner or later, to be found out," "The condition of perfection is idleness, the aim of perfection is youth," and the like.

These and many other sparkles of Oscar's inverted mind had been applauded over and over again by Londoners flocking in throngs to St. James's and the Haymarket to see and hear his masterly comedies, and certainly it was not for a man of Carson's caliber to destroy the fame which these witticisms had won for themselves.

The court ordeal became more threatening when the barrister began to press Wilde on the subject of the following letter which he once wrote from Torquay to Lord Alfred who was then in London, staying at the Savoy:

> My Own Boy,
>
> Your sonnet is quite lovely, and it is a marvel that those red rose-leaf lips of yours should have been no less for music of song than for madness of kisses. Your slim gilt soul walks between passion and poetry. I know Hyacinthus, whom Apollo loved so madly, was you in Greek days.
>
> Why are you alone in London, and when do you go to Salisbury? Do go there to cool your hands in the grey twilight of Gothic things, and come here whenever you like. It is a lovely place—it only lacks you; but go to Salisbury first.
>
> Always, with undying love,
>
> Yours,
>
> Oscar.

This piece of "prose poetry" was subsequently rendered into "rhymed poetry" by Pierre Louÿs, who styled himself "a poet of no importance." The sonnet appeared on the first page of one of the issues of *The Spirit Lamp*.[1] Here it is:

Hyacinthus! ô mon cœur! jeune dieu doux et blond!
Tes yeux sont la lumière de la mer! ta bouche,
Le sang rouge du soir où mon soleil se couche. . . .
Je t'aime, enfant câlin, cher aux bras d'Apollon.

Tu chantais, et ma lyre est moins douce, le long
Des rameaux suspendus que la brise effarouche,
A frémir, que ta voix à chanter, quand je touche
Tes cheveux couronnés d'acanthe et de houblon.

Mais tu pars! tu me fuis pour les Portes d'Hercule;
Va! rafraîchis tes mains dans le clair crépuscule
Des choses où descend l'âme antique. Et reviens,

Hyacinthe adoré! hyacinthe! hyacinthe!
Car je veux voir toujours dans les bois syriens
Ton beau corps étendu sur la rose et l'absinthe.

"Why," asked Carson, "should a man of your age address a boy nearly twenty years younger as 'My Own Boy'?"

—I was fond of him [answered the witness]—I have always been fond of him.

—Do you adore him?

—No, but I have always liked him. I think it is a beautiful letter. It is a poem. I was not writing an ordinary letter. You might as well cross-examine me as to whether *King Lear* or a sonnet of Shakespeare was proper.

—Apart from art, Mr. Wilde?

—I cannot answer apart from art.

—Suppose a man who was not an artist had written this letter, would you say it was a proper letter?

—A man who was not an artist could not have written that letter.

—Why?

—Because nobody but an artist could write it. He certainly could not write the language unless he were a man of letters.

—I can suggest, for the sake of your reputation, that there is nothing very wonderful in this "red rose-leaf lips of yours"?

—A great deal depends upon the way it is read.

—"Your slim gilt soul walks between passion and poetry." Is that a beautiful phrase?

—Not as you read it, Mr. Carson. You read it very badly.

—I do not profess to be an artist; and when I hear you give evidence, I am glad I am not.

This verbal duel having lasted for some time, Carson finally turned to Wilde's embarrassing liaisons with Wood and Allen, *alias* Pea, and Cliburn and Taylor, some of whom were subsequently sentenced to penal servitude for blackmail and fraud. For a pronounced æsthete and fashionable artist to have deliberately mingled with butlers and grooms was something an ordinary jury would naturally consider suspicious. In fact, what could have prompted Wilde to take Alfred Wood to supper at the Florence Restaurant and to entertain him there in a private room? Why did Oscar pay him the sum of £30? Why should Wilde have invited Edward Shelley, an obscure office boy in the publishing firm of Messrs. Elkin Mathews and John Lane, to dine with him at the Albemarle Hotel and afterwards at his Tite Street house and several London clubs? Why did Wilde give money to such infamous rascals as Allen and Cliburn?—All these vexing questions could not be brushed aside by mere paradoxes and flashy repartee. However, Wilde having steadily denied improper conduct with any of these youths, thus far no *legal* proof of his guilt had been produced.

The first day of the trial came to a close with the amusing story of Wilde's intimate acquaintance with a young lad named Alphonse Conway. Carson asked the witness if Conway was selling newspapers at the kiosk on the pier at Worthing. Wilde promptly answered: "It is the first I have heard of his connection with literature."—"Was his conversation literary?"—"On the contrary," retorted the poet, "quite simple and easily understood. He had been to school, where naturally he had not learned much."

In the course of the cross-examination it developed that

Wilde had taken Conway to Brighton and provided him with a suit of blue serge.

—And a straw hat with a band of red and blue? [interjected Carson].
—That, I think, was his unfortunate selection.
—But you paid for it?
—Yes.

In conclusion, Carson asked Wilde this rather maladroit question: "I believe you have written an article to show that Shakespeare's Sonnets were suggestive of unnatural vice?"— "On the contrary," replied Wilde, "I have written an article to show that they are not."

However, much as Wilde's performance in the witness-box on that first day may have been brilliant, his doom was predestined by the fact that everybody in London was convinced of his guilt. The moment the trial assumed the unfortunate course which, foolishly, Sir Edward had mapped out for himself—just as soon as the character of Oscar, and not that of Queensberry, became the center of the legal storm—Wilde's action was bound to collapse. Here were twelve plain and fiercely virtuous Englishmen in the jury-box listening to Wilde's love-sonnets addressed to Lord Alfred; to scandalous stories filled with homosexual allusions; to breezy hotel and beach episodes skillfully knitted together and woven into a shady picture—what must their reaction have been to all the filth that was exhibited to them with neither fig-leaf nor veil?— In the case of an ordinary creature, perhaps, the feeling of pity or compassion might have softened the hearts of these stern judges of the facts. Ah, but not in the case of Oscar, with all his fame and insolence and genius and wit; not in the case of an "arrogant coxcomb," as some people nicknamed him, who had so persistently and conspicuously shown contempt for England and her moral code, for society and its bourgeois virtues, for a firmly established social order and its secret vices. Wasn't this a unique chance to strike back at the poet whose lyre, to the commonplace Britisher, was much too disturbing; whose philosophy planted seeds of amorality in the minds of the young;

and whose reputation was mordantly mirrored in that *Green Carnation*[2] which, in those days, was fast threatening to become a "best seller."

It is idle to contend that the Grainger incident on the second day of Wilde's cross-examination decided his case.—Walter Grainger was a servant at a certain house in High Street, Oxford, where Lord Alfred and Oscar used to have rooms. In answer to Carson's question: "Did you ever kiss Grainger?"—Oscar indignantly exclaimed: "Oh, dear, no! He was a peculiarly plain boy. He was, unfortunately, extremely ugly. I pitied him for it."

Of course, this was not a particularly happy way of disposing of counsel's vulgar insinuation. But Oscar's alleged affection for Grainger was something neither better nor worse than his other amours which had been brought to light at the Old Bailey. Carson's question was indeed, pertinently insolent, and the witness did lose his temper. In fact, there was a moment when, unable to control his feelings, he began several answers almost inarticulately, finishing none of them. Nevertheless, from a legal point of view, it was utterly unimportant why Oscar did *not* kiss Granger, whether it was because the lad was ugly "as a door-mat," or for any other reason. The plain fact remains that, during the ordeal of the trial, Wilde had been compelled to make a number of admissions which, in their conjunction, did prove fatal.

When, on April 5, all this preliminary evidence was finally summed up in Carson's speech, it became clear that the jury would be sure to acquit the Marquis. It is a question whether, in justice to his client, Sir Edward Clarke should have hoisted the white flag before the case had actually come to a close, but it is generally understood that his unexpected interposition was made for the explicit purpose of preventing Queensberry's witnesses giving their disgusting testimonies.

As things turned out, Sir Edward did withdraw from the prosecution and he did submit to a verdict of "not guilty." The Judge charged the jury accordingly, and, after a few moments consultation, the foreman announced that they had found the libel to be true. Immediately, Lord Queensberry was discharged amidst the cheers of his friends, whoever they may have been.

When, on the sullen stage of the Old Bailey, the curtain had thus dropped, Wilde must have realised that this was the beginning of his tragic end, or rather, the end of his triumphant beginning as lord of the English language.

CHAPTER XXX

OSCAR'S RUIN

JUST as soon as the result of the Queensberry trial had become known, the newspapers, with ferocious glee and bestial cruelty, began to hound Wilde. In the afternoon of April 5, *The Echo,* a London evening daily of the period, printed the following leader:

> And so a most miserable case is ended. Lord Queensberry is triumphant, and Mr. Oscar Wilde is "damned and done for." He may now change places with Lord Queensberry, and go into the dock himself, and have Lord Queensberry's evidence against him. He appears to have illustrated in his life the beauty and truthfulness of his teachings. He said, in cross-examination, that he considered there was no such thing as morality, and he seems to have harmonised his practices with his theory. The counsel for the prosecution, the judge, and jury are entitled to public thanks for abruptly terminating the trial, and so preventing the publication of probably revolting revelations. The best thing for everybody now is to forget all about Oscar Wilde, his perpetual posings, his æsthetical teachings, and his theatrical productions. If not tried himself, let him go into silence, and be heard of no more.

Editorially commenting on the outcome of Wilde's action against the Marquis of Queensberry, *The Westminster Gazette* stated:

> The case proves that it is untrue to say that art has nothing to do with morality. Wilde's art rests on a basis of rottenness and corruption.

Scarcely any more generous was the article in *The Daily Telegraph:*

> It was a just verdict and must be held to include with Wilde the tendency of his peculiar career, the meaning and the influence of his

teachings and all the shallow and specious arts by which he attempted to establish a cult and even set up new schools of literature and social thought.

Pour sauver les apparences, Wilde hastily drew up a communiqué and sent it to *The Evening News,* explaining the reason for his spectacular withdrawal from the case:

> It would have been impossible for me to have proved my case without putting Lord Alfred Douglas in the witness-box against his father. Lord Alfred Douglas was extremely anxious to go into the box, but I would not let him do so. Rather than put him into so painful a position, I determined to retire from the case, and to bear on my own shoulders whatever ignominy and shame might result from my prosecuting Lord Queensberry.

So long as Oscar stayed in court facing the inquisitive looks of so many heartless spectators, he tried to appear indifferent, if not cheerful. But in truth, Queensberry's victory crushed him and broke his morale. He left the battlefield unnoticed by the crowd but watchfully followed by two detectives. He was driven in a brougham drawn by two brown cobs to the Holborn Viaduct Hotel, where he had reserved a sitting room. He was soon joined by Lord Alfred, Lord Douglas of Hawick and Robert Ross. After luncheon, they all proceeded to St. James's Square; Lord Alfred cashed a check at the London and Westminster Bank, but Wilde, without stopping, drove straight to the Cadogan Hotel, Sloane Street. His entourage urged him to leave at once for Dover and try to reach Calais. But, having lapsed into morbid apathy, Oscar kept saying that it was too late and that the last train to Dover had gone. He asked Ross to call on Mrs. Wilde and to report to her the sad news.

Poor Constance! What could she do?—She was heartbroken and wept helplessly. "I hope," she said, "Oscar is going away abroad!" Yet nothing would move the poet to action. Silent, he sat in his arm-chair, drinking hock and seltzer, impassively waiting for the dreadful blow to fall on his discrowned head.

In the meantime, Charles Russell, Queensberry's solicitor,

probably acting under instructions from his client, dispatched the following letter to Hamilton Cuffe, Director of Prosecutions:

> Dear Sir,
>
> In order that there be no miscarriage of justice, I think it my duty at once to send you a copy of all our witnesses' statements together with a copy of the shorthand notes of the trial.

This step placed the authorities under obligation to act at once. On the same day Mr. Asquith, then the Home Secretary, Sir F. Lockwood, the Solicitor-General, and Sir Robert Reid, the Attorney-General, held a conference, at which it was decided that a warrant for Wilde's arrest should at once be issued. Several hours later, Sir John Bridge, Chief Magistrate, signed the warrant and handed it to Detective-Inspector Brockwell. At 7:30 that evening, Wilde was found at the Cadogan Hotel. He was immediately arrested and driven by the police officers in a four-wheeled cab to Scotland Yard. At about eight o'clock, he was taken to Bow Street. There, he was charged with committing acts of gross indecency with other male persons, to which charge Wilde made no reply. After a thorough search he was conveyed to one of the cells. Lord Alfred visited the station with a view to bailing out his friend, but much to his distress he was informed that his application could not be entertained.

On April 6, 11 and 19, 1895, preliminary proceedings were held before Sir John Bridge at Bow Street. Oscar Wilde was charged with the violation of Clause 10 of Section XI of the Criminal Law Amendment Act of January 1, 1886, which is worded thus:

> Any male person who, in public or private, commits, or is a party to the commission of, or procures or attempts to procure the commission by any male person of any act of gross indecency with another male person, shall be guilty of a misdemeanour, and, being convicted thereof, shall be liable, at the discretion of the Court, to be imprisoned for any term not exceeding two years with or without hard labour.

Alfred Taylor was also kept under arrest on a charge of conspiring with Wilde in the perpetration of the above offence.

Sir Edward Clarke represented Wilde, while Mr. Arthur Newton acted as counsel for Taylor. Altogether, twenty-two witnesses were called for the prosecution, among them the brothers Parker, Charles and William, Alfred Wood, Atkins and Sidney Mavor.

Some of them were individuals of a most suspicious character—notorious blackmailers, professional extortionists and petty swindlers. These young miscreants are said to have been fatly paid by the Marquis for appearing as witnesses against Oscar Wilde. The bulk of their testimony was conspicuously weak, flimsy and inconclusive.

Mavor, for one, proved decidedly disappointing to Mr. Gill, who appeared on behalf of the Public Prosecutor. While the lad was waiting in the corridor to give evidence, Lord Alfred went up and shook hands with him. "Surely," he said, "you are not going to testify against Oscar?" But Mavor whispered, "Well, what can I do? I daren't refuse to give evidence now: they got a statement out of me!"—"For God's sake," exclaimed Douglas, "remember you are a gentleman and a Public School boy. . . . When Counsel asks you the questions, deny the whole thing, and say you made the statement because you were frightened by the police. They can't do anything to you."

So, when Mr. Gill asked Mavor what had happened at the Albemarle Hotel where he had once spent a night on Oscar's invitation, the witness laconically answered: "Nothing." Of course, Counsel "dropped him like a hot brick."

On April 19, both defendants were committed for trial and, four days later, the Grand Jury found true bills in the case of Oscar Fingall O'Flahertie Wills Wilde and Alfred Waterhouse Somerset Taylor on the various counts in the indictment.

Among Wilde's biographers there is a consensus of opinion as to the consequence of Wilde's imprisonment.

On his arrest [states Sherard] immediate ruin followed. His sources of income dried up in an hour; his books were withdrawn from sale; the managers suspended the performance of his plays. His creditors clamoured for payment, judgments were obtained against him, and an execution was put into the house in Tite Street. From affluence he passed suddenly to dire poverty at a time when money was needed for his defence, when the utter lack of resources seemed to hold out the menace that he would be left to face the terrible charges which were being accumulated against him without the means to fee counsel or to prepare evidence.

Stuart Mason in his *Bibliography* has reproduced the text of the title page of the catalogue of that disgraceful auction plunder or "pillage of an unprotected house." It reads:

> By order of the Sheriff. A.D. 1895. 16 Tite Street, Chelsea. Catalogue of the Library of Valuable Books, Pictures, Portraits of Celebrities, Arundel Society Prints, Household Furniture, Carlyle's Writing Table, Chippendale and Italian Chairs, Old Persian Carpets and Rugs, Brass Fenders, Moorish and Oriental Curiosities, Embroideries, Silver and Plated Articles, Old Blue and White China, Moorish Pottery, Handsome Ormolu Clock, and numerous Effects: Which will be sold by Auction, By Mr. Bullock, on the Premises, on Wednesday, April 24, 1895, at One O'Clock. . . .

On that day, Wilde's "house beautiful" presented a pitiful picture: it was overrun by a whole crowd of curiosos, idlers and rumour-mongers. Doors were broken open, valuables were stolen, and the sale was carried on amidst scenes of chaotic disorder. Eventually, the police were summoned to eject the disturbers.

Most lots were disposed of at ridiculously low prices. A fine Whistler, a picture of a girl with the artist's butterfly signature, was knocked down for six pounds. Rothenstein bought a Monticelli for eight pounds which he sold later for Wilde's benefit at a much higher price. An "old painting" of Will Hughes, the work of Charles Ricketts, was purchased for only a guinea. An original manuscript poem by Keats was bought for thirty-eight shillings. Oscar's pride—his precious library with presentation copies from famous men of letters—was sold and dispersed. The last lot was a rabbit hutch, which brought only a couple of shillings. At the same time, some of Wilde's papers, including the original manuscripts of the essay *The Incomparable and Ingenious History of Mr. W. H.* and *The Woman Covered with Jewels,* mysteriously disappeared and have never since been discovered.

Now Wilde was an outcast and a pauper. A few months later he was brought from Reading Gaol, manacled between two policemen, to appear before the Court of Bankruptcy. He recorded this incident in his *De Profundis,* and he told there the touching story of a friend who "waited in the long dreary corridor that, before the whole crowd, whom an action so sweet and simple hushed into silence, he might gravely raise his hat to me, as, handcuffed and with bowed head, I passed him by." "Men," added Wilde, "have gone to Heaven for smaller things than that."

During the whole period from April 6 until May 7, Wilde was kept incarcerated in a special cell in Holloway Prison. One of the London dailies at the time gave an accurate description of that hideously furnished, ill-lighted and unsanitary abode: it was about ten feet broad, twelve feet long and eleven feet high. Light was supplied through an iron-barred window placed high up and well out of the prisoner's reach. A table made of hard white wood was placed on the right-hand side of the window. Oscar was supplied by the prison authorities with a water jug and a Bible gratis. In the corner near the fireplace there was a small camp bedstead, so narrow that it was almost impossible for a man of Oscar's massive construction to recline with any ease within so limited a space. Prisoners were permitted to sleep only upon hard mattresses, and the bed was "adorned" by a cover quilt made up of patches of all colours of the rainbow.

Lord Alfred Douglas recounts:

> I used to see Oscar every day at Holloway in the ghastly way that "visits" are arranged in prisons. The visitor goes into a box rather like the box of a pawnshop. . . . There is a whole row of these boxes, each occupied by a visitor, and opposite, facing each visitor is the prisoner whom he is visiting. The two sides of visitors and prisoners are separated by a corridor about a yard in width, and a warder paces

up and down the corridor. . . . Visitor and prisoner have to shout to make their voices heard above the voices of other prisoners and visitors. Nothing more revolting and cruel and deliberately malignant could be devised by human ingenuity. And it is to be remembered that I am speaking of a remand prison, where prisoners are awaiting trial, and possibly quite innocent of any offence whatever. Poor Oscar was rather deaf. He could hardly hear what I said in the babel. He looked at me with tears running down his cheeks and I looked at him. Such as it was, as he told me in nearly every letter he wrote (and he wrote every day with clockwork regularity), this interview was the only bright spot in the day.

In winding up his account, Lord Alfred stated:

Certainly, whatever poor Oscar had done, from the moment the prison gates closed upon him, he began to redeem himself by suffering, and even to shine in contrast to the conduct of his enemies. At the noble game of hitting a man when he is down the English can give points to any other nation on earth.

However, not only enemies, but "friends" as well, had given, in the case of Wilde, ample evidence of how despicable, vile and trivial human nature really is. Let us discount the miserable scribes with their petty pens dipped—to use Poushkin's phrase—in the "opium of ink mixed with a mad hound's venom of saliva." But shall we forget "the divine Sarah," whose delicate nerves Oscar, the irresistible charmer, in his happy days of fame, used to tickle so delightfully by his platonic courtship and literary hosannas?

Mr. Sherard has bequeathed to posterity the story of her infamous conduct when she was called upon to contribute a negligible sum of 7000 francs for meeting the expense of counsel's fee in the forthcoming trial. "Well," she said, assuming a perfect dramatic pose—"we'll see. What I can do I will—the utmost—out of friendship for a great artist, who is also a man of good heart, and who, I am sure, is suffering most unjustly."

As soon as Sherard had left Sarah's house, he drove to the nearest telegraph office and dispatched a long telegram to his friend in Holloway Gaol, describing the sympathy and affection with which the great actress had spoken of him. Of course, not a penny had come out of Madame's generous purse, and at last Mr. Sherard was forced to write Wilde an apologetic letter for having unwittingly aroused in him false hopes. He explained how Sarah had kept him on the run, deceiving and evading him for a whole week.

In answer to Sherard's report, Wilde wrote him this beautiful letter:

L.P.
C. 4

From *Wilde,*
H. M. Prison,
Holloway,
16–4–1895.

*B.*2–4
3.56.

My Dear Robert,—You good, daring, reckless friend! I was delighted to get your letter, with all its wonderful news. For myself, I am ill—apathetic. Slowly life creeps out of me. Nothing but Alfred Douglas' daily visits quicken me into life, and even him I only see under humiliating and tragic conditions.

Don't fight more than 6 duels a week! I suppose Sarah is hopeless; but your chivalrous friendship—your fine, chivalrous friendship—is worth more than all the money in the world.—

Yours,
Oscar

And it will be remembered that this incident happened at a time when Madame Bernhardt had already accepted *Salomé* and had promised Wilde to produce the play at her own theatre at Porte St. Martin. One hardly needs to add that Oscar's arrest had instantaneously caused a change in her plans, and bowing with a graceful *révérence* to the democratic Tartuffes across the Channel, the "noble" actress withdrew the drama from her repertoire. What, then, was the difference between Madame Bernhardt and the managers of the Lyceum Theatre, in which at that time *An Ideal Husband* was running, who decided—lest the gentle Broadway folks be shocked—to remove the author's name from the bills and programs?—After all, the New York producers merely followed the example set by their London confrère, Sir George Alexander, in the case of *The Importance of Being Earnest.*

Verily, when the crash came, Wilde must have discovered the true price of false friendship and he may have then recalled Plautus' wise saying: *Pauci ex multis amici sunt homini qui certi sunt.*[1]

CHAPTER XXXI

FIAT JUSTITIA

ONLY three days after the Grand Jury found true bills in the case of Oscar Wilde and Alfred Taylor, they were brought for trial at the Old Bailey before Mr. Justice Arthur Charles. This was on Friday, April 26, 1895. Every available seat in the courtroom was occupied, and the reporters noted that Earl Russell was among the earliest arrivals.

As a result of the enforced confinement, Wilde looked haggard and worn; his long hair hung in disorder.

Mr. C. F. Gill again took charge of the prosecution. Sir Edward Clarke, assisted by Mr. Charles Mathews and Mr. Travers Humphreys, acted for Wilde. Mr. J. P. Grain and Mr. Paul Taylor appeared as counsel for the defendant Alfred Taylor.

There were twenty-five counts in the indictment relating to acts of gross indecency alleged to have been committed by Wilde, Taylor being accused of the procuring of these acts. The defendants were also jointly charged with conspiring and agreeing to procure the commission of acts of gross indecency by Wilde. Both men pleaded not guilty.

The trial lasted five days. Lord Alfred Douglas, having left England, was not called to testify. Charles Parker and Alfred Wood appeared as star witnesses for the Crown. Their disreputable conduct was fully demonstrated in the course of Sir Edward's cross-examination. Another of Queensberry's "foundlings," by the name of Frederick Atkins, after having denied under oath that he had ever been arrested for demanding money from a gentleman he had taken to his rooms and robbed, was later compelled to admit that he had lied to the jury and that, in fact, he had been kept in custody at Rochester Row. Edward Shelley, still another among Wilde's accusers, pressed by Sir Edward, confessed that "sometimes he was not very sane" and that he had assaulted his own father. Finally, Sidney Mavor, also a State's witness, most emphatically denied that he had ever been guilty of any offence with Wilde.

On May 1, the Judge framed the following questions to the jury:

(1) Do you think that Wilde committed indecent acts with Edward Shelley and Alfred Wood and with a person or persons unknown at the Savoy Hotel or with Charles Parker?

(2) Did Taylor procure or attempt the commission of these acts or any of them?

(3) Did Wilde and Taylor or either of them attempt to get Atkins to commit indecencies?

(4) Did Taylor commit indecent acts with Charles Parker or with William Parker?

The jury retired at twenty-five minutes to two, and it was nearly a quarter past five when they returned.

His lordship then said:

Gentlemen of the Jury, I have received a communication from you to the effect that with the exception of the minor question which I put to you in regard to Atkins you are unable to arrive at an agreement.

The foreman confirmed this statement, reporting also that the jurors were unable to agree on any of the sub-divisions of questions (1) and (4).

That being so [the Judge ruled] I do not feel justified in retaining you any longer.

Upon the specific direction of the Court, the jury returned a verdict of acquittal on the charges of conspiracy as well as on four counts relating to Mavor and Wood.

After the discharge of the jury, Sir Edward Clarke made an application that Wilde be admitted to bail. Notwithstanding the result of the trial, the Judge again refused to accede to counsel's motion on the formal ground that, in his opinion, it should be renewed in the ordinary way before a judge in chambers.

Under the circumstances, however, Oscar's release from Holloway was only a matter of time, as the problem of raising cash for bail had been previously solved by Lord Alfred's brother, Percy: he undertook to supply the bulk of the money, while Ernest Leverson, the husband of Ada Leverson, the "Sphinx" of *Punch,* agreed to make up the balance, whatever that sum might be.

Evidently, Wilde had been informed about this arrangement because, on April 17, he wrote Ada from prison one of those lovely letters of his which so clearly divulge the genuine kindness of his heart:

> I hear that wonderful things are being done for me—by people of noble beautiful souls and natures. Of course, I cannot thank you. Words may not bear such burdens. I cannot even try. I merely say that you will always remain in a niche of a heart—half-broken already—as a most dear image of all that in life has love and pity in it. As for me, the wings of great love encompass me! holy ground.
>
> With deep affection and gratitude
>
> Yours,
>
> Oscar

It was not until May 7, that Wilde was released. The amount of the bail was fixed for two sureties at £1250 each, and for the defendant himself in the sum of £2500. One of the bailors—Reverend Stewart Headlam—a perfect stranger to Wilde—consented to act for the poet, as a matter of principle. He did not actually put up the money, for the sum of £1800 was supplied by Percy, and the balance of £700 by Ernest Leverson.

After all formalities had been completed, Wilde was permitted to leave the court and he drove to the Midland Hotel at St. Pancras.

Infuriated by the collapse of the case against Wilde, the old Marquis proceeded at once to that hotel and denounced

Oscar to the manager. What followed has been vividly described by Sherard in *The Story of an Unhappy Friendship:*

> It was late in the evening. Two rooms were engaged for him [Wilde] and dinner was ordered. Just as he had sat down at the table the manager roughly entered the room and said, "You are Oscar Wilde, I believe." Then he added, "You must leave the house at once." From this hotel he drove to another in a distant part of London where he was not known or recognized. He had sunk down exhausted on the bed of the room he had engaged when the landlord appeared. He had been followed from his last refuge by a band of men, prize-fighters, and had been denounced in the hall below. The landlord expressed his regret, but insisted on his leaving. "The men say they will sack the house and raze the street if you stay here a moment longer."

At last, long past midnight, Willy Wilde, in his mother's house in Oakley Street, heard a feeble rap at the front door. Opening it, he saw his brother, who, white as death, reeled forward into the passage. "Give me shelter, Willy," he cried. "Let me lie on the floor, or I shall die in the streets." "He came like a hunted stag," said Willy, "and fell down on the threshold."

Though Oscar worshipped his mother, he could not have felt happy at her house: even aside from the terrible nervous strain to which he had been subjected ever since the day of his arrest, what comfort could Lady Wilde or Willy offer him? Having lived through the humiliating experience of an English court ordeal, Oscar clearly visualised what was coming. He knew that the next trial, which he was now facing, would bring nothing but further disgrace and added torture to body and mind. And forgetful of Seneca's wise maxim, "long for the inevitable," he dreaded the grey future into which he was slowly drifting.

Sherard, who came over from Paris to see Oscar after his release from Holloway, painted a pathetic picture of the condition in which he found his friend:

> He was lying on a small camp-bedstead in a corner between the

fireplace and the wall, and in a glass on the mantelpiece was an arum lily, sere and yellow, which drooped lamentably down over his head. His face was flushed and swollen, his voice was broken, he was a man altogether collapsed. I sat down on the bed and took his hand in mine. . . .

There were moments when Wilde was seriously contemplating suicide. Sherard strongly urged him to forfeit the bail and leave England for the Continent. Lord Alfred wrote his brother Percy from Calais to tell Oscar that he was at liberty to flee if he would and could. Lord Douglas of Hawick, who had assumed responsibility for the largest part of the bail, said, "It will practically ruin me if I lose all that money at the present moment, but if there is a chance even of his conviction, in God's name let him go."

Likewise, Frank Harris tried to persuade Wilde to adopt the course which had been mapped out for him. More than that, Constance called on him one day, while he was staying with the Leversons, and implored him to leave the country at once, since the next trial would prove fatal.

All arrangements for the flight had been made, and, as a matter of fact, the poet, who was at no time under police surveillance, could easily have journeyed to some Continental port. What a temptation this must have been! Would it not have been a blessed relief to forget once and forever the mortifying mise en scène of the Old Bailey with its justices and prosecutors and warders and docks, and to breathe like a free man in a free country, amidst animated crowds and brightly lit boulevards, in an atmosphere of gladness and mirthful jests and that *joie de vivre* which in days past—alas, no longer!—used to be the greatest charm of Paris!

But then he started asking himself if he had the right to yield to temptation. Would it be honourable for him to betray the confidence of his sureties and friends?—The moral norm, which hitherto seemed never to have bothered Oscar's conscience, suddenly awoke in him and shook him to his very foundations. Lady Wilde, his beloved mother, told him she would never speak to him again if he dared to attempt a disgraceful escape. To the bitter end, she believed in the innocence of her son. Hers was a pathetic sorrow into which the sympathy of the most devoted friends dared not intrude; it was "the grief over that death in life, the loss of honour that to the noble and upright is more precious than life itself."[1] And there, again, was Willy, who kept telling Oscar that, being an Irish gentleman, he would have to stay "to face the music."

This was moral agony. To the few who were permitted to call at the mourning house in Oakley Street, it was pitiful to watch Oscar during those long hours when he sat there in his room, silent, fiercely fighting his inner battle, oscillating between hope and despair, regretting his folly and seeking in vain to banish from his fatigued mind the ghastly phantom of Fate. In ordinary circumstances, it is a real privilege of the mind to forget the things which no longer need to be remembered, but, as Sherard said, Wilde was suffering "all the tortures of brain-fever without its merciful coma."

At last, he said to himself that pride and self-respect should prevail over the seductive prospect of freedom. "I cannot see myself," he declared, "slinking about the Continent, a fugitive from justice." He declined Harris's offer to flee from England in a yacht which had been kept under steam at Erith on the Thames waiting to bring him over to the hospitable shores of France. He also promptly notified Lord Alfred of his decision "to face the music."

He wrote me a very touching letter [says Douglas] giving his reasons for not going. It made me weep at the time, and even now I don't like to think of it, but I have thought since a hundred times, that it was an insane thing not to go, and that it would really have been a braver thing to do. Oscar said in his letter that he could not "run away" and "hide" and "let down" his bails (but my brother wanted him to go on my account, and Mr. Headlam would not have been affected in the least). He wrote: "A dishonoured name, a hunted life are not for me to whom you have been revealed on that high hill where beautiful things are transfigured."

But even having thus cut the Gordian knot, Oscar continued to feel miserable in his cheerless Oakley Street refuge, with its dark and heavy curtains over the windows which kept it artificially plunged into a sad *crépuscule*. Besides, he must have been greatly annoyed by his brother's patronising air and the continual reminders of things which it would have been gratifying to forget. "That house," he complained, "is depressing. Willy makes such a merit of giving me shelter; he means well, I suppose; but it is all dreadful." This fact is fully corroborated by Ada Leverson in her sketchy *Letters to The Sphinx from Oscar Wilde*. She gives there most interesting details of Oscar's brief sojourn at their house in Courtfield Gardens just before his last trial:

He seemed so unhappy with his family at this time that we asked him to stay with us, feeling that he would be more at ease with friends than with relatives. Before he came, we called all the servants together, parlour-maid, house-maid, cook, kitchen-maid and our old nurse, Mrs. Field, who acted as my maid. We told them who was coming, offering them a month's wages if they wished to leave at once. For the affair was now such a scandal as had rarely been known. Little else was talked of in London; the papers were full of it. . . . Each servant in turn refused to leave. . . . Then I went to fetch Oscar. He accepted with joy. And he came back with me in the little pill-box brougham. When we arrived I showed him his room. . . . While all our friends, as well as the whole public, were discussing Oscar, no one had any idea he was under our roof. He made certain rules in order to avoid any embarrassment for us. He never left the nursery floor till six o'clock. He had breakfast, luncheon and tea up there, and received all his loyal friends there. He never would discuss his troubles before me; such exaggerated delicacy seems to-day almost incredible. But every day at six he would come down dressed for dinner, and talk to me for a couple of hours in the drawing-room. As always he was most carefully dressed, there was a flower in his buttonhole, and he had received his usual daily visit from the old hairdresser who shaved him and waved his hair. His ambition was always to look like a Roman bust. . . .

And this is what "Sphinx" recorded about Wilde's farewell moments at her house:

> The morning came when he was to leave for his ordeal. The night before he had asked me to put a sleeping-draught on his mantelpiece. He never intended to take it, but just the presence of it had, he said, a magical effect. In the hall he suddenly turned to me and said, for the first time in a faltering voice, "If the worst comes to the worst, Sphinx, you'll write me?" Then he and his friend, Mr. Adey, left in the little pill-box brougham which I had hired for him.

This was on May 20, 1895.

At eleven o'clock sharp, the usher at the Old Bailey gave the signal, and Mr. Justice Wills (Sir Alfred) took his seat on the Bench. As the Judge entered the court, Taylor was placed in the dock and Wilde, accompanied by the Reverend Stewart Headlam and Lord Douglas of Hawick, came in by a door near the jury-box. When the Clerk of Arraigns called out the names of the defendants, Wilde stepped into the dock. Mental worry was noticeable on his face.

Sir Frank Lockwood, the Solicitor-General, Mr. Gill and Mr. Avory appeared for the prosecution, Sir Edward Clarke, Mr. Charles Mathews and Mr. Travers Humphreys acting as counsel for Oscar Wilde.

Before the jurors had been sworn in, Sir Edward moved that the defendants be tried separately on the ground that at the first trial there was an indictment of conspiracy which had subsequently been withdrawn. Mr. Grain, on behalf of Taylor, concurred. Over the objection of the Solicitor-General, the Court ruled that the defendants be tried separately. But the Judge denied Sir Edward's application that his client's case be taken first.

There is no necessity of going into Taylor's trial. The fact, however, should be mentioned that the jury found Taylor guilty on two counts alleging indecency with Charles and William Parker, and not guilty on the charge of procuring Wood for Wilde.

Meanwhile, on Wednesday morning, May 22, the Marquis

of Queensberry and his eldest son, Lord Douglas of Hawick, were charged at the Marlborough Street Police Court with disorderly conduct in Piccadilly on the previous afternoon.

Police Constable Morrell said that while he was on duty at the corner of Bond Street, his attention was called to a large crowd outside Scotts, the hatters. He went there and found the Marquis and his son engaged in a fist fight. He separated them, after which they again closed; once more, he stopped the row but a minute later he saw the combatants exchanging blows near a confectionery shop. Thereupon, witness arrested the good Marquis, while Percy was taken in charge by another "bobby." Evidently what had happened was this: Lord Douglas and a friend were walking in Piccadilly when they saw Queensberry crossing the street. The latter had just come out of a post office whence he had dispatched the following telegram to Percy's wife:

> To Lady Douglas—Must congratulate on verdict. Cannot on Percy's appearance. Looked like a dug up corpse. Fear too much madness in kissing. Taylor guilty. Wilde's turn tomorrow.—Queensberry.

Percy stopped the Marquis and asked him if he intended to further pester his wife with letters of any kind. A street fight ensued. It is difficult to ascertain who had struck the first blow: it was a close match, but one of the witnesses thought Queensberry was quicker, to which the Magistrate remarked: "He naturally would be, seeing that the Marquis is a boxer." Both defendants were bound over in their own sureties of £500 to keep the peace for six months.

The incident, perhaps, would not be worth mentioning at all were it not for the fact that it throws additional light upon the maniacal personality of Lord Queensberry.

On the same day when that petty family quarrel was deliberated upon at the Police Court, the second and final trial of Oscar Wilde began at the Old Bailey. Mr. Justice Wills took his seat at half-past ten, and then Wilde stepped into the dock.

The Clerk of Arraigns read out the indictment, which alleged that the accused, being a male person, unlawfully committed on diverse dates acts of gross indecency with Charles Parker, Alfred Wood, Edward Shelley and two other unidentified male persons. To this indictment, the defendant pleaded not guilty.

Substantially, the evidence produced at this trial, which lasted four days in succession, differed little from that given before Mr. Justice Charles.

In his eloquent speech to the jury, Sir Edward Clarke vigorously denounced the criminal conduct of Charles Parker and Wood and commented severely upon "the tender care taken of these witnesses by the Crown." "This trial," he said, "seems to be operating as an act of indemnity for all blackmailers in London. Wood and Parker, in giving evidence, have established for themselves a sort of statute of limitations. In testifying on behalf of the Crown they have secured immunity for past rogueries and indecencies." Counsel concluded his plea with this statement:

> If on examination of the evidence you felt it your duty to say that the charges had not been proved, I am sure you will be glad that the brilliant promise which had been clouded by these accusations, and the bright reputation which was so nearly quenched in the torrent of prejudice which a few weeks ago had been sweeping through the Press, had been saved by your verdict from absolute ruin; and that it left him, a distinguished man of letters and a brilliant Irishman, to live among us a life of honour and repute, and to give in the maturity of his genius gifts to our literature of which he had given only the promise in his early youth.

Mr. Justice Wills, who throughout the trial had been by no means lenient toward the defendant, admitted, in his summing up, that Wood's story of the visit to Wilde's house in Tite Street was not convincing at all. His lordship thought that it might have been possible to obtain some corroboration of the story told by that witness, but this Counsel for the prosecution had failed to do. Likewise, the Judge expressed the opinion that the evidence of the Savoy Hotel servants, given as it was, after a long lapse of time, should not be entirely relied upon. However, on the whole, it was observed in more than one instance that the Judge, while placing two issues before the jury in fair and objective enough language, "yet imparted to his delivery, his tones and his manner a significance which deprived his statements of that appearance of impartiality that is usually expected of the Bench."

On May 25, at half-past three in the afternoon, the jury retired to consider their verdict. There seems to have been a general belief that the trial would again end in a disagreement and that the Crown would then have to issue a *Nolle Prosequi*. The Solicitor-General is said to have remarked to Sir Edward, "You'll dine your man in Paris tomorrow." But defence counsel entertained no such hopes.

Around 6 P.M., the jury returned to their seats, and Wilde was again placed in the dock.

There was dead silence in the room when the Clerk of Arraigns asked the jurors: "Gentlemen, have you agreed upon your verdict?" The foreman answered: "We have." Then came the questions and answers:

The Clerk of Arraigns: Do you find the prisoner at the bar guilty of an act of gross indecency with Charles Parker at the Savoy Hotel on the night of his first introduction to him?

The Foreman of the Jury:—*Guilty*.

2. Do you find him guilty of a similar offence a week later?—*Guilty*.

3. Do you find him guilty of the offence at St. James's Place?—*Guilty*.

4. Do you find him guilty of this offence at about the same period?—*Guilty*.

5. Do you find him guilty of a similar offence with Alfred Wood at Tite Street?—*Guilty*.

6. Do you find him guilty of the offence in Room No. 362 of the Savoy Hotel?—*Guilty*.

7. Do you find him guilty of the offence in Room No. 346 of the Savoy Hotel?—*Guilty*.

Do you find him guilty on all counts in the indictment except that relating to Edward Shelley?—Yes; *Not Guilty* on that count.

After the jury returned their verdict, Alfred Taylor was placed in the dock beside Oscar Wilde. Then Sir Alfred Wills, Knight, and a Justice of Her Majesty's High Court, spoke as follows:

Oscar Wilde and Alfred Taylor, the crime of which you have been convicted is so bad that one has to put stern restraint upon one's self to prevent one's self from describing, in language which I would rather not use, the sentiments which must rise to the breast of every man of honour who has heard the details of these two terrible trials.

That the jury have arrived at a correct verdict in this case I cannot persuade myself to entertain the shadow of a doubt; and I hope, at all events, that those who sometimes imagine that a judge is half-hearted in the cause of decency and morality because he takes care no prejudice shall enter into the case, may see that that is consistent at least with the utmost sense of indignation at the horrible charges brought home to both of you.

It is no use for me to address you. People who can do these things must be dead to all sense of shame, and one cannot hope to produce any effect upon them. It is the worst case I have ever tried. That you, Taylor, kept a kind of male brothel it is impossible to doubt. And that you, Wilde, have been the center of a circle of extensive corruption of the most hideous kind among young men, it is equally impossible to doubt.

I shall, under such circumstances, be expected to pass the severest sentence that the law allows. In my judgment it is totally inadequate for such a case as this.

The sentence of the court is that each of you be imprisoned and kept to hard labour for two years.

The obvious cruelty of the sentence caused live commotion in the courtroom. Cries were heard: "Oh, oh!" "Shame!" Taylor received his sentence with calm indifference. But Wilde seemed crushed and heartbroken. Sherard, who was present on the last day of the trial, said that Oscar's face flushed purple, his eyes protruded, and over all was an expression of extreme horror:

When the judge had finished speaking, and whilst a whirl of satisfaction buzzed through the Court, Wilde, who had recovered himself, said: "And I? May I say nothing, my lord?" But the judge made no answer—only an impatient sign with his hand. . . . Warders touched my poor friend on the shoulder. He shuddered and gave one wild look round the Court. Then he turned and lumbered forward to the head of the stairs which led to the bottomless pit. He was swept down and disappeared.

The news of the tragic outcome of the trial quickly spread outside the Old Bailey and came as a signal for ugly and frantic street demonstrations of fiendish joy over the ruin and disgrace which had befallen an aristocrat of the spirit and a man of genius who had unfolded to the world so many visions full of noble truth and undying beauty.

Now at last the vilest scum of the nation, from top to bottom, were given a chance to unbridle their basest instincts and to indulge in a savage orgy of blind hate and brutish vengeance. News-venders, tearing through the streets, triumphantly yelled: "GUILTY!—TWO YEARS HARD LABOUR!" "WILDE VERDICT! OSCAR GUILTY!" Glaring placards announcing Wilde's fate were promptly posted all over London. The rabble, men and women, joined by harlots lifting their ragged skirts, cheering themselves hoarse, leaped and hopped around in a grim and hideous *carmagnole*.

What a triumph! Now at last the donkey was free to kick with his democratic hoof at the mortally wounded heraldic lion.

CHAPTER XXXII

READING GAOL

WILDE began to serve his sentence at Wandsworth Gaol, in a suburb of London. On the very first evening of his confinement, he received his initiation into the soul-degrading ignominy of the English prison routine when, much to his repugnance, he was ordered to enter a filthy bath in which other prisoners had preceded him.

He was kept in solitary confinement, and subjected to a regime of dead silence. For a man of enormous intellectual power such as his, unbroken silence must have been relentless torture. This psychic state has been pathetically described by Dostoievsky at the time when, pending his trial, he was committed to SS. Peter and Paul Fortress in St. Petersburg:

> It is now five months [he wrote to his brother Michael] or so, that I have been existing on my own assets, that is, on my brain and nothing else. So far, the engine has not fallen apart, and it goes on functioning. But continuous thinking, and thinking alone, with no impressions from the outside world to regenerate and assist the thought—this is dreadful! . . . Everything from within me went to my head, and from my head—to thought, absolutely everything, yet in spite of this, the brain work grows more intense every day.

The shock of the three trials; Holloway; the loss of home, wife, children; the brutal manifestations of public contempt; the vengeance of mocking enemies; the treason of false friends; the humiliating experience of bankruptcy—what more could a man endure, with how much less to sustain him could he exist? Though physically alive, spiritually Wilde no longer belonged to the Kingdom of this World. This was stagnation, the paralysing immobility of the grave in which human beings had been locked and left forsaken to expiate their sins in the darkness of oblivion. "Here," he said, "I have the horror of death with the still greater horror of living."

Such was Oscar's present—the terrible sequel to his past. As for the future—there was none, just gray nothingness, *un néant vaste et noir,* in Baudelaire's poetic language. Remorse, Solitude, Silence and Despair, like huge spiders, kept peering at him day and night from out of the four corners of that loathsome cell. "Thought," remarked Wilde once, "to those that sit alone and silent and in bonds, is no 'winged living thing,' as Plato feigned it, but a thing dead, breeding what is horrible like a slime that shows monsters to the moon."

As one morning he was monotonously tramping round the yard at Wandsworth, a poor thief whispered to him in the husky prison voice men acquire from long and compulsory silence: "I am sorry for you; it is harder for the likes of you than for the likes of us." The miserable convict perceived the depth of Wilde's mental agony more clearly and with a sense of greater compassion than such a distinguished *littérateur* as Alphonse Daudet, who, as we know, expressed a typically *petit bourgeois* satisfaction with the barbaric sentence which Mr. Justice Wills imposed upon the poet.

On August 26, 1895, Wilde became entitled to his first quarterly visit. Mr. Sherard, who then called on him, was much struck by his resignation. The sad interview took place in a vaulted room which was divided by a double row of iron bars.

> In the passage between stood a warder who kept his eyes fixed on a noisy clock which hurried the spare allowance of minutes along. . . . I noticed that his [Wilde's] hands were disfigured, and that his nails were broken and bleeding; also that his head and face were untidy with growth of hair. And that is all that I noticed, for I looked at his face all the time, and if he was in some hideous uniform I did not see it. He was greatly depressed, and at one time had tears in his eyes.

While Oscar was still at Wandsworth, by special permission of the Home Office, Constance also came to see him. This was on September 21, 1895. The experience of this visit proved shocking to her; in fact, it was more dreadful than she had ever anticipated.

On November 13, 1895, Wilde was ordered to be removed from that prison to Reading Gaol. Here is his own account of the disgraceful journey:

> I was brought down here from London. From two o'clock till half-past two on that day I had to stand on the centre platform of Clapham Junction in convict dress, and handcuffed, for the world to look at. I had been taken out of the hospital ward without a moment's notice being given to me. Of all possible objects I was the most grotesque. When people saw me they laughed. Each train as it came up swelled the audience. Nothing could exceed their amusement. That was, of course, before they knew who I was. As soon as they had been informed they laughed still more. For half an hour I stood there in the grey November rain surrounded by a jeering mob.

What a brave lot these virtuous Philistines must have been!

The transfer to Reading Gaol in no measure relieved Wilde's situation. In fact, the old school of penology taught that a penitentiary, to fulfill its purpose, had to bear all the marks of an elaborate device for intimidation. Accordingly, the prison personnel at Reading in Wilde's time was mostly composed of men who hated the inmates and treated them with execrable brutality. The regulations there were—if it is possible—even more rigorous than at Wandsworth. Conversation of any kind was strictly forbidden. Reading was not permitted. Food was served in filthy receptacles and was uneatable. The very smell and sight of it made one's stomach turn.

Oscar's cell, C.3.3., was three steps wide and three steps long. Daylight never penetrated into it and it had practically no ventilation. The air was stifling and one could hardly breathe. Visits were allowed only four times every twelve months and they took place under shocking conditions. Such was the general picture of the Reading Inferno.

> Words [Wilde told Harris] cannot convey the cumulative effect of a myriad discomforts, brutal handling and slow starvation. Surely like Dante I have written on my face the fact that I have been in hell.

Only Dante never imagined any hell like an English prison; in his lowest circle people could move about; could see each other; and hear each other groan; there was some change, some human companionship in misery. . . .

And on top of all this shame and anguish, our poet had the great misfortune to be sent to a gaol which at the time was governed by the notorious Lieutenant Colonel H. Isaacson. He was a brute with no sense of pity and no sign of sympathy for human sorrow—"a horrible creature, a cruel Jew without imagination," as Wilde called him. "I will see to it," he told Wilde, with vicious delight, "that your whims be plucked out of your system."

As a result, punishment was mercilessly applied to the poet for every slightest breach of the innumerable prison regulations. And, of course, it is true that all these statutes have been, as Renier suggested, framed and devised in such a way that no human being could possibly fail to break them. "Find out what the children are doing, and tell them not to," the Victorian mother used to instruct the nurse. "See what prisoner C.3.3. is doing, and punish him for it," seems to have been the spirit in which Wilde was treated under the governorship of Isaacson.

André Gide in his *Recollections* has told how Wilde was caught one day talking with a fellow-inmate. Both culprits—C.3.3. and C.4.8.—were at once sent before the Governor. Isaacson tried his best to find out who had spoken first because, under prison rules, the man who had begun the conversation received a double penalty, usually a fortnight in the dark cell. Wilde's companion confessed that he was the first to break the rule. Yet Wilde, anxious to spare the poor devil from undergoing a severe penalty, told the Governor that it was he who had started the incriminating dialogue. Isaacson grew furious, his face went scarlet and he said: "This I can't understand. I should have thought one of you must have spoken first. I shall have to give you both double punishment."

Wilde was very popular among his unfortunate comrades

and greatly beloved by them. They knew he was a man who, having been flung into the gutter even as they, belonged to those chosen few who were still able to look at the stars. The mental superiority of this unusual prisoner must have made a strange impression upon those downtrodden creatures. Besides, they could not help but admire his kind heart and the unpretentious generosity which he invariably manifested in his intercourse with them. Above all, however, they respected him for his loyalty to them as companions in a common calamity.

Like Dostoievsky, the most penetrating of all mind-readers of our age, Wilde had grasped the fact that, in the souls of the humblest of these ragged beggars and common-law criminals, there dwelt genuinely humane and strangely touching emotions which lifted them from the "lower depths" of a bestial existence to the lofty heights of the moral ideal.

> The poor [Wilde said in *De Profundis*] are wiser, more charitable, more kind, more sensitive than we are. In their eyes prison is a tragedy in a man's life, a misfortune, a casualty, something that calls for sympathy in others. They speak of one who is in prison as of one who is "in trouble" simply. It is the phrase they always use, and the expression has the perfect wisdom of love in it.

And throughout the two years of his prison slavery, Wilde himself tried, as much as circumstances would permit, to show kindness to his fellow inmates and they in turn did their best, in their humble way, to comfort him and to relieve his pain.

From time to time, illness would compel Wilde to seek relief in the gaol infirmary. But there he was always suspected of simulation and, as a rule, was promptly ordered to his cell, warders being instructed to watch the poor man with double zeal. And when, in the enlightened opinion of the jailers, Wilde had been guilty of an attempt to deceive the prison Esculapios, he would promptly be punished.

The truth is that in the hospital the very association with other human beings, the fact that there he was not alone, would automatically restore to Wilde his splendid vitality, and then the breath of life would animate his features and his innate wit would come back to him. At such moments, fleeting though they were, the convicts in the ward listened to him with beaming faces, his stories made them laugh and their enjoyment brought gladness to him, reviving his whole person and making outsiders imagine that he was full of vigour and in excellent spirits. It was thus that Wilde appeared to two officials who were sent down from the Home Office to report on his health and who, unknown to him, watched him through a spy-hole in the infirmary for half an hour. "He was sitting on his bed and discoursing," said Sherard, "and all the patients were in high delight. In consequence, the two gentlemen returned to London and reported that C.3.3. was in enviable physical and mental condition."

Wilde's friends, however, had every reason to fear that this kind of prison régime would completely ruin his health. In a letter to More Adey, Ross gave this description of the appearance of Wilde only a few weeks after his transfer to Reading:

> He is much thinner and is now clean-shaven, so that his emaciated condition is more apparent. His face is dull brick colour . . . his eyes are horribly vacant. I noticed he had lost a great deal of hair. . . . He always had great quantities of thick hair, but there is now a bald patch on the crown. It is also streaked with white and grey. . . . The remarkable part of the interview was that Oscar hardly talked at all, except to ask if there was any chance of his being let out, what the attitude of the press and public would be. . . . He said he had nothing to say and wanted to hear *us* [Ross and Sherard] talk. . . . *He is not allowed pencil or paper.* . . . Each person has his view as to what constitutes a decayed mind, but if I was asked about Oscar before a commission I should say that "confinement, apart from all labour or treatment, had made him temporarily silly." . . . If asked whether he was going to die, "it seems quite possible within the next few months, even if his constitution remained unimpaired." . . . I should be less surprised to hear of dear Oscar's death than of Aubrey Beardsley's, and you know what he looks like.

As early as November, 1895, a petition to Her Majesty the Queen was drawn up and signed by Professor Frederick York

Powell, of Oxford, in which, among other things, it was stated that

> if the Prisoner should survive and complete his sentence it is greatly to be feared he would ultimately be incapacitated from following his profession, and thus would be deprived, in the prime of life, of the means of earning a livelihood.

This application, as well as a later one, was never submitted to the authorities, because information was received from the Home Secretary, in a letter dated September 24, 1896, that, the case of Wilde having been carefully considered, "no grounds, medical or other," were found which would justify any mitigation of the sentence. There is probably much truth in what Charles Ricketts wrote to Jean Paul Raymond that even if the great Victorians, Morris, for example, or Meredith or Watts, had wished to alleviate Wilde's suffering, they would have been powerless to save him.

> In France [says Ricketts] a celebrity can appeal to the public, here [in England] this is not allowed, it would disturb the general dead level of mediocrity we wish to perpetuate. Our eminent men . . . are subject to censorships, police interference; a book can be suppressed by a magistrate without jury or witness exactly as in Bolshevik Russia.

An additional misfortune was wrought upon Wilde shortly after his removal to Reading: on February 3, 1896, Lady Wilde died at her residence. The proud Jane Francesca Agnes Speranza was simply unable to survive the conviction of her son. Upon learning of Lady Wilde's passing, Constance, who had fled from England to Italy, at once went back to London. She must have felt that it was her last duty toward her dishonoured husband to convey to him the sad news with that gentle grace which only a loving woman is capable of bestowing upon a broken man living through a great sorrow.

In *De Profundis,* Wilde perpetuated this act of mercy in a heartbreaking passage which ranks among the most marvellous lines that have ever been recorded in the English tongue.

> No one knew [he wrote there, referring to his mother] how deeply

I loved and honoured her. Her death was terrible to me; but I, once a lord of language, have no words in which to express my anguish and my shame. Never even in the most perfect days of my development as an artist could I have found words fit to bear so august a burden; or to move with sufficient stateliness of music through the purple pageant of my incommunicable woe. She and my father had bequeathed me a name they had made noble and honoured, not merely in literature, art, archæology, and science, but in the public history of my own country, in its evolution as a nation. I had disgraced that name eternally. I had made it a low by-word among low people. I had dragged it through the very mire. I had given it to brutes that they might make it brutal, and to fools that they might turn it into a synonym for folly. What I suffered then, and still suffer, is not for pen to write or paper to record. My wife, always kind and gentle to me, rather than that I should hear the news from indifferent lips, travelled, ill as she was, all the way from Genoa to England to break to me herself the tidings of so irreparable, so irredeemable, a loss.

This was the last time that Oscar saw Constance: shortly before his release from prison he signed a formal deed of separation, by virtue of which he agreed to give her full custody over Cyril and Vyvyan and she, in turn, undertook to allow him £150 a year on condition that the "pension" was to be withdrawn if he should ever again start living under the same roof with Lord Alfred.

That Oscar felt boundlessly grateful to Constance for her Samaritan kindness in coming to visit him after Lady Wilde's death is clearly perceived from his letter to Ross, in which he asked the latter to write a solicitor about his wife's settlement on him:

I feel [he stated] that I have brought such unhappiness on her and such wrong on my children that I have no right to go against her wishes in anything. She was gentle and good to me here when she came to see me. I have full trust in her. Please have this done *at once*, and thank my friends for their kindness—I feel I am acting rightly in leaving this to my wife.

In the "dead house" where Wilde lay buried, the hours and days crept by in slow, weary and monotonous succession. "Even if I get out of this loathsome place," he wrote from Reading, "I know that there is nothing for me but a life of a pariah, of disgrace and penury and contempt." And a few days later, he added to that confession:

> No man of my position can fall into the mire of life without getting a great deal of pity from his inferiors: and I know that when plays last too long spectators tire. *My* tragedy has lasted far too long; and I am quite conscious of the fact that when the end *does* come I shall return an unwelcome visitant to a world that does not want me . . . as one whose face is grey with long imprisonment and crooked with pain. Horrible as are the dead when they rise from their tombs, the living who come out from their tombs are more horrible still.

Even the news of the marked success of the première of *Salomé* at the Théâtre de L'Œuvre in Paris, with Lugné-Poë, the director, in the part of Herod, failed to assuage the mental suffering of the poet. His mind merely registered this event without filling him with joy. There is this brief allusion to it in a letter to Ross of March 10, 1896:

> Please write to Stuart Merrill in Paris, or Robert Sherard, to say how gratified I was at the performance of my play, and have my thanks conveyed to Lugné-Poë: it is something that at a time of disgrace and shame I should be still regarded as an artist; I wish I could feel more pleasure, but I seem dead to all emotions except those of anguish and despair.

Meanwhile, the rumours of Wilde's ill-treatment had finally leaked out of the dark depths of the tombs. After much delay, Sir Evelyn Ruggles Brise of the Home Office issued instructions that the poet be accorded certain privileges, including the right to receive books from friends.

Of course, this was but a relative alleviation, for Wilde was still required to sleep on his plank bed and to shred the hard ropes into oakum till his fingertips grew dull with pain. He still had to perform the menial offices of his daily routine, turning the crank that supplied the prison with water and scrubbing on his knees the floor of his cell. He still wore the dreadful dress "that made sorrow grotesque to look at," and he was still subjected to dead solitude and perplexing silence. But now at least he could read, he could keep company with the masters of language and the princes of thought.

Just as soon as this permission had been granted, Wilde wrote Ross a letter requesting a whole library. Among the authors and books for which he asked were Merimée, Anatole France, Pierre Louÿs, Montaigne, a French Bible and an English one, a French-English Dictionary, Yeats' *The Secret Rose,* two novels by A. E. W. Mason, English translations of Calderón's plays, Dante, a number of works on *The Divine Comedy.* Wilde's list, it goes without saying, had to be submitted to the prison censor, who made thereon many curious notes, passing certain books and refusing others: for instance, he permitted Flaubert's *Salammbô* but struck out *La Tentation de St. Antoine;* Strindberg was passed, but Ibsen was barred, apparently on the theory that he was a dangerous social dreamer; Sienkiewicz's *Quo Vadis* shared the fate of *Doctor Stockmann* and *Hedda Gabler;* so also did three books by John Addington Symonds and Arthur Morrison's Criminology Series; he was allowed a copy of *Salomé,* yet not the reviews of it. The most disappointing of all refusals was that of his request for manuscript books, pencils and foolscap paper, which were heavily scored through, presumably as being in shocking discord with the prison regulations.

Coincident with the permission to receive books was an event which made Wilde's confinement less miserable than it had been before: his cell was placed under the immediate supervision of Warder T. Martin, one of the few officers at Reading who refused to regard the prisoners as mere beasts kept behind iron bars. Exceptionally intelligent for a man of his position, Martin did not at all fit into the grim picture of that obsolete prison, and as a matter of record, shortly after Wilde's release he was dismissed for having given some biscuits to children in prison there.

Fortunately, Martin developed a great affection for the martyred poet. There are in existence several scribbles which

Wilde managed to smuggle to his keeper, some of them written on torn bits of paper, others on the inside of envelopes—mere fragments which, however, shed a sympathetic light on both prisoner and warder. For instance, this one:

> My dear friend, What have I to write about except that if you had been an officer in Reading Prison a year ago my life would have been much happier. Every one tells me I am looking much happier. That is because I have a good friend who gives me the *Chronicle* and *promises* me ginger biscuits!
>
> O. W.

Another of Wilde's notes to Martin reads:

> You must get me his address some day—He is such a good fellow—Of course I would not for worlds get such a friend as you are into *any danger*—I quite understand your feelings. *The Chronicle* is capital today. You must get A 3/2 to come out and clean on Saturday morning and I will give him my note then—myself.[1]

Naturally, it was a great comfort for Wilde to get a warder as kindhearted as Martin. A still happier tiding was awaiting our poet: on July 1, 1896, Major J. O. Nelson was given charge of Reading Gaol, Lieutenant-Colonel Isaacson having received the governorship of Lewes Prison. Nelson was an amiable man who also took a sympathetic interest in Wilde's dreadful fate.

One day, the new Governor called Wilde into his office and told him that henceforth he would be allowed to use writing materials. This, indeed, was an unexpected joy: from now on, his braincuffed genius was enabled once more to express its ideas and meditations in tangible symbols and not merely in the evanescent workings of thought. It is due to the granting of this privilege that mankind has been enriched by *De Profundis,* that mighty symphony of a repentant soul, one of the deepest, most touching and loftiest creations in world literature.

This pathetic poem in prose was written by special permission of the Home Secretary during the last six months of Wilde's imprisonment. Originally, it was cast in the form of a letter to an unnamed friend (Lord Alfred Douglas). The manuscript of eighty close-written pages on twenty folio sheets was handed to Ross by the poet himself on the day of his release. A reduced facsimile of a portion of Wilde's manuscript appears in Mason's *Bibliography* (pages 448–449). The somewhat unusual story of its publication has been explained by Ross in his prefatory dedication of *De Profundis* to Doctor Max Meyerfeld:

> But for you I do not think the book would have ever been published. When first you asked me about the manuscript which you heard Wilde wrote in prison, I explained to you vaguely that some day I hoped to issue portions of it, in accordance with the writer's wishes; though I thought it would be premature to do so at that moment. You begged however that Germany (which already held Wilde's plays in the highest esteem) should have the opportunity of seeing a new work by one of her favourite authors. I rather reluctantly consented to your proposal; and promised, at a leisured opportunity, to extract such portions of the work as might be considered of general public interest. I fear that I postponed what was to me a rather painful task; it was only your visits and more importunate correspondence . . . that brought about the fulfilment of your object. There was no idea of issuing the work in England; but after dispatching to you a copy for translation in *Die Neue Rundschau,* it occurred to me that the simultaneous publication of the original might gratify Wilde's English friends and admirers who had expressed curiosity on the subject.

Thus, the extracts of Wilde's long epistle to Douglas appeared first in a German version under the title *Aufzeichnungen und Briefe aus dem Zuchthause in Reading.* This was in 1905. In the same year, Messrs. Methuen and Company brought out an English edition of the original manuscript with such deletions as had been made by Ross. It would seem that Wilde had given Ross full instructions with regard to those parts of his prison manuscript which he wished published, but he allowed his friend absolute discretion in the matter.[2]

In England, the book caused an extraordinary sensation; the press devoted long columns to this remarkable work, which was compared now with Rousseau's *Confessions,* now with De

Quincey's *Confessions of an English Opium-Eater,* and other less known literary self-denunciations.

As a piece of prose, *De Profundis* is, of course, a *magnum opus* of the highest order. Its rhythmical properties have reached that stage of perfection where the dividing line between poetry and prose is almost altogether effaced. In this, Wilde merely followed the method, principles and genre originally conceived by Pater and which our poet had incarnated in his *L'Envoi, Intentions* and Fairy Tales. In those earlier creations, however, his style, as we know, was still flowery and, in parts at least, artificial; it also suffered from an over-elaboration of detail. But *De Profundis,* as Ingleby observed,

> is purged of all the faults—one might say the faults of excellence. . . . Just as the man himself was purged and purified in mind by the terrible experiences of prison, so his style also became stronger and more beautiful,

acquiring "the harmony and strength of a great wind blowing through a forest."

And also, just as the man grew sincere and simple, so the mode of his expression became sincere in its simplicity, and simple in its sincerity. It is marked with an artistic self-restraint and that tact of omission with which only the great masters of the written or spoken word are blessed. The very handling of the material is devoid of any formal plan or artificially devised scheme: with a surprising flexibility, the poet registers his changing moods and fluid emotions, the pulsations of his vibrating ego, one after another, as they arose in his troubled soul during those gloomy hours of his confinement.

However, the chief interest of *De Profundis* lies not in the excellence of its style, nor in the bewitching cadence of its musical periods, but in its contents rather, in the revelation of a complex human drama, in the slow ascent of the spirit to the snowy heights of wisdom. Albeit Wilde had no intention of writing a treatise on philosophy or a textbook on ethics, or a *précis* on logic, and though he made it quite clear that neither conventional morality nor pharisaical religion was likely to show him the way to salvation, nevertheless, *De Profundis* is at once a philosophical poem and a faithful record of the resurrection of a man whose whole life had been shattered by the grim law of retribution.

Prison taught Wilde the lesson of humility and made him understand the dignity of suffering. In days past, when he was happy, how could he have known that the tears of sorrow are often more precious than the pearls of beauty?

> The gods [he said] had given me almost everything. I had genius, a distinguished name, high social position, brilliancy, intellectual daring; I made art a philosophy and philosophy an art: I altered the minds of men and the colours of things: there was nothing I said or did that did not make people wonder. I took the drama, the most objective form known to art, and made it as personal a mode of expression as the lyric or sonnet. . . . Drama, novel, poem in prose, poem in rhyme, subtle or fantastic dialogue, whatever I touched, I made beautiful in a new mode of beauty. . . . I treated art as the supreme reality and life as a mere mode of fiction. I awoke the imagination of my century so that it created myth and legend around me. I summed up all systems in a phrase and all existence in an epigram.

It was because of this state of self-sufficiency and self-conceit that he had been lured into what he himself termed "long spells of senseless and sensual ease"; and it was thus that he yielded to the temptation of becoming a man of fashion instead of aspiring to become a man of genius. The sighs of grief and the ache of mourning were of no concern to him. He may have talked—as he did in *The Soul of Man* or in *The Young King*—about the burdens of the poor and the misery of the outcast, but his heart was at war with his mind, and for things genuinely spiritual he never did evince a great passion. He admitted them for the sake of contrast with his own feasts of thought and his own luxury of living. But the bitterness and scorn, the horrible disgrace, the wild despair, the impotent rage, which he had experienced while in prison, kindled in his soul a new light, not as dazzling perhaps as the flames of fame and the glare of notoriety amidst which he had been moving, yet how much more penetrating and even! Suffering helped him to find his own soul and that something hidden away in him, which was humbleness.

At last he had discovered the true meaning of Dostoievsky's secret, the strange devotion of the great Russian clairvoyant to all those "poor folk," "downtrodden and insulted," to those saintly "idiots" and God-seeking "possessed," who live and love and suffer in his immortal creations. In Wilde's spiritual growth, these revelations proved a point of departure to realms that hitherto had remained unexplored by him. It was, or at least he hoped it was, the beginning of a *vita nuova*. Now he could truthfully say about himself:

> I am completely penniless, and absolutely homeless. Yet there are worse things in the world than that. I am quite candid when I say that rather than go out from this prison with bitterness in my heart against the world, I would gladly and readily beg my bread from door to door. If I got nothing from the house of the rich I would get something at the house of the poor. Those who have much are often greedy; those who have little always share. . . . The external things of life seem to me now of no importance at all. You can see to what intensity of individualism I have arrived—or am arriving rather, for the journey is long, and "where I walk there are thorns."

Thorns of Sorrow which penetrate into one's heart and make it bleed "when any hand but that of love touches it."

In this battle against his own boundless pride, Wilde scored a victory more glorious than any he had won before. Yet even this triumph was not a decisive one: he found a new and noble moral law, but he failed to grasp the fact that an ethical norm, to be binding upon man's conduct, must have a heteronomous, or divine, sanction, and that it cannot be an autonomous precept of man's own will or whim. However, a conception such as this would have led Wilde from the shrine of reason to the temple of God, in Whom he had no belief. He confessed to himself that religion was impotent to help him. And it is significant that from among all the gospels only one appealed to his intellect: not even the Fifth apocryphal Evangel of St. Clement of Alexandria, but *La Vie de Jésus,* that Sixth Gospel which is Thomas's record of eternal doubt, or man's attempt to achieve virtue without Christ.

There are in *De Profundis* fascinating pages about Christ, passages full of beauty and romantic pathos. Still, what Wilde accepted in Jesus was not His divinity but His humanity. It pleased him to treat Christ as a supreme individualist and an inspired poet—and it is Wilde who semi-blasphemously asserted that Shelley and Sophocles are of our Saviour's company. Paganism in Wilde was so deeply rooted that even when his thought turned to the Son of Man, Golgotha always remained covered by the shadow of Olympus. The nearest Wilde ever got to the mystery of the New Testament is where he speaks of Christ's earthly life as "an idyll," though it ended with the darkness "coming over the face of the earth."

> One always thinks of him as a young bridegroom with his companions, as indeed he somewhere describes himself; as a shepherd straying through a valley with his sheep in search of green meadow or cool stream; as a singer trying to build out of the music the walls of the City of God; or as a lover for whose love the whole world was too small. . . . I see no difficulty at all in believing that such was the charm of his personality that his mere presence could bring peace to souls in anguish, and that those who touched his garments or his hands forgot their pain; or that as he passed by on the highway of life people who had seen nothing of life's mystery saw it clearly, and others who had been deaf to every voice but that of pleasure heard for the first time the voice of love and found it as "musical as Apollo's lute."

Thus, in Wilde's mind heathen realism prevailed over Christian mysticism. He entered the gates of the House of Sorrow without ever having known what sorrow was. He left Reading, though purified, yet groping in the dark, with the name of Christ on his lips but the symbol of the Cross sadly absent from his broken heart. And hope, which had returned to him, was supported by neither love nor faith. He knew not whence to start nor whither to go on his pilgrimage along the barren roads of earthly existence. That is why the concluding chords in *De Profundis* are pitched in a minor key, reminding one of the mournful sounds of a requiem dropping upon the marble face of Death, rather than of a radiant prelude to the hymn of Life, praising its joys and many wonders.

Society, as we have constituted it [said Wilde] will have no place for me, has none to offer; but Nature, whose sweet rains fall on unjust and just alike, will have clefts in the rocks where I may hide, and secret valleys in whose silence I may weep undisturbed. She will hang the night with stars so that I may walk abroad in the darkness without stumbling, and send the wind over my footprints so that none may track me to my hurt: she will cleanse me in great waters, and with bitter herbs make me whole.

CHAPTER XXXIII

A FUGITIVE FROM FATE

TO ONE, said Voltaire, who has lost everything—life is a disgrace and death a duty.

Reading Gaol to Wilde was a nightmare from which he awoke only to find himself at the threshold of his own grave. There, within the four walls of his cell, he was a prisoner of Fate; after his release he became at once a fugitive from Fate. Destiny made him a pilgrim without destination, a man without a name, or rather with one that was not his own, for he re-entered the world under the pseudonym "Sebastian Melmoth."[1] His heart was broken, his will crushed. Bitter memories of the past—those pitiless thieves that rob one of the present—invaded his wearied brain and brought to it the sad tale

> of other years,
> Of hopes that bloomed to die,
> Of sunny smiles that set in tears
> And loves that mouldering lie.

Oscar's aimless wanderings, his vagabondage, began on the very day when he was put outside Wandsworth with that symbolic half sovereign, the earnings of two years' hard labour, which represented all that he retained in the way of earthly possessions. His was a state of misery so abject that even his clothes had to be provided by friends—whether by Ross or Harris is unimportant.[2]

On May 19, 1897, when Wilde was set free, he drove to Brompton Oratory and asked there to see one of the priests, probably Father Sebastian Bowden. This was Oscar's first impulsive move. What could have been the motive of that visit?—Was it a recurring whim to join the Catholic Church?

Or was it a vague hope of learning in the Chapel something he proved unable to grasp in prison—an attempt, perhaps, to bridge the gap between agnosticism and religion, to find some sort of a compromise between Renan and Christ? Who knows? —There is no record of what transpired between Wilde and the friar who received him. All we know is that the interview led to nothing, and that, accompanied by Ross and Reginald Turner, he promptly departed for Dieppe via New Haven.

Why was Dieppe chosen?—No doubt, Wilde had to get out of the country. He knew "his" England too well, and consequently, had every reason to believe that life there would be made intolerable for him. Why, even the tailor refused to take his order for two suits! One can easily imagine what kind of treatment would have been accorded Wilde by his former acquaintances, shopkeepers, hotel managers and restaurateurs.

Still, from among all places whither he could have gone, Dieppe was about the worst that could have been designated for him. In fact, while still in prison, Oscar wrote to Ross:

> I now hear that Dieppe has again been decided on. I dislike it as I am so well known there. . . .

His presentiment about that unattractive French port unfortunately proved true: time and again, he was publicly insulted there not only by his compatriots but also by Frenchmen who were catering to an English clientele. On one occasion, a Dieppe hostler declined to serve dinner to Wilde because English people threatened to withdraw their custom if he were permitted to patronise the place. Altogether, the Dieppe experience was a dreadful one. Referring to that period, Martin Birnbaum notes in his *Memoirs:*

> The one pleasant incident in the record of this part of his career is his meeting with Fritz Thaulow at Dieppe. Wilde had been insulted by some English residents of the town in the presence of the big Northerner, when the painter walked up to the poet, and said in a clear voice which all the prudes could hear, "Mr. Wilde, my wife and I would feel honoured to have you dine with us *en famille* this evening." There he found Charles Conder, the decorator of exquisite

fans, and both men recovered something of their former gaiety in the charming atmosphere of the Thaulow home, filled with golden-haired children and their infectious laughter.

Naturally, Wilde could not have stayed at Dieppe and it was imperative for him to find some other spot nearby where he could live in complete retirement, in the quiet of utter obliteration.

After a great deal of hesitation, he finally selected for his hiding-place, Berneval-sur-Mer, a little village on the seacoast not far from Dieppe. He took two rooms there in a clean and agreeably situated *auberge*. He was treated with kindness and attention by the hotel staff, while the proprietress, "a perfect dear," as Wilde christened her, became really devoted to him. His *appartement* was arranged with taste; there were many books and the tall pedestal in the corner supported a pretty Gothic madonna.

Hôtel de la Plage—this was the high-sounding name of the inn—was an old-fashioned establishment, hopelessly provincial and, needless to say, typically French! Early in June, Oscar wrote Ross inviting him to spend a few days with him at Berneval.

> As for your room [he remarked humourously] the charge will be nominally 2 fr. 50 a night, but there will be *lots* of extras, such as *bougie, bain* and hot water: all cigarettes smoked in the bedroom are charged extra: washing is extra: and if any one does not take the extras, of course he is charged more.
> *Bain*—25c.
> *Pas de bain*—50c.
> *Cigarette dans la chambre à coucher*—10c. *chaque cigarette.*
> *Pas de cigarette dans la chambre à coucher*—20c. *chaque cigarette.*

"This," he added, "is the *système* in all good hotels."

Not much time elapsed before Oscar had become a favourite of those simple Berneval fisherfolk, who felt quite proud of their *Monsieur Melmoth,* who, to them, probably personified the dignity of the British Empire. The village youngsters were particularly fond of him—they simply worshipped him. On

June 27, during Queen Victoria's jubilee days, Wilde gave a feast to some forty school children and the whole school, with the teacher at their head, turned out for the occasion.[3] Everybody enjoyed the party immensely and when Wilde was about to leave, the people started shouting, *Vivent Monsieur Melmoth et la Reine d'Angleterre!*

He made friends with the douane officers; to cure them of their boredom he gave them the novels of Dumas père. Constant Trop-Hardy, the old curé of the tiny grey stone chapel of Notre Dame de Liesse, took a sincere fancy to the distinguished exile. There was even a time when Oscar thought seriously of confessing to him that he was in great disgrace. The humble servant of Christ had a charming little cottage and a *jardin potager*. Oscar enjoyed his company, and the two used to take long walks by the sea.

Although Wilde complained at the time that he had neither watch nor clock and that the sun at Berneval "was hours in advance," so that he had to rely "on the unreliable moon," nevertheless he rose every day rather punctually at half-past seven and took his morning swim. He was in bed by ten. His was a simple life, and never had he been in such perfect health. Not only his body but his soul as well seemed to live in perfect unison with nature, that deep blue sky and opal sea and the glorious sunshine and the fresh breath of the wandering winds. Writing from Berneval to Rothenstein, our poet thus summed up the moods and feelings which animated him at the time:

> I know, dear Will, you will be pleased to know that I have not come out of prison an embittered or disappointed man. On the contrary. In many ways I have gained much. I am not ashamed of having been in prison: I often was in more shameful places: but I am really ashamed of having led a life unworthy of an artist. I don't say that Messalina is a better companion than Sporus, or that the one is all right and the other all wrong: I know simply that a life of definite and studied materialism, and a philosophy of appetite and cynicism, and a cult of sensual and senseless ease, are bad things for an artist: they narrow the imagination, and dull the more delicate sensibilities. . . . Of course I have lost much, but still . . . when I reckon up all that

is *left* to me, the sun and the sea of this beautiful world; its dawns dim with gold and its nights hung with silver; many books, and all flowers, and a few good friends, and a brain and body to which health and power are not denied—really I am *rich* . . . and as for money, my money did me horrible harm. . . .

Friends who came to see Wilde for a day at that little Berneval inn were delighted to find him his old self, in intellectual vigour and sensitiveness to the play of life. Yet the impression of Oscar's appearance was merely a superficial one.

Here is what he wrote to Frank Harris two weeks after he had moved to the Hôtel de la Plage:

. . . While I am cheerful, happy, and have sustained to the full that passionate interest in life and art that was the dominant chord of my nature, and made all modes of existence and all forms of expression utterly fascinating to me always—still I need rest, quiet, and often complete solitude. . . . I have no *storage* of nervous force. When I expend what I have, in an afternoon, nothing remains. I look to quiet, to a simple mode of existence, to nature in all the infinite meanings of an infinite world, to charge the cells for me. Every day, if I meet a friend, or write a letter longer than a few lines, or even read a book that makes, as all fine books do, a direct claim on me, a direct appeal, an intellectual challenge of any kind, I am utterly exhausted in the evening and often sleep badly.

Wilde settled at Berneval on May 28, 1897. Forthwith he wrote a number of letters, all of them nuanced, to his various friends at Reading, those wretched creatures with whom he had spent two unhappy years. Then he instructed Ross to enclose money orders in each of them. "Those are my debts of honour," he said, "and I must pay them."

In those days, Wilde was full of ideas and literary plans. He contemplated writing two Biblical plays—*Pharaoh* and one entitled *Ahab and Jezebel.* He meant to finish *The Florentine Tragedy,* and it was at Berneval that he conceived *The Ballad of Reading Gaol,* which proved his swan song. Jokingly, he announced to his friends that "in his heavier moments" he had even started compiling a Political Economy, the first law of which he had framed as follows: "Wherever there exists a demand there is *no* supply."

It was his cherished hope to make a grand comeback as an artist and thus to pick up the thread of life which he let fall at the gates of Reading. He felt that nothing but creative work could revive his spirit and restore to him that position in the world which he had lost when the heavy hand of Fate had forced him to his knees only to make him scrub the filthy floor of his shameful cell.

One day he said to Gide, who had come to visit him at Berneval:

> The public is dreadful; it judges only by what one has done last. If I returned to Paris it would see only the condemned man. I shall not appear again until I write a play.

For a while, this instinct of self-preservation urged him to shun the perilous temptations of the Sodoms of our epoch and to stay at Berneval:

> I adore this place [he wrote to a friend]. The whole country is lovely, and full of forest and deep meadow. It is simple and healthy. If I live in Paris I may be doomed to things I don't desire. I am afraid of big towns. . . . I am frightened of Paris—I want to live here.

In his impulsive enthusiasm for unsophisticated life, he had even planned to rent a charming chalet within a two minutes' walk from the hospitable village. On June 5, 1897, he rather emphatically made known his decision to Ross:

> I propose to *live* at Berneval. I will *not* live in Paris, nor in Algiers, nor in Southern Italy.

It was in this mood that Wilde composed at Berneval his mighty and sombre *Ballad of Reading Gaol,* which Birnbaum justly called "one of the most perfect poems of its kind," and which Mr. Monahan described "as the best fruit of Wilde's talent—indeed the one work that has united all suffrages." Though the poet may have been influenced in a measure by Coleridge's meters, his creation is original all through, and as an indictment of capital punishment, it ranks with such a heart-breaking story as Andreev's *The Seven That Were Hanged,* or Prince Mishkin's unforgettable account, in *The Idiot,* of the confused feelings of a man sentenced to die just before the moment when he is ordered to ascend the scaffold of the guillotine.

The grim realism of the *Ballad,* despite the limitations inherent in poetry, is as powerful as that achieved by Zola in *Germinal,* or by Tolstoy in *The Death of Ivan Ilyich.* The six-line stanza,

> I walked, with other souls in pain,
> Within another ring,
> And was wondering if the man had done
> A great or little thing,
> When a voice behind me whispered low,
> *"That fellow's got to swing"*—

has become a classic, and the whole *Ballad,* as Arthur Symons suggested, is a "symbol of the obscure deaths of the heart, the unseen violence upon souls, the martyrdom of hope."

The biographical significance of the piece was thus summed up by Richard Butler Glaenzer:

> In the wrath of remembered tortures, in the emotion of their quickening into the nascent word, in the agony of their parturition, Wilde's mind gave way. Like his opalescent art, it *seemed* most alive the moment before its dissipation. And so *The Ballad of Reading Gaol,* this last child of a wayward intellect, may be said to have earned that distinction by having been the first to follow his release from prison. For its creation, crucified talents were resurrected and forced to labour by a supreme and final effort of will.

Indeed, Wilde's was a Pyrrhic victory which his soul was unable to survive and after which "he closed his imperial lips forever." The dull seclusion of a French village soon began to weigh upon his mind. A typical product of urban civilisation, he not only loved but pathetically needed the animation of crowded cities—their clubs, and shows and manifold seductive diversions, that whirl and swirl, that vivacious tempo of life which, in his pagan days, used to exhilarate him on the misty banks of the Thames. Yes, he craved all that, and above all—he longed for London, which he never did or could forget, that London in whose fogs, as La Jeunesse put it, "he had found all his triumphs and which, in his vanity, he had transformed into a monstrous garden of flowers and palaces of subtlest suggestion and discreetest charm."

Now that London was denied to him, he began to dream about Paris as the next best place to satisfy his cosmopolitan tastes. He began to be restless, and in a letter to "dearest Robbie" he had to confess:

> I simply cannot stand Berneval—I nearly committed suicide there last Thursday, I was so bored.

Again, as in Reading Gaol, he was alone, a culprit and an outcast, in a state of terrible isolation, with all the burdensome thoughts revolving in his head as in a vicious circle. Friends sought to kindle his dimmed genius into a flame of creative work. He made a number of gallant efforts; he did try his best to build up his spirit, to find that Archimedean point of support which, he felt, would enable him to lift with the lever of his will the oppressive weight of his shattered hopes. But all was in vain. He had no strength to discipline himself into submission to the monotony of colourless rustic vegetation, and he fled from Berneval.

First, he proceeded to Rouen, where his reunion with Lord Alfred took place.

> The meeting [says Douglas] was a great success. . . . Poor Oscar cried when I met him at the station. We walked about all day arm in arm, or hand in hand, and were perfectly happy. Next day he went back to Berneval, and I returned to Paris, but we had settled that when I went to Naples about six weeks later he was to join me there.

This was the end of Wilde's probation period. From now on, he began drifting from place to place, moving about without purpose like one of those inorganic particles helplessly suspended in a Brownian solution.

He made his appearance in Paris, but he arrived there without his play, a defeated and "convicted man." As might have been expected, French literary circles took a snobbish attitude toward the broken poet. Zola, who during Wilde's imprisonment refused to sign the petition for his release "for fear of being compromised in some enterprise against good morals"; Stuart Merrill, who described Wilde in his plea as *un malheureux fou;* Pierre Louÿs, Henri de Régnier, Schwob—they all gave the poor man to understand that he was no longer one of their illustrious company. Even Jean Lorrain and several other notorious homosexuals broke off their acquaintance with Oscar.

> Lorrain [Mr. O'Sullivan informs us] was a journalist. . . . his employers told him that if he published a line in defence of Wilde anywhere they would put him off the morning paper from which he derived a good income. The attitude of the others is described in a phrase of one of them: *Je ne fréquente pas les forçats.*

Wilde did not remain long in Paris, and he left for Naples to join Douglas. Again, what was it that prompted Oscar to journey to Italy?—Perhaps he was hoping against hope that companionship, homage, warm hospitality, in place of solitude and hostility, would galvanise his dying soul. This is what, in fact, he wrote Douglas almost on the eve of his departure for Naples:

> My own darling Boy, I feel that my only hope of doing beautiful work in art is being with you—it was not so in old days, but now it is different. . . . I feel that only with you can I do anything at all.

Alas, there was nothing in the whole world that could have restored Wilde to that *vita nuova* about which he had dreamt in his Reading cell. He was no longer capable of any consistent mental effort.

At *bella Napoli,* the two friends stayed for a fortnight at the Hotel Royal, and from there they went to Lord Alfred's suburban villa at Posilipo. Douglas described their sojourn at Naples as "fairly happy," even though they quarrelled at times and had little money to spend. Oscar's income was limited to a modest allowance of £3 a week from his wife, while Lord Alfred at the time was not very much better off.

As for creative work, Wilde accomplished practically nothing: he merely put the finishing touches to his *Ballad,* and, being in need of money, he wrote to Leonard Smithers, his London publisher, asking for £20 as an advance on the poem:

> Application to you for a personal loan may, and, I have no doubt will, follow later on, but up to the present time our relations have been merely the usual ones of poet and publisher, with the usual complete victory for the latter. . . . I also—such is the generosity of my nature—send enclosed four more verses of great power and romantic-realistic suggestion, twenty-four lines in all, each worth a guinea in any of the market-places for poetry.[4]

The Naples idyll came to an abrupt end: Lord Alfred's mother, upon hearing that he was living under the same roof with Oscar, wrote to her son, threatening him with the discontinuance of his allowance unless he left his friend at once. This ultimatum came as a bombshell. As neither Oscar nor Douglas was in a position to raise a penny, the association had to be broken up. Lord Alfred left the grieving poet in the villa with three months' rent paid in advance, and also with £200 which Lady Douglas sent to her son for Oscar.

What could he have undertaken next?—He went to Sicily; but what was the object in going there, except, perhaps, the one Goethe defined in his lyrical gem, *Gefunden,* as

> To look for nothing
> Such was my aim.[5]

And so Wilde wandered back to Naples, feeling miserable and ill, as ever pursued by the dreadful phantom of loneliness and facing what he himself described as "a tragi-comedy of an existence, pervaded by all-devouring ennui." Yet Naples was no better than Palermo: both places bored him and neither offered him any comfort.

In this state of depression, he left for Paris. He had no more ambitions—just one *idée fixe,* to efface everything from his memory, to forget himself, his poverty, his disgrace, the innumerable insults with which the world greeted him on his unwelcome reappearance on the weary stage of life. Now it was just a mad flight from reality into the sad realm of oblivion. Even before he had started on his Italian journey, he wrote Rothenstein: "I don't know where I shall go. . . . I am not in the mood to do the work I want—and I fear I shall never be. The intense energy of creation has been kicked out of me. I don't care now to struggle to get back what, when I had it, gave me little pleasure." This was the beginning of a mortal agony. He sought to relieve it with absinthe which he poured in ever-increasing doses into the shell of his sick body. With sardonic humour he remarked:

Je viens de faire une découverte: l'alcool pris en dose suffisante produit tous les effets de l'ivresse.

During those dreary hours he must often have repeated to himself Rabelais' dying phrase: "Let down the curtain—the farce is over."

Unaware of the psychic condition to which the great poet had been reduced, people still took interest in him. Now and then, flattering offers were made to him: stage producers demanded new plays, the newspapers wanted him to write articles for them.

And Wilde [recounts Vance Thompson] lifted his heavy-lidded eyes and promised—and could not write. This was the real tragedy. His brain was dead. He tried to waken it with alcohol. I remember his coming into Henry's bar one evening—a slow-moving, bloated phantom, an enormous caricature—where I was sitting with Rowland Strong. The barmen drove him away. We followed him and saw him go into the Chatham bar, only to be chased out with ignominy. Tears were running out of his pale eyes and his thick mouth was quivering as he drifted away into the night.

The few faithful friends who did not turn their backs on the unhappy man supplied him from time to time with money, but he spent it recklessly with no thought of the future, as one who knows he is doomed and that his days are numbered. "I have been a King," he said once, "and now I want to be a beggar."[6] Accordingly, his purse was always empty. Leonard Smithers, who had generously helped Beardsley, came also to Wilde's aid. Birnbaum reproduced in his *Fragments* a sad letter from Oscar to his publisher, which, indeed, requires no comment.

June 23, 1898.

My dear Smithers—Please send me £10.—and you will receive the MS. with its due corrections—I don't think you can receive it if you don't, as I am quite penniless, and on the brink of expulsion from my hotel—I do not receive anything till July 1st—I hope you will make up your mind about this coming to Paris, as Robbie has a suit of clothes for me and if you don't come I shall have to wait till I can pay the duty. I have gone to a little inn at Nogent—

Address—
M. Sebastian Melmoth
L'Idée
Le Perreux
Nogent-sur-Marne

as I dare not go back to my Hotel and at Nogent I have credit.—

Do please do this for me *at once.*

Yours
O. W.

Upon his arrival in Paris, Wilde took a room at the Hôtel Alsace, 13 rue des Beaux Arts. This was a shabby, cheap and unsanitary place with no drainage, a typical *maison de cinquième catégorie,* whose chief lure at the time must have been either the traditional gilded clock *à la Louis XVI,* or the *"sonnerie électrique,"* an innovation which Monsieur J. Dupoirier, the proprietor, proudly advertised on the hotel stationery. Oscar's monthly bill, *café-au-lait y compris,* amounted to only 110 francs.

Oscar was not happy there: aside even from the ugliness of the furnishings and the wretched vulgarity of that neighbourhood, the thing that troubled him most was the feeling of insecurity, the fear of being entirely at the mercy of the management.

> All houses in Paris [he explained in a letter to Ross] where there are furnished rooms are a form of hotel—other people live there—and might object to my living at the same address. The *propriétaire* wd. of course find out my real name and ask me to go.

The thought that he might be "found out" seems to have haunted Wilde to the end of his life.

No sooner had he settled at the Hôtel Alsace, than he hastened to decamp for Nogent; thence he promptly returned to Paris, and, after only a short sojourn there, he went to Chanmerières to enjoy the lovely Seine with her placid backwaters and willows and water-lilies and "tourquoise kingfishers."

In December of the same year, he left with Frank Harris for Napoule near Cannes. On the *Côte d'Azure* he spent about two months. While at Nice, Oscar went to see Sarah Bernhardt in *La Tosca*. Their "reunion" must have given Wilde much pleasure: the actress embraced him and wept and the whole evening, he said, "was wonderful."

On April 7, 1898, following an operation, Constance Wilde passed away at Genoa. In the month of February of the next year, Oscar made a trip to that town to visit his wife's grave.

> It is very pretty [he wrote Ross from Switzerland], a marble cross with dark ivy leaves inlaid in a good pattern—the cemetery is a garden at the foot of the lovely hills that climb into the mountains. . . . It was very tragic seeing her name carved on a tomb—her surname—my name not mentioned of course—just "Constance Mary, daughter of Horace Lloyd, Q.C." and a verse from Revelations—I brought some flowers—I was deeply affected—with a sense, also, of the uselessness of all regrets—Nothing could have been otherwise—and life is a very terrible thing.

Having completed his pilgrimage to Genoa, Wilde proceeded to Gland on *Lac Léman,* where he stayed as a guest of M. Mellor. While in Switzerland, Oscar received word from Ross of Willy Wilde's death, which, it seems, left no painful impression on our poet.

Like all other places, Gland bored Wilde, and soon he resumed his aimless wanderings. "The chill virginity of the Swiss Alps" no longer appealed to him; now he was dreaming of "the red flowers of life that stain the feet of summer in Italy." And he fled from Geneva. In May, 1899, he drifted back to Paris, where first he took a room at the Hôtel de la Néva, but was turned out. Then he went to the Hôtel Marsollier off the Avenue de l'Opéra: unable to pay a small bill of £5, he was again forced to leave and the landlord kept Oscar's effects as a sort of pawn. From this hotel, he turned once more to the rue des Beaux Arts, where he had first met Monsieur Dupoirier.

> Wilde told the kindhearted little man of his grievous plight and Dupoirier immediately bade him in God's name come back to his old room, and set off to redeem his new lodger's belongings in pawn at the Hôtel Marsollier. Here Wilde lived the thirteen months of life that remained to him, here at number 13 of the rue des Beaux Arts, and it was with Dupoirier alone watching his bedside that he died, while Ross and Turner were for a moment out of the room.[7]

As a matter of fact, however, early in 1900, Wilde stayed ten days at Gland, and in the spring of that year, in April and May, he again visited Palermo, Genoa, Naples and Rome.

The Eternal City aroused anew Wilde's religious emotions. As in 1875 and 1877, Catholicism filled him with joy and almost made him believe that "his walking stick showed signs of budding," kindling a spark of faith in his empty heart. He was in a state of pious exaltation. Referring to a ceremony at St. Peter's, where the Pope made his appearance before the people, Wilde wrote:

> And when I saw the old white Pontiff, successor of the Apostles and Father of Christendom, pass, carried high above the throng, and in passing turn and bless me where I knelt I felt my sickness of body and soul fall from me like a worn garment, and I was made whole.[8]

One day, Oscar went to the Vatican Gallery, and, upon

leaving the building, he found that the Papal gardens were opened to some Bohemian and Portuguese pilgrims.

I at once [he reported to Ross] spoke both languages fluently—explained that my English dress was a form of penance, and entered that waste, desolate Park—with its faded Louis XIV gardens, its sombre avenues, its sad woodland— The peacocks screamed, and I understood why tragedy dogged the gilt feet of each Pontiff. But I wandered in exquisite melancholy for an hour.

Finally, Wilde came back to Paris, to his miserable quarters at the Hôtel d'Alsace. He knew that he was desperately ill, suffering from what he once described to Harris as "softening of the brain." In one of his letters to Ross he candidly admitted:

I have no future. . . . I don't think I am equal to intellectual architecture of thought. . . .

But he still retained much of his former charm and chivalry. Comtesse de Brémont, who came across Wilde in the autumn of 1900, on the quaint *bâteau-mouche* going in the direction of St. Cloud, found him purified through suffering. He was, as ever, gentle and gallant. In answer to her question why he did not write, he said:

I have no time to write—if I willed. My time is short—my work is done—and when I cease to live, that work will begin to live. Ah! my work will live as long as men live to read it; my work will be my great monument! Contessa [he went on], don't sorrow for me, but watch and pray—it will not be for long—watch and pray.

Another account of Wilde's conduct in Paris during the same period is given by Graham Robertson in his book, *Time Was*. He tells of Mr. Augustin Daly's sudden death, and how Wilde, "a wanderer and an exile, unrecognised by nearly all his former friends," came to the assistance of Mrs. Daly and Miss Ada Rehan, who had been staying with the poor widow.

Arrangements had to be made and Mrs. Daly was not equal to taking them in hand. "I," said Ada, "seemed to be all alone and so confused and frightened. And then Oscar Wilde came to me and was more good and helpful than I can tell you—just like a very kind brother. I shall always think of him as he was to me through those few dreadful days."

Yet Wilde himself was rapidly sinking. His bodily frame was falling apart, and, while probably nothing could have been done to arrest the corrosion of his brain, it is certain that he did everything to aggravate his condition. He insisted on drinking absinthe, which to him was deadly poison. He ate little and irregularly; he took no exercise, but he consumed brandy in large quantities—a litre bottle would hardly see him through the night—and "*café-cognac*" appeared as a steady item on his hotel bills. He could not get up before late in the afternoon, and then he used to go to a little *bistro* for a drink. He must have sat there with the one immobile thought of the silent shadows that were slowly, but threateningly, gathering around him. His nerves were shattered; he could no longer control his actions. When, on rare occasions, some old friend would call on him, the ill-starred man strained himself in a desperate effort to revive, for a few brief moments, that brilliancy which, in days past, was the sparkling essence of his irresistible charm. "It was," Thompson relates, "as if he were trying to tell everything at once—and he hiccoughed out fantasies and dreams, plays, stories, shining paradoxes and memories," all of which he was going to write . . . some day. Says La Jeunesse:

> Words fail to paint properly the chaos of hope, of words and laughter, the mad sequence of half-concluded sentences into which the poet plunged, proving to himself his still inextinguished fancy, his battling against surrender, his smiling at fate; or to suggest the grim dark into which he always must turn, daily fearing death in the narrow chamber of a sordid inn.

Meanwhile, Wilde began to suffer from dreadful headaches; the pains grew so intolerable that the doctors suggested an operation, which the patient could not afford, since, to quote his own words, it would have made him die "beyond his means."

> He must have suffered terribly [said Dupoirier] for he kept raising his hands to his head to try to ease the torture. He cried out again and again. We used to put ice on his head. I was ever giving him injections of morphine.

This must have been some form of cerebral meningitis. As early as in July, 1900, Wilde by wire cancelled an appointment with Louis Wilkinson, who was to travel from Dieppe to Paris to meet the ailing poet: "*Je suis très malade. Ne venez pas cette semaine*"—such was Wilde's laconic message. In October of the same year he had to take to his bed. Several days later he rallied. On October 10, he even underwent a minor operation for a growth in the ear, which apparently made him feel better. But his recovery proved only temporary; on October 30, he drove to the *Bois*. This was the last time he was able to leave his room.

Through November, Wilde grew steadily weaker and, according to Ransome, he was often hysterical and delirious. "I am very ill," he wrote Ross, "and the doctor is making all kinds of experiments. My throat is a limekiln, my brain a furnace and my nerves a coil of angry adders." Reginald Turner and Dupoirier faithfully nursed him. When the poet's condition became alarming, Turner by wire summoned Ross from Nice to Paris. On the 29th, Ross brought to Wilde's bedside Father Dunn, a Catholic priest, who baptised the poet and administered extreme unction. Early in the afternoon, on the 30th of November, Wilde sank into a coma. Now he was ready to start on his last voyage and to take, what Hobbes called, "a great leap into the dark":

> At 1:45 [recorded Ross] the time of his breathing altered . . . his pulse began to flutter. He heaved a deep sigh . . . the limbs seemed to stretch involuntarily, the breathing became fainter. He passed at ten minutes to two exactly.

Such was the end of the earthly drama of Oscar Wilde,

whose genius, surviving his dust, continues to live and shine among the immortals of all lands and ages.

Oscar Wilde was buried according to the rites of the Catholic Church on December 3, 1900, in the Cemetery of Bagneux, on the outskirts of Paris.

The requiem Mass was officiated by Father Dunn and two other priests in the Chapel of the Sacred Heart at the beautiful old Church of Saint Germain-les-Près. There was no music, and the absolution having been intoned in English, the liturgic Latin, as La Jeunesse remarked, was turned to a non-conformist jumble.

At the funeral Lord Alfred took the part of chief mourner. Only a few friends joined the funeral *cortège,* among them five ladies in deep mourning. There were altogether twenty-four wreaths of flowers—some were sent anonymously. Monsieur Dupoirier, to whom Oscar remained indebted in the sum of over 2000 francs, supplied a beaded trophy on which there was the pathetic inscription, "*A mon locataire.*" Another of the same kind was from *Le service de l'Hôtel.*

Wilde's body was buried in a temporary concession rented in the name of Robert Ross, in the Seventeenth Grave of the Eighth Row of the Fifteenth Division. The laconic inscription on the tomb was as follows:

OSCAR WILDE
Oct. 16th., 1854 Nov. 30th., 1900
Verbis meis addere nihil audebant et super illos stillabat
eloquiem meum.
Job XXIX. 22.
R. I. P.

On July 20, 1909, Wilde's remains were moved by Ross to Père Lachaise, a Pantheon of Fame in which Balzac, Musset, Sarah Bernhardt, Bizet, Adelina Patti, Chopin and many other illustrious men and women have found their last repose. Wilde's grave is in the Eighty-ninth Division facing the Avenue

Carette. Engraved on the back of the headstone is a brief *curriculum vitae* of his, accompanied by these fitting lines:

> And alien tears will fill for him
> Pity's long-broken urn,
> For his mourners will be outcast men,
> And outcasts always mourn.[9]

Alas, a despicable and ugly monument was placed over the ashes of the Apostle of Beauty, perhaps "to prevent any one from praying at his grave."

The Epstein monstrosity was the last grimace that Fate pulled at him whose immortal soul had soared into the vast domain of Eternity.

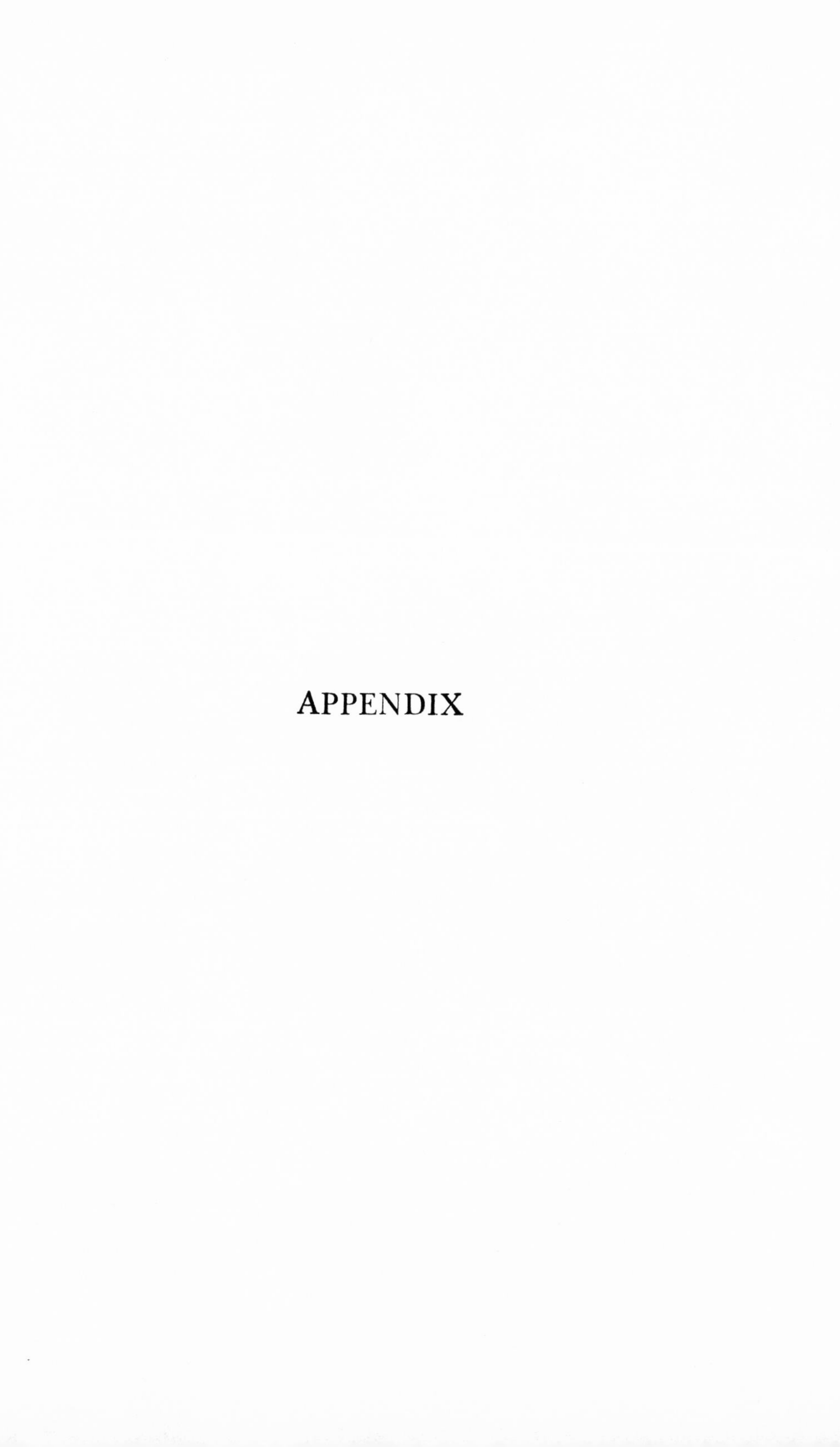

APPENDIX

OSCAR WILDE

CHRONOLOGICAL INDEX

The Index printed below does not purport to give an exhaustive chronological record of the biographical and literary events in Oscar Wilde's career. However, the student may find it useful in that it lists some of the more important facts relating to the life and work of the poet. Substantially, the Index covers the period from October 16, 1854, *i.e.,* the date of Wilde's birth, until November 30, 1900, when he died in Paris. Only a few dates preceding and succeeding this period have been inserted for the convenience of the reader. For many of the references dealing with Wilde's literary achievements the author is indebted to Mr. Stuart Mason (C. S. Millard), whose *Bibliography* is an inexhaustible well of authentic information. Much useful material was also extracted from the anonymous work, *The Writings of Oscar Wilde,* London, 1907, and *Decorative Art in America, A Lecture by Oscar Wilde Together with Letters, Reviews, and Interviews,* edited with an Introduction by Richard Butler Glaenzer, New York, 1906. As to the strictly biographical data, a rather careful examination had to be made of the various books and magazine articles on Wilde. The chronology of Wilde's trials and of the last period of his life is admirably summed up in *Oscar Wilde: Three Times Tried,* London, 1912, *After Reading, Letters of Oscar Wilde to Robert Ross,* and *Oscar Wilde, A Collection of Original Manuscripts, Letters and Books,* a catalogue of the auction sale published by Messrs. Dulau & Co., London, 1928. All dates were carefully checked by the author and corrected wherever mistakes appeared in the various original sources. Many important dates were found in the author's collection of Oscar Wilde's unpublished letters.

1851

Doctor William Wilde married in Dublin Miss Jane Francesca Elgee (born in 1826).

1852

The first child, William, was born to Doctor and Mrs. William Wilde.

1854

OCTOBER 16—O. W. was born at 21 Westland Row, Dublin.

1855

APRIL 26—O. W. baptised at St. Mark's, Dublin.

OSCAR WILDE

1856

Doctor William and Mrs. Wilde moved into their mansion at 1, Merrion Square, Dublin.

1857

Oscar I, King of Sweden, conferred upon Doctor William Wilde the Order of the Polar Star.

1864

O. W. was sent to Portora Royal School at Enniskillen.

Lord Carlisle, Viceroy of Ireland, conferred knighthood upon Doctor William Wilde in recognition of his services to statistical science.

1867

FEBRUARY 23—Isola Wilde, sister of O. W., died.

1871

O. W. graduated from Portora Royal School.

OCTOBER 10—O. W. matriculated as a junior freshman at Trinity College, Dublin.

OCTOBER 26—O. W. passed an entrance scholarship examination at Trinity College and was elected a "Queen's Scholar."

1872

JANUARY 31—In the "Examination for Honours" in Classics at Trinity College, O. W. was third out of eight in the First Rank.

APRIL 29—O. W. at Trinity College won the Michaelmas prize.

1873

JUNE 9—O. W. was elected at Trinity College to a University Scholarship on the Foundation entitling him to an annual sum of £20.

1874

O. W. at Trinity College took the Berkeley Gold Medal for an examination in the fragments of the Greek comic poets as edited by Meineke.

J. P. Mahaffy in the preface to his *Social Life in Greece from Homer to Menander* acknowledged his obligation to O. W. for making improvements and corrections throughout that book.

OCTOBER 17—O. W. matriculated at Magdalen College, Oxford.

1875

O. W. made an extensive tour through Northern Italy, visiting Milan, Padua, Venice, Verona, etc.

JUNE 15–O. W., at Magdalen College, wrote his poem, "Graffiti d'Italia. I. San Miniato."

NOVEMBER–*The Dublin University Magazine* published O. W.'s "Chorus of Cloud Maidens," adapted from "Aristophanes," the earliest known of O. W.'s published writings.

1876

(Michaelmas term) *Kottabos* published O. W.'s "Θρηνῳδία."

JANUARY–*The Dublin University Magazine* published O. W.'s poem, "From Spring Days to Winter (for music)."

MARCH–*The Dublin University Magazine* published O. W.'s poem, "Graffiti d'Italia. I. San Miniato."

APRIL 19–Sir William Wilde died.

JUNE–*The Dublin University Magazine* published O. W.'s poem, "The Dole of the King's Daughter (for painting)."

SEPTEMBER–*The Irish Monthly* published O. W.'s "The True Knowledge."

The Dublin University Magazine published O. W.'s "Αἴλινον, αἴλινον 'εἰπὲ τὸ δ' εῦ νικάτω."

The Month published O. W.'s poem, "Graffiti d'Italia." Reprinted in *Poems* under the title "Rome Unvisited."

OCTOBER–*Kottabos* published O. W.'s poem, "The Rose of Love, and With a Rose's Thorn."

1877

(Michaelmas term) *Kottabos* published O. W.'s poem, "Wasted Days."

(Hilary term) *Kottabos* published O. W.'s "A Fragment from the Agamemnon of Æschylus. A Night vision."

FEBRUARY–*The Irish Monthly* published O. W.'s poem, "Lotus Leaves."

MARCH–O. W. departed for Greece via Genoa.

MARCH–O. W. wrote his sonnet, "Holy Week at Genoa."

JUNE–*The Irish Monthly* published O. W.'s sonnet, "Salve Saturnia Tellus." Reprinted with revisions under the title, "Sonnet on Approaching Italy," in *Poems,* London, 1881.

JUNE–*The Illustrated Monitor* published O. W.'s sonnet, "Urbs Sacra Æterna."

JULY–*The Irish Monthly* published O. W.'s article, "The Tomb of Keats." At its close is the sonnet "The Grave of Keats" under the original title, "Heu Miserande Puer."

JULY–*The Dublin University Magazine* published O. W.'s article, "The Grosvenor Gallery."

JULY–*The Illustrated Monitor* published O. W.'s "Sonnet Written During Holy Week."

Autumn—O. W. was fined £45 by the Magdalen dons for failure to return to college on time from his journey to Greece and Italy.

December—*The Irish Monthly* published O. W.'s sonnet "ΠΟΝΤΟΣ ΑΤΡΥΓΕΤΟΣ."

1878

April—*The Irish Monthly* published O. W.'s poem, "Magdalen Walks."

May 1—Mrs. George Morrell gave a ball at Headington Hill Hall, Oxford, at which O. W. appeared in a costume à la Prince Rupert.

June 26—O. W. recited in the Sheldonian Theatre, Oxford, his poem, "Ravenna," for which he was awarded the Newdigate prize.

July—*The Irish Monthly* published O. W.'s poem, "Ave Maria Gratia Plena."

July 15—*Ravenna* was published in book form by Thos. Shrimpton and Son, Oxford.

1879

O. W. wrote "The Rise of Historical Criticism" for the Chancellor's English Essay Prize at Oxford.

(Michaelmas term) *Kottabos* published "Ave Maria."

(Hilary term) *Kottabos* published O. W.'s ballad, "La Belle Marguerite."

April—O. W.'s poem, "The Conqueror of Time," was published in *Time*. Reprinted in *Poems* (1881) under the title, "Athanasia."

May 5—*Saunders' Irish Daily News* printed O. W.'s notice on "Grosvenor Gallery."

June—O. W.'s sonnet, "Easter Day," was published in *Waifs and Strays*. Reprinted in *Poems* (1881).

June 11—*The World* published O. W.'s sonnet "To Sarah Bernhardt." Reprinted in *Poems* under the title "Phèdre."

July—O. W.'s poem, "The New Helen," published in *Time*.

July 16—O. W.'s "Queen Henrietta Maria (Charles I, act III)" published in *The World*.

1880

Routledge's Christmas Annual published "Sen Artysty; or The Artist's Dream" by Madame Helena Modjeska. "Translated from the Polish by Oscar Wilde." [?]

January 14—O. W.'s sonnet, "Portia" published in *The World*.

March—*Waifs and Strays* published O. W.'s poem, "Impression de Voyage."

August—*The Biograph and Review* published a notice, "Oscar Wilde," which was the first biographical sketch of O. W.

August 25—O. W.'s "Ave Imperatrix, A Poem on England," published in *The World*.

SEPTEMBER—*Vera: or The Nihilists* published in London by Ranken & Co.

SEPTEMBER 25—*Pan* published O. W.'s poem, "Pan—A Villanelle."

NOVEMBER 10—O. W.'s sonnet, "Libertatis Sacra Fames," published in *The World.*

1881

JANUARY—*The Burlington* published O. W.'s sonnet, "The Grave of Keats."

JANUARY 8—*Pan* published O. W.'s sonnet, "To Helen (Serenade of Paris)." Reprinted in *Poems* under the title "Serenade (for music)."

FEBRUARY 12—*Punch* published "Maudle on the Choice of a Profession," with reference to O. W.

FEBRUARY—*Punch* attacked O. W. in "Beauty Not at Home."

MARCH 2—*The World* published O. W.'s poem, "Impression du Matin." Subsequently, on February 26, 1895, the facsimile of the manuscript was reproduced in *The Picture Magazine* under the heading "To My Friend Luther Munday."

APRIL 9—*Punch* published "A Maudle In Ballad To His Lily."

APRIL 23—*Pan* published O. W.'s "Impressions. I. Les Silhouettes. II. La Fuite de la Lune."

APRIL 30—*Punch* printed "The First of May," "An Æsthetic Rondeau," "Substitution."

MAY 7—*Punch* published "A Design for an Æsthetic Theatrical Poster, 'Let Us Live Up To It.'"

MAY 7—*Punch* printed "A Padded Cell."

MAY 14—*Punch* published "Philistia Defiant."

MAY 14—*Punch* published "A Fashionable Nursery Rhyme."

MAY 14—*Punch* printed "The Grosvenor Gallery."

MAY 17—O. W. entered into a written agreement with David Bogue for the publication of *Poems.*

MAY 28—*Punch* printed "Some Æsthetic Notes."

MAY 28—E. J. Milliken's parody of O. W.'s "La Fuite de la Lune" (*Pan,* April 23, 1881), under the title "More Impressions. La Fuite des Oies, by Oscuro Wildegoose," was printed in *Punch.*

JUNE—First printing of O. W.'s *Poems* (David Bogue, London).

JUNE 25—*Punch's* "Fancy Portraits, No. 37, 'O. W.'"

JUNE 25—*Punch* attacked O. W. in "Æsthetics at Ascot."

JULY 23—*Punch* printed "Maunderings at Marlow. By Our Own Æsthetic Bard."

JULY 23—*Punch* published "Swinburne and Water."

JULY 23—*Athenæum* printed a long review of O. W.'s *Poems.*

AUGUST 20—*Punch* printed "Too-Too Awful, A Sonnet of Sorrow."

AUGUST 20—*Punch* published "Croquis, by Dumb-Crambo, Junior."

SEPTEMBER 17—*Punch* printed a parody on O. W.'s poem, "Impression de l'Automme (stanzas by our muchly admired Poet Drawit Milde)."

SEPTEMBER 22—*Patience* produced at the Standard Theatre on Broadway, New York.

SEPTEMBER 30—Colonel W. F. Morse cabled O. W. from New York offering a fifty-lectures engagement tour in the U. S.

OCTOBER 1—O. W.'s *Poems* published in America by Roberts Brothers, Boston.

OCTOBER 1—O. W. cabled to Colonel W. F. Morse his consent in principle to fill the lecture engagements in the U. S.

OCTOBER 1—*Punch* published "The Æsthete to the Rose. (By Wildegoose, after Waller)."

OCTOBER 29—*Punch* printed a parody, "Spectrum Analysis" on O. W.'s "The Burden of Itys" ("By the Wilde-Eyede Poet").

NOVEMBER 12—*Punch* printed a skit on O. W.'s *Poems* under the title, "A Sort of 'Sortes.' "

NOVEMBER 19—*Punch* ridiculed O. W. in its "Poet's Corner: Or, Nonsense Rhymes on Well-Known Names."

NOVEMBER 26—*Punch* printed a parody on O. W., "Theoretikos (put into plain English for the benefit of Philistia) by Oscuro Wildegoose."

NOVEMBER 26—*Punch* printed "The Downfall of the Dado."

NOVEMBER 30—*The World* printed a notice on the withdrawal of *Vera* from the repertoire of the Adelphi Theatre, London, where the play was to have been produced December 17, 1881.

DECEMBER 6—*Punch's Almanack for 1882* printed a parody, "More Impressions des Sornettes, by Oscuro Wildegoose."

DECEMBER 10—*Punch* printed "Impressions du Théâtre."

DECEMBER 17—*Vera* was to have been produced at the Adelphi Theatre, London, but the play was withdrawn from the repertoire (See November 30, 1881).

DECEMBER 24—O. W. sailed on *S.S. Arizona* from England to New York.

DECEMBER 24—"Mr. Punch's 'Mother Hubbard' Fairy Tale Grinaway Christmas Cards—(Second Series)" was published in *Punch*.

DECEMBER 31—*Punch* attacked O. W. in "Mrs. Langtry as 'Lady Macbeth.' "

1882

O. W. entered into an agreement with Hamilton Griffin in New York to write a five-act tragedy for Miss Mary Anderson.

While in America O. W. wrote "L'Envoi" to Rennell Rodd's *Rose Leaf and Apple Leaf*, a collection of poems which was published in Philadelphia, 1882, by J. M. Stoddart & Co.

JANUARY 2—O. W. arrived in New York.

JANUARY 5—Mr. and Mrs. A. A. Hayes, Jr., of New York, gave a reception in honour of O. W.

JANUARY 7—*Punch* printed "A New Departure."

JANUARY 7—*Punch* printed "In Earnest."

JANUARY 7—*Punch* printed "Clowning and Classicism."

JANUARY 8—O. W. interviewed by a representative of *The New York Daily Tribune.*

JANUARY 8—*The New York World* published O. W.'s (?) sonnet, "Sul Mare."

JANUARY 8—Mrs. John Bigelow gave a dinner in honour of O. W.

JANUARY 9—O. W. lectured at Chickering Hall in New York on "The English Renaissance."

JANUARY 10—*The New York World* published O. W.'s (?) sonnet, "Ave Rosina (Impressions du Théâtre)."

JANUARY 14—*Punch* printed an "Impressions du Théâtre."

JANUARY 14—*Punch* printed "To An Æsthetic Poet."

JANUARY 14—*Punch* published "Murder Made Easy. A Ballad à la Mode. By 'Brother Jonathan' Wilde" (with cartoon).

JANUARY 14—*Punch* printed "Æsthetic Ladies' Hair."

JANUARY 14—*Punch* published "Oscar Interviewed."

JANUARY 15—O. W.'s unpublished letter to Norman Forbes Robertson, from New York, giving an account of his experience there. (Author's Collection.)

JANUARY 16—O. W. arrived in Philadelphia, and attended a reception at the home of Robert Stewart Davis.

JANUARY 17—O. W. lectured at Horticultural Hall in Philadelphia, after which he attended a reception at J. M. Stoddart's home.

JANUARY 18—O. W. was entertained at breakfast by Professor S. H. Grosse, Philadelphia.

JANUARY 18—O. W. visited the Women's School of Design, Philadelphia.

JANUARY 18—O. W. visited, in the afternoon, Walt Whitman at Camden, N. J.

JANUARY 18—O. W. was entertained at dinner by George W. Childs, Philadelphia.

JANUARY 19—O. W. neglected to attend a party which was given in his honour by Mr. and Mrs. Charles Carroll at Baltimore, and proceeded to Washington, D. C., stopping at the Arlington Hotel.

JANUARY 23—O. W. lectured at Lincoln Hall in Washington, D. C.

JANUARY 24—David Bogue published fifth edition of O. W.'s *Poems.*

JANUARY 27—O. W. lectured at the Albany Music Hall.

JANUARY 28—O. W. arrived in Boston, stopping at the Vendôme Hotel.

JANUARY 31—O. W. lectured at the Boston Music Hall.

FEBRUARY 1—O. W. lectured in New Haven at Peck's Opera House.

FEBRUARY 2—O. W. lectured at the Hartford Opera House.

FEBRUARY 3—O. W. lectured at the Brooklyn Academy of Music.

FEBRUARY 4—*Punch* ridiculed O. W. in "Distinctly Precious Pantomime."

FEBRUARY 4—*Punch* printed "A Poet's Day: Ariadne in Naxos; Or, Very Like a Wail."

FEBRUARY 4—*Punch* published "Sketches from 'Boz.' Oscar Wilde as Harold Skimpole."

FEBRUARY 6—O. W. lectured at Utica, N. Y.

FEBRUARY 7—O. W. lectured at the Grand Opera House, Rochester, N. Y., on "The English Renaissance."

FEBRUARY 8—O. W. lectured at the Buffalo Academy of Music.

FEBRUARY 9—O. W. visited Niagara Falls.

FEBRUARY 10—O. W. arrived in Chicago.

FEBRUARY 15—*Our Continent* (Philadelphia) published O. W.'s poem, "Impressions. I. Le Jardin. II. La Mer."

FEBRUARY 15—A letter from Whistler appeared in *The World,* entitled "To Mr. Wilde in America."

FEBRUARY 17—O. W. lectured at the Detroit Music Hall.

FEBRUARY 18—*Punch* attacked O. W. in "Lines by Mrs. Cimabue Brown."

FEBRUARY 18—O. W. lectured in Case Hall, Cleveland.

FEBRUARY 21—O. W. lectured at the Masonic Temple, Louisville, Ky.

FEBRUARY 22—*The World* published a letter from Whistler about O. W., entitled "Disguised in Careful Timidity."

FEBRUARY 28—O. W. at Springfield, Ill.

MARCH 1—O. W. in Dubuque, Iowa.

MARCH 2—O. W. lectured at the Dubuque Opera House.

MARCH 3—*The New York Herald* printed O. W.'s letter to Joaquin Miller.

MARCH 4—O. W. lectured at Racine, Wis.

MARCH 5—O. W. lectured at the Grand Opera House, Milwaukee.

MARCH 11—*Punch* printed "Ossian (with variations)."

MARCH 11—*Punch* printed "The Poet Wilde's Unkissed Kisses."

MARCH 11—O. W. lectured at the Chicago Central Music Hall.

MARCH 16—O. W. lectured at the Opera House, St. Paul, Minn.

MARCH 17—O. W. spoke at a St. Patrick's Day celebration at the St. Paul Opera House.

MARCH 20—O. W. in Sioux City, Iowa.

MARCH 21—O. W. lectured at the Social Art Club, Omaha, Neb.

MARCH 27—O. W. lectured at Platt's Hall in San Francisco. On this date O. W. wrote a long letter to Norman Forbes Robertson describing his journey across the American Continent. (Author's Collection.)

MARCH 28—O. W. lectured at Oakland, Calif.

MARCH 29—O. W.'s second lecture at Platt's Hall, San Francisco.

MARCH 30—O. W. lectured at San José, Calif.

MARCH 31—O. W. lectured at Sacramento, Calif.

APRIL 1—*Punch* printed "The Poet Wilde."

APRIL 1—O. W.'s third lecture at Platt's Hall, San Francisco.

APRIL 1—*Punch* printed "A Philistine to An Æsthete."

APRIL 5—O. W.'s fourth lecture at Platt's Hall, San Francisco.

APRIL 8—*Punch* published "Impression de Gaiety Théâtre. By Ossian Wilderness."

APRIL 10—O. W. at Salt Lake City.

APRIL 11—O. W. lectured at Salt Lake City.

APRIL 12—O. W. lectured in Denver, Colo.

APRIL 13—O. W. lectured at the Tabor Grand Opera House, Leadville, Colo.

APRIL 14—O. W. lectured at Colorado Springs.

APRIL 15—O. W.'s second lecture in Denver.

APRIL 17—O. W. lectured at the Coates Opera House, Kansas City, Mo.

APRIL 18—O. W. lectured in St. Joseph, Mo.

APRIL 20—O. W. lectured in Topeka, Kans.

APRIL 21—O. W. lectured in Lawrence, Kans.

APRIL 22—*Punch* printed "Likely."

APRIL 26—O. W. lectured in Des Moines, Iowa.

APRIL 27—O. W. lectured at the Iowa City Opera House.

APRIL 28—O. W. lectured at Cedar Rapids, Iowa.

MAY 2—O. W. lectured in Dayton, Ohio.

MAY 3—O. W. lectured at the Comstock Opera House, Columbus, Ohio.

MAY 11—O. W. lectured at Wallack's Theatre, New York, on "Decorative Art in America."

MAY 12—O. W. at Montreal.

MAY 13—O. W. lectured at Ottawa.

MAY 15—O. W. at Toronto.

JUNE 2—O. W. lectured at the Globe Theatre, Boston.

JUNE 10—*Harper's Bazaar* published an article attacking Wilde, "Something on *Us*. Something to 'Live Up to' in America."

JUNE 11—O. W. lectured at the Grand Opera House, Cincinnati, Ohio.

JUNE 12—O. W. lectured at Leubrie's Theatre, Memphis, Tenn.

JUNE 14—O. W. at Vicksburg.

JUNE 16—O. W. lectured at the New Orleans Grand Opera House.

JUNE 19—O. W. lectured at the Pavilion, Galveston, Tex.

JUNE 21—O. W. lectured in San Antonio, Tex.

JUNE 24—O. W. returned to New Orleans.

JUNE 26—O. W. lectured at Spanish Fort, La.

JUNE 27—O. W. left New Orleans and stopped at Beauvoir, where he visited Jefferson Davis.

JUNE 28—O. W. lectured at the Amusement Park, Mobile, Ala.

JUNE 29—O. W. lectured in Montgomery, Ala.

JUNE 30—O. W. lectured in Columbus, Ga.

JULY 3—O. W. lectured at Rolston Hall, Macon, Ga.

JULY 4—O. W. lectured at De Give's Opera House, Atlanta, Ga.

JULY 5—O. W. lectured at the Savannah Theatre, Savannah, Ga.

JULY 6—O. W. lectured in Augusta, Ga.

JULY 7—O. W. lectured at the Academy, Charleston, S. C.

JULY 9—O. W. lectured in Wilmington, Del.

JULY 10—O. W. lectured at Van Wyck's Academy, Norfolk, Va.

JULY 12—O. W. lectured at the Richmond Theatre, Richmond, Va.

JULY 15—O. W. lectured at the Casino, Newport, R. I.

JULY 29—O. W. visited Henry Ward Beecher at Peekskill, N. Y.

AUGUST 9—O. W. lectured at Gould Hall, Ballston Spa, N. Y.

AUGUST 10—O. W. lectured in the Congress Hall ballroom, Saratoga, N. Y.

SEPTEMBER 9—*Harper's Weekly* ridiculed O. W. in an article "Oscar Wilde on Our Cast-Iron Stoves: Another American Institution Sat Down On."

SEPTEMBER 26—O. W. lectured in Providence, R. I.

SEPTEMBER 28—O. W. lectured in Pawtucket, R. I.

SEPTEMBER 29—O. W. lectured in North Attleboro, Mass.

OCTOBER 3—O. W. lectured in Bangor, Me.

OCTOBER 8—O. W. at Halifax.

OCTOBER 12—O. W. was arrested at Moncton, N. B., for breach of a lecture contract and was released upon payment of $100.

OCTOBER 13—O. W. lectured at St. John, N. B.

OCTOBER 23—O. W. met Mrs. Langtry in N. Y. at the boat.

NOVEMBER 4—*Punch* attacked O. W. in "Not Generally Known."

NOVEMBER 7—*The New York Herald* printed O. W.'s review of *An Unequal Match,* by Tom Taylor, in which Mrs. Langtry made her first appearance in New York, at Wallack's Theatre on November 6, 1882.

NOVEMBER 10—O. W. had breakfast with Marie Prescott and her husband, William Perzel, at Delmonico's, New York, at which time the details of the production *Vera* were discussed.

NOVEMBER 14—O. W. was swindled at a card game in N. Y.

NOVEMBER 26—*Punch* printed "What! No Soap! Or, Pop Goes the Langtry Bubble."

DECEMBER 27—O. W. sailed from New York for Liverpool on *SS. Bothnia.*

1883

JANUARY 6—O. W. arrived in Liverpool.

FEBRUARY—O. W. met Robert Sherard in Paris.

MARCH 15—O. W. finished in Paris his *Duchess of Padua.*

MARCH 31—*Punch* printed "Sage Green (By a Fading-out Æsthete)."

MARCH 31—*Punch* printed "To Be Sold."

MAY 5—O. W. in Paris wrote a letter to Robert Sherard in re "L'Envoi" and "The Sphinx." (See Chap. XV.)

MAY 5—O. W. dined at M. Edmond de Goncourt's home in Paris.

MAY 6—O. W. wrote a letter from Paris to Marie Prescott in which reference is made to his agreement with the actress for the production of *Vera* in N. Y.

MAY 12—*Punch* published "Our Academy Guide. No. 163.—Private Frith's View.—Members of the Salvation Army, led by General Oscar Wilde, joining in a hymn."

JUNE—O. W. arranged with Colonel Morse in London for a lecture tour through England and Scotland.

JUNE 30—O. W.'s lecture to the students of the Royal Academy at their club in Golden Square, Westminster.

JULY 9—O. W.'s lecture at Prince's Hall, Piccadilly, on "Personal Impressions of America."

JULY 30—O. W.'s lecture at Southport, England.

AUGUST 2—O. W. went to Liverpool to welcome Mrs. Langtry on her return from America.

AUGUST 2—O. W. left for New York from Liverpool.

AUGUST 12—O. W. arrived in New York to supervise the last rehearsals of *Vera.*

AUGUST 12—*The New York Herald* printed O. W.'s letter to Miss Marie Prescott, endorsing her selections for the cast of *Vera* at the Union Square Theatre, New York.

AUGUST 12—*The New York Herald* printed under the general heading "Amusement Notes" O. W.'s letter to Marie Prescott on *Vera.*

AUGUST 20—First performance of O. W.'s *Vera* at Union Square Theatre, New York.

AUGUST 25—*The New York Mirror* printed a long review of the performance of *Vera* at the Union Square Theatre.

SEPTEMBER 1—*Punch* printed "The Play's (not) the Thing."

SEPTEMBER 24—O. W.'s lecture at Wandsworth Town Hall on his "Impressions of America."

NOVEMBER—O. W. announced to Robert Sherard his engagement to Miss Constance Lloyd.

November 3—*Punch* attacked O. W. in "Sartorial Sweetness and Light."

November 10—*Punch* printed "Counter Criticism."

November 14—Exchange of telegrams between O. W. and Whistler printed in *The World.* Reprinted in Whistler's *The Gentle Art of Making Enemies.*

November 17—*Punch* published "Cheap Telegrams."

November 17—*Punch* printed "Another Invitation to Amerikay."

November 24—*Punch* printed "And Is This Fame?"

1884

March 5—O. W.'s lecture at the Crystal Palace on his "Impressions of America."

May—O. W.'s poem "Under the Balcony" was published in *Shakepearean Show Book,* a collection of original contributions, illustrations and music which was brought out for the benefit of the Chelsea Hospital for Women.

May 29—O. W. married Miss Constance Lloyd at the Paddington Parish Church of St. James, Sussex Gardens, London.

May 29—Mr. and Mrs. Oscar Wilde left from Charing Cross Station for Paris on their honeymoon trip.

May 30—Mr. and Mrs. Oscar Wilde arrived in Paris on their honeymoon trip, engaging rooms at the Hôtel Wagram, rue Rivoli.

June 14—*Punch* published "The Town. II. Bond Street."

August 23—*Punch* printed "The Town. No. XI—'Form.' A Legend of Modern London. Part I."

August 30—*Punch* published "A Legend of Modern London. Part II."

October 14—*The Pall Mall Gazette* published O. W.'s "On Woman's Dress." Reprinted in *The Pall Mall Budget,* October 17, 1884.

October 17—*The World* published an excerpt from Whistler's letter to Mr. Godwin, authority on costume, concerning O. W.'s "æsthetic" dress.

November 11—*The Pall Mall Gazette* printed O. W.'s article "More Radical Ideas upon Dress Reform." Reprinted in *The Pall Mall Budget,* November 14, 1884.

1885

In a Good Cause published O. W.'s poem, "Impressions de Paris. Le Jardin de Tuileries."

February 20—Whistler delivered his "Ten O'Clock" lecture at Prince's Hall.

February 21—*The Pall Mall Gazette* printed O. W.'s review of "Mr. Whistler's Ten O'Clock." Reprinted in *The Pall Mall Budget,* February 27, 1885.

FEBRUARY 25—O. W.'s letter to Whistler, "Dear Butterfly," printed in *The World*. Reprinted in Whistler's *The Gentle Art of Making Enemies.*

FEBRUARY 25—*The World* published a letter from Whistler, entitled "The Naïveté of the Poet," in reply to O. W.'s review of his lecture at Prince's Hall.

FEBRUARY 28—*The Pall Mall Gazette* published O. W.'s article, "The Relation of Dress to Art: A Note in Black and White on Mr. Whistler's Lecture." Reprinted in *The Pall Mall Budget,* March 6, 1885.

MARCH 7—*The Pall Mall Gazette* published O. W.'s article "Dinners and Dishes." Reprinted in *The Pall Mall Budget,* March 13, 1885.

MARCH 13—*The Pall Mall Gazette* published O. W.'s article, "A Modern Epic" (review of *Melchior* by H. G. Wells). Reprinted in *The Pall Mall Budget,* March 20, 1885.

MARCH 14—*The Dramatic Review* published O. W.'s article, "Shakespeare on Scenery."

MARCH 27—*The Pall Mall Gazette* published O. W.'s article, "A Bevy of Poets." Reprinted in *The Pall Mall Budget,* April 3, 1885.

APRIL 1—*The Pall Mall Gazette* published O. W.'s article, "Parnassus versus Philology."

APRIL 11—*The Dramatic Review* published O. W.'s poem, "The Harlot's House."

MAY—*The Nineteenth Century* published O. W.'s article, "Shakespeare and Stage Costume." Reprinted in 1891 in *Intentions* under the title "The Truth of Masks."

MAY 9—*The Dramatic Review* published O. W.'s review of *Hamlet* at the Lyceum.

MAY 15—*The Pall Mall Gazette* published O. W.'s review, "Two Novels." Reprinted in *The Pall Mall Budget,* May 22, 1885.

MAY 23—*The Dramatic Review* published O. W.'s review of *Henry the Fourth* at Oxford.

MAY 27—*The Pall Mall Gazette* published O. W.'s article, "Modern Greek Poetry." Reprinted in *The Pall Mall Budget,* May 29, 1885.

MAY 29—*The Dramatic Review* published O. W.'s review of *Olivia,* a play in four acts by H. G. Wells, at the Lyceum.

MAY 30—*Punch* attacked O. W. in "Ben Trovato."

JUNE 6—*The Dramatic Review* published O. W.'s review of *As You Like It* at Coombe House.

JUNE 27—*Punch* published "Interiors and Exteriors. No. 13. At Burlington House. The 'Swarry.' "

JULY 4—*Society* (*Midsummer Dreams*) published O. W.'s poem, "Roses and Rue." Reprinted in *Poems* (1908) under the title "To L. L."

NOVEMBER 18—*The Pall Mall Gazette* published O. W.'s article, "A Handbook to Marriage."

DECEMBER 7—*Punch* ridiculed O. W. in its "Almanack for 1886. The Walnut Season. Here Y'ar! Ten a Penny. All Cracked."

1886

JANUARY 15—*The Pall Mall Gazette* published O. W.'s article, "Half Hours with the Worst Authors." Reprinted in *The Pall Mall Budget,* January 21, 1886.

JANUARY 23—*The Dramatic Review* published O. W.'s "Sonnet On The Recent Sale by Auction of Keats' Love Letters."

FEBRUARY 1—*The Pall Mall Gazette* published O. W.'s article, "One of Mr. Conway's Remainders." Reprinted in *The Pall Mall Budget,* February 4, 1886.

FEBRUARY 8—*The Pall Mall Gazette* published O. W.'s article, "To Read or Not to Read." Reprinted in *The Pall Mall Budget* under the title "The Best Hundred Books," February 11, 1886.

FEBRUARY 20—*The Dramatic Review* published O. W.'s review of *Twelfth Night* at Oxford.

MARCH 6—*The Pall Mall Gazette* published O. W.'s article, "The Letters of a Great Woman." Reprinted in *The Pall Mall Budget,* March 11, 1886.

APRIL 12—*The Pall Mall Gazette* published O. W.'s article, "News from Parnassus." Reprinted in *The Pall Mall Budget,* April 15, 1886.

APRIL 14—*The Pall Mall Gazette* published O. W.'s review on "Some Novels." Reprinted in *The Pall Mall Budget,* April 15, 1886.

APRIL 17—*The Pall Mall Gazette* published O. W.'s article, "A Literary Pilgrim." Reprinted in *The Pall Mall Budget,* April 22, 1886.

APRIL 21—*The Pall Mall Gazette* published O. W.'s article, "Béranger in England." Reprinted in *The Pall Mall Budget,* April 22, 1886.

MAY 13—*The Pall Mall Gazette* published O. W.'s article, "The Poetry of the People."

MAY 15—*The Dramatic Review* published O. W.'s notice on *The Cenci,* a production by the Shelley Society at the Grand Theatre, Islington.

JULY—*The Century Guild Hobby Horse* published O. W.'s "Keats' Sonnet on Blue."

AUGUST 4—*The Pall Mall Gazette* published O. W.'s article, "Pleasing and Prattling." Reprinted in *The Pall Mall Budget,* August 5, 1886.

SEPTEMBER 13—*The Pall Mall Gazette* published O. W.'s article, "Balzac in English." Reprinted in *The Pall Mall Budget,* September 16, 1886.

SEPTEMBER 16—*The Pall Mall Gazette* published O. W.'s article, "Two New Novels."

SEPTEMBER 20—*The Pall Mall Gazette* published O. W.'s article, "Ben Jonson." Reprinted in *The Pall Mall Budget,* September 23, 1886.

SEPTEMBER 26—*The Pall Mall Gazette* published O. W.'s article, "The Poet's Corner." Reprinted in *The Pall Mall Budget,* September 30, 1886.

October 8–*The Pall Mall Gazette* published O. W.'s article, "A Ride Through Morocco." Reprinted in *The Pall Mall Budget,* October 14, 1886.

October 14–*The Pall Mall Gazette* published O. W.'s article, "The Children of the Poets." Reprinted in *The Pall Mall Budget,* October 21, 1886.

October 28–*The Pall Mall Gazette* published O. W.'s article, "New Novels."

November 3–*The Pall Mall Gazette* published O. W.'s article, "A Politician's Poetry." Reprinted in *The Pall Mall Budget* under the title "Lord Carnavon's 'Odyssey,'" November 4, 1886.

November 6–*The Pall Mall Gazette* published O. W.'s (?) article signed "Oxoniensis": "Mr. Swinburne and *The Quarterly Review.*" Reprinted in *The Pall Mall Budget,* November 11, 1886.

November 10–*The Pall Mall Gazette* published O. W.'s review, "Mr. Symond's History of the Renaissance."

November 18–*The Pall Mall Gazette* published O. W.'s article, "A 'Jolly' Art Critic."

November 24–O. W.'s letter to Whistler ("Atlas, this is very sad . . .") printed in *The World.* Reprinted in Whistler's *The Gentle Art of Making Enemies.*

December 1–*The Pall Mall Gazette* published O. W.'s article, "A 'Sentimental Journey' Through Literature."

December 11–*The Pall Mall Gazette* published O. W.'s article, "Two Biographies of Sir Philip Sidney."

1887

January 8–*The Pall Mall Gazette* published O. W.'s article, "Common Sense in Art."

February 1–*The Pall Mall Gazette* published O. W.'s article, "Miner a Minor Poet." Reprinted in *The Pall Mall Budget* under the title "A Miner Poet," February 3, 1887.

February 17–*The Pall Mall Gazette* published O. W.'s article, "The Poets and the People. By one of the latter."

February 17–*The Pall Mall Gazette* published O. W.'s notice "A New Calendar." Reprinted in *The Pall Mall Budget,* February 24, 1887.

February 23–*The Court and Society Review* published O. W.'s story, "The Canterville Ghost." (Concluded in the March 2, 1887 issue.)

March 8–*The Pall Mall Gazette* published O. W.'s article, "The New Poet's Corner."

March 23–*The Court and Society Review* published O. W.'s article, "The American Invasion."

March 28–*The Pall Mall Gazette* published O. W.'s article, "Great

Writers by Little Men." Reprinted in *The Pall Mall Budget,* March 31, 1887.

MARCH 31—*The Pall Mall Gazette* published an article by O. W., "A New Book on Dickens." Reprinted in *The Pall Mall Budget,* April 7, 1887.

APRIL 12—*The Pall Mall Gazette* published O. W.'s article, "Our Book Shelf." Reprinted in *The Pall Mall Budget,* April 14, 1887.

APRIL 13—*The Court and Society Review* published O. W.'s article, "The Great Ormond Street Child's Hospital."

APRIL 13—*The Court and Society Review* published O. W.'s article, "The American Man" (anonymous).

APRIL 13—*The Court and Society Review* published O. W.'s review of *Held by the Enemy,* a drama by William Gillette (anonymous—under the title "The New Play.")

APRIL 18—*The Pall Mall Gazette* published O. W.'s article, "A Cheap Edition of a Great Man."

APRIL 20—*The Court and Society Review* published an article by O. W. entitled "The Butterfly's Boswell" on Walter Dowdeswell's account of Whistler (anonymous).

APRIL 20—*The Court and Society Review* published an article by O. W. entitled "The Child-Philosopher" (anonymous).

APRIL 25—O. W.'s story, "Lady Alroy," published in *The World.* Reprinted under the title "The Sphinx Without a Secret" in *Lord Arthur Savile's Crime and Other Stories.* (1891).

APRIL 26—*The Pall Mall Gazette* published O. W.'s article, "Mr. Morris's Odyssey." Reprinted in *The Pall Mall Budget,* April 28, 1887.

APRIL 27—*The Court and Society Review* published an article by O. W. entitled "The Rout of R. A." (anonymous).

APRIL 30—*The Pall Mall Gazette* published O. W.'s article, "The Poet's Corner."

MAY 2—*The Pall Mall Gazette* published O. W.'s article, "A Batch of Novels." Reprinted in *The Pall Mall Budget,* May 5, 1887.

MAY 4—*The Court and Society Review* published an article by O. W. entitled "Should Geniuses Meet?" (anonymous).

MAY 7—*The Saturday Review* published O. W.'s review of "Some Novels."

MAY 11—*The Court and Society Review* published O. W.'s "Lord Arthur Savile's Crime." (Continued in the May 18 and 25, 1887 issues.)

JUNE—O. W. assumed editorship of *The Woman's World.*

JUNE 11—*The Pall Mall Gazette* published O. W.'s article, "Mr. Pater's Imaginary Portraits."

JUNE 22—O. W.'s story, "The Model Millionaire," published in *The World.* Reprinted in *Lord Arthur Savile's Crime and Other Stories* (1891).

AUGUST 8—*The Pall Mall Gazette* published O. W.'s review of "A Good Historical Novel." Reprinted in *The Pall Mall Budget,* November 17, 1887.

AUGUST 20—*The Saturday Review* published O. W.'s review of "New Novels."

SEPTEMBER 14—*The Court and Society Review* published O. W.'s review of *The Winter's Tale* at the Lyceum and also the articles, "Comedy Theatre" and "The Blue Bells of Scotland" (anonymous).

SEPTEMBER 27—*The Pall Mall Gazette* published O. W.'s article, "Two Biographies of Keats." Reprinted in *The Pall Mall Budget,* September 29, 1887.

OCTOBER 15—*The Pall Mall Gazette* published O. W.'s article, "Sermons in Stones at Bloomsbury: The Sculpture Room at the British Museum." Reprinted in *The Pall Mall Budget,* October 20, 1887.

OCTOBER 24—*The Pall Mall Gazette* published O. W.'s article, "A Scotchman on Scottish Poetry." Reprinted in *The Pall Mall Budget,* October 27, 1887.

NOVEMBER—O. W.'s article, "Literary and Other Notes," published in *The Woman's World.*

NOVEMBER 9—*The Pall Mall Gazette* published O. W.'s article, "Mr. Mahaffy's New Book." Reprinted in *The Pall Mall Budget,* November 17, 1887.

NOVEMBER 24—*The Pall Mall Gazette* published O. W.'s article, "Mr. Morris's Completion of the Odyssey." Reprinted in *The Pall Mall Budget,* December 1, 1887.

NOVEMBER 30—*The Pall Mall Gazette* printed O. W.'s article, "Sir Charles Bowen's Vergil." Reprinted in *The Pall Mall Budget,* December 1, 1887.

DECEMBER—*The Lady's Pictorial* (Christmas Number) published O. W.'s poem, "Fantaisies Décoratives" in two parts. "I. Le Paneau. II. Les Ballons."

DECEMBER—O. W.'s "Literary and Other Notes" published in *The Woman's World.*

DECEMBER 10—*Punch* attacked O. W. in "Our Booking-Office: The Woman's World."

DECEMBER 12—*The Pall Mall Gazette* printed O. W.'s notice, "The Unity of the Arts: A Lecture and A Five O'Clock."

DECEMBER 13—*The Court and Society Review* published O. W.'s sonnet, "Un Amant de Nos Jours."

DECEMBER 16—*The Pall Mall Gazette* printed O. W.'s article, "Aristotle at Afternoon Tea." Reprinted in *The Pall Mall Budget,* December 22, 1887.

DECEMBER 17—*The Pall Mall Gazette* published O. W.'s review, "Early Christian Art in Ireland."

DECEMBER 25—*The Sunday Times* published O. W.'s article, "Art at Willis's Rooms."

1888

JANUARY—O. W.'s "Literary and Other Notes" published in *The Woman's World.*

JANUARY 20—*The Pall Mall Gazette* published O. W.'s reviews under the title, "The Poet's Corner."

FEBRUARY—O. W.'s "Literary and Other Notes" published in *The Woman's World.*

FEBRUARY 15—*The Pall Mall Gazette* published O. W.'s reviews under the title, "The Poet's Corner." Reprinted in *The Pall Mall Budget,* February 16, 1888.

FEBRUARY 24—*The Pall Mall Gazette* published O. W.'s article, "Venus or Victory?"

MARCH—O. W.'s "Literary and Other Notes" published in *The Woman's World.*

APRIL 6—*The Pall Mall Gazette* published O. W.'s reviews under the title, "The Poet's Corner."

APRIL 14—*The Pall Mall Gazette* published O. W.'s review, "M. Caro on George Sand."

MAY—O. W.'s *The Happy Prince and Other Tales* was published by Walter Crane and Jacob Hood, London.

JUNE 12—Walter Pater wrote O. W. a letter giving enthusiastic praise to *The Happy Prince and Other Tales.*

JUNE 15—O. W. wrote a letter to George Herbert Kersley giving his views on *The Happy Prince and Other Tales.*

JULY 13—O. W. in a letter to Thomas Hutchinson explained his views on "The Nightingale and the Rose."

OCTOBER 24—*The Pall Mall Gazette* published O. W.'s reviews under the title, "The Poet's Corner."

NOVEMBER 2—*The Pall Mall Gazette* published a report of O. W.'s on William Morris's lecture on "Tapestry."

NOVEMBER 9—*The Pall Mall Gazette* published a report of O. W.'s on a lecture of George Simonds, "Sculpture," at the Arts and Crafts.

NOVEMBER 16—*The Pall Mall Gazette* published O. W.'s reviews under the title, "Poet's Corner."

NOVEMBER 16—*The Pall Mall Gazette* published O. W.'s report, "Printing and Printers: Lecture at the Arts and Crafts," which Emery Walker delivered at the Arts and Crafts Exhibition on November 15, 1888.

NOVEMBER 17—*The World* published a letter from Whistler to the National Art Exhibition on the subject of O. W.

NOVEMBER 23—*The Pall Mall Gazette* published O. W.'s article, "The Beauties of Bookbinding: Mr. Cobden-Sanderson at the Arts and Crafts." Reprinted in *The Pall Mall Budget,* November 29, 1888.

NOVEMBER 30—*The Pall Mall Gazette* published O. W.'s notice, "The Close of the Arts and Crafts: Mr. Walter Crane's lecture on Design."

DECEMBER—*The Woman's World* printed O. W.'s review, "A Fascinating Book. (Embroidery and Lace . . . by Ernest Lefebure)."

DECEMBER—O. W.'s reviews under the heading, "A Note on Some Modern Poets," published in *The Woman's World.*

DECEMBER—*The Lady's Pictorial* (Christmas Number) published O. W.'s tale, "The Young King."

DECEMBER 7—*The Times* printed an article highly commending *The Woman's World* under the editorship of O. W.

DECEMBER 8—*The Queen* published O. W.'s article, "English Poetesses."

DECEMBER 11—*The Pall Mall Gazette* published O. W.'s review, "Sir Edwin Arnold's Last Volume."

DECEMBER 14—*The Pall Mall Gazette* published O. W.'s review, "Australian Poets." Reprinted in *The Pall Mall Budget,* December 20, 1888.

DECEMBER 20—*The St. Moritz Post Davos and Maloja News* published in a special Christmas number O. W.'s poem, "Autumn," which was originally published, under the title "Le Jardin," in *Our Continent,* February 15, 1882.

1889

JANUARY—*The Fortnightly Review* published O. W.'s essay, "Pen, Pencil and Poison."

JANUARY—Second Edition of *The Happy Prince and Other Tales* (David Nutt, London).

JANUARY—O. W.'s "Some Literary Notes" published in *The Woman's World.*

JANUARY—*The Nineteenth Century* published O. W.'s essay, "The Decay of Lying." Reprinted in 1891 in *Intentions.*

JANUARY 3—*The Pall Mall Gazette* published O. W.'s review, "Poetry and Prison. Mr. Wilfrid Blunt's 'In Vinculis.'"

JANUARY 3—*The Pall Mall Gazette* published O. W.'s review, "Mr. Andrew Lang's 'Grass of Parnassus.'"

JANUARY 5—*Punch* attacked Wilde in "Our Booking-Office. Article in The Fortnightly."

JANUARY 25—*The Pall Mall Gazette* published O. W.'s article, "The Gospel According to Walt Whitman."

JANUARY 26—*The Pall Mall Gazette* published O. W.'s article, "The New President."

FEBRUARY—O. W.'s "Some Literary Notes" published in *The Woman's World.*

FEBRUARY—*The Eclectic Magazine* reprinted from *The Nineteenth Century* (January, 1889) O. W.'s "The Decay of Lying."

FEBRUARY 5—*The Centennial Magazine* published O. W.'s poem, "Symphony in Yellow."

FEBRUARY 12—*The Pall Mall Gazette* published O. W.'s article, "One of the Bibles of the World." Reprinted in *The Pall Mall Budget,* February 14, 1889.

FEBRUARY 15—*The Pall Mall Gazette* published O. W.'s review, "Poetical Socialists."

FEBRUARY 27—*The Pall Mall Gazette* published O. W.'s review, "Mr. Brander Matthews's Essays."

MARCH—O. W.'s "Some Literary Notes" published in *The Woman's World.*

MARCH 2—*The Pall Mall Gazette* published O. W.'s review, "Mr. William Morris's Last Book."

MARCH 25—*The Pall Mall Gazette* published O. W.'s review, "Adam Lindsay Gordon." Reprinted in *The Pall Mall Budget,* March 28, 1889.

MARCH 30—*The Pall Mall Gazette* published O. W.'s reviews under the title, "The Poet's Corner."

MARCH 30—*Paris Illustré* published O. W.'s "The Birthday of the Little Princess," which was reprinted in *A House of Pomegranates* under the title, "The Birthday of the Infanta."

APRIL—O. W.'s "Some Literary Notes" published in *The Woman's World.*

APRIL 13—*The Pall Mall Gazette* published O. W.'s review, "Mr. Froude's Blue Book." Reprinted in *The Pall Mall Budget,* April 18, 1889.

MAY—O. W.'s "Some Literary Notes" published in *The Woman's World.*

MAY 17—*The Pall Mall Gazette* published O. W.'s review, "Ouida's New Novel." Reprinted in *The Pall Mall Budget,* May 23, 1889.

JUNE—O. W.'s "Some Literary Notes" published in *The Woman's World.*

JUNE 5—*The Pall Mall Gazette* published O. W.'s review, "A Reader's Novel."

JUNE 24—*The Pall Mall Gazette* published O. W.'s reviews under the title, "The Poet's Corner."

JUNE 27—*The Pall Mall Gazette* published O. W.'s review, "Mr. Swinburne's Last Volume." Reprinted in *The Pall Mall Budget,* July 4, 1889.

JUNE—*Blackwood's Edinburgh Magazine* published O. W.'s "The Portrait of Mr. W. H."

JULY 6—*Punch* printed an advertisement of *Blackwood's Magazine,* containing "The Portrait of Mr. W. H. by Oscar Wilde."

JULY 12—*The Pall Mall Gazette* published O. W.'s review, "Three New Poets." (W. B. Yeats, Caroline Fitzgerald and Richard Le Gallienne.)

August—*The Eclectic Magazine* reprinted from *Blackwood's Edinburgh Magazine,* July, 1889, O. W.'s "The Portrait of Mr. W. H."

October 5—*Punch* published "Appropriate Subject."

December—*The Lady's Pictorial* (Christmas Number) published O. W.'s poem, "To the Forest."

1890

January 2—*Truth* published a letter from Whistler on the subject of O. W.'s plagiarism.

January 9—*Truth* printed O. W.'s letter, "Reply to Whistler."

January 10—*Truth* published a letter from Whistler about O. W.

February 8—*The Speaker* published O. W.'s review, "A Chinese Sage." (Chang Tzu.)

March 22—*The Speaker* published O. W.'s review, "Mr. Pater's Last Volume."

May 24—*The Pall Mall Gazette* published O. W.'s review, "Primavera."

June 20—*Lippincott's Monthly Magazine* published O. W.'s novel, "The Picture of Dorian Gray."

June 26—*The St. James's Gazette* printed O. W.'s letter under the heading, "Mr. Wilde's 'Bad Case'" (re "Dorian Gray"). Reprinted in *St. James's Budget,* June 27, 1890.

June 27—*The St. James's Gazette* printed O. W.'s letter under the heading, "Mr. Oscar Wilde Again."

June 28—*The St. James's Gazette* printed O. W.'s letter under the heading, "Mr. Oscar Wilde's Defense."

June 30—*The St. James's Gazette* printed O. W.'s letter under the heading, "Mr. Oscar Wilde's Defense." This letter and those printed in the issues of June 27 and 28, 1890, were reprinted in *The St. James's Budget,* July 4, 1890.

July—*The Nineteenth Century* published the first part of O. W.'s essay, "The True Function and Value of Criticism; With Some Remarks on the Importance of Doing Nothing." Reprinted in *Intentions* under the title, "The Critic as Artist. Part I."

July 12—*The Scots Observer* printed O. W.'s letter under the heading, "Mr. Wilde's Rejoinder," which was a reply to a criticism of "The Picture of Dorian Gray" by "Thersites" in the July issue of *Lippincott's Monthly Magazine.*

July 19—*Punch* attacked Oscar Wilde in "Our Booking-Office. Dorian Gray."

August 2—*The Scots Observer* printed O. W.'s letter under the heading, "Art and Morality."

August 16—*The Scots Observer* printed O. W.'s letter under the heading, "Art and Morality."

SEPTEMBER—*The Nineteenth Century* published the second (concluding) part of O. W.'s essay, "The True Function and Value of Criticism; With Some Remarks on the Importance of Doing Nothing." Reprinted in 1891 in *Intentions* under the title, "The Critic as Artist. Part II."

SEPTEMBER 20—*Punch* ridiculed O. W. in "Development."

DECEMBER 25—*Punch* ran an article, "Punch Among the Planets."

1891

JANUARY 26—O. W.'s *The Duchess of Padua* under the title *Guido Ferranti* was produced anonymously at the Broadway Theatre, New York, by Laurence Barrett.

JANUARY 27—*The New York Tribune* in an account of the anonymous production of *Guido Ferranti* at the Broadway Theatre, New York, disclosed O. W.'s identity as its author.

FEBRUARY—*The Fortnightly Review* published O. W.'s "The Soul of Man Under Socialism."

MARCH—*The Fortnightly Review* published O. W.'s "A Preface to Dorian Gray."

MARCH 14—*Punch* printed "Desdemona to the Author of 'Dorian Gray.'" (Apropos of his paragraphic Preface.)

MARCH 14—*Punch* published "Wilde Flowers."

APRIL—*The Eclectic Magazine* reprinted from *The Fortnightly Review* (February, 1891) O. W.'s "The Soul of Man Under Socialism."

APRIL 24—O. W.'s *The Picture of Dorian Gray* published in book form by Ward Lock and Co., London.

MAY 2—O. W.'s *Intentions* published in book form by James Osgood, McIlvaine and Co., London.

MAY 30—*Punch* attacked O. W. in "Our Booking-Office. Intentions."

SUMMER—Lionel Johnson introduced Lord Alfred Douglas to O. W. at the latter's home in Tite Street.

JULY—O. W.'s *Lord Arthur Savile's Crime and Other Stories* published in book form by James R. Osgood, McIlvaine and Co., London.

JULY—Enthusiastic review of *Intentions* printed in *The Photographic American Review.*

JULY 1—Ward Lock and Co. published a new edition of *The Picture of Dorian Gray* limited to 250 copies each signed by O. W. (Author's Collection No. 30.)

SEPTEMBER 26—*The Times* printed O. W.'s letter under the heading, "An Anglo-Indian's Complaint."

OCTOBER 24—O. W. entered into an agreement with Elkin Matthews for the publication of the Sixth edition of *Poems.*

NOVEMBER—O. W.'s *A House of Pomegranates* published in book form by James R. Osgood, McIlvaine and Co., London.

EARLY DECEMBER—O. W. in Paris.

DECEMBER 5—*The Speaker* printed O. W.'s letter under the heading, "A House of Pomegranates."

DECEMBER 11—*The Pall Mall Gazette* published O. W.'s letter on his "A House of Pomegranates."

1892

FEBRUARY 20—First performance of *Lady Windermere's Fan* at the St. James's Theatre.

FEBRUARY 20—*The Daily Telegraph* printed O. W.'s letter entitled "Puppets and Actors."

FEBRUARY 27—*The St. James's Gazette* printed O. W.'s letter under the heading, "Mr. Oscar Wilde Explains." (re *Lady Windermere's Fan.*)

MARCH 5—*Punch* commented on O. W.'s *Lady Windermere's Fan* in an article, "A Wilde 'Tag' to a Tame Play." With a cartoon by J. Bernard Partridge.

MARCH 12—*Punch* published "Lord Wildermere's Mother-in-Law."

MARCH 12—*Punch* printed "A Pathetic Description of the Present State of Mr. George Alexander."

APRIL 27—O. W. left London for Paris.

APRIL 30—*Punch* published "Staircase Scenes.—No. 1, Private View, Royal Academy."

MAY—Messrs. Elkin Matthews and John Lane issued the Sixth edition of O. W.'s *Poems,* reprint of Bogue's fifth edition.

MAY 19—*The Poet and the Puppets,* a musical travesty by Charles Brookfield and J. M. Clover, caricaturing *Lady Windermere's Fan,* was produced at the Comedy Theatre, London.

JUNE—*Salomé* was rehearsed for production at the Palace Theatre, London, by Madame Sarah Bernhardt.

JUNE—O. W. in Bad-Homburg.

JUNE 25—*Punch* printed "The Playful Sally."

JUNE 29—O. W.'s interview re *Salomé* published in *The Pall Mall Gazette.* Reprinted June 30, 1892, in *The Pall Mall Budget.*

JUNE 29 [?]—O. W.'s letter to the *Gaulois* on the suppression of *Salomé.*

JULY 2—*Punch* ridiculed O. W. in "A Difficulty."

JULY 9—*Punch* printed a cartoon by J. Bernard Partridge representing O. W. as a French conscript. "A Wilde Idea. Or, More Injustice to Ireland!" referring to O. W.'s announcement that he intended to become a French citizen because of the decision of the Lord Chamberlain to withhold the license for the production of *Salomé.*

JULY 9—*The Spectator* published William Watson's humorous "Lines to Our New Censor" in connection with the decision of the Lord Chamberlain to withhold the license for the production of *Salomé.*

JULY 16—*Punch* published "Racine, With the Chill Off."

JULY 16—*Punch* published "On the Fly-Leaf of An Old Book."

SEPTEMBER—O. W. first met Sidney Mavor.

OCTOBER 3—O. W. ordered Thornhills in Bond Street to send a cigarette case to Sidney Mavor.

DECEMBER 6—O. W.'s sonnet, "The New Remorse," was published in *The Spirit Lamp.*

1893

JANUARY 19—*Punch* printed "To Rome for Sixteen Guineas."

FEBRUARY—Acting edition of *Lady Windermere's Fan* for the production of the play in Palmer's Theatre, New York.

FEBRUARY—O. W. went to Paris in connection with the publication of *Salomé* accompanied by Fred Atkins.

FEBRUARY 17—O. W.'s "The House of Judgment" was published in *The Spirit Lamp.*

FEBRUARY 22—O. W.'s *Salomé* published by Librairie de l'Art Indépendant, Paris.

MARCH—O. W. engaged rooms at the Savoy Hotel, London, and started living there.

MARCH 2—*The Times* printed O. W.'s letter to the editor under the heading, "Mr. Oscar Wilde on 'Salomé.' " Reprinted in *The Times Weekly Edition,* March 3, 1893.

MARCH 13—O. W. met Charles Parker at Kettner's and went with him to the Savoy Hotel.

MARCH 29—O. W. left the Savoy Hotel, London.

APRIL 19—O. W.'s *A Woman of No Importance* was produced by Herbert Beerbohm Tree at the Haymarket Theatre, London.

APRIL 22—*Punch* attacked O. W. in "The B. and S. Drama at the Adelphi."

APRIL 29—*Punch* ridiculed O. W. in "The Premier at the Haymarket Last Wednesday."

APRIL 29—*Punch* printed "Stray Thoughts on Play-Writing."

MAY 4—*The Spirit Lamp* published the "Sonnet on *Hyacinthe*" by Pierre Louÿs prefaced by these words, "A letter written in prose by Mr. Oscar Wilde to a friend and translated into rhymed verse by a poet of no importance."

MAY 6—*Punch* published "A Work of Some Importance."

MAY 13—*Punch* printed "Wilder Ideas; Or, Conversation as he is spoken at the Haymarket."

MAY 27—*Punch* published "A Wylde Vade Mecum (By Professor H-xl-y)."

JUNE—O. W. stayed in a cottage at Goring.

JUNE 3—*Punch* printed "Second Title for the Play at the Haymarket."

JUNE 6—O. W.'s "The Disciple" was published in *The Spirit Lamp.*

JULY 15—*Punch* printed "The Play is Not the Thing."

JULY 15—*Punch* ridiculed O. W. in "An Afternoon Party."

JULY 29—*Punch* published "At the T. R. H."

AUGUST 26—*Punch* printed "Still Wilder Ideas (Possibilities for the next O. Wilde Play)."

OCTOBER 13—*Punch* attacked O. W. in "The O. B. C. (Limited)."

NOVEMBER 9—Messrs. Elkin Matthews and John Lane published O. W.'s *Lady Windermere's Fan.*

DECEMBER—O. W. and Lord Alfred Douglas went to Cairo.

DECEMBER 30—*Punch* printed "New Year's Eve at Latterday Hall. An Incident. Dorian Gray Taking Juliet in to Dinner."

1894

FEBRUARY 9—Messrs. Elkin Matthews and John Lane (London), Copeland and Day (Boston), published *Salomé* translated from the French by Lord Alfred Douglas, with illustrations by Aubrey Beardsley.

FEBRUARY 17—*Punch* attacked O. W. in "Blushing Honours."

MARCH 10—*Punch* printed "She-Notes. By Borgia Smudgiton."

APRIL 27—O. W. departed for Paris.

MAY 3—O. W. in Paris at the Hôtel de Deux Mondes.

JUNE—The Marquis of Queensberry called on O. W. at his house in Tite Street and, after insulting his host, was expelled.

JUNE 11—Messrs. Elkin Mathews and John Lane (London) published O. W.'s *The Sphinx,* with decorations by Charles Rickets.

JULY—*The Fortnightly Review* published O. W.'s "Poems in Prose."

JULY 21—*Punch* published "The Minx.—A Poem in Prose."

AUGUST 4—*Punch* published "Our Charity Fête."

AUGUST 5—*The Weekly Sun* published over O. W.'s name a poem "The Shamrock," which, however, the poet never wrote.

SEPTEMBER 15—In the Pioneer Series of Heinemann's Novels *The Green Carnation* by Robert Hichens was published anonymously.

SEPTEMBER 20—*The Pall Mall Gazette* published O. W.'s article, "The Ethics of Journalism, I."

SEPTEMBER 25—*The Pall Mall Gazette* published O. W.'s second article, "The Ethics of Journalism, II." Both articles were reprinted in *The Pall Mall Budget,* September 27, 1894.

OCTOBER 2—*The Pall Mall Gazette* printed a letter of O. W. on "The Green Carnation."

OCTOBER 9—John Lane published in London O. W.'s *A Woman of No Importance.*

October 20—*Punch* printed "The Blue Gardenia. (A Colourable Imitation.)"

October 27—*Punch* ridiculed O. W. in "Morbidezza."

November 10—*Punch* published "The Decadent Guys. (A Colour-Study in Green Carnations.)"

November 24—*To-Day* published an interview with Constance Wilde entitled "Mrs. Oscar Wilde at Home."

December 1 (?)—The first and only number of *The Chameleon* was published by Messrs. Gay and Bird, London, in which appeared "The Priest and the Acolyte," wrongly attributed to O. W. In the same issue appeared O. W.'s *Phrases and Philosophies for the Use of the Young.*

December 15—*Punch* attacked O. W. in "The Truisms of Life (Note 12).

1895

January 3—O. W.'s *An Ideal Husband* first produced by Messrs. Lewis Waller and H. H. Morell at the Royal Theatre, London.

January 12—*Punch* printed "An Overheard Fragment of a Dialogue."

January 19—*Punch* published "A Penny Plain—But Oscar Coloured."

January 19—*Punch* published "To Rome for Sixteen Guineas."

February 2—*Punch* published "A God in the Os-car."

February 2—*Punch* printed "A Wilde 'Ideal Husband.' "

February 14—O. W.'s *The Importance of Being Earnest* produced by Mr. George Alexander at the St. James's Theatre, London.

February 18—The Marquis of Queensberry left at 4:30 p.m. with Sidney Wright, hall porter, at the Albemarle Club, an insulting visiting card for O. W.

February 23—*Punch* printed "The O. W. Vade Mecum."

February 26—*The Picture Magazine* reproduced facsimile of O. W.'s manuscript of the poem, "To My Friend Luther Munday."

February 28—O. W. received at the Albemarle Club Queensberry's insulting card.

February 28—O. W., by letter from the Hotel Avondale, advised Ross about Queensberry's insulting card.

February 28—At 11:30 p.m. O. W. and Ross had a conference at the Avondale Hotel about the course to take in connection with Queensberry's insulting card.

March 1—O. W. went to consult Mr. Charles Octavius Humphreys, senior partner in the solicitors' firm, C. O. Humphreys, Son and Kershaw, in anticipation of a libel action against Queensberry.

March 1—O. W. applied at the Police Court for a warrant for Queensberry's arrest on a charge of the publication of a libellous statement.

CHRONOLOGICAL INDEX

MARCH 2—The Marquis of Queensberry was arrested by Inspector Greet at Carter's Hotel, Piccadilly, under O. W.'s warrant.

MARCH 2—The Marquis of Queensberry was charged at the Marlborough Street Police Court with publishing a libel concerning O. W. and his case was adjourned for a week, William Tyser and the defendant having produced the required bail.

MARCH 2—*Punch* ridiculed O. W. in "The Rivals at the A. D. C."

MARCH 9—The hearing in the Queensberry case was resumed at the Marlborough Street Police Court, and the Marquis was committed for trial.

MARCH 12—O. W.'s *An Ideal Husband* produced at the Lyceum Theatre, New York.

MARCH 16—*Punch* published "The Advantage of Being Consistent."

MARCH 31—O. W. and Lord Alfred Douglas examined Queensberry's plea of justification at the office of Humphreys.

APRIL 2—*Punch* printed "The Advisability of Not Being Born in a Handbag."

APRIL 3—The trial of the Libel action against Queensberry began at the Old Bailey before Mr. Justice Henn Collins.

APRIL 4—Second day of the trial at the Old Bailey of Queensberry's case.

APRIL 4—*The New York Herald* reproduced in its columns the "Prose Sonnet" (O. W.'s letter to Lord Alfred Douglas).

APRIL 5—Third and last day of the trial of Queensberry's case at the Old Bailey. Collapse of the prosecution and Queensberry's acquittal.

APRIL 5—Charles Russell, Queensberry's solicitor, forwarded to Hamilton Cuffe, Director of Prosecutions, copies of all witnesses' statements "in re Oscar Wilde."

APRIL 5—Home Secretary, Mr. H. H. Asquith, the Attorney-General, Sir Robert Reid, and the Solicitor-General, Sir F. Lockwood, held a conference in reference to O. W.'s case and it was agreed that a warrant for his arrest should be applied for.

APRIL 5—*The Evening News and Post* printed O. W.'s letter giving his reasons for withdrawing from the libel action against the Marquis of Queensberry.

APRIL 5—O. W. arrested at 7:30 P.M. at the Cadogan Hotel, driven to Scotland Yard and at 8 P.M. taken to Bow Street, where he was charged with committing acts of gross indecency with other male persons.

APRIL 5—Lord Alfred Douglas at 9 P.M. called at Bow Street Station in an attempt to bail out O. W. and his application was turned down.

APRIL 6—*Punch* published "April Foolosophy. (By one of Them.)"

APRIL 6—*Punch* printed "Concerning a Misused Term: viz. Art, as recently applied to a certain form of Literature."

APRIL 6—O. W. sent to Holloway Prison.

APRIL 6—First day of preliminary proceedings against O. W. at Bow Street before Sir John Bridge.

APRIL 9—St. Louis and Newark public libraries removed O. W.'s books.

APRIL 11—Second day of preliminary proceedings against O. W. at Bow Street before Sir John Bridge.

APRIL 13—*Punch* attacked O. W. in "The Long and Short of It."

APRIL 16—O. W. wrote Robert Sherard from Holloway Prison thanking him for his endeavours to obtain a loan from Madame Sarah Bernhardt.

APRIL 17—O. W. wrote Ada Leverson from Holloway Prison expressing his gratitude for her kindness and that of her husband in arranging bail.

APRIL 19—Third day of preliminary proceedings against O. W. at Bow Street before Sir John Bridge. O. W. and Alfred Taylor committed for trial.

APRIL 23—Grand Jury found true bills in the case of O. W. and Alfred Taylor.

APRIL 24—By order of the Sheriff the auction sale of O. W.'s belongings at 16 Tite Street took place.

APRIL 24—Mr. Charles Willie Matthews applied at the Central Criminal Court on behalf of O. W. for the postponement of his client's trial until the May Sessions, which motion was denied by Mr. Justice Charles.

APRIL 26—The first day of O. W.'s trial at the Old Bailey before Mr. Justice Charles.

APRIL 27—The second day of O. W.'s trial at the Old Bailey before Mr. Justice Charles.

APRIL 29—The third day of O. W.'s trial at the Old Bailey before Mr. Justice Charles.

APRIL 30—The fourth day of O. W.'s trial at the Old Bailey before Mr. Justice Charles.

MAY 1—The fifth and concluding day of O. W.'s trial at the Old Bailey before Mr. Justice Charles. The jury disagreed and the verdict "not guilty" was given on certain counts. Sir Edward Clarke's application on behalf of O. W. for bail was denied.

MAY 3—Mr. Charles Matthews made an application before Mr. Baron Pollock in chambers to allow O. W. out on bail until the time of his new trial.

MAY 4—Mr. Baron Pollock in chambers announced that he had decided to fix the amount of O. W.'s bail at £5000.

MAY 7—Hearing at Bow Street Police Station with reference to the proposed bail of O. W., who was released on that day from Holloway Prison.

MAY 7—Following his release from Holloway, O. W. drove to the Midland Hotel at St. Pancras. At midnight on the same day, O. W., having been refused admission at several hotels, found shelter at Lady Wilde's house in Oakley Street.

MAY 12—O. W. moved to Mr. and Mrs. Ernest Leverson's house in Courtfield Gardens, where he stayed until May 20, 1895.

MAY 20—The first day of O. W.'s second trial at the Old Bailey before Mr. Justice Wills. On motion of Sir Edward Clarke, Alfred Taylor's case was separated from that of O. W., and the court ruled that Taylor's case be tried first.

MAY 21—Alfred Taylor tried at the Old Bailey before Mr. Justice Wills was found "guilty" on the counts alleging indecency with Charles and William Parker and "not guilty" on the count alleging the procuring of Wood for O. W.

MAY 22—The Marquis of Queensberry and his son, Percy Douglas, were charged at the Marlborough Street Police Court with disorderly conduct (street fight) in Piccadilly on the preceding day.

MAY 22—O. W.'s second trial was resumed before Mr. Justice Wills at the Old Bailey.

MAY 23—O. W.'s second trial before Mr. Justice Wills continued at the Old Bailey.

MAY 24—O. W.'s second trial before Mr. Justice Wills at the Old Bailey continued.

MAY 25—Last day of O. W.'s second trial at the Old Bailey before Mr. Justice Wills. The jury, having found O. W. guilty on all counts, except that relating to Edward Shelley, Mr. Justice Wills sentenced O. W. and Taylor to two years of hard labour in prison.

MAY 27—O. W. was removed to Pentonville Prison and, later, to Wandsworth Gaol, where he began to serve his sentence.

MAY 30—O. W.'s *The Soul of Man* (*Under Socialism*) was privately printed by the Chiswick Press, London.

AUGUST 26—Robert Sherard called on O. W. at Wandsworth Gaol.

SEPTEMBER 21—Constance Wilde visited O. W. at Wandsworth.

OCTOBER—Ward Lock and Co. published a 6 sh. edition of *The Picture of Dorian Gray.*

NOVEMBER—Prof. Fred. York Powell of Oxford drew up a petition to Her Majesty the Queen of England for the mitigation of O. W.'s sentence. (The petition was never actually presented.)

NOVEMBER—Bankruptcy proceedings against O. W.

NOVEMBER 13—O. W. was removed from Wandsworth Gaol to Reading Gaol, where he continued to serve his sentence.

1896

FEBRUARY 3—Lady Wilde, O. W.'s mother, died at her residence, 146 Oakley Street, London.

FEBRUARY 11—The first performance of *Salomé* by Mr. A. F. Lugné-Poë at the Théâtre de L'Œuvre, Paris.

MARCH 10—O. W. wrote a letter to Ross from Reading Gaol re the production of *Salomé* in Paris.

JULY 1—Major J. O. Nelson appointed Governor of Reading Gaol, his predecessor, Lieut. Col. H. Isaacson, having received the governorship of Lewes Prison.

SEPTEMBER 24—The Home Secretary refused the mitigation of O. W.'s sentence.

OCTOBER (?)—O. W. wrote a letter to Ross from Reading Gaol giving a detailed account of his psychic state.

1897

MARCH—O. W., while in Reading Gaol, completed his *Epistola,* which later was given by Ross the title, *De Profundis.*

APRIL 1—O. W. wrote a letter to Ross giving him charge of all his literary works.

APRIL 6—O. W. wrote a letter to Ross requesting him to send him a number of books.

MAY 19—O. W. was released from prison.

MAY 19—O. W., upon his release from prison, went to Brompton Oratory and had an interview with Father Sebastian Bowden. (?)

MAY 19—O. W. left England via Newhaven and proceeded to Dieppe.

MAY 19—*L'Eclaireur* printed a notice of O. W.'s arrival in Dieppe.

MAY 28—O. W. moved from Dieppe to the Hôtel de la Plage at Berneval-sur-Mer. On this day he wrote a long letter to Robert Ross.

MAY 28—*The Daily Chronicle* published O. W.'s article, "The Case of Warder Martin: Some Cruelties of Prison Life."

MAY 30—O. W. wrote Robert Ross (from Berneval) re his article in *The Daily Chronicle.* (See May 28, 1897.)

MAY 31—O. W. from Berneval wrote a long letter to Robert Ross telling him about his future plans and his desire to rent a chalet near Berneval.

JUNE 2—O. W. wrote from Berneval to Robert Ross, advising him that he had determined to finish *The Florentine Tragedy.*

JUNE 3—*L'Eclaireur* printed notice of O. W.'s arrival in Berneval.

JUNE 5—O. W. in a letter to Ross from Berneval announced his decision to live there.

JUNE 7—O. W. rented Chalet Bourgeat near Berneval.

JUNE 9—O. W. wrote letter to William Rothenstein describing his psychic state.

JUNE 12—William Rothenstein arrived in Berneval on a visit to O. W.

JUNE 13—O. W. wrote from Berneval a long letter to Frank Harris, giving a detailed account of his psychic state after release from Reading.

June 27—O. W. gave a children's party at Berneval.

August 14—Robert Ross and Robert Sherard visited O. W. at Berneval.

August 14—O. W. wrote a letter to William Rothenstein enclosing a short biographical sketch of himself.

August 20—O. W. in a letter to William Rothenstein advised him of his intentions to go to Rouen.

August 24—O. W. wrote a letter to William Rothenstein confessing his creative apathy.

August 24—O. W. finished at Berneval his *Ballad of Reading Gaol.*

September 2—O. W. wrote Rothenstein from Berneval thanking him for a check of £15 the proceeds from the sale of a painting which had formerly belonged to O. W.

September 5 (?)—O. W. met Lord Alfred Douglas at Rouen, where they spent one day at the Hôtel de la Poste.

1898

January 8—O. W. wrote from Naples an important letter to Leonard Smithers in re *The Ballad of Reading Gaol* and its American edition.

February 13—Leonard Smithers published O. W.'s *The Ballad of Reading Gaol.* ("by C. 3. 3.")

February 24—The second edition of *The Ballad of Reading Gaol* was published in London.

March 4—Leonard Smithers (London) published third "author's" edition of *The Ballad of Reading Gaol* limited to 99 copies. On the same date the fourth edition of 1200 copies of *The Ballad* was printed.

March 17—Leonard Smithers (London) published the fifth edition of *The Ballad of Reading Gaol* (1000 copies).

March 24—*The Daily Chronicle* published O. W.'s article, "Don't Read This If You Want to be Happy To-day."

April 7—Constance Wilde, following an operation, died at Genoa.

May 21—Leonard Smithers (London) published the sixth edition of *The Ballad of Reading Gaol.*

June 23—O. W.'s pathetic letter to Smithers from Nogent-sur-Marne, asking for £10.

July 29—O. W. wrote Ross from Paris a postcard admitting the inadequacy of *The Duchess of Padua* from a literary standpoint.

October 3—O. W., writing from Paris to Ross, advised him of his intention to go to Napoule with Frank Harris.

October 13—O. W. wrote from Hôtel d'Alsace, Paris, a letter to Frank Harris in re the latter's criticism of Rodin's "Balzac."

December 3—O. W., writing from Paris to Ross, admitted his intellectual impotence.

DECEMBER 27—O. W. arrived in Napoule, A.M., stopping at the Hôtel des Bains.

DECEMBER 31 (?)—O. W. went to Nice and saw there Madame Sarah Bernhardt in *La Tosca.*

1899

FEBRUARY—O. W. visited his wife's grave in Genoa.

FEBRUARY—Leonard Smithers & Co., London, published O. W.'s *The Importance of Being Earnest.*

FEBRUARY 25—O. W. in Nice en route to Gland, Switzerland.

MARCH 15—Leonard Smithers wrote O. W. advising him that he intended printing more copies of *The Ballad of Reading Gaol.*

MARCH 15—O. W.'s letter to Ross from Gland, Switzerland, thanking him for wiring about Willy Wilde's death.

MARCH 21—O. W.'s letter to Ross from Gland, Switzerland, re O. W.'s bankruptcy and his intention to leave for Genoa.

MAY—O. W. returned from Geneva to Paris and met M. Dupoirier, proprietor of the Hôtel d'Alsace, where he took lodgings.

MAY 29—O. W. at the Hôtel Marsollier, Paris.

JUNE 23—Seventh edition of *The Ballad of Reading Gaol* of 2000 copies published by Leonard Smithers. In this edition, for the first time, the author's full name appeared in brackets.

JULY—Leonard Smithers & Co., London, published O. W.'s *An Ideal Husband.*

1900

APRIL 16—O. W. in Rome, where he spent, with intervals, over a month, until May 28, journeying to Palermo, Tivoli, etc.

APRIL 16—O. W. wrote from Rome a long letter to Robert Ross recounting his experiences at Palermo.

APRIL and MAY—(April 12 (?) to May 15) O. W. in Rome.

MAY 15—O. W. left Rome for Naples.

AUGUST—O. W. returned to Paris and settled at the Hôtel d'Alsace.

OCTOBER—O. W. was confined to his bed.

OCTOBER 10—O. W. underwent a minor operation not connected with his illness.

OCTOBER 17—Robert Ross visited O. W. in Paris.

OCTOBER 22—O. W. left his room for the first time after his operation.

OCTOBER 30—O. W. drove to the Bois. This was the last time he was able to leave his room.

NOVEMBER—O. W.'s last letter to Ross, describing his physical and mental suffering.

NOVEMBER 12—O. W.'s farewell to Robert Ross.

NOVEMBER 13—Robert Ross left Paris for Nice.

NOVEMBER 29—Ross brought Father Dunn, a Catholic priest, to O. W.'s bedside. O. W. was baptised and received extreme unction.

NOVEMBER 29—Robert Ross telegraphed Lord Alfred Douglas and Frank Harris advising them of O. W.'s grave condition.

NOVEMBER 30—O. W., after sinking into a coma, died at 1:50 in the afternoon at the Hôtel d'Alsace.

DECEMBER 3—O. W. was buried in the Cemetery of Bagneux, Paris.

DECEMBER 10—Lord Alfred Douglas wrote a sonnet, "To Oscar Wilde" (later entitled "The Dead Poet").

1905

JANUARY and FEBRUARY—Dr. Max Meyerfeld published the German version of O. W.'s *De Profundis* in *Die Neue Rundschau,* Berlin, under the title, "Aufzeichnungen und Briefe aus dem Zuchthause in Reading."

FEBRUARY 23—Messrs. Methuen and Co., London, published O. W.'s *De Profundis.*

1909

JULY 20—Ross had the remains of O. W. removed to the Cemetery of Père Lachaise, Paris.

BIBLIOGRAPHY

(BOOKS AND PERIODICALS CONSULTED)

A. B. W., "Lady Windermere's Fan," *The Speaker,* February 27, 1892, London. "An Ideal Husband," *The Speaker,* January 12, 1895, London. "The Importance of Being Earnest," *The Speaker,* February 23, 1895, London.

Aristophanes, *Comedies,* Transl. by M. Artaud (in Russian), St. Petersburg, 1897.

Arnold, Matthew, *Essays, Literary and Critical,* J. M. Dent & Co., London, 1909.

Athenæum, The, London, September 1, 1888, "The Happy Prince and Other Stories," by Oscar Wilde; June 6, 1891, "Intentions"; June 27, 1891, "The Picture of Dorian Gray."

Atkinson, G. T., "Oscar Wilde at Oxford," *The Cornhill Magazine,* May, 1929, London.

Baudelaire, Charles, *Les Fleurs du Mal,* Editions d'Art, Edouard Pelletan, Paris, 1928.

Bendz, Ernst, *Oscar Wilde, A Retrospect,* Alfred Hölder, Vienna, 1921.

Birnbaum, Martin, *Oscar Wilde, Fragments and Memories,* Elkin Mathews, London, 1920.

Blomfield, Reginald, *The Mistress Art,* Edward Arnold, London, 1908.

Bock, Edward J., "Walter Pater's Einfluss ueber Oscar Wilde," *Bonner's Studien zur Englischen Philologie,* Heft VIII, Bonn, 1913.

Brasol, Boris, *The Mighty Three, Poushkin–Gogol–Dostoievsky,* William Farquhar Payson, New York, 1934.

Braybrooke, Patrick, *Oscar Wilde, A Study,* Braithwate & Miller, Ltd., London, 1930.

Brazile, Cécil Georges, "Les Derniers Jours d'Oscar Wilde," *La Revue Hebdomadaire,* Vol. XI, pp. 387–399, November, 1925.

Brémont, Anna, Comtesse de, *Oscar Wilde and His Mother,* Everett & Co., Ltd., London, 1911.

Brewer, Rev. E. Cobham, *Dictionary of Phrase and Fable,* Cassell & Co., Ltd., London, 1895.

Butler, Samuel, *Shakespeare's Sonnets Reconsidered,* Longmans, Green & Co., London, 1899.

BIBLIOGRAPHY

Cambridge History of English Literature, The, Edited by Sir A. W. Ward and A. R. Walles, Vol. XIV, The Nineteenth Century, Cambridge University Press, Cambridge, 1934.

Catalogue, *Autograph Letters and Historical Documents,* published by Messrs. Maggs Bros., Ltd. (London, N604, Christmas 1934, and N628, Summer, 1936. Under *Wilde, Oscar.*)

Chesterton, G. K., *The Victorian Age in Literature,* Williams & Norgate, Ltd., London, 1925.

Chislett, William, Jr., "The New Hellenism of Oscar Wilde," *The Sewanee Review,* Tennessee, July, 1915.

Clutton-Brock, A., *Essays on Art,* 2d ed., Methuen & Co., London, 1920.

Coleridge, Gilbert, "Oscar Wilde," *The Nineteenth Century and After,* London, April, 1922.

Cook, E. Wake, *Anarchism in Art and Chaos in Criticism,* London, 1904.

Cook, H. Lucius, "French Sources of Oscar Wilde's 'Picture of Dorian Gray,'" *Romanic Review,* Vol. XIX, pp. 25–34, 1928.

Currie, Mary Montgomerie, "Concerning Some of the 'Enfants Trouvés' of Literature," *The Nineteenth Century and After,* London, July, 1904.

Dostoievsky, F. M., *The Possessed, The Brothers Karamazov, The Injured and Insulted, A Writer's Diary, The Idiot* (in Russian), St. Petersburg, 1895.

Douglas, Lord Alfred, *The Autobiography of Lord Alfred Douglas,* Secker, London, 1929.

"Salomé." A Critical Review, *The Spirit Lamp,* May, 1893.

My Friendship with Oscar Wilde, Coventry House, New York, 1932.

A Letter from Alfred Douglas to Robert Sherard on André Gide's Lies about Himself and Oscar Wilde, Calvi (Corsica), 1933.

Dulau & Company, Ltd., *A Collection of Original Manuscripts, Letters and Books of Oscar Wilde* (Catalogue), London, 1928.

Early Work of Aubrey Beardsley, The, with a prefatory note by H. C. Marillier, John Lane, London, 1920.

Ellis, Havelock, *The Criminal,* 5th ed., Charles Scribner's Sons, London—New York, 1916.

Studies in the Psychology of Sex, two parts, Macmillan, Toronto, 1936.

Evening Telegram, The, New York, April 6, 1895, "Oscar Wilde's Shame."

Forel, Doctor August, *The Sexual Question,* Physicians' and Surgeons' Book Co., New York, 1925.

Foster, Joseph, *Alumni Oxonienses,* 1715–1886, Oxford, 1886.

Fry, John Hemming, *The Revolt Against Beauty,* Putnam's Sons, New York, 1934.

Gide, André, *Corydon,* Librairie Gallimard, Paris, 1932.
Si le Grain ne Meurt, Librairie Gallimard, Paris, 1933.

Glaenzer, Richard Butler, "The Story of 'The Ballad of Reading Gaol,'" *The Bookman,* June, 1911, New York.

Gleichen-Russwurm, Alexander von, *Dandies and Don Juans. Concerning Fashions and Love Among the Great,* A. A. Knopf, New York, 1928.

Goethe, Wolfgang, *Conversations with Eckermann,* M. Walter Dunne, London, 1901.

Graham, David, *Common Sense and the Muses,* William Blackwood & Sons, Edinburgh and London, 1925.

Great Reign, The, Mills & Boon, Ltd., London, 1922.

Great Victorians, The, 3d ed., Ivor Nicholson & Watson, Ltd., London, 1932.

Grey, C., Lieut-Gen., *The Early Years of His Royal Highness The Prince Consort,* Harper & Bros., New York, 1867.

Hagemann, Carl, *Oscar Wilde* (in German), Deutsche Verlagsanstalt, Berlin, 1925.

Hamilton, Clayton, *The Theory of the Theatre,* Grant Richards, Ltd., London, 1910.

Hamilton, Walter, *The Æsthetic Movement in England,* Reeves & Turner, London, 1892.

Harris, Frank, and Douglas, Lord Alfred, New Preface to *The Life and Confessions of Oscar Wilde,* Fortune Press, London, 1925.

Harris, Frank, *Oscar Wilde, His Life and Confessions,* Two Volumes. Author's edition, New York, 1918.

Hichens, Robert Smythe, *The Green Carnation,* Mitchell Kennerley, New York, 1894.

Hirschberg, Doctor Magnus, *Die Homosexualität,* Berlin, 1914.

Hopkins, R. Thurston, *Oscar Wilde, A Study of the Man and His Work,* Lynwood & Co., Ltd., 2d ed., London, 1913.

Housman, Laurence, *Echo de Paris,* Appleton & Co., New York, 1924 (copyright James B. Pinker & Son, London).

Howe, P. P., *Dramatic Portraits,* Mitchell Kennerley, New York, 1913.

Huneker, James Gibbon, *Essays* (Essay on "O. W."), Charles Scribner's Sons, New York, 1929.

Illustrated Sporting and Dramatic News, The, February 27, 1892, London, "Lady Windermere's Fan."

In Memoriam Oscar Wilde, 3d ed., Insel Verlag, Leipzig, 1911.

Ingleby, Leonard Cresswell, *Oscar Wilde,* T. Werner Laurie, London, 1907.
Oscar Wilde, Some Reminiscences, T. Werner Laurie, London, 1912.

Jackson, Holbrook, *The Eighteen Nineties,* Alfred Knopf, New York, 1927.

Jung, C. G., *Psychological Types or The Psychology of Individuation,* Harcourt, Brace & Co., New York, 1924.

Kant, Immanuel, *Sämtliche Werke,* Vol. II, Kritik der reinen Vernunft, L. Voss, Leipzig, 1838–1842.

Kenilworth, Walter Winston, *A Study of Oscar Wilde,* R. F. Fenno & Co., New York, 1912.

Krafft-Ebing, Doctor R. von, *Psychopathia Sexualis,* Physicians' and Surgeons' Book Co., New York, 1924.

Lachmann, Hedwig, *Oscar Wilde* (in German), Berlin-Leipzig, 1905.

Lamb, Charles, *The Last Essays of Elia,* with introduction by The Right Honourable Augustine Birrell, Blackie & Son, Ltd., London-Glasgow (year not given).

Lefroy, Edward Cracroft, *Echoes from Theocritius,* with an introduction by John Addington Symonds, E. P. Dutton & Co., New York, 1922.

Legacy of Greece, The, Essays, Edited by R. W. Livingstone, Clarendon Press, Oxford, 1928.

Le Gallienne, Richard, "Intentions," *The Academy,* July 4, 1891, London.

Lemonnier, Léon, "Oscar Wilde en exil, d'après des documents nouveaux," *La Grande Revue,* Janvier, 1931, pp. 373–398.

Leverson, Ada, *Letters to "the Sphinx" from Oscar Wilde,* Duckworth, London, 1930.

Lewis, Lloyd, and Smith, Henry Justin, *Oscar Wilde Discovers America,* Harcourt, Brace & Co., New York, 1936.

Literature (publ. by *The Times*), March 26, 1898, London, "The Ballad of Reading Gaol by C. 3. 3."

Lynd, Robert, *The Art of Letters* (Chapter XVII on Oscar Wilde), Charles Scribner's Sons, New York, 1926.

Maeterlinck, Maurice, *The Blind,* transl. by Richard Hovey, New York, 1916.

Les Sept Princesses, Paris, 1891.

Magnus, Laurie, *A Dictionary of European Literature,* George Routledge & Sons, Ltd., London, 1927.

Mahaffy, John Pentland, *Social Life in Greece from Homer to Menander,* 1874, 3d ed., London, 1877.

Rambles and Studies, London, 1892.

Marjoribanks, Edward, *The Life of Lord Carson,* Times Book Club, London, 1932.

Mason, A. E. W., *Sir George Alexander and the St. James Theatre,* Macmillan & Co., Ltd., London, 1935.

Mason, Stuart, *Bibliography of Oscar Wilde,* T. Werner Laurie, Ltd., London, 1914.

Maxwell, W. B., Autobiography, *Time Gathered,* Hutchinson & Co., London, 1937.

Merejkovsky, D. S., Essay "Acropolis" in *Eternal Satellites* (in Russian), St. Petersburg, 1911.

Moderwell, Hiram Kelly, *The Theatre of Today,* John Lane Co., New York, 1914.

Moll, Doctor Albert, *The Sexual Life of the Child,* The Macmillan Co., New York, 1921.

Monahan, Michael, *Nemesis,* Frank Maurice, Inc., New York, 1926.

O'Donaghue, David J., *The Poets of Ireland, A Biographical Dictionary,* Author's edition, London, 1892–1893.

Oscar Wilde: Three Times Tried, The Ferrestone Press, Ltd., London, 1912.

O'Sullivan, Vincent, *Aspects of Wilde,* Henry Holt & Co., New York, 1936.

Pacq, Hilary, *Le Procès d'Oscar Wilde,* Gallimard, Paris, 1933.

Parrott, Thomas Marc, *William Shakespeare, A Handbook,* Charles Scribner's Sons, New York, 1934.

Pater, Walter, *The Renaissance,* with an introduction by Arthur Symons, The Modern Library, New York (year not given).

"A Novel by Oscar Wilde (The Picture of Dorian Gray)," *The Bookman,* November, 1891.

Petronius, Arbiter, *The Satyricon,* transl. by William Burnaby, The Modern Library, New York (year not given).

Platon, *Le Banquet,* transl. by Léon Robin, Société d'Edition, "Les Belles Lettres," Paris, 1929.

Powys, John Cowper, *Suspended Judgments,* G. Arnold Shaw, New York, 1916.

Essays on Joseph Conrad and Oscar Wilde, Haldeman-Julius, Girard, Kansas, 1923.

Priest and the Acolyte, The, with an introductory protest by Stuart Mason, Lotus Press, London, 1907.

Ransome, Arthur, "Oscar Wilde in Paris," *The Bookman,* May, 1911, New York.

Oscar Wilde, A Critical Study, Mitchell Kennerley, New York, 1913.

Recollections of Oscar Wilde, Ernest La Jeunesse, André Gide and Franz Blei, transl. by Percival Pollard, Haldeman-Julius, Girard, Kansas, 1906.

Renan, Ernest, *Prière sur l'Acropole,* A. Ferroud, Paris, 1920.

Marc Aurèle et la Fin du Monde Antique, Calmann-Lévy, Paris, 1912.

St. Paul, Paris, 1869.

Renier, G. J., *Oscar Wilde,* Appleton & Co., New York, 1933.

Ricketts, Ch. S., *Some Recollections of Oscar Wilde,* The Nonesuch Press, Bloomsbury, 1932.

Robinson, C. E., *Everyday Life in Ancient Greece,* Clarendon Press, Oxford, 1933.

Rodd, Rennell, *Rose-Leaf and Apple-Leaf,* J. M. Stoddart & Co., Philadelphia, 1882.

BIBLIOGRAPHY

Ruskin, John, *Modern Painters,* J. M. Dent & Sons, Ltd., London, 1923.

Seven Lamps of Architecture, J. M. Dent & Sons, Ltd., London, 1932.

The Crown of Wild Olive, The Platt & Peck Co., New York, 1919.

Saturday Review of Politics, Literature, Science and Art, The, London.

July 23, 1881, "Recent Poetry" (Poems by Oscar Wilde).

October 21, 1888, "The Happy Prince and Other Stories" by Oscar Wilde.

Schuré, Edouard, *Les Prophètes de la Renaissance,* 15th ed., Perrin et Cie, Paris, 1929.

Sex Life of the Unmarried Adult, The, An Inquiry and Interpretation of Current Sex Practices, edited by Ira S. Wile, New York, 1934.

Seyffert, Oscar, *A Dictionary of Classical Antiquities,* London, 1891.

Shaw, George Bernard (G. B. S.), "An Ideal Husband," *The Saturday Review,* January 12, 1895, London.

Sherard, Robert Harborough, *Oscar Wilde, The Story of an Unhappy Friendship,* Privately Printed, Hermes Press, London, 1902.

The Real Oscar Wilde, T. Werner Laurie, Ltd., London, 1915.

The Life of Oscar Wilde, Dodd, Mead & Co., New York, 1928.

Oscar Wilde, Drunkard and Swindler, Calvi (Corsica), 1933.

Bernard Shaw, Frank Harris & Oscar Wilde, T. Werner Laurie, Ltd., London, 1936.

Sherman, Stuart Pratt, *Critical Woodcuts* (Chapter XIV), "Oscar Wilde, A Dandy of Letters," Charles Scribner's Sons, New York, 1926.

Short, Ernest H., *The House of God,* London, 1925.

Sixteen Letters from Oscar Wilde (to William Rothenstein), with notes by John Rothenstein, Faber & Faber, London, 1930.

Speaker, The, July 5, 1890, London, "Profuse and Perfervid" ("The Picture of Dorian Gray" by Oscar Wilde).

July 4, 1891, London, "Intentions."

Stoddart, Doctor W. H. B., *Mind and Its Disorders,* 5th ed., P. Blakiston's Son & Co., Philadelphia, 1926.

Swinburne, Algernon Charles, *Studies in Prose and Poetry,* Chatto & Windus, London, 1915.

Symons, Arthur, "The Ballad of Reading Gaol," *The Saturday Review,* March 12, 1898, London.

Studies in Prose and Verse, Dent & Sons, Ltd., London, 1910.

Theatre, The, June 1, 1891, London, "The Picture of Dorian Gray."

Theocritus, Bion and Moschus, with introduction by A. Lang, Macmillan & Co., Ltd., London, 1932.

Thompson, Vance, "The Two Deaths of Oscar Wilde," *The Leaflet,* No. 2, San Francisco, November, 1930.

Times, The, London, February 22, 1892, "St. James's Theatre ('Lady Windermere's Fan')."

February 23, 1893, "Salomé."

April 20, 1893, "A Woman of No Importance."

February 15, 1895, "St. James's Theatre ('The Importance of Being Earnest')."

Truth, February 21, 1895, London, "The Importance of Being Oscar."

Turgenev, Ivan S., *Fathers and Sons* (in Russian), St. Petersburg, 1897.

The Song of Triumphant Love (in Russian), St. Petersburg, 1897.

Turquet-Milnes, G., *Oscar Wilde,* Constable & Co., Ltd., London, 1913.

The Influence of Baudelaire in France and England.

Volynsky, A. L., *Struggle for Idealism,* Essay on Oscar Wilde (in Russian), St. Petersburg, 1900.

Wells, H. G., "Socialism in the Middle Classes," *Fortnightly Review,* November, 1906, London.

Whistler, James McNeill, *The Gentle Art of Making Enemies,* edited by Sheridan Ford, Frederick Stokes & Brother, New York, 1890.

Wiegler, Paul, *Genius in Love and Death,* Albert & Charles Boni, New York, 1929.

Wilde, Constance, "Children's Dresses in this Century," *The Woman's World,* Vol. I, London, 1888.

Wilde, Jane Francesca Speranza, *Poems,* Dublin, 1864.

Wilde, Oscar, *After Reading, Letters to Robert Ross,* Beaumont Press, London, 1921.

Decorative Art in America, With Letters, Reviews and Interviews, by Richard Butler Glaenzer, Brentano's, New York, 1906.

Impressions of America, edited with an introduction by Stuart Mason, Keystone Press, Sunderland, 1906.

Letters to Sarah Bernhardt, Haldeman-Julius Co., Girard, Kansas, 1924.

Some hitherto unpublished Letters of the Last Phase to Louis Wilkinson, *The Forum,* January, 1914, Vol. 31, No. 1.

Wingfield-Stratford, Esme, *The Victorian Tragedy,* George Routledge & Sons, Ltd., London, 1931.

Woodbridge, Homer E., "Oscar Wilde: A Study in Decadent Romanticism," *Harvard Monthly,* Vol. 41, pp. 214–227, 1905.

Writings of Oscar Wilde, The, London, 1907.

WORKS BY OSCAR WILDE

(Referred to in the Text)

WORKS BY OSCAR WILDE

WORKS BY OSCAR WILDE

NOTES

NOTES

INTRODUCTORY, *Page xiii*

(1) *The Sex Life of the Unmarried Adult.* An Inquiry and Interpretation of Current Sex Practices. Edited by Ira S. Wile, N. Y., 1934.

CHAPTER I, *Page 4*

(1) In addition to the three mentioned artists, there were four others who formed the nucleus of the pre-Raphaelite movement in England: James Collinson, William Michael Rossetti, the younger brother of Gabriel, George Stephens and Thomas Woolner, the sculptor. Their creed, based on "an entire adherence to the simplicity of art," was formulated in a manifesto printed on the cover of the first number (January 1, 1850) of *The Germ*, the short-lived official organ of the rebels.

CHAPTER III, *Page 19*

(1) "*Figaro*," April 1, 1907.

Page 21

(2) Incredible though it may seem, the day and even the year of Oscar Wilde's birth have been stated incorrectly in a number of textbooks, encyclopedias and other so-called "reliable sources of information." Hedwig Lachmann in his *Oscar Wilde* (Berlin, 1905), on page 12, told that Wilde was born on October 15, 1856. Walter Hamilton (*The Æsthetic Movement in England*) and even some of the more recent biographers, for example, Alexander von Gleichen-Russwurm (*Dandies and Don Juans*, N. Y., 1928), have unhesitatingly repeated the same mistake. The *Dictionary of National Biography*, Volume XXII, Supplement (Smith, Elder and Company, London, 1909, page 1385), gives the year of Oscar Wilde's birth as 1856. Moreover, *Encyclopedia Britannica* (Volume XXIII, 14th Edition, 1929, page 596) maintains that Wilde was born in Dublin "October 15, 1856," both the day of the month and the year being wrong. The same error was made by Laurie Magnus in his *Dictionary of European Literature* (page 582, George Routledge and Sons, Ltd., London, 1927). On the other hand, David J. O'Donaghue in his biographical dictionary, *The Poets of Ireland*, London, 1893, states that Oscar Wilde was born at No. 1 Merrion Square, Dublin, on October 16, 1855.

(3) In most biographies, the place of Oscar Wilde's birth is given as 1, Merrion Square, Dublin. However, R. Thurston Hopkins in his *Oscar Wilde: A Study of the Man and His Work* (London, Lynwood & Company, Ltd., 1913) and Arthur Ransome in *Oscar Wilde: A Critical Study*, page 26

(Mitchell Kennerley, New York, 1913) have both stated that the poet was born at 21 Westland Row, Dublin. The same address appears on the back of the Wilde monument at Père Lachaise. In order to have the matter of Wilde's place of birth authoritatively ascertained, the author communicated with the Lord Mayor of Dublin, requesting him to send a photostat copy of Oscar Wilde's birth certificate. In answer to this inquiry, the Assistant Registrar-General of Ireland wrote the following:

General Register Office,
Custom House,
Dublin, C. 10
27th April, 1937

Sir,

I beg to acknowledge the receipt of your communication of the 16th ultimo addressed to the Lord Mayor and transmitted to this office for attention, and to say that there are no records in this office of any births which occurred before the 1st January 1864, the date on which the Births and Deaths Registration (Ireland) Acts came into force.

This office is therefore not in a position to supply you with the copy you require of a record of birth of Oscar Wilde.

It may however be of interest to you to know that his father's address is given in the Dublin Street Directory (Thom's) for 1855 as 21, Westland Row, whereas the 1856 edition gives it as 1, Merrion Square N., i.e. the change of address would have taken place after October, 1854 but before October 1855 when the material for the 1856 edition was being compiled. On this reasoning the inscription on the tomb in the Père Lachaise Cemetery would be correct.

I am, Sir,
Your obedient Servant,
[signed] M. McDowling
Asst. Registrar-General.

B. Brasol, Esq.,
230, Riverside Drive,
New York City,
U. S. A.

It appears from the above that Oscar was born not at 1 Merrion Square, but at 21 Westland Row, and that the Wildes moved into their mansion at 1 Merrion Square one year after the poet's birth.

Chapter VIII, *Page 49*

(1) There is a great deal of confusion regarding the time when, in 1877, Wilde departed for Greece. The generally accepted version may be summed up thus: in the Spring of 1877, Oscar Wilde proceeded from England to Genoa, and from there he intended to visit Rome on his way to Greece. However, Mahaffy, having joined Wilde in Genoa, persuaded him to go directly to Greece via Corfu, without visiting Rome. After a more or less protracted sojourn in Greece, Wilde went to Rome. It is not known how much time he had actually spent there, but he was supposed to have been late for his Autumn term at Oxford, and, accordingly, the Magdalen dons imposed upon him a fine of £45. To what extent

this account may be considered trustworthy will be perceived from the following facts:

1. In the year 1877, Easter Sunday came on April 1.

2. *The Illustrated Monitor* (Dublin) published in its July issue Wilde's *Sonnet Written During Holy Week*, marked in the Ms. "Genoa 1877."

3. Thus, the Sonnet must have been written between the 25th and 31st of March.

4. If we were to accept the official version of Wilde's moves, it would appear that Wilde must have arrived in Greece early in April, 1877.

5. The fact of his journey to Greece is reflected: (*a*) in the sonnet, *Santa Decca*, marked "Corfu" and (*b*) in the sonnet, *Impression de Voyage*, with its last line, "I stood upon the soil of Greece at last," marked "*Katakolo, 1877*."

6. However, in the July, 1877, issue of *The Dublin University Magazine* Wilde's article, *The Grosvenor Gallery*, was printed. This is a notice of the first exhibition held at that Gallery on *May* 1, 1877, so that, judging by this paper, one would be inclined to think that early in May Wilde must have been in London.

7. Furthermore, *The Irish Monthly* in its July issue for the same year printed Wilde's article, *The Tomb of Keats*, which is marked "*Rome, 1877*," and on July 7, 1877, Rev. Matthew Russell, editor of that magazine, wrote Wilde a letter from which it appears that by that date the poet had read the proof of his article and had it returned with his criticisms. Therefore, it is legitimate to presume that Wilde visited Rome some time in May, 1877.

8. All the more so as in the *June* issue of *The Illustrated Monitor* we find Wilde's Sonnet, *Urbs Sacra Aeterna*, marked "Rome, 1877." Obviously, to have appeared in the June number, the sonnet must have been written in the latter part of April, or *at the latest*, early in May, which, in turn, would suggest that in April, or early in May, Wilde was in Rome.

9. That Wilde could not have visited Greece later during the summer of 1877, is evidenced by the fact that in Mr. Gabriel Wells's possession there are several unpublished letters of Wilde to Richard Harding (Kitten) dating to July and August, 1877, all of which were addressed from *Ireland* (Dublin and Illaunroe Lodge, Lough Fee). In one of these undated letters there is a specific reference to Wilde's article on the Grosvenor Gallery ("Did I tell you of my wonderful letter from Pater . . . on my Grosvenor Gallery . . . Pater gives me great praise, so I am vainer than usual . . ."). This proves that the letter was written after July 1, 1877.

10. In another letter marked "1 Merrion Square N." Wilde writes: "I send you a little notice of Keats' grave I have just written . . . I visited it with Bouncer and Dunsline." This letter, then, must have been written *after* July 1, 1877.

Page 49

(2) Wilde undertook an extensive journey through Northern Italy in the summer of 1875. He recorded his impressions in several long letters to his mother. In one of these he wrote: ". . . Venice in beauty of architecture and colour is beyond description—it is the meeting place of the Byzantine and Italian art . . . belonging to the *East* as much as to the West. . . . The Cathedral—outside most elaborate in pinnacles and statues awfully out of proportion with the rest of the building—inside most

impressive through its huge size and giant pillars supporting the roof—some good old stained glass and a lot of hideous modern windows—these moderns don't see that the use of a window in a church is to show a beautiful massing together and blending of colour—a good old window has the rich pattern of a Turkey carpet—the figures are quite subordinate and only serve to show the sentiment of the designer—a modern fresco style of window has *sûa naturâ* to compete with painting and of course looks monstrous and theatrical—the Cathedral is an awful failure—outside the design is monstrous and inartistic—the over-elaborate details stuck high up where no one can see them—everything is vile in it. It is, however, imposing and gigantic as a failure." (Quoted from Messrs. Dulau & Co.'s Catalogue, p. 85.)

Page 56

(3) Author's translation.

CHAPTER IX, *Page 60*

(1) Time and again it was rumored that on the instance of Lady Wilde, Oscar at the age of eight or nine was baptized a Catholic. Obviously, the source of this rumor should be sought in the story printed some time ago by Father Fox in *Donahoe's Magazine* (Boston). Because this fact, if it were true, would stand in conflict with several important subsequent events in Wilde's life (Portora; his first move after the release from Reading Gaol; his baptism on the eve of his death, etc.) the author communicated with the Archbishop of Dublin as per letter printed below:

March 6, 1937

His Eminence Archbishop of Dublin,
Dublin, Ireland

Your Eminence:

I have been engaged for some time in writing a complete and unbiased biography of Oscar Wilde.

It is known that when he lay on his deathbed in a small hotel in Paris, perhaps twelve hours before his troubled soul left his agonizing body, a friend of his, Robert Ross, induced him to embrace the Roman Catholic faith, and thus he was baptized *in articulo mortis*.

This fact, which is conceded by all Wilde's biographers, stands in strange contradiction with a letter of the late Reverend Lawrence Charles Prideaux Fox, a Roman Catholic priest of the Oblates of Mary Immaculate, which was published in 1905, in *Donahoe's Magazine*, Boston, Massachusetts. In one of the articles written by him in April, 1905 (Volume LIII, No. 4, page 397), there appears a portrait of Lady Wilde, the poet's mother, below which is the inscription: "Whose son, Oscar, I baptized." Father Fox, who was then stationed at St. Kevin's, Glencree, which, I understand, is about fifteen miles from Dublin, referring to the incident of Oscar's alleged baptism, gives the following story:

"When stationed at the reformatory I sometimes called on Sir William Wilde, who was reported to be one of the cleverest oculists of his time. He was bitterly opposed to reformatories, and made no secret of his animosity; not so, however, his talented and patriotic wife, Lady Wilde, who was better known by her *nom de plume*, Speranza. She used to take lodgings every summer for herself and her children at a farmhouse, at the foot of the vale of Glencree, belonging to a worthy family of the name of Evans, intimate friends of mine. On my calling there one day she asked my permission to bring her children to our chapel to assist at Mass on Sundays. As we had a tribune in the chapel from which the boys and the altar could be seen without actual communication I readily acceded to her request, and after the Mass was over, I enjoyed many a pleasant hour with this excellent lady. I am not sure whether she ever became a Catholic herself, but it was not long before she asked me to instruct two of her children, one of them being that future erratic genius, Oscar Wilde. After a few weeks I baptized these two children, Lady Wilde herself being present on the occasion. At her request I called on their father, and told him what I had done, his sole remark being that he did not care what they were so long as they became as good as their mother. I presume I must have been removed from Glencree soon after that time, as I never met any of the family again."

I should like to add that this report recounts an episode dating back to 1862, or 1863, when Oscar Wilde was eight or nine years old.

Your Eminence will realize the great importance of either authoritatively corroborating the account of Father Fox or refuting it.

I imagine that the records of the church of the Oblates of Mary Immaculate for the years 1862, and 1863, would reveal the fact that Oscar had been baptized and received in the Roman Catholic Church.

I am applying to Your Eminence with the humblest and earnest request to have the said church records carefully searched, which would definitely decide the question of Wilde's Roman Catholicism in one way or another.

Permit me, Your Eminence, to thank you in advance for any assistance which you might be willing to render me in this connection, and believe me, I am

Your humble servant,
BORIS BRASOL

The Archbishop's office had Father Fox's story checked and thereupon advised the author as follows:

5th May, 1937.

Boris Brasol, Esq.
230 Riverside Drive,
New York City.

Dear Sir,

In answer to your letter dated March 6th and addressed to His Grace the Archbishop of Dublin, I am to say that enquiries have been made and that there is *no record* or tradition in Glencree or district that Oscar Wilde was baptized a Catholic there.

Very faithfully yours,
P. DUNNE
Secretary.

Page 62

(2) This sonnet was first published in the July, 1877, issue of *The Illustrated Monitor*. There, the first and second lines of the first tercet read:

Outside, a little child came singing clear,
"Jesus, the Blessed Master, has been slain"— . . .

and the first line of the second tercet reads:

Ah, God! ah, God! these sweet and honied hours . . .

Page 65

(3) Edouard Schuré, *Les Prophètes de la Renaissance*, p. 83, 15th ed., Paris, 1929. Author's translation.

CHAPTER X, *Page 68*

(1) The phonetic arrangement of Wilde's antistrophe has a touch of originality in that it combines the amphibrachic and the anapæstic metres.

Cloud maidens that bring the rain shower,
  To the Pallas-loved land let us wing,
To the land of stout heroes and Power,
  Where Kekrops was hero and king,
Where honour and silence is given
  To the mysteries that none may declare,
Where are gifts to the high gods in heaven
  When the house of the gods is laid bare,
Where are lofty roofed temples; and statues
  Well carven and fair.

The rhythm here remotely reminds one of Poe's *Ulalume*, and despite its irregularity, it has a certain musical swing that makes the delineation of the poem most attractive.

Page 69

(2) As a mere example, the following excerpt from *Lotus Leaves* may be cited:

Eastward the silver arrows fall
Splintering the veil of holy night,
And a long wave of yellow light
Breaks silently on tower and hall.

From this strophe, one would imagine that the poet uses a trochee arrangement, since both "eastward" and "splintering"—the opening words in the two first lines—would be naturally accented on the first syllables, respectively. And yet, the poem as a whole is unmistakably an iambic ensemble. The same mistreatment of the metrical form is conspicuous in the fragment from *Agamemnon of Æschylus*. Here again, the five-foot iamb adopted in the initial chant of the chorus:

Thy prophecies are but a lying tale,

is suddenly broken by a line such as this:

Crying for sorrow of its dreary days.

It is out of the question, of course, to place the phonetic emphasis in "crying" on the second syllable, though it is only by pronouncing the word as "cry*íng*" that the iambic rhythm can be saved.

Page 70

(3) Unlike the majority of our poets, who have been indulging—alas! with so little success—in the difficult art of "ringing the sonnet," Wilde, contrary to Lord Alfred Douglas's assertion, did, in part at least, master its stern canon: in *Heu Miserande Puer* his two quatrains, with the according words *pain, lain—slain, chain,* yield unblemished "girdled rhymes" which convey to the build of the stanzas a touch of subtle beauty. But it is true that Wilde, too, missed many a fine point of the exacting classical sonnet etiquette as distinguished from the less formal Elizabethan pattern. Without going into unnecessary details, the following may be observed: traditionally, sonnets are five-foot iambic verses where the phonetic stress is on the second vowel. Now, the first and fifth lines in *Heu Miserande Puer* begin with the words "Rid of" and "Fair as," respectively, which is a distinct violation of that rule of English prosody which views with disfavour the accentuation of articles, conjunctions and prepositions. Again, in many of his tercets, as in *Italia*, the *Holy Week*, *On Approaching Italy*, and so forth, Wilde arranges his rhymes in the a-f, b-e, c-d order, instead of following the customary a-d, b-e, c-f sequence. On the other hand, in sonnets *de stricte observance*, if the build of the particular language permits it, the masculine and feminine rhymes must alternate in both the quatrains and tercets, a rule which Wilde has often disregarded even though upon the successive recurrence of the mounting and subsiding sounds, those phonetic crescendos and diminuendos, the exquisite grace of a sonnet is altogether dependent. But these and similar poetic "misdemeanors," in a young minstrel, should not be censured too severely, since in this respect even Byron was far from infallible, not only in the sense that he repeatedly violated Boileau's forgotten maxim:

Ni qu'un mot déjà mis osa s'y remontrer,

but also because in some of his sonnets, in those written *To Genevra*, for instance, there appear lines with a distinctly deformed measure.

Chapter XI, *Page 75*

(1) See Mason's *Bibliography*, p. 282.

Chapter XIII, *Page 95*

(1) Shortly after Wilde's arrival in New York, *The World* published two sonnets, *Sul Mare* and *Ave Rosina*, both signed "O. W!" which may or may not have been written by Oscar Wilde. Mr. Vyvyan Holland, to whom these pieces were submitted, expressed his opinion that these are but parodies. As a matter of fact, neither *Sul Mare* nor *Ave Rosina* has ever been included in any of the collections of Wilde's poems. (*Poems*, 1881; Vol. I, of The Complete Works of Oscar Wilde, Connoisseurs' Edition, N. Y., 1927; Bernard Tauchnitz's pirated edition of *The Poems*, Leipzig, 1911, etc.). However, from a literary standpoint, both sonnets are interest-

ing and for this reason they are here reproduced as they appeared in *The World.*

(*The World,* January 8, 1882)

SUL MARE

(*For the World*)

The Spirit of the Sea lies strangely still;
Her long, lithe, yellow-olive limbs, all prone,
Throb soft and tremble languidly. A moan—
A rapturous, slumberous, passion-haunted thrill—
Fills all the star-pierced space of sky and air.
Why thus, O Lady of my boyhood's dreams?
Why thus, O wild Sea Spirit? "Ah! meseems,"
She answers, "'tis in vain that I am fair."

"In vain I hold in leash my tempest might,
And veil with am'rous mists my fiery thought.
The poet has no gleam of rapture caught."
Oh, stay, thou Bride of Passion! Glad my sight
With Boreal storms or lightning from the South
And I will kiss thine angry, foam-flecked mouth!

ENVOI

I bring an argosy to this new land
For him who yearns, not slaves who understand;
For him who finds the Beautiful most grand
Unrobed—save one white lily in her hand.

O. W.!

(*The World,* January 10, 1882)

AVE ROSINA!

(*Impression du Théâtre.*)

Ave Rosina! Queen of Mimes and Mirth!
I've looked on thee and turned me toward the sun.
With thine own silver laugh the streamlets run
And ripple out their gladness to the earth.
Thy happy soul informs the song-bird's flight;
The weird, gray symphonies of winter skies
Reflect the languid witchery of thine eyes.
Thy gold-dusk hair is all there is of night!

And yet, the joyaunce of that lovely mien
I'd turn to fire, or death, or sob, or groan.
Dear Heart, I dare not lose my minor tone;
I must be Wild, Despairing and Unclean,
To clasp thee in a charnel house! Oh, bliss!
The Gorged Asp of Passion asks but this!

O. W.!

NOTES

Page 96

(2) February 29, 1936, p. 12, article by Dr. A. S. W. Rosenbach, *Letters That We Ought to Burn.*

Page 100

(3) Author's translation.

CHAPTER XIV, *Page 102*

(1) Commenting upon the financial returns of the Chickering Hall lecture, Lloyd Lewis and Henry J. Smith (*Oscar Wilde Discovers America,* p. 60) noted:

"Wilde's lecture had brought a full $1,000 into the box-office. . . . Only a few American lecturers—and they long-established idols like Robert G. Ingersoll, Henry Ward Beecher . . . Wendell Phillips—could consistently beat that figure."

Page 109

(2) Reprinted from Martin Birnbaum's *Oscar Wilde. Fragments and Memories,* pp. 21, 22.

Page 110

(3) Quoted from an unpublished letter to Norman Forbes Robertson. Author's collection.

CHAPTER XV, *Page 114*

(1) Nor are Pater's views on music altogether "original." No doubt, he was influenced by Schopenhauer who in his *World as Will and Idea* (Vol. I, p. 239, 6th Ed.) speaks of music as "a universal language" resembling geometrical figures and numbers "which are the universal forms of all possible objects of experience. . . ."

Page 120

(2) Moschus, *Idyl IX.* Translated by Ernest Myers.

CHAPTER XVI, *Page 123*

(1) Mr. Stuart Mason on page 270 of his *Bibliography* erroneously asserted that "Wilde returned from America in *April 1883.* . . ." As stated in the text, Wilde sailed from New York for England on December 27, 1882, on the Cunarder S.S. *Bothnia* arriving in Liverpool on January 6, 1883. Mr. Sherard advised the author that he made acquaintance of Wilde in Paris, in *February,* 1883. Messrs. Maggs Bros. have reproduced in their Catalogue of *Autograph Letters and Historical Documents* N628 (summer, 1936) Wilde's letter to Charles Waller dated Paris, *March 26,* 1883, whilst *The Duchess of Padua* was finished by Wilde in Paris on *March 15* of that year. Obviously, then, Wilde could not have "returned from America in April 1883."

Page 127

(2) "On the whole Wilde in Paris did not make a familiar figure."

Page 128

(3) See letter to Norman Robertson about "the great train robber and murderer, Jesse James," April 19, 1882. Author's collection.

CHAPTER XVII, *Page 134*

(1) See Robert Ross's *Note* to *The Duchess of Padua* in Wyman-Fogg Company's edition of Oscar Wilde's *Complete Works*, Boston, 1905. Ross further states that *The Duchess* was produced in New York on November 14, 1891, at the Hammerstein Opera House. This is correct, but he should have added that anonymously the play, under the title *Guido Ferranti*, was first produced on January 26, 1891, at the Broadway Theatre in New York.

Page 134

(2) Arthur Ransome, curiously, suggested that "*The Sphinx among other poems*, as well as much else of Wilde's work, was written in Paris. *The Sphinx* perhaps was written as early as 1874 *at the Hôtel Voltaire* . . ." ("Oscar Wilde in Paris," *The Bookman*, May, 1911, pp. 268-272). As a matter of fact, Wilde lived at the Hôtel Voltaire in *1883*, and not in 1874. Besides, it is a mystery what other poems, besides *The Sphinx*, Wilde could have written in Paris.

Page 135

(3) There seems to have developed some friction between Wilde and Messrs. Mathews and Lane about the publication of *The Sphinx*. The latter apparently blamed the poet for the delay in submitting to them the final text of his manuscript. In answer to these accusations, Wilde wrote (1893) his publishers: "The MS has been in Ricketts's hands for *more than one year*, during which time I have waited very patiently as I did not wish to interfere with the production of *The Sphinx*—or to cause any trouble. I am pleased to note that in the last letter received by me no absurd statements are made about the Members of the Firm not having read the work and so being relieved from any honourable responsibility to publish it. There is no objection to publishers reading the works they produce before publication but if they enter into an agreement with an author to publish his work, they, if they desire to be considered an honest and honourable Firm, cannot plead their own carelessness or lack of intellectual interest as an excuse for the non-performance of their agreement. . . . I am at present in favour of entrusting my plays to Mr. Mathews, whose literary enthusiasm about them has much gratified me, and to leave to Mr. Lane the incomparable privilege of publishing *The Sphinx*, *Salomé* and my beautiful story on Shakespeare's Sonnets. . . ." (Quoted from Maggs Bros'. Catalogue N628, summer, 1936, pp. 107-108.)

NOTES

Chapter XX, *Page 165*

(1) How sincerely Wilde was devoted to his wife appears conclusively from a hitherto unpublished letter which on December 16, 1884, he wrote her from Edinburgh:

Dear and Beloved,

Here am I; and you at the Antipodes: O execrable facts, that keep our lips from kissing, though our souls are one.

What can I tell you by letter—? alas! nothing that I would tell you. The messages of the gods to each other travel not by pen and ink and indeed your bodily presence here would not make you more real: for I feel your fingers in my hair, and your cheek brushing mine. The air is full of the music of your voice, my soul and body seem no longer mine, but mingled in some exquisite ecstasy with yours——

Ever and ever
Yours
Oscar

(*From the J. P. Morgan collection.*)

Page 169

(2) Here is another of Wilde's letters relating to the editorial policies of *The Woman's World*. It was addressed to Mrs. Louise Chandler Moulton, an American poetess and fiction writer whose book, *Ourselves and Our Neighbours*, Wilde reviewed in the February, 1888, issue of that magazine.

16 Tite Street.
Chelsea, S.W.

Dear Mrs. Moulton,

I have been asked to become literary adviser to one of the monthly magazines, and am anxious to make it an organ through which women of culture and position will be able to express their views.

Will you write me a short article about seven or eight pages? on any subject you like— Would American poetesses please you? with illustrations—as the magazine will be illustrated—or Boston Literary Society? with anecdotes of men like Longfellow, or Emerson— I think the last should make a charming article—the magazine will not make its new departure for some months, so you will have lots of time. Do Boston for me.

The honorarium will be the same as that paid by the *Fortnightly* and *XIX Century*—a pound a page.

Believe
Oscar Wilde

(*From the collection in the Library of Congress.*)

Chapter XXIV, *Page 201*

(1) *The Decay of Lying* (January, 1889); *The Critic as Artist* (July-September, 1890); *The Truth of Masks* (May, 1885); and *Pen, Pencil & Poison, Fortnightly Review* (January, 1889).

Page 203

(2) Author's translation. First quoted in his *The Mighty Three* (pp. 264-265).

(3) July 4, 1891. *Page 203*

(4) "This anxiety and this sublime distress." *Page 206*

Page 207

(5) Wainewright's *Essays and Criticisms* were first collected in 1880, and published by Reeves & Turner with an account of the author by W. C. Hazlitt. Interesting observations on the twisted personality of Wainewright will be found in Havelock Ellis's *The Criminal*, Fifth Ed., London-New York, 1916 (pp. 222-223).

CHAPTER XXV, *Page 211*

(1) In the summer of 1935, the author visited Mr. Sherard in London. On this occasion the question of the origin of Wilde's homosexuality was brought up, and Mr. Sherard, basing himself upon the authority of a person whose name he did not disclose at the time, made the following statement:

Oscar Wilde, he said, while at Oxford, had contracted syphilis for the cure of which mercury injections were administered. It was probably due to these treatments that Wilde's teeth subsequently grew black and became decayed. Before proposing to Miss Constance Lloyd, Wilde went to see in London a doctor who assured the poet that he had been completely cured and that there was no pathological obstacle to his marriage. However, shortly after the birth of Vyvian, Wilde discovered that syphilis, which apparently had been altogether dormant, had broken out in his system. He clearly realized that if he were to continue marital intercourse with his wife, a syphilitic child might have been born. Naturally, from that time on he was actually forced to give up physical relations with Constance. It was then that one of his friends initiated him into homosexual practices of which even Reading Gaol, apparently, did not cure him.

If the above hypothesis has any foundation, it would seem that the syphilitic toxin must have exercised a fatal effect upon Oscar's heart and that he died, not of cerebral meningitis, but of heart failure. It is interesting to note that Mr. Paul Wiegler in his *Genius in Love and Death*, referring to the last days of Wilde at the Hôtel d'Alsace, made this statement:

"The physician, Dr. Tucker, finds that he has all the symptoms of syphilis and calls in a specialist, Dr. Kleiss" (page 123).

This passage may be of some importance as corroborating the statement made by Mr. Sherard to the author.

The author sought to ascertain the real cause of Wilde's death through Dr. Edmond Locard, one of the most illustrious European criminologists of our age, now in charge of the Lyon Police Laboratory. Unfortunately, every endeavor on Dr. Locard's part to find the record of Wilde's last illness proved unsuccessful.

NOTES

Page 211

(2) *The Court and Society Review*, 1887.

Page 213

(3) *The Real Oscar Wilde*, Robert H. Sherard, page 362.

CHAPTER XXVI, *Page 220*

(1)

THE QUEEN

No, no, these are not tears, my child. It is not the same thing as tears . . . Nothing has happened . . . Nothing has happened.

THE PRINCE

Where are my seven cousins?

THE QUEEN

Here, here, attention, attention . . . let us not speak too loud; they are still sleeping; one should not speak of those who are sleeping.

THE PRINCE

They are sleeping? . . . Are all the seven still living?

THE QUEEN

Yes, yes, yes; be careful, be careful . . . They are sleeping here; they are always sleeping.

THE PRINCE

They are always sleeping? . . . What? What? What? Are . . . all the seven . . . all the seven?

THE QUEEN

Oh, oh, oh! What did you think! . . . What did you dare to think of, Marcellus, Marcellus! Be careful!

(*Author's translation from the French.*)

(2)

Page 221

HEROD

There is a wind blowing. Is there not a wind blowing?

HERODIAS

No, there is no wind.

HEROD

I tell you there is a wind that blows. . . . And I hear in the air something that is like the beating of wings, like the beating of vast wings. Do you not hear it?

HERODIAS

I hear nothing.

HEROD

I hear it no longer. But I heard it. It was the blowing of the wind, no doubt. It has passed away. But no, I hear it again. Do you hear it? It is just like the beating of wings.

(*Translated from the French by Lord Alfred Douglas.*)

NOTES

Chapter XXVI, *Page 222*

(3) SALOMÉ

à Oscar W.

A travers le brouillard lumineux des sept voiles
La courbe de son corps se cambre vers la lune
Elle se touche avec sa chevelure brune
Et ses doigts caressants où luisent des étoiles.

Le rêve d'être un paon qui déploierait sa queue
La fait sourire sous son éventail de plumes
Elle danse au milieu d'un tourbillon d'écumes
Où flotte l'arc léger de son écharpe bleue.

Presque nue, avec son dernier voile, flot jaune,
Elle fuit, revient, tourne, et passe. Aubord du thrône
Le tétrarque tremblant la supplie et l'appelle.

Fugitive, qui danse avec des roses soires
Et traîne dans le sang avec ses pieds barbares
L'ombre terrible de la lune derrière elle.

Pierre

Page 222

(4) "But this is heraldic; one might say, a fresco. . . . The word must fall like a pearl upon a crystal disk; no rapid movements, stylized gestures."

Page 222

(5) *The Spirit Lamp*, May 1893, p. 26
(6) By Victorien Sardou. *Page 223*

Page 224

(7) Wilde appears to have been dissatisfied with the publishers' proposed cover of *Salomé*. In a letter to Messrs. Mathews and Lane quoted in Maggs Bros. Catalogue N604 (Christmas, 1934, pp. 100-101) the poet commented as follows: "The cover of *Salomé* is quite dreadful—don't spoil a lovely book. Have simply a folded vellum wrapper with the design in scarlet—much deeper and much better—the texture of the present cover is coarse and common—it is quite impossible—and spoils the real beauty of the interior. Use up this horrid Irish stuff for stories, etc.—don't inflict it on a work of art like *Salomé*. It really will do you a great deal of harm—everyone will say that it is coarse and inappropriate. I loathe it. So does Beardsley."

Chapter XXVIII, *Page 243*

(1) Falsehood is the particular danger of the romantic genre.

NOTES

Chapter XXIX, *Page 261*

(1) *The Spirit Lamp*, May, 1893, Vol. IV, No. 1, P. A.

Page 264

(2) A burlesque anonymously published on September 15, 1894. The *Pall Mall Gazette* at the time suggested that Wilde himself was the author of the book which the poet emphatically denied in a letter to the Editor of that newspaper. As a matter of fact, it was Robert Smythe Hichens who was the author of the satire which was obviously inspired by the queer habits and poses of our poet. Referring to *The Green Carnation*, Wilde proudly admitted that he was the inventor of that "magnificent flower."

Chapter XXX, *Page* 274

(1) Few out of the many friends are men who can be trusted.

Chapter XXXI, *Page 280*

(1) Anna de Brémont, *Oscar Wilde and His Mother*, p. 153.

Chapter XXXII, *Page 298*

(1) Another letter which, on the eve of his release, Wilde handed to Martin is printed in *Dulau's Catalogue* (page 30). It reads:

> Please find out for me the name of A.2.11, also the names of the children who are in for the rabbits and the amount of the fine. Can I pay this and get them out? If so I will get them out to-morrow. Please, dear friend, do this for me. I must get them out. Think what a thing for me it would be to be able to help three little children. I wd. be delighted beyond words. If I can do this by paying the fine tell the children that they are to be released to-morrow by a friend and ask them to be happy and not to tell anyone.

Facsimile of this note appears on an inbound leaf facing page 576, Vol. II, of Harris's *Life and Confessions*.

Page 299

(2) In 1909, Ross presented the complete text of Wilde's original manuscript to the Trustees of the British Museum, where it is kept at the present, but it is not shown to visitors. In 1912, T. W. N. Crosland published the hitherto unpublished portions of *De Profundis*, and on September 22, 1912, Mr. Paul R. Reynolds of New York published fifteen copies of these extracts under the title *The Suppressed Portion of "De Profundis" by Oscar Wilde. Now for the First Time Published by His Literary Executor, Robert Ross.* This pamphlet was entered for copyright at the Library of Congress, Washington, D. C., on September 24, 1913. A copy of the Reynolds edition is now in possession of Paul R. Reynolds, Jr., son of the publisher. The expurgated parts of this work of Wilde are not altogether unknown to the public, since some passages therefrom were read into the record

during the hearing of the libel action which, in 1913, Lord Alfred brought against Arthur Ransome (King's Bench Division), and were reported by the London newspapers (April 18 and 19, 1913). Moreover, Frank Harris, in his *Oscar Wilde. His Life and Confessions* (Author's Edition, New York, 1916) reprinted that part of the unpublished portion of *De Profundis* which was read in court. See Vol. II, pp. 552 to 575.

CHAPTER XXXIII, *Page 305*

(1) *Melmoth the Wanderer*, a novel which was written in the early part of the nineteenth century by C. R. Maturin, Oscar Wilde's great-uncle. From that novel Wilde took his pseudonym, Sebastian Melmoth. Shortly after his release from Reading Gaol, Wilde, in a letter to Louis Wilkinson, explained that he assumed the name of Melmoth "to prevent postmen having fits."

Page 305

(2) Sherard, in his last book, *Bernard Shaw, Frank Harris and Oscar Wilde* (pp. 231-235), has ably demonstrated that it was Ross, and not Harris, who had provided Wilde with clothes after his release from prison.

Page 308

(3) Léon Lemonnier in *La Grande Revue* (January, 1931) gives the "menu" which was arranged for that occasion: "*fraises à la crême, bisquits, confiture, thé.*" Wilde himself waited on his young guests. This information was conveyed to Mr. Lemonnier by Mr. Léon Detoisien, who in 1930, was the school teacher at Berneval.

Page 314

(4) Reprinted from Mason's *Bibliography* (p. 411).

Page 314

(5) Und nichts zu suchen
Das war mein Sinn.

Page 562

(6) Before Wilde was released from Reading Gaol, on the initiative of Robert Ross, a fund of £800 for the benefit of the poet was raised by some of his friends. According to Lord Alfred Douglas, the largest contributor was Miss Adela Schuster. However, it should be noted that Ross failed to ask Lord Alfred to subscribe to this fund. Lord Alfred Douglas alone, during the first ten months of 1900, sent to Wilde from Chantilly £332 which are listed chronologically in an appendix to Lord Alfred's *My Friendship with Oscar Wilde* (p. 305). But, in addition, sporadic contributions were made to the poet by some of his other friends—Sir George Alexander, Smithers, etc.

Page 318

(7) Sherard, *Bernard Shaw, Frank Harris and Oscar Wilde* (p. 283).

Page 318

(8) Reprinted from O'Sullivan's *Aspects of Wilde* (p. 176). This letter should be compared with the following passage from Wilde's letter to Ross dated "Roma. Saturday" (1900):

> By the way did I tell you that on Easter Sunday I was completely cured of my mussel-poisoning? it is true and I always knew I would be: five months under a Jewish physician at Paris not merely did not heal me, but made me worse: the blessing of the Vicar of Christ made me whole. *Dulau's Catalogue* p. 76).

According to Paul Wiegler, Wilde contracted, in 1900, a skin disease which spread on his arms, breast and back. See: *Genius in Love and Death,* page 121, Albert & Charles Boni, New York, 1929.

Page 323

(9) "Oscar Wilde, Author of *Salomé* and other beautiful works, was born at 21 Westland Row, Dublin, October 16, 1854. He was educated at Portora Royal School, Enniskillen and Trinity College, Dublin, where he obtained scholarship and won the Berkeley Gold Medal for Greek in 1874. Sometime Demy of Magdalen College in Oxford he gained a first class in Classical Moderations in 1876: a first class in Literæ Humaniores and the Newdigate Prize for English verse in 1878. He died fortified by the Sacrament of the Church on November 30, 1900, at the Hôtel d'Alsace, 13, rue des Beaux Arts, Paris. R.I.P. *Verbis mei addere nihil audebant et super illos stillabat eloquiem meum.*

Job, caput XXIX, 22

And alien tears will fill for him
Pity's long broken urn,
For his mourners will be outcast men
And outcasts always mourn.

"This tomb, the work of Jacob Epstein, was given by a lady as a memorial of her admiration of the Poet."

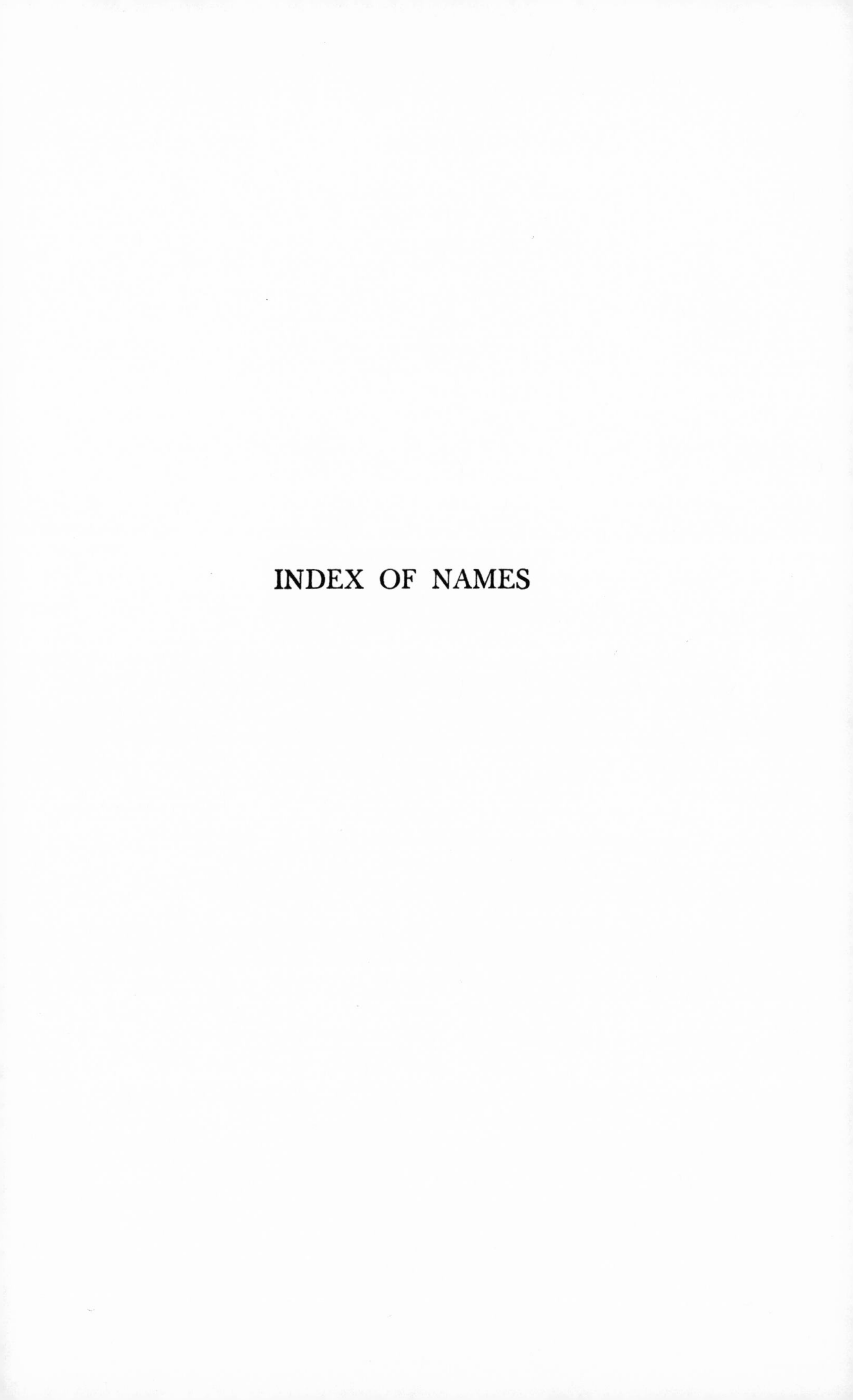

INDEX OF NAMES

INDEX OF NAMES

INDEX OF NAMES

INDEX OF NAMES

INDEX OF NAMES

INDEX OF NAMES

INDEX OF NAMES

INDEX OF NAMES